Praise for *Cloud Native Go*

This book does a great job of bringing the high level concept of "Cloud Native" down to earth and implemented using the modern computing language Go. The marriage of the two concepts works well, and the result is great inspiration.

—*Lee Atchison*
Owner, Atchison Technology LLC

This is the first book I've come across that covers such a breadth and depth of modern cloud native practices in such a practical way. The patterns presented here have clear examples to solve real problems that are faced by engineers on a daily basis.

—*Alvaro Atienza*
Site Reliability Engineer, Flatiron Health

Matt's expertise in the art and science of building reliable systems in a fundamentally unreliable world are clearly (and humorously) captured in the pages within. Join him as he introduces you to the fundamental building blocks and system designs that enable large scale, reliable systems to be constructed from the ephemeral and unreliable components that comprise the underlying cloud infrastructure of today's modern computing environment.

—*David Nicponski*
Principal Engineer, Robinhood

Over the past few years, two infrastructure trends have been happening: Go has been increasingly used for infrastructure, in addition to backend; and the infrastructure is moving to the cloud. This book summarizes the state of the art of the combination of the two.

—*Natalie Pistunovich*
Lead Developer Advocate, Aerospike

I came in knowing next to nothing about Go, and left feeling like an expert. I would go so far as to say that simply reading this book made me a better engineer.

—*James Quigley*
Systems Reliability Engineer, Bloomberg

Cloud Native Go

Building Reliable Services in
Unreliable Environments

Matthew A. Titmus

Beijing · Boston · Farnham · Sebastopol · Tokyo

Cloud Native Go

by Matthew A. Titmus

Published by O'Reilly Media, Inc., 1005 Gravenstein Highway North, Sebastopol, CA 95472.

O'Reilly books may be purchased for educational, business, or sales promotional use. Online editions are also available for most titles (*http://oreilly.com*). For more information, contact our corporate/institutional sales department: 800-998-9938 or *corporate@oreilly.com*.

Acquisitions Editor: Suzanne McQuade
Production Editor: Daniel Elfanbaum
Proofreader: nSight, Inc.
Interior Designer: David Futato
Illustrator: Kate Dullea

Development Editor: Amelia Blevins
Copyeditor: Piper Editorial Consulting, LLC
Indexer: nSight, Inc.
Cover Designer: Karen Montgomery

April 2021:   First Edition

Revision History for the First Edition
2021-04-20:   First Release

See *http://oreilly.com/catalog/errata.csp?isbn=9781492076339* for release details.

978-1-492-07633-9

[LSI]

For you, Dad.

Your gentleness, wisdom, and humility are dearly missed.

Also, you taught me to code, so any mistakes in this book are technically your fault.

Table of Contents

Part II.   Cloud Native Go Constructs

Part III. The Cloud Native Attributes

Preface

It's a magical time to be a technologist.

We have Docker to build containers, and Kubernetes to orchestrate them. Prometheus lets us monitor them. Consul lets us discover them. Jaeger lets us trace the relationships between them. These are just a few examples, but there are many, many more, all representative of a new generation of technologies: all of them are "cloud native," and all of them are written in *Go*.

The term "cloud native" feels ambiguous and buzzwordy, but it actually has a pretty specific definition. According to the Cloud Native Computing Foundation, a sub-foundation of the renowned Linux Foundation, a cloud native application is one that's designed to be scalable in the face of a wildly changing load, resilient in the face of environmental uncertainty, and manageable in the face of ever-changing requirements. In other words, a cloud native application is built for life in a cruel, uncertain universe.

Incorporating lessons learned from years of building cloud-based software, Go was created about a decade ago as the first major language designed specifically for the development of cloud native software. This was largely because the common server languages in use at the time simply weren't a great fit for writing the kinds of distributed, process-intensive applications that Google produces a lot of.

Since that time, Go has emerged as the *lingua franca* of cloud native development, being used in everything from Docker to Harbor, Kubernetes to Consul, InfluxDB to CockroachDB. Ten out of fifteen of the Cloud Native Computing Foundation's graduated projects, and forty-two of sixty-two[1] of its projects overall, are written mostly or entirely in Go. And more arrive every day.

---

1 Including CNCF Sandbox, Incubating, and Graduated code-based (non-specification) projects, as of February 2021.

Who Should Read This Book

This book is directed at intermediate-to-advanced developers, particularly web application engineers and DevOps specialists/site reliability engineers. Many will have been using Go to build web services, but may be unfamiliar with the subtleties of cloud native development—or even have a clear idea of what "cloud native" is—and have subsequently found their services to be difficult to manage, deploy, or observe. For these readers, this work will provide a solid foundation in not just how to build a cloud native service, but it will show why these techniques matter at all, as well as offer concrete examples to understand this sometimes abstract topic.

It's expected that many readers may be more familiar with other languages, but lured by Go's reputation as the language of cloud native development. For these readers, this book will present best practices for adopting Go as their cloud native development language, and help them solve their own cloud native management and deployment issues.

Why I Wrote This Book

The way that applications are designed, built, and deployed is changing. Demands of scale are forcing developers to spread their services' efforts across legions of servers: the industry is going "cloud native." But this introduces a host of new problems: how do you develop or deploy or manage a service running on ten servers? A hundred? A thousand? Unfortunately, the existing books in the "cloud native" space focus on abstract design principles, and contain only rudimentary examples of how to do any of this, or none at all. This book seeks to fill a need in the marketplace for a practical demonstration of complex cloud native design principles.

Conventions Used in This Book

The following typographical conventions are used in this book:

Italic
> Indicates new terms, URLs, email addresses, filenames, and file extensions.

`Constant width`
> Used for program listings, as well as within paragraphs to refer to program elements such as variable or function names, databases, data types, environment variables, statements, and keywords.

`Constant width bold`

Shows commands or other text that should be typed literally by the user.

`Constant width italic`

Shows text that should be replaced with user-supplied values or by values determined by context.

 This element signifies a tip or suggestion.

 This element signifies a general note.

 This element indicates a warning or caution.

Using Code Examples

Supplemental material (code examples, exercises, etc.) is available for download at *https://github.com/cloud-native-go/examples*.

This book is here to help you get your job done. In general, if example code is offered with this book, you may use it in your programs and documentation. You do not need to contact us for permission unless you're reproducing a significant portion of the code. For example, writing a program that uses several chunks of code from this book does not require permission. Selling or distributing examples from O'Reilly books does require permission. Answering a question by citing this book and quoting example code does not require permission. Incorporating a significant amount of example code from this book into your product's documentation does require permission.

We appreciate, but do not require, attribution. An attribution usually includes the title, author, publisher, and ISBN. For example: "*Cloud Native Go* by Matthew A. Titmus (O'Reilly). Copyright 2021 Matthew A. Titmus, 978-1-492-07633-9."

If you feel your use of code examples falls outside fair use or the permission given above, feel free to contact us at *permissions@oreilly.com*.

O'Reilly Online Learning

 For more than 40 years, *O'Reilly Media* has provided technology and business training, knowledge, and insight to help companies succeed.

Our unique network of experts and innovators share their knowledge and expertise through books, articles, and our online learning platform. O'Reilly's online learning platform gives you on-demand access to live training courses, in-depth learning paths, interactive coding environments, and a vast collection of text and video from O'Reilly and 200+ other publishers. For more information, visit *http://oreilly.com*.

How to Contact Us

Please address comments and questions concerning this book to the publisher:

O'Reilly Media, Inc.
1005 Gravenstein Highway North
Sebastopol, CA 95472
800-998-9938 (in the United States or Canada)
707-829-0515 (international or local)
707-829-0104 (fax)

We have a web page for this book, where we list errata, examples, and any additional information. You can access this page at *https://oreil.ly/cloud-native-go*.

Email *bookquestions@oreilly.com* to comment or ask technical questions about this book.

For more information about our books, courses, conferences, and news, see our website at *http://www.oreilly.com*.

Find us on Facebook: *http://facebook.com/oreilly*

Follow us on Twitter: *http://twitter.com/oreillymedia*

Watch us on YouTube: *http://www.youtube.com/oreillymedia*

Acknowledgments

First and foremost, I'd like to thank my wife and son. You're the motivation for every good thing I've done since you've entered my life, and the guiding stars that let me keep my direction true and my eyes on the sky.

To my dad, who we lost recently. You were the closest thing to a true Renaissance man I've ever known while still managing to be the kindest, most humble person I've ever known. I still want to be just like you when I grow up.

To Mary. Who feels his absence more profoundly than anyone. You're family, and you'll always be family, even if I don't call you as often as I should. Dad would be so proud of your strength and grace.

To Sarah. I'm always amazed by your strength and grit. Your sharp mind has made you both my staunchest ally and fiercest adversary since you could first speak. Don't tell Nathan, but you're my favorite sibling.

To Nathan. If we all inherited one third of dad's genius, you got his heart. I don't say it often enough, but I'm so proud of you and your accomplishments. Don't tell Sarah, but you're my favorite sibling.

To Mom. You're strong and smart, colorful and unconventional. Thank you for teaching me to always do what actually needs doing, regardless of what people think. Stay weird, and remember to feed the chickens.

To Albert. You have a huge heart and a bottomless well of patience. Thank you for joining our family; we're better for having you.

To the rest of my family. I don't get to see you nearly as often as I'd like, and I miss you all dearly, but you're always there when I need you. Thank you for celebrating the wins with me, and for supporting me through the losses.

To Walt and Alvaro, whom I can't seem to get away from, even by changing jobs. Thank you for your enthusiastic support when I need it, and your stark realism when I need that instead. You both make me a better engineer. Also, thank you for introducing me to Will Wight's Cradle series, and for the crippling addiction that followed.

To "Jeff Classic," "New Jeff," Alex, Markan, Priyanka, Sam, Owen, Matt M., Marius, Peter, Rohit, and all of my friends and colleagues at Flatiron Health. Thanks for going beyond just allowing me to divert my focus onto this endeavor, but also for supporting me and my work, serving as sounding boards, acting as beta readers and critics, and for both encouraging me and being my enablers.

To all of my friends at CoffeeOps in New York and around the world. You've graciously allowed me to bounce thoughts off of you and to challenge you, and you've challenged me in return. This book is better because of your input.

To Liz Fong-Jones, the renowned observability expert and oracle. Your guidance, direction, and code samples were invaluable, and without your generosity this book would have been a lot harder to write, and the result would have been a lot poorer.

To my technical reviewers Lee Atchison, Alvaro Atienza, David Nicponski, Natalie Pistunovich, and James Quigley. Thank you for having the patience to read every single word I wrote (even the footnotes). This is a much better book because of your sharp eyes and hard work.

And finally, to the entire team of hardworking editors and artists at O'Reilly Media whom I was fortunate enough to work with, especially Amelia Blevins, Danny Elfanbaum, and Zan McQuade. 2020 turned out to be a very interesting year, but your kindness, patience, and support carried me through it.

PART I

Going Cloud Native

## CHAPTER 1

What Is a "Cloud Native" Application?

The most dangerous phrase in the language is, "We've always done it this way."[1]

—Grace Hopper, *Computerworld (January 1976)*

If you're reading this book, then you've no doubt at least heard the term *cloud native* before. More likely, you've probably seen some of the many, many articles written by vendors bubbling over with breathless adoration and dollar signs in their eyes. If this is the bulk of your experience with the term so far, then you can be forgiven for thinking the term to be ambiguous and buzzwordy, just another of a series of markety expressions that might have started as something useful but have since been taken over by people trying to sell you something. See also: Agile, DevOps.

For similar reasons, a web search for "cloud native definition" might lead you to think that all an application needs to be cloud native is to be written in the "right" language[2] or framework, or to use the "right" technology. Certainly, your choice of language can make your life significantly easier or harder, but it's neither necessary nor sufficient for making an application cloud native.

Is cloud native, then, just a matter of *where* an application runs? The term *cloud native* certainly suggests that. All you'd need to do is pour your kludgy[3] old application into a container and run it in Kubernetes, and you're cloud native now, right? Nope. All you've done is make your application harder to deploy and harder to manage.[4] A kludgy application in Kubernetes is still kludgy.

---

1 Surden, Esther. "Privacy Laws May Usher in Defensive DP: Hopper." *Computerworld*, 26 Jan. 1976, p. 9.

2 Which is Go. Don't get me wrong—this is still a Go book after all.

3 A "kludge" is "an awkward or inelegant solution." It's a fascinating word with a fascinating history.

4 Have you ever wondered why so many Kubernetes migrations fail?

So, what *is* a cloud native application? In this chapter, we'll answer exactly that. First, we'll examine the history of computing service paradigms up to (and especially) the present, and discuss how the relentless pressure to scale drove (and continues to drive) the development and adoption of technologies that provide high levels of dependability at often vast scales. Finally, we'll identify the specific attributes associated with such an application.

The Story So Far

The story of networked applications is the story of the pressure to scale.

The late 1950s saw the introduction of the mainframe computer. At the time, every program and piece of data was stored in a single giant machine that users could access by means of dumb terminals with no computational ability of their own. All the logic and all the data all lived together as one big happy monolith. It was a simpler time.

Everything changed in the 1980s with the arrival of inexpensive network-connected PCs. Unlike dumb terminals, PCs were able to do some computation of their own, making it possible to offload some of an application's logic onto them. This new multitiered architecture—which separated presentation logic, business logic, and data (Figure 1-1)—made it possible, for the first time, for the components of a networked application to be modified or replaced independent of the others.

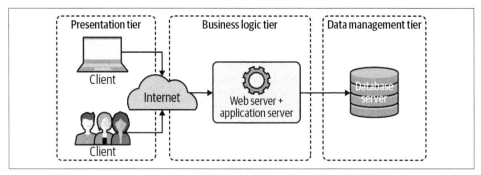

Figure 1-1. A traditional three-tiered architecture, with clearly defined presentation, business logic, and data components

In the 1990s, the popularization of the World Wide Web and the subsequent "dot-com" gold rush introduced the world to software as a service (SaaS). Entire industries were built on the SaaS model, driving the development of more complex and resource-hungry applications, which were in turn harder to develop, maintain, and deploy. Suddenly the classic multitiered architecture wasn't enough anymore. In response, business logic started to get decomposed into subcomponents that could be developed, maintained, and deployed independently, ushering in the age of microservices.

In 2006, Amazon launched Amazon Web Services (AWS), which included the Elastic Compute Cloud (EC2) service. Although AWS wasn't the *first* infrastructure as a service (IaaS) offering, it revolutionized the on-demand availability of data storage and computing resources, bringing Cloud Computing—and the ability to quickly scale—to the masses, catalyzing a massive migration of resources into "the cloud."

Unfortunately, organizations soon learned that life at scale isn't easy. Bad things happen, and when you're working with hundreds or thousands of resources (or more!), bad things happen *a lot*. Traffic will wildly spike up or down, essential hardware will fail, upstream dependencies will become suddenly and inexplicably inaccessible. Even if nothing goes wrong for a while, you still have to deploy and manage all of these resources. At this scale, it's impossible (or at least wildly impractical) for humans to keep up with all of these issues manually.

Upstream and Downstream Dependencies

In this book we'll sometimes use the terms *upstream dependency* and *downstream dependency* to describe the relative positions of two resources in a dependency relationship. There's no real consensus in the industry around the directionality of these terms, so this book will use them as follows:

Imagine that we have three services: A, B, and C, as shown in the following figure:

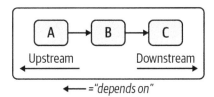

In this scenario, Service A makes requests to (and therefore depends on) Service B, which in turn depends on Service C.

Because Service B depends on Service C, we can say that Service C is a *downstream dependency* of Service B. By extension, because Service A depends on Service B which depends on Service C, Service C is also a *transitive downstream dependency* of Service A.

Inversely, because Service C is depended upon by Service B, we can say that Service B is an *upstream dependency* of Service C, and that Service A is a *transitive upstream dependency* of Service A.

What Is Cloud Native?

Fundamentally, a truly cloud native application incorporates everything we've learned about running networked applications at scale over the past 60 years. They are scalable in the face of wildly changing load, resilient in the face of environmental uncertainty, and manageable in the face of ever-changing requirements. In other words, a cloud native application is built for life in a cruel, uncertain universe.

But how do we *define* the term *cloud native*? Fortunately for all of us,[5] we don't have to. The Cloud Native Computing Foundation (*https://oreil.ly/621yd*)—a subfoundation of the renowned Linux Foundation, and something of an acknowledged authority on the subject—has already done it for us:

> Cloud native technologies empower organizations to build and run scalable applications in modern, dynamic environments such as public, private, and hybrid clouds….
>
> These techniques enable loosely coupled systems that are resilient, manageable, and observable. Combined with robust automation, they allow engineers to make high-impact changes frequently and predictably with minimal toil.[6]
>
> —Cloud Native Computing Foundation, *CNCF Cloud Native Definition v1.0*

By this definition, cloud native applications are more than just applications that happen to live in a cloud. They're also *scalable, loosely coupled, resilient, manageable,* and *observable*. Taken together, these "cloud native attributes" can be said to constitute the foundation of what it means for a system to be cloud native.

As it turns out, each of those words has a pretty specific meaning of its own, so let's take a look.

Scalability

In the context of cloud computing, *scalability* can be defined as the ability of a system to continue to behave as expected in the face of significant upward or downward changes in demand. A system can be considered to be scalable if it doesn't need to be refactored to perform its intended function during or after a steep increase in demand.

Because unscalable services can seem to function perfectly well under initial conditions, scalability isn't always a primary consideration during service design. While this might be fine in the short term, services that aren't capable of growing much beyond their original expectations also have a limited lifetime value. What's more, it's

---

5 Especially for me. I get to write this cool book.

6 Cloud Native Computing Foundation. "CNCF Cloud Native Definition v1.0," GitHub, 7 Dec. 2020. *https:// oreil.ly/KJuTr*.

often fiendishly difficult to refactor a service for scalability, so building with it in mind can save both time and money in the long run.

There are two different ways that a service can be scaled, each with its own associated pros and cons:

Vertical scaling
> A system can be *vertically scaled* (or *scaled up*) by upsizing (or downsizing) the hardware resources that are already allocated to it. For example, by adding memory or CPU to a database that's running on a dedicated computing instance. Vertical scaling has the benefit of being technically relatively straightforward, but any given instance can only be upsized so much.

Horizontal scaling
> A system can be *horizontally scaled* (or *scaled out*) by adding (or removing) service instances. For example, this can be done by increasing the number of service nodes behind a load balancer or containers in Kubernetes, or another container orchestration system. This strategy has a number of advantages, including redundancy and freedom from the limits of available instance sizes. However, more replicas mean greater design and management complexity, and not all services can be horizontally scaled.

Given that there are two ways of scaling a service—up or out—does that mean that any service whose hardware can be upscaled (and is capable of taking advantage of increased hardware resources) is "scalable"? If you want to split hairs, then sure, to a point. But how scalable is it? Vertical scaling is inherently limited by the size of available computing resources, so a service that can only be scaled up isn't very scalable at all. If you want to be able to scale by ten times, or a hundred, or a thousand, your service really has to be horizontally scalable.

So what's the difference between a service that's horizontally scalable and one that's not? It all boils down to one thing: state. A service that doesn't maintain any application state—or which has been very carefully designed to distribute its state between service replicas—will be relatively straightforward to scale out. For any other application, it will be hard. It's that simple.

The concepts of scalability, state, and redundancy will be discussed in much more depth in Chapter 7.

Loose Coupling

Loose coupling is a system property and design strategy in which a system's components have minimal knowledge of any other components. Two systems can be said to be *loosely coupled* when changes to one component generally don't require changes to the other.

For example, web servers and web browsers can be considered to be loosely coupled: servers can be updated or even completely replaced without affecting our browsers at all. In their case, this is possible because standard web servers have agreed that they would communicate using a set of standard protocols.[7] In other words, they provide a *service contract*. Imagine the chaos if all the world's web browsers had to be updated each time NGINX or httpd had a new version![8]

It could be said that "loose coupling" is just a restatement of the whole point of microservice architectures: to partition components so that changes in one don't necessarily affect another. This might even be true. However, this principle is often neglected, and bears repeating. The benefits of loose coupling—and the consequences if it's neglected—cannot be understated. It's very easy to create a "worst of all worlds" system that pairs the management and complexity overhead of having multiple services with the dependencies and entanglements of a monolithic system: the dreaded *distributed monolith*.

Unfortunately, there's no magic technology or protocol that can keep your services from being tightly coupled. Any data exchange format can be misused. There are, however, several that help, and—when applied with practices like declarative APIs and good versioning practices—can be used to create services that are both loosely-coupled *and* modifiable.

These technologies and practices will be discussed and demonstrated in detail in Chapter 8.

Resilience

Resilience (roughly synonymous with *fault tolerance*) is a measure of how well a system withstands and recovers from errors and faults. A system can be considered *resilient* if it can continue operating correctly—possibly at a reduced level—rather than failing completely when some part of the system fails.

When we discuss resilience (and the other the other "cloud native attributes" as well, but especially when we discuss resilience) we use the word "system" quite a lot. A *system*, depending on how it's used, can refer to anything from a complex web of interconnected services (such as an entire distributed application), to a collection of closely related components (such as the replicas of a single function or service instance), or a single process running on a single machine. Every system is composed of several subsystems, which in turn are composed of sub-subsystems, which are themselves composed of sub-sub-subsystems. It's turtles all the way down.

---

7 Those of us who remember the Browser Wars of the 1990s will recall that this wasn't always strictly true.

8 Or if every website required a different browser. That would stink, *wouldn't it?*

In the language of systems engineering, any system can contain defects, or *faults*, which we lovingly refer to as *bugs* in the software world. As we all know too well, under certain conditions, any fault can give rise to an *error*, which is the name we give to any discrepancy between a system's intended behavior and its actual behavior. Errors have the potential to cause a system to fail to perform its required function: a *failure*. It doesn't stop there though: a failure in a subsystem or component becomes a fault in the larger system; any fault that isn't properly contained has the potential to cascade upwards until it causes a total system failure.

In an ideal world, every system would be carefully designed to prevent faults from ever occurring, but this is an unrealistic goal. You can't prevent every possible fault, and it's wasteful and unproductive to try. However, by assuming that all of a system's components are certain to fail—which they are—and designing them to respond to potential faults and limit the effects of failures, you can produce a system that's functionally healthy even when some of its components are not.

There are many ways of designing a system for resiliency. Deploying redundant components is perhaps the most common approach, but that also assumes that a fault won't affect all components of the same type. Circuit breakers and retry logic can be included to prevent failures from propagating between components. Faulty components can even be reaped—or can intentionally fail—to benefit the larger system.

We'll discuss all of these approaches (and more) in much more depth in Chapter 9.

Resilience Is Not Reliability

The terms *resilience* and *reliability* describe closely related concepts, and are often confused. But, as we'll discuss in Chapter 9, they aren't quite the same thing:[9]

- The resilience of a system is the degree to which it can continue to operate correctly in the face of errors and faults. Resilience, along with the other four cloud native properties, is just one factor that contributes to reliability.

- The reliability of a system is its ability to behave as expected for a given time interval. Reliability, in conjunction with attributes like availability and maintainability, contributes to a system's overall dependability.

---

[9] If you're interested in a complete academic treatment, I highly recommend *Reliability and Availability Engineering* (*https://oreil.ly/80wGT*) by Kishor S. Trivedi and Andrea Bobbio.

Manageability

A system's *manageability* is the ease (or lack thereof) with which its behavior can be modified to keep it secure, running smoothly, and compliant with changing requirements. A system can be considered *manageable* if it's possible to sufficiently alter its behavior without having to alter its code.

As a system property, manageability gets a lot less attention than some of the more attention-grabbing attributes like scalability or observability. It's every bit as critical, though, particularly in complex, distributed systems.

For example, imagine a hypothetical system that includes a service and a database, and that the service refers to the database by a URL. What if you needed to update that service to refer to another database? If the URL was hardcoded you might have to update the code and redeploy, which, depending on the system, might be awkward for its own reasons. Of course, you could update the DNS record to point to the new location, but what if you needed to redeploy a development version of the service, with its own development database?

A manageable system might, for example, represent this value as an easily modified environment variable; if the service that uses it is deployed in Kubernetes, adjustments to its behavior might be a matter of updating a value in a ConfigMap. A more complex system might even provide a declarative API that a developer can use to tell the system what behavior she expects. There's no single right answer.[10]

Manageability isn't limited to configuration changes. It encompasses all possible dimensions of a system's behavior, be it the ability to activate feature flags, or rotate credentials or TLS certificates, or even (and perhaps especially) deploy or upgrade (or downgrade) system components.

Manageable systems are designed for adaptability, and can be readily adjusted to accommodate changing functional, environmental, or security requirements. Unmanageable systems, on the other hand, tend to be far more brittle, frequently requiring ad hoc—often manual—changes. The overhead involved in managing such systems places fundamental limits on their scalability, availability, and reliability.

The concept of manageability—and some preferred practices for implementing them in Go—will be discussed in much more depth in Chapter 10.

---

10 There are some wrong ones though.

Observability

The *observability* of a system is a measure of how well its internal states can be inferred from knowledge of its external outputs. A system can be considered *observable* when it's possible to quickly and consistently ask novel questions about it with minimal prior knowledge, and without having to reinstrument or build new code.

On its face, this might sound simple enough: just sprinkle in some logging and slap up a couple of dashboards, and your system is observable, right? Almost certainly not. Not with modern, complex systems in which almost any problem is the manifestation of a web of multiple things going wrong simultaneously. The Age of the LAMP Stack is over; things are harder now.

This isn't to say that metrics, logging, and tracing aren't important. On the contrary: they represent the building blocks of observability. But their mere existence is not enough: data is not information. They need to be used the right way. They need to be rich. Together, they need to be able to answer questions that you've never even thought to ask before.

The ability to detect and debug problems is a fundamental requirement for the maintenance and evolution of a robust system. But in a distributed system it's often hard enough just figuring out *where* a problem is. Complex systems are just too...*complex*. The number of possible failure states for any given system is proportional to the product of the number of possible partial and complete failure states of each of its components, and it's impossible to predict all of them. The traditional approach of focusing attention on the things we expect to fail simply isn't enough.

---

11 Plus, they both start with *M*. Super confusing.

Emerging practices in observability can be seen as the evolution of monitoring. Years of experience with designing, building, and maintaining complex systems have taught us that traditional methods of instrumentation—including but not limited to dashboards, unstructured logs, or alerting on various "known unknowns"—just aren't up to the challenges presented by modern distributed systems.

Observability is a complex and subtle subject, but, fundamentally, it comes down to this: instrument your systems richly enough and under real enough scenarios so that, in the future, you can answer questions that you haven't thought to ask yet.

The concept of observability—and some suggestions for implementing it—will be discussed in much more depth in Chapter 11.

Why Is Cloud Native a Thing?

The move towards "cloud native" is an example of architectural and technical adaptation, driven by environmental pressure and selection. It's evolution—survival of the fittest. Bear with me here; I'm a biologist by training.

Eons ago, in the Dawn of Time,[12] applications would be built and deployed (generally by hand) to one or a small number of servers, where they were carefully maintained and nurtured. If they got sick, they were lovingly nursed back to health. If a service went down, you could often fix it with a restart. Observability was shelling into a server to run top and review logs. It was a simpler time.

In 1997, only 11% of people in industrialized countries, and 2% worldwide, were regular internet users. The subsequent years saw exponential growth in internet access and adoption, however, and by 2017 that number had exploded to 81% in industrialized countries and 48% worldwide[13]—and continues to grow.

All of those users—and their money—applied stress to services, generating significant incentive to scale. What's more, as user sophistication and dependency on web services grew, so did expectations that their favorite web applications would be both feature-rich and always available.

The result was, and is, a significant evolutionary pressure towards scale, complexity, and dependability. These three attributes don't play well together, though, and the traditional approaches simply couldn't, and can't, keep up. New techniques and practices had to be invented.

---

12 That time was the 1990s.

13 International Telecommunication Union (ITU). "Internet users per 100 inhabitants 1997 to 2007" and "Internet users per 100 inhabitants 2005 to 2017." *ICT Data and Statistics (IDS)*.

Fortunately, the introduction of public clouds and IaaS made it relatively straightforward to scale infrastructure out. Shortcomings with dependability could often be compensated for with sheer numbers. But that introduced new problems. How do you maintain a hundred servers? A thousand? Ten thousand? How do you install your application onto them, or upgrade it? How do you debug it when it misbehaves? How do you even know it's healthy? Problems that are merely annoying at small scale tend to become very hard at large scale.

Cloud native is a thing because scale is the cause of (and solution to) all our problems. It's not magic. It's not special. All fancy language aside, cloud native techniques and technologies exist for no other reasons than to make it possible to leverage the benefits of a "cloud" (quantity) while compensating for its downsides (lack of dependability).

Summary

In this chapter, we talked a fair amount about the history of computing, and how what we now call "cloud native" isn't a new phenomenon so much as the inevitable outcome of a virtuous cycle of technological demand driving innovation driving more demand.

Ultimately, though, all of those fancy words distill down to a single point: today's applications have to dependably serve a lot of people. The techniques and technologies that we call "cloud native" represent the best current practices for building a service that's scalable, adaptable, and resilient enough to do that.

But what does all of this to do with Go? As it turns out, cloud native infrastructure requires cloud native tools. In Chapter 2, we'll start to talk about what that means, exactly.

Why Go Rules the Cloud Native World

> Any intelligent fool can make things bigger, more complex, and more violent. It takes a touch of genius—and a lot of courage—to move in the opposite direction.[1]
>
> —E.F. Schumacher, *Small Is Beautiful (August 1973)*

The Motivation Behind Go

The idea of Go emerged in September of 2007 at Google, the inevitable outcome of putting a bunch of smart people in a room and frustrating the heck out of them.

The people in question were Robert Griesemer, Rob Pike, and Ken Thompson; all already highly regarded for their individual work in designing other languages. The source of their collective ire was nothing less than the entire set of programming languages that were available at the time, which they were finding just weren't well-suited to the task of describing the kinds of distributed, scalable, resilient services that Google was building.[2]

Essentially, the common languages of the day had been developed in a different era, one before multiple processors were commonplace, and networks were quite so ubiquitous. Their support for multicore processing and networking—essential building blocks of modern "cloud native" services[3]—was often limited or required extraordinary efforts to utilize. Simply put, programming languages weren't keeping up with the needs of modern software development.

---

1 Schumacher, E.F. "Small Is Beautiful." *The Radical Humanist*, August 1973, p. 22.

2 These were "cloud native" services before the term "cloud native" was coined.

3 Of course, they weren't called "cloud native" at the time; to Google they were just "services."

Features for a Cloud Native World

Their frustrations were many, but all of them amounted to one thing: the undue complexity of the languages they were working with was making it harder to build server software. These included, but weren't limited to:[4]

Low program comprehensibility
Code had become too hard to read. Unnecessary bookkeeping and repetition was compounded by functionally overlapping features that often encouraged cleverness over clarity.

Slow builds
Language construction and years of feature creep resulted in build times that ran for minutes or hours, even on large build clusters.

Inefficiency
Many programmers responded to the aforementioned problems by adopting more fluid, dynamic languages, effectively trading efficiency and type safety for expressiveness.

High cost of updates
Incompatibilities between even minor versions of a language, as well as any dependencies it may have (and its transitive dependencies!) often made updating an exercise in frustration.

Over the years, multiple—often quite clever—solutions have been presented to address some of these issues in various ways, usually introducing additional complexity in the process. Clearly, they couldn't be fixed with a new API or language feature. So, Go's designers envisioned a modern language, the first language built for the cloud native era, supporting modern networked and multicore computing, expressive yet comprehensible, and allowing its users to focus on solving their problems instead of struggling with their language.

The result, the Go language, is notable as much for the features it explicitly *doesn't have* as it is for the ones it does. Some of those features (and nonfeatures) and the motivation behind them are discussed in the following sections.

Composition and Structural Typing

Object-oriented programming, which is based on the concept of "objects" of various "types" possessing various attributes, has existed since the 1960s, but it truly came into vogue in the early to mid-1990s with the release of Java and the addition of

---

4 Pike, Rob. "Go at Google: Language Design in the Service of Software Engineering." Google, Inc., 2012. *https://oreil.ly/6V9T1*.

object-oriented features to C++. Since then, it has emerged as the dominant programming paradigm, and remains so even today.

The promise of object-oriented programming is seductive, and the theory behind it even makes a certain kind of intuitive sense. Data and behaviors can be associated with *types* of things, which can be inherited by *subtypes* of those things. *Instances* of those types can be conceptualized as tangible objects with properties and behaviors—components of a larger system modeling concrete, real-world concepts.

In practice however, objected-oriented programming using inheritance often requires that relationships between types be carefully considered and painstakingly designed, and that particular design patterns and practices be faithfully observed. As such, as illustrated in Figure 2-1, the tendency in object-oriented programming is for the focus to shift away from developing algorithms, and towards developing and maintaining taxonomies and ontologies.

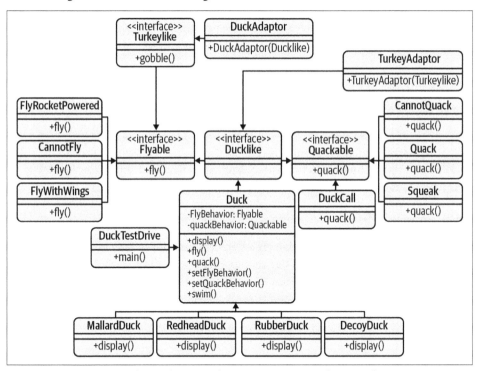

Figure 2-1. Over time, objected-oriented programming trends towards taxonomy

That's not to say that Go doesn't have object-oriented features that allow polymorphic behavior and code reuse. It, too, has a type-like concept in the form of *structs*, which can have properties and behaviors. What it rejects is inheritance and the elaborate relationships that come with it, opting instead to assemble more complex types by *embedding* simpler ones within them: an approach known as *composition*.

Specifically, where inheritance revolves around extending "is a" relationships between classes (i.e., a car "is a" motored vehicle), composition allows types to be constructed using "has a" relationships to define what they can do (i.e., a car "has a" motor). In practice, this permits greater design flexibility while allowing the creation of business domains that are less susceptible to disruption by the quirks of "family members."

By extension, while Go uses interfaces to describe behavioral contracts, it has no "is a" concept, so equivalency is determined by inspecting a type's definition, not its lineage. For example, given a Shape interface that defines an Area method, any type with an Area method will implicitly satisfy the Shape interface, without having to explicitly declare itself as a Shape:

```
type Shape interface {             // Any Shape must have an Area
    Area() float64
}

type Rectangle struct {            // Rectangle doesn't explicitly
    width, height float64          // declare itself to be a Shape
}

func (Rectangle r) Area() float64 {  // Rectangle has an Area method; it
    return r.width * r.height        // satisfies the Shape interface
}
```

This *structural typing* mechanism, which has been described as *duck typing*[5] at compile time, largely sheds the burdensome maintenance of tedious taxonomies that saddle more traditional object-oriented languages like Java and C++, freeing programmers to focus on data structures and algorithms.

Comprehensibility

Service languages like C++ and Java are often criticized for being clumsy, awkward to use, and unnecessarily verbose. They require lots of repetition and careful bookkeeping, saddling projects with superfluous boilerplate that gets in the way of programmers who have to divert their attention to things other than the problem they're trying to solve, and limiting projects' scalability under the weight of all the resulting complexity.

---

5 In languages that use duck typing, the type of an object is less important than the methods it defines. In other words, "if it walks like a duck and it quacks like a duck, then it must be a duck."

Go was designed with large projects with lots of contributors in mind. Its minimalist design (just 25 keywords and 1 loop type), and the strong opinions of its compiler, strongly favor clarity over cleverness.[6] This in turn encourages simplicity and productivity over clutter and complexity. The resulting code is relatively easy to ingest, review, and maintain, and harbors far fewer "gotchas."

CSP-Style Concurrency

Most mainstream languages provide some means of running multiple processes concurrently, allowing a program to be composed of independently executed processes. Used correctly, concurrency can be incredibly useful, but it also introduces a number of challenges, particularly around ordering events, communication between processes, and coordination of access to shared resources.

Traditionally, a programmer will confront these challenges by allowing processes to share some piece of memory, which is then wrapped in locks or mutexes to restrict access to one process at a time. But even when well-implemented, this strategy can generate a fair amount of bookkeeping overhead. It's also easy to forget to lock or unlock shared memory, potentially introducing race conditions, deadlocks, or concurrent modifications. This class of errors can be fiendishly difficult to debug.

Go, on the other hand, favors another strategy, based on a formal language called Communicating Sequential Processes (CSP), first described in Tony Hoare's influential paper of the same name[7] that describes patterns of interaction in concurrent systems in terms of message passing via channels.

The resulting concurrency model, implemented in Go with language primitives like `goroutines` and `channels`, makes Go uniquely[8] capable of elegantly structuring concurrent software without depending entirely on locking. It encourages developers to limit sharing memory, and to instead allow processes to interact with one another *entirely* by passing messages. This idea is often summarized by the Go proverb:

> Do not communicate by sharing memory. Instead, share memory by communicating.
>
> —Go Proverb

---

6 Cheney, Dave. "Clear Is Better than Clever." *The Acme of Foolishness*, 19 July 2019. *https://oreil.ly/vJs0X*.

7 Hoare, C.A.R. "Communicating Sequential Processes." *Communications of the ACM*, vol. 21, no. 8, Aug. 1978, pp. 666–77. *https://oreil.ly/CHiLt*.

8 At least among the "mainstream" languages, whatever that means.

Concurrency Is Not Parallelism

Computational concurrency and parallelism are often confused, which is understandable given that both concepts describe the state of having multiple processes executing during the same period of time. However, they are most definitely not the same thing:[9]

- *Parallelism* describes the simultaneous execution of multiple independent processes.

- *Concurrency* describes the composition of independently executing processes; it says nothing about when processes will execute.

Fast Builds

One of the primary motivations for the Go language was the maddeningly long build times for certain languages of the time,[10] which even on Google's large compilation clusters often require minutes, or even hours, to complete. This eats away at development time and grinds down developer productivity. Given Go's primary purpose of enhancing rather than hindering developer productivity, long build times had to go.

The specifics of the Go compiler are beyond the scope of this book (and beyond my own expertise). Briefly, however, the Go language was designed to provide a model of software construction free of complex relationships, greatly simplifying dependency analysis and eliminating the need for C-style include files and libraries and the overhead that comes with them. As a result, most Go builds complete in seconds, or occasionally minutes, even on relatively humble hardware. For example, building all 1.8 million lines[11] of Go in Kubernetes v1.20.2 on a MacBook Pro with a 2.4 GHz 8-Core Intel i9 processor and 32 GB of RAM required about 45 seconds of real time:

```
mtitmus:~/workspace/kubernetes[MASTER]$ time make

real    0m45.309s
user    1m39.609s
sys     0m43.559s
```

---

9 Gerrand, Andrew. "Concurrency Is Not Parallelism." *The Go Blog*, 16 Jan. 2016. *https://oreil.ly/WXf4g*.

10 C++. We're talking about C++.

11 Not counting comments; Openhub.net. "Kubernetes." *Open Hub*, Black Duck Software, Inc., 18 Jan. 2021. *https://oreil.ly/y5Rty.*

Not that this doesn't come without compromises. Any proposed change to the Go language is weighed in part against its likely effect on build times; some otherwise promising proposals have been rejected on the grounds that they would increase it.

Linguistic Stability

Go 1 was released in March of 2012, defining both the specification of the language and the specification of a set of core APIs. The natural consequence of this is an explicit promise, from the Go design team to the Go users, that programs written in Go 1 will continue to compile and run correctly, unchanged, for the lifetime of the Go 1 specification. That is, Go programs that work today can be expected to continue to work even under future "point" releases of Go 1 (Go 1.1, Go 1.2, etc.).[12]

This stands in stark contrast to many other languages, which sometimes add new features enthusiastically, gradually increasing the complexity of the language—and anything written in it—in time, leading to a once elegant language becoming a sprawling featurescape that's often exceedingly difficult to master.[13]

The Go Team considers this exceptional level of linguistic stability to be a vital feature of Go; it allows users to trust Go and to build on it. It allows libraries to be consumed and built upon with minimal hassle, and dramatically lowers the cost of updates, particularly for large projects and organizations. Importantly, it also allows the Go community to use Go and to learn from it; to spend time writing with the language rather than writing the language.

This is not to say that Go won't grow: both the APIs and the core language certainly *can* acquire new packages and features,[14] and there are many proposals for exactly that,[15] but not in a way that breaks existing Go 1 code.

That being said, it's quite possible[16] that there will actually *never* be a Go 2. More likely, Go 1 will continue to be compatible indefinitely; and in the unlikely event that a breaking change is introduced, Go will provide a conversion utility, like the `go fix` command that was used during the move to Go 1.

---

12 The Go Team. "Go 1 and the Future of Go Programs." *The Go Documentation. https://oreil.ly/Mqn0I.*

13 Anybody remember Java 1.1? I remember Java 1.1. Sure, we didn't have generics or autoboxing or enhanced for loops back then, but we were happy. Happy, I tell you.

14 I'm on team generics. Go, fightin' Parametric Polymorphics!

15 The Go Team. "Proposing Changes to Go." *GitHub*, 7 Aug. 2019. *https://oreil.ly/folYF.*

16 Pike, Rob. "Sydney Golang Meetup—Rob Pike—Go 2 Draft Specifications" (video). *YouTube*, 13 Nov. 2018. *https://oreil.ly/YmMAd.*

Memory Safety

The designers of Go have taken great pains to ensure that the language is free of the various bugs and security vulnerabilities—not to mention tedious bookkeeping—associated with direct memory access. Pointers are strictly typed and are always initialized to some value (even if that value is nil), and pointer arithmetic is explicitly disallowed. Built-in reference types like maps and channels, which are represented internally as pointers to mutable structures, are initialized by the make function. Simply put, Go neither needs nor allows the kind of manual memory management and manipulation that lower-level languages like C and C++ allow and require, and the subsequent gains with respect to complexity and memory safety can't be overstated.

For the programmer, the fact that Go is a garbage-collected language obviates the need to carefully track and free up memory for every allocated byte, eliminating a considerable bookkeeping burden from the programmer's shoulders. Life without malloc is liberating.

What's more, by eliminating manual memory management and manipulation—even pointer arithmetic—Go's designers have made it effectively immune to an entire class of memory errors and the security holes they can introduce. No memory leaks, no buffer overruns, no address space layout randomization. Nothing.

Of course, this simplicity and ease of development comes with some tradeoffs, and while Go's garbage collector is incredibly sophisticated, it does introduce some overhead. As such, Go can't compete with languages like C++ and Rust in pure raw execution speed. That said, as we see in the next section, Go still does pretty well for itself in that arena.

Performance

Confronted with the slow builds and tedious bookkeeping of the statically typed, compiled languages like C++ and Java, many programmers moved towards more dynamic, fluid languages like Python. While these languages are excellent for many things, they're also very inefficient relative to compiled languages like Go, C++, and Java.

Some of this is made quite clear in the benchmarks of Table 2-1. Of course, benchmarks in general should be taken with a grain of salt, but some results are particularly striking.

Table 2-1. Relative benchmarks for common service languages (seconds)[a]

	C++	Go	Java	NodeJS	Python3	Ruby	Rust
Fannkuch-Redux	8.08	8.28	11.00	11.89	367.49	1255.50	7.28
FASTA	0.78	1.20	1.20	2.02	39.10	31.29	0.74
K-Nucleotide	1.95	8.29	5.00	15.48	46.37	72.19	2.76
Mandlebrot	0.84	3.75	4.11	4.03	172.58	259.25	0.93
N-Body	4.09	6.38	6.75	8.36	586.17	253.50	3.31
Spectral norm	0.72	1.43	4.09	1.84	118.40	113.92	0.71

[a] Gouy, Isaac. The Computer Language Benchmarks Game. 18 Jan. 2021. *https://oreil.ly/bQFjc*.

On inspection, it seems that the results can be clustered into three categories corresponding with the types of languages used to generate them:

- Compiled, strictly typed languages with manual memory management (C++, Rust)
- Compiled, strictly typed languages with garbage collection (Go, Java)
- Interpreted, dynamically typed languages (Python, Ruby)

These results suggest that, while the garbage-collected languages are generally slightly less performant than the ones with manual memory management, the differences don't appear to be great enough to matter except under the most demanding requirements.

The differences between the interpreted and compiled languages, however, is striking. At least in these examples, Python, the archetypal dynamic language, benchmarks about *ten to one hundred times slower* than most compiled languages. Of course, it can be argued that this is still perfectly adequate for many—if not most—purposes, but this is less true for cloud native applications, which often have to endure significant spikes in demand, ideally without having to rely on potentially costly upscaling.

Static Linking

By default, Go programs are compiled directly into native, statically linked executable binaries into which all necessary Go libraries and the Go runtime are copied. This produces slightly larger files (on the order of about 2MB for a "hello world"), but the resulting binary has no external language runtime to install,[17] or external library

---

17 Take that, Java.

dependencies to upgrade or conflict,[18] and can be easily distributed to users or deployed to a host without fear of suffering dependency or environmental conflicts.

This ability is particularly useful when you're working with containers. Because Go binaries don't require an external language runtime or even a distribution, they can be built into "scratch" images that don't have parent images. The result is a very small (single digit MB) image with minimal deployment latency and data transfer overhead. These are very useful traits in an orchestration system like Kubernetes that may need to pull the image with some regularity.

Static Typing

Back in the early days of Go's design, its authors had to make a choice: would it be *statically typed*, like C++ or Java, requiring variables to be explicitly defined before use, or *dynamically typed*, like Python, allowing programmers to assign values to variables without defining them and therefore generally faster to code? It wasn't a particularly hard decision; it didn't take very long. Static typing was the obvious choice, but it wasn't arbitrary, or based on personal preference.[19]

First, type correctness for statically typed languages can be evaluated at compile time, making them far more performant (see Table 2-1).

The designers of Go understood that the time spent in development is only a fraction of a project's total lifecycle, and that any gains in coding velocity with dynamically typed languages is more than made up for by the increased difficulty in debugging and maintaining such code. After all, what Python programmer hasn't had their code crash because they tried to use a string as an integer?

Take the following Python code snippet, for example:

```
my_variable = 0

while my_variable < 10:
    my_varaible = my_variable + 1    # Typo! Infinite loop!
```

See it yet? Keep trying if you don't. It can take a second.

Any programmer can make this kind of subtle misspelling error, which just so happens to also produce perfectly valid, executable Python. These are just two trivial examples of an entire class of errors that Go will catch at compile time rather than (heaven forbid) in production, and generally closer in the code to the location where

---

18 Take that, Python.

19 Few arguments in programming generate as many snarky comments as Static versus Dynamic typing, except perhaps the Great Tabs versus Spaces Debate, on which Go's unofficial position is "shut up, who cares?"

---

they are introduced. After all, it's well-understood that the earlier in the development cycle you catch a bug, the easier (read cheaper) it is to fix it.

Finally, I'll even assert something somewhat controversial: typed languages are more readable. Python is often lauded as especially readable with its forgiving nature and somewhat English-like syntax,[20] but what would you do if presented with the following Python function signature?

```
def send(message, recipient):
```

Is `message` a string? Is `recipient` an instance of some class described elsewhere? Yes, this could be improved with some documentation and a couple of reasonable defaults, but many of us have had to maintain enough code to know that that's a pretty distant star to wish on. Explicitly defined types can guide development and ease the mental burden of writing code by automatically tracking information the programmer would otherwise have to track mentally by serving as documentation for both the programmer and everybody who has to maintain their code.

Summary

If Chapter 1 focused on what makes a *system* cloud native, then this chapter can be said to have focused on what makes a *language*, specifically Go, a good fit for building cloud native services.

However, while a cloud native system needs to be scalable, loosely coupled, resilient, manageable, and observable, a language for the cloud native era has to be able to do more than just build systems with those attributes. After all, with a bit of effort, pretty much any language can, technically, be used to build such systems. So what makes Go so special?

It can be argued that all of the features presented in this chapter directly or indirectly contribute to the cloud native attributes from the previous chapter. Concurrency and memory safety can be said to contribute to service scalability, and structural typing to allow loose coupling, for example. But while Go is the only mainstream language I know that puts all of these features in one place, are they *really* so novel?

Perhaps most conspicuous of Go's features are its baked-in—not bolted-on—concurrency features, which allow a programmer to fully and more safely utilize modern networking and multicore hardware. Goroutines and channels are wondrous, of course, and make it far easier to build resilient, highly concurrent networked services, but they're technically not unique if you consider some less common languages like Clojure or Crystal.

---

20 I, too, have been lauded for my forgiving nature and somewhat English-like syntax.

I would assert that where Go really shines is in its faithful adherence to the principle of clarity over cleverness, which extends from an understanding that source code is written by humans for other humans.[21] That it compiles into machine code is almost immaterial.

Go is designed to support the way people actually work together: in teams, which sometimes change membership, whose members also work on other things. In this environment, code clarity, the minimization of "tribal knowledge," and the ability to rapidly iterate are critical. Go's simplicity is often misunderstood and unappreciated, but it lets programmers focus on solving problems instead of struggling with the language.

In Chapter 3, we'll review many of the specific features of the Go language, where we'll get to see that simplicity up close.

---

21 Or for the same human after a few months of thinking about other things.

## PART II

Cloud Native Go Constructs

Go Language Foundations

A language that doesn't affect the way you think about programming is not worth knowing.[1]

—Alan Perlis, *ACM SIGPLAN Notices (September 1982)*

No programming book would be complete without at least a brief refresher of its language of choice, so here we are!

This chapter will differ slightly from the ones in more introductory level books, however, in that we're assuming that you're at least familiar with common coding paradigms but may or may not be a little rusty with the finer points of Go syntax. As such, this chapter will focus as much on Go's nuances and subtleties as its fundamentals. For a deeper dive into the latter, I recommend either *Introducing Go* by Caleb Doxsey (O'Reilly) or *The Go Programming Language* by Alan A. A. Donovan and Brian W. Kernighan (Addison-Wesley Professional)

If you're relatively new to the language, you'll definitely want to read on. Even if you're somewhat comfortable with Go, you might want to skim this chapter: there will be a gem or two in here for you. If you're a seasoned veteran of the language, you can go ahead and move on to the next chapter (or read it ironically and judge me).

---

1 Perlis, Alan. *ACM SIGPLAN Notices* 17(9), September 1982, pp. 7–13.

Basic Data Types

Go's basic data types, the fundamental building blocks from which more complex types are constructed, can be divided into three subcategories:

- Booleans that contain only one bit of information—`true` or `false`—representing some logical conclusion or state.
- Numeric types that represent simple—variously sized floating point and signed and unsigned integers—or complex numbers.
- Strings that represent an immutable sequence of Unicode code points.

Booleans

The Boolean data type, representing the two logical truth values, exists in some form[2] in every programming language ever devised. It's represented by the `bool` type, a special 1-bit integer type that has two possible values:

- `true`
- `false`

Go supports all of the typical logical operations:

```
and := true && false
fmt.Println(and)        // "false"

or := true || false
fmt.Println(or)         // "true"

not := !true
fmt.Println(not)        // "false"
```

> Curiously, Go doesn't include a logical XOR operator. There *is* a ^ operator, but it's reserved for bitwise XOR operations.

---

2 Earlier versions of C, C++, and Python lacked a native Boolean type, instead representing them using the integers 0 (for `false`) or 1 (for `true`). Some languages like Perl, Lua, and Tcl still use a similar strategy.

Simple Numbers

Go has a small menagerie of systematically named, floating point, and signed and unsigned integer numbers:

Signed integer
    int8, int16, int32, int64

Unsigned integer
    uint8, uint16, uint32, uint64

Floating point
    float32, float64

Systematic naming is nice, but code is written by humans with squishy human brains, so the Go designers provided two lovely conveniences.

First, there are two "machine dependent" types, simply called int and uint, whose size is determined based on available hardware. These are convenient if the specific size of your numbers isn't critical. Sadly, there's no machine-dependent floating-point number type.

Second, two integer types have mnemonic aliases: byte, which is an alias for uint8; and rune, which is an alias for uint32.

 For most uses, it generally makes sense to just use int and float64.

Complex Numbers

Go offers two sizes of *complex numbers*, if you're feeling a little imaginative:[3] complex64 and complex128. These can be expressed as an *imaginary literal* by a floating point immediately followed by an i:

```
var x complex64 = 3.1415i
fmt.Println(x)              // "(0+3.1415i)"
```

Complex numbers are very neat but don't come into play all that often, so I won't drill down into them here. If you're as fascinated by them as I hope you are, *The Go Programming Language* by Donovan and Kernighan gives them the full treatment they deserve.

---

3 See what I did there?

Strings

A *string* represents a sequence of Unicode code points. Strings in Go are immutable: once created, it's not possible to change a string's contents.

Go supports two styles of string literals, the double-quote style (or interpreted literals) and the back-quote style (or raw string literals). For example, the following two string literals are equivalent:

```
// The interpreted form
"Hello\nworld!\n"

// The raw form
`Hello
world!`
```

In this interpreted string literal, each \n character pair will be escaped as one newline character, and each \" character pair will be escaped as one double-quote character.

Behind the scenes, a string is actually just a wrapper around a slice of UTF-8 encoded byte values, so any operation that can be applied to slices and arrays can also be applied to strings. If you aren't clear on slices yet, you can take this moment to read ahead to "Slices" on page 37.

Variables

Variables can be declared by using the var keyword to pair an identifier with some typed value, and may be updated at any time, with the general form:

```
var name type = expression
```

However, there is considerable flexibility in variable declaration:

- With initialization: `var foo int = 42`
- Of multiple variables: `var foo, bar int = 42, 1302`
- With type inference: `var foo = 42`
- Of mixed multiple types: `var b, f, s = true, 2.3, "four"`
- Without initialization (see "Zero Values" on page 33): `var s string`

> Go is very opinionated about clutter: it *hates* it. If you declare a variable in a function but don't use it, your program will refuse to compile.

Short Variable Declarations

Go provides a bit of syntactic sugar that allows variables within functions to be simultaneously declared and assigned by using the := operator in place of a `var` declaration with an implicit type.

Short variable declarations have the general form:

```
name := expression
```

These can be used to declare both single and multiple assignments:

- With initialization: `percent := rand.Float64() * 100.0`
- Multiple variables at once: `x, y := 0, 2`

In practice, short variable declarations are the most common way that variables are declared and initialized in Go; `var` is usually only used either for local variables that need an explicit type, or to declare a variable that will be assigned a value later.

 Remember that := is a declaration, and = is an assignment. A := operator that only attempts to redeclare existing variables will fail at compile time.

Interestingly (and sometimes confusingly), if a short variable declaration has a mix of new and existing variables on its left-hand side, the short variable declaration acts like an assignment to the existing variables.

Zero Values

When a variable is declared without an explicit value, it's assigned to the *zero value* for its type:

- Integers: 0
- Floats: 0.0
- Booleans: `false`
- Strings: "" (the empty string)

To illustrate, let's define four variables of various types, without explicit initialization:

```
var i int
var f float64
var b bool
var s string
```

Now, if we were to use these variables we'd find that they were, in fact, already initialized to their zero values:

```
fmt.Printf("integer: %d\n", i)    // integer: 0
fmt.Printf("float: %f\n", f)      // float: 0.000000
fmt.Printf("boolean: %t\n", b)    // boolean: false
fmt.Printf("string: %q\n", s)     // string: ""
```

You'll notice the use of the `fmt.Printf` function, which allows greater control over output format. If you're not familiar with this function, or with Go's format strings, see the following sidebar.

Formatting I/O in Go

Go's `fmt` package implements several functions for formatting input and output. The most commonly used of these are (probably) `fmt.Printf` and `fmt.Scanf`, which can be used to write to standard output and read from standard input, respectively:

```
func Printf(format string, a ...interface{}) (n int, err error)
func Scanf(format string, a ...interface{}) (n int, err error)
```

You'll notice that each requires a `format` parameter. This is its *format string*: a string embedded with one or more *verbs* that direct how its parameters should be interpreted. For output functions like `fmt.Printf`, the formation of these verbs specifies the format with which the arguments will be printed.

Each function also has a parameter a. The `...` (*variadic*) operator indicates that the function accepts zero or more parameters in this place; `interface{}` indicates that the parameter's type is unspecified. Variadic functions will be covered in "Variadic Functions" on page 54; the `interface{}` type in "Interfaces" on page 59.

Some of the common verb flags used in format strings include:

```
%v    The value in a default format
%T    A representation of the type of the value
%%    A literal percent sign; consumes no value
%t    Boolean: the word true or false
%b    Integer: base 2
%d    Integer: base 10
%f    Floating point: decimal point but no exponent, e.g. 123.456
%s    String: the uninterpreted bytes of the string or slice
%q    String: a double-quoted string (safely escaped with Go syntax)
```

If you're familiar with C, you may recognize these as somewhat simplified derivations of the flags used in the `printf` and `scanf` functions. A far more complete listing can be found in Go's documentation for the `fmt` package (*https://oreil.ly/Qajzp*).

The Blank Identifier

The *blank identifier*, represented by the _ (underscore) operator, acts as an anonymous placeholder. It may be used like any other identifier in a declaration, except it doesn't introduce a binding.

It's most commonly used as a way to selectively ignore unneeded values in an assignment, which can be useful in a language that both supports multiple returns and demands there be no unused variables. For example, if you wanted to handle any potential errors returned by fmt.Printf, but don't care about the number of bytes it writes,[4] you could do the following:

```
str := "world"

_, err := fmt.Printf("Hello %s\n", str)
if err != nil {
    // Do something
}
```

The blank identifier can also be used to import a package solely for its side effects:

```
import _ "github.com/lib/pq"
```

Packages imported in this way are loaded and initialized as normal, including triggering any of its init functions, but are otherwise ignored and need not be referenced or otherwise directly used.

Constants

Constants are very similar to variables, using the const keyword to associate an identifier with some typed value. However, constants differ from variables in some important ways. First, and most obviously, attempting to modify a constant will generate an error at compile time. Second, constants *must* be assigned a value at declaration: they have no zero value.

Both var and const may be used at both the package and function level, as follows:

```
const language string = "Go"

var favorite bool = true

func main() {
    const text = "Does %s rule? %t!"
    var output = fmt.Sprintf(text, language, favorite)

    fmt.Println(output)    // "Does Go rule? true!"
}
```

---

4 Why would you?

To demonstrate their behavioral similarity, the previous snippet arbitrarily mixes explicit type definitions with type inference for both the constants and variables.

Finally, the choice of fmt.Sprintf is inconsequential to this example, but if you're unclear about Go's format strings you can look back to "Formatting I/O in Go" on page 34.

Container Types: Arrays, Slices, and Maps

Go has three first-class container types that can be used to store collections of element values:

ArrayArray
> A fixed-length sequence of zero or more elements of a particular type.

Slice
> An abstraction around an array that can be resized at runtime.

Map
> An associative data structure that allows distinct keys to be arbitrarily paired with, or "mapped to," values.

As container types, all of these have a length property that reflects how many elements are stored in that container. The len built-in function can be used to find the length of any array, slice (including strings), or map.

Arrays

In Go, as in most other mainstream languages, an *array* is a fixed-length sequence of zero or more elements of a particular type.

Arrays can be declared by including a length declaration. The zero value of an array is an array of the specified length containing zero-valued elements. Individual array elements are indexed from 0 to N-1, and can be accessed using the familiar bracket notation:

```
var a [3]int            // Zero-value array of type [3]int
fmt.Println(a)          // "[0 0 0]"
fmt.Println(a[1])       // "0"

a[1] = 42               // Update second index
fmt.Println(a)          // "[0 42 0]"
fmt.Println(a[1])       // "42"

i := a[1]
fmt.Println(i)          // "42"
```

Arrays can be initialized using array literals, as follows:

```
b := [3]int{2, 4, 6}
```

You can also have the compiler count the array elements for you:

```
b := [...]int{2, 4, 6}
```

In both cases, the type of b is [3]int.

As with all container types, the len built-in function can be used to discover the length of an array:

```
fmt.Println(len(b))         // "3"
fmt.Println(b[len(b)-1])    // "6"
```

In practice, arrays aren't actually used directly very often. Instead, it's much more common to use *slices*, an array abstraction type that behaves (for all practical purposes) like a resizable array.

Slices

Slices are a data type in Go that provide a powerful abstraction around a traditional array, such that working with slices looks and feels to the programmer very much like working with arrays. Like arrays, slices provide access to a sequence of elements of a particular type via the familiar bracket notation, indexed from 0 to N-1. However, where arrays are fixed-length, slices can be resized at runtime.

As shown in Figure 3-1, a slice is actually a lightweight data structure with three components:

- A pointer to some element of a backing array that represents the first element of the slice (not necessarily the first element of the array)
- A length, representing the number of elements in the slice
- A capacity, which represents the upper value of the length

If not otherwise specified, the capacity value equals the number of elements between the start of the slice and the end of the backing array. The built-in len and cap functions will provide the length and capacity of a slice, respectively.

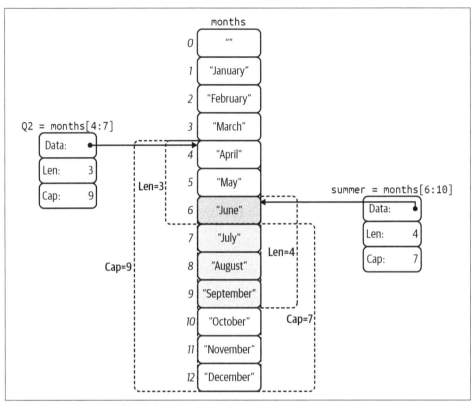

Figure 3-1. Two slices backed by the same array

Working with slices

Creating a slice is somewhat different from creating an array: slices are typed only according to the type of their elements, not their number. The make built-in function can be used to create a slice with a nonzero length as follows:

```
n := make([]int, 3)      // Create an int slice with 3 elements

fmt.Println(n)           // "[0 0 0]"
fmt.Println(len(n))      // "3"; len works for slices and arrays

n[0] = 8
n[1] = 16
n[2] = 32

fmt.Println(n)           // "[8 16 32]"
```

As you can see, working with slices feels a lot like working with arrays. Like arrays, the zero value of a slice is a slice of the specified length containing zero-valued elements, and elements in a slice are indexed and accessed exactly like they are in an array.

A slice literal is declared just like an array literal, except that you omit the element count:

```
m := []int{1}            // A literal []int declaration
fmt.Println(m)           // "[1]"
```

Slices can be extended using the append built-in, which returns an extended slice containing one or more new values appended to the original one:

```
m = append(m, 2)         // Append 2 to m
fmt.Println(m)           // "[1 2]"
```

The append built-in function also happens to be *variadic*, which means it can accept a variable number of arguments in addition to the slice to be appended. Variadic functions will be covered in more detail in "Variadic Functions" on page 54:

```
m = append(m, 2)         // Append to m from the previous snippet
fmt.Println(m)           // "[1 2]"

m = append(m, 3, 4)
fmt.Println(m)           // "[1 2 3 4]"

m = append(m, m...)      // Append m to itself
fmt.Println(m)           // "[1 2 3 4 1 2 3 4]"
```

Note that the append built-in function returns the appended slice rather than modifying the slice in place. The reason for this is that behind the scenes, if the destination has sufficient capacity to accommodate the new elements, then a new slice is constructed from the original underlying array. If not, a new underlying array is automatically allocated.

Note that append *returns* the appended slice. Failing to store it is a common error.

The slice operator

Arrays and slices (including strings) support the *slice operator*, which has the syntax s[i:j], where i and j are in the range 0 ≤ i ≤ j ≤ cap(s).

For example:

```
s0 := []int{0, 1, 2, 3, 4, 5, 6}   // A slice literal
fmt.Println(s0)                     // "[0 1 2 3 4 5 6]"
```

In the previous snippet, we define a slice literal. Recall that it closely resembles an array literal, except that it doesn't indicate a size.

If the values of i or j are omitted from a slice operator, they'll default to 0 and len(s), respectively:

```
s1 := s0[:4]
fmt.Println(s1)                    // "[0 1 2 3]"

s2 := s0[3:]
fmt.Println(s2)                    // "[3 4 5 6]"
```

A slice operator will produce a new slice backed by the same array with a length of j - i. Changes made to this slice will be reflected in the underlying array, and subsequently in all slices derived from that same array:

```
s0[3] = 42              // Change reflected in all 3 slices
fmt.Println(s0)         // "[0 1 2 42 4 5 6]"
fmt.Println(s1)         // "[0 1 2 42]"
fmt.Println(s2)         // "[42 4 5 6]"
```

This effect is illustrated in more detail in Figure 3-1.

Strings as slices

The subject of how Go implements strings under the hood is actually quite a bit more complex than you might expect, involving lots of details like the differences between bytes, characters, and runes; Unicode versus UTF-8 encoding; and the differences between a string and a string literal.

For now it's sufficient to know that Go strings are essentially just read-only slices of bytes that typically (but aren't *required* to) contain a series of UTF-8 sequences representing Unicode code points, called runes. Go even allows you to cast your strings into byte or rune arrays:

```
s := "foö"        // Unicode: f=0x66 o=0x6F ö=0xC3B6
r := []rune(s)
b := []byte(s)
```

By casting the string s in this way, we're able to uncover its identity as either a slice of bytes or a slice of runes. We can illustrate this by using fmt.Printf with the %T (type) and %v (value) flags (which we presented in "Formatting I/O in Go" on page 34) to output the results:

```
fmt.Printf("%T %v\n", s, s)     // "string foö"
fmt.Printf("%T %v\n", r, r)     // "[]int32 [102 111 246]"
fmt.Printf("%T %v\n", b, b)     // "[]uint8 [102 111 195 182]"
```

Note that the value of the string literal, foö, contains a mix of characters whose encoding can be contained in a single byte (f and o, encoded as 102 and 111, respectively) and one character that cannot (ö, encoded as 195 182).

 Remember that the byte and rune types are mnemonic aliases for uint8 and int32, respectively.

Each of these lines print the type and value of the variables passed to it. As expected, the string value, foö, is printed literally. The next two lines are interesting, however. The uint8 (byte) slice contains four bytes, which represent the string's UTF-8 encoding (two 1-byte code points, and one 2-byte code point). The int32 (rune) slice contains three values that represent the code points of the individual characters.

There's far, far more to string encoding in Go, but we only have so much space. If you're interested in learning more, take a look at Rob Pike's "Strings, Bytes, Runes and Characters in Go" on *The Go Blog* (*https://oreil.ly/mgku7*) for a deep dive into the subject.

Maps

Go's *map* data type references a *hash table*: an incredibly useful associative data structure that allows distinct keys to be arbitrarily "mapped" to values as key-value pairs. This data structure is common among today's mainstream languages: if you're coming to Go from one of these then you probably already use them, perhaps in the form of Python's dict, Ruby's Hash, or Java's HashMap.

Map types in Go are written map[K]V, where K and V are the types of its keys and values, respectively. Any type that is comparable using the == operator may be used as a key, and K and V need not be of the same type. For example, string keys may be mapped to float32 values.

A map can be initialized using the built-in make function, and its values can be referenced using the usual name[key] syntax. Our old friend len will return the number of key/value pairs in a map; the delete built-in can remove key/value pairs:

```
freezing := make(map[string]float32)     // Empty map of string to float32

freezing["celsius"] = 0.0
freezing["fahrenheit"] = 32.0
freezing["kelvin"] = 273.2

fmt.Println(freezing["kelvin"])          // "273.2"
fmt.Println(len(freezing))               // "3"
```

```
    delete(freezing, "kelvin")          // Delete "kelvin"
    fmt.Println(len(freezing))          // "2"
```

Maps may also be initialized and populated as *map literals*:

```
freezing := map[string]float32{
    "celsius":    0.0,
    "fahrenheit": 32.0,
    "kelvin":     273.2,                 // The trailing comma is required!
}
```

Note the trailing comma on the last line. This is not optional: the code will refuse to compile if it's missing.

Map membership testing

Requesting the value of a key that's not present in a map won't cause an exception to be thrown (those don't exist in Go anyway) or return some kind of null value. Rather, it returns the zero value for the map's value type:

```
foo := freezing["no-such-key"]          // Get non-existent key
fmt.Println(foo)                         // "0" (float32 zero value)
```

This can be a very useful feature because it reduces a lot of boilerplate membership testing when working with maps, but it can be a little tricky when your map happens to actually contain zero-valued values. Fortunately, accessing a map can also return a second optional bool that indicates whether the key is present in the map:

```
newton, ok := freezing["newton"]        // What about the Newton scale?
fmt.Println(newton)                      // "0"
fmt.Println(ok)                          // "false"
```

In this snippet, the value of newton is 0.0. But is that really the correct value,[5] or was there just no matching key? Fortunately, since ok is also false, we know the latter to be the case.

Pointers

Okay. Pointers. The bane and undoing of undergraduates the world over. If you're coming from a dynamically typed language, the idea of the pointer may seem alien to you. While we're not going to drill down *too* deeply into the subject, we'll do our best to cover it well enough to provide some clarity on the subject.

Going back to first principles, a "variable" is a piece of storage in memory that contains some value. Typically, when you refer to a variable by its name (foo = 10) or by

---

5 In fact, the freezing point of water on the Newton scale actually is 0.0, but that's not important.

an expression (s[i] = "foo"), you're directly reading or updating the value of the variable.

A *pointer* stores the *address* of a variable: the location in memory where the value is stored. Every variable has an address, and using pointers allows us to indirectly read or update the value of their variables (illustrated in Figure 3-2):

Retrieving the address of a variable
> The address of a named variable can be retrieved by using the & operator. For example, the expression p := &a will obtain the address of a and assign it to p.

Pointer types
> The variable p, which you can say "points to" a, has a type of *int, where the * indicates that it's a pointer type that points to an int.

Dereferencing a pointer
> To retrieve the value of the value a from p, you can *dereference* it using a * before the pointer variable name, allowing us to indirectly read or update a.

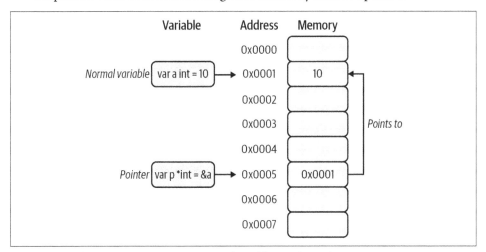

Figure 3-2. The expression p := &a gets the address of a and assigns it to p

Now, to put everything in one place, take a look at the following:

```
var a int = 10

var p *int = &a       // p of type *int points to a
fmt.Println(p)        // "0x0001"
fmt.Println(*p)       // "10"

*p = 20               // indirectly update a
fmt.Println(a)        // "20"
```

Pointers can be declared like any other variable, with a zero value of nil if not explicitly initialized. They're also comparable, being equal only if they contain the same address (that is, they point to the same variable) or if they are both nil:

```
var n *int
var x, y int

fmt.Println(n)              // "<nil>"
fmt.Println(n == nil)       // "true" (n is nil)

fmt.Println(x == y)         // "true" (x and y are both zero)
fmt.Println(&x == &x)       // "true" (*x is equal to itself)
fmt.Println(&x == &y)       // "false" (different vars)
fmt.Println(&x == nil)      // "false" (*x is not nil)
```

Because n is never initialized, its value is nil, and comparing it to nil returns true. The integers x and y both have a value of 0, so comparing their values yields true, but they are still distinct variables, and comparing pointers to them still evaluates to false.

Control Structures

Any programmer coming to Go from another language will find its suite of control structures to be generally familiar, even comfortable (at first) for those coming from a language heavily influenced by C. However, there are some pretty important deviations in their implementation and usages that might seem odd at first.

For example, control structure statements don't require lots of parentheses. Okay. Less clutter. That's fine.

There's also only one loop type. There is no while; only for. Seriously! It's actually pretty cool, though. Read on, and you'll see what I mean.

Fun with for

The for statement is Go's one and only loop construct, and while there's no explicit while loop, Go's for can provide all of its functionality, effectively unifying all of the entry control loop types to which you've become accustomed.

Go has no do-while equivalent.

The general for statement

The general form of for loops in Go is nearly identical to that of other C-family languages, in which three statements—the init statement, the continuation condition, and the post statement—are separated by semicolons in the traditional style. Any variables declared in the init statement will be scoped only to the for statement:

```
sum := 0

for i := 0; i < 10; i++ {
    sum += 1
}

fmt.Println(sum)        // "10"
```

In this example, i is initialized to 0. At the end of each iteration i is incremented by 1, and if it's still less than 10, the process repeats.

 Unlike most C-family languages, for statements don't require parentheses around their clauses, and braces are required.

In a break from traditional C-style languages, Go's for statement's init and post statements are entirely optional. As shown in the code that follows, this makes it considerably more flexible:

```
sum, i := 0, 0

for i < 10 {            // Equivalent to: for ; i < 10;
    sum += i
    i++
}

fmt.Println(i, sum)     // "10 45"
```

The for statement in the previous example has no init or post statements, only a bare condition. This is actually a big deal, because it means that for is able to fill the role traditionally occupied by the while loop.

Finally, omitting all three clauses from a for statement creates a block that loops infinitely, just like a traditional while (true):

```
fmt.Println("For ever...")

for {
    fmt.Println("...and ever")
}
```

Because it lacks any terminating condition, the loop in the previous snippet will iterate forever. On purpose.

Looping over arrays and slices

Go provides a useful keyword, range, that simplifies looping over a variety of data types.

In the case of arrays and slices, range can be used with a for statement to retrieve the index and the value of each element as it iterates:

```
s := []int{2, 4, 8, 16, 32}      // A slice of ints

for i, v := range s {            // range gets each index/value
    fmt.Println(i, "->", v)      // Output index and its value
}
```

In the previous example, the values of i and v will update each iteration to contain the index and value, respectively, of each element in the slice s. So the output will look something like the following:

```
0 -> 2
1 -> 4
2 -> 8
3 -> 16
4 -> 32
```

But what if you don't need both of these values? After all, the Go compiler will demand that you use them if you declare them. Fortunately, as elsewhere in Go, the unneeded values can be discarded by using the "blank identifier," signified by the underscore operator:

```
a := []int{0, 2, 4, 6, 8}
sum := 0

for _, v := range a {
    sum += v
}

fmt.Println(sum)    // "20"
```

As in the last example, the value v will update each iteration to contain the value of each element in the slice a. This time, however, the index value is conveniently ignored and discarded, and the Go compiler stays content.

Looping over maps

The range keyword may be also be used with a for statement to loop over maps, with each iteration returning the current key and value:

```
m := map[int]string{
    1: "January",
    2: "February",
    3: "March",
    4: "April",
}

for k, v := range m {
    fmt.Println(k, "->", v)
}
```

Note that Go maps aren't ordered, so the output won't be either:

```
3 -> March
4 -> April
1 -> January
2 -> February
```

The if Statement

The typical application of the `if` statement in Go is consistent with other C-style languages, except for the lack of parentheses around the clause and the fact that braces are required:

```
if 7 % 2 == 0 {
    fmt.Println("7 is even")
} else {
    fmt.Println("7 is odd")
}
```

 Unlike most C-family languages, `if` statements don't require parentheses around their clauses, and braces are required.

Interestingly, Go allows an initialization statement to precede the condition clause in an `if` statement, allowing for a particularly useful idiom. For example:

```
if _, err := os.Open("foo.ext"); err != nil {
    fmt.Println(err)
} else {
    fmt.Println("All is fine.")
}
```

Note how the `err` variable is being initialized prior to a check for its definition, making it somewhat similar to the following:

```
_, err := os.Open("foo.go")
if err != nil {
    fmt.Println(err)
} else {
    fmt.Println("All is fine.")
}
```

The two constructs aren't exactly equivalent however: in the first example `err` is scoped only to the `if` statement; in the second example `err` is visible to the entire containing function.

The switch Statement

As in other languages, Go provides a switch statement that provides a way to more concisely express a series of if-then-else conditionals. However, it differs from the traditional implementation in a number of ways that make it considerably more flexible.

Perhaps the most obvious difference to folks coming from C-family languages is that there's no fallthrough between the cases by default; this behavior can be explicitly added by using the fallthrough keyword:

```
i := 0

switch i % 3 {
case 0:
    fmt.Println("Zero")
    fallthrough
case 1:
    fmt.Println("One")
case 2:
    fmt.Println("Two")
default:
    fmt.Println("Huh?")
}
```

In this example, the value of i % 3 is 0, which matches the first case, causing it to output to word Zero. In Go, switch cases don't fall through by default, but the existence of an explicit fallthrough statement means that the subsequent case is also executed and One is printed. Finally, the absence of a fallthrough on that case causes the resolution of the switch to complete. All told, the following is printed:

```
Zero
One
```

Switches in Go have two interesting properties. First, case expressions don't need to be integers, or even constants: the cases will be evaluated from top to bottom, running the first case whose value is equal to the condition expression. Second, if the switch expression is left empty it'll be interpreted as true, and will match the first case whose guarding condition evaluates to true. Both of these properties are demonstrated in the following example:

```
hour := time.Now().Hour()

switch {
case hour >= 5 && hour < 9:
    fmt.Println("I'm writing")
case hour >= 9 && hour < 18:
    fmt.Println("I'm working")
default:
```

```
    fmt.Println("I'm sleeping")
}
```

The switch has no condition, so it's exactly equivalent to using switch true. As such, it matches the first statement whose condition also evaluates to true. In my case, hour is 23, so the output is "I'm sleeping."[6]

Finally, just as with if, a statement can precede the condition expression of a switch, in which case any defined values are scoped to the switch. For example, the previous example can be rewritten as follows:

```
switch hour := time.Now().Hour(); {  // Empty expression means "true"
case hour >= 5 && hour < 9:
    fmt.Println("I'm writing")
case hour >= 9 && hour < 18:
    fmt.Println("I'm working")
default:
    fmt.Println("I'm sleeping")
}
```

Note the trailing semicolon: this empty expression implies true, so that this expression is equivalent to switch hour := time.Now().Hour(); true and matches the first true case condition.

Error Handling

Errors in Go are treated as just another value, represented by the built-in error type. This makes error handling straightforward: idiomatic Go functions may include an error-typed value in its list of returns, which if not nil indicates an error state that may be handled via the primary execution path. For example, the os.Open function returns a non-nil error value when it fails to open a file:

```
file, err := os.Open("somefile.ext")
if err != nil {
    log.Fatal(err)
    return err
}
```

The actual implementation of the error type is actually incredibly simple: it's just a universally visible interface that declares a single method:

```
type error interface {
    Error() string
}
```

---

6 Clearly this code needs to be recalibrated.

This is very different from the exceptions that are used in many languages, which necessitate a dedicated system for exception catching and handling that can lead to confusing and unintuitive flow control.

Creating an Error

There are two simple ways to create error values, and a more complicated way. The simple ways are to use either the `errors.New` or `fmt.Errorf` functions; the latter is handy because it provides string formatting too:

```
e1 := errors.New("error 42")
e2 := fmt.Errorf("error %d", 42)
```

However, the fact that `error` is an interface allows you to implement your own error types, if you need to. For example, a common pattern is to allow errors to be nested within other errors:

```
type NestedError struct {
    Message string
    Err     error
}

func (e *NestedError) Error() string {
    return fmt.Sprintf("%s\n  contains: %s", e.Message, e.Err.Error())
}
```

For more information about errors, and some good advice on error handling in Go, take a look at Andrew Gerrand's "Error Handling and Go" on *The Go Blog* (*https://oreil.ly/YQ6if*).

Putting the Fun in Functions: Variadics and Closures

Functions in Go work a lot like they do in other languages: they receive parameters, do some work, and (optionally) return something.

But Go functions are built for a level of flexibility not found in many mainstream languages, and can also do a lot of things that many other languages can't, such as returning or accepting multiple values, or being used as first-class types or anonymous functions.

Functions

Declaring a function in Go is similar to most other languages: they have a name, a list of typed parameters, an optional list of return types, and a body. However, Go function declaration differs somewhat from other C-family languages, in that it uses a dedicated `func` keyword; the type for each parameter follows its name; and return types are placed at the end of the function definition header and may be omitted entirely (there's no void type).

A function with a return type list must end with a return statement, except when execution can't reach the end of the function due to the presence of an infinite loop or a terminal panic before the function exits:

```
func add(x int, y int) int {
    return x + y
}

func main() {
    sum := add(10, 5)
    fmt.Println(sum)        // "15"
}
```

Additionally, a bit of syntactic sugar allows the type for a sequence of parameters or returns of the same type to be written only once. For example, the following definitions of func foo are equivalent:

```
func foo(i int, j int, a string, b string) { /* ... */ }
func foo(i, j int, a, b string)             { /* ... */ }
```

Multiple return values

Functions can return any number of values. For example, the following swap function accepts two strings, and returns two strings. The list of return types for multiple returns must be enclosed in parentheses:

```
func swap(x, y string) (string, string) {
    return y, x
}
```

To accept multiple values from a function with multiple returns, you can use multiple assignment:

```
a, b := swap("foo", "bar")
```

When run, the value of a will be "bar," and b will be "foo."

Recursion

Go allows *recursive* function calls, in which functions call themselves. Used properly, recursion can be a very powerful tool that can be applied to many types of problems. The canonical example is the calculation of the factorial of a positive integer, the product of all positive integers less than or equal to n:

```
func factorial(n int) int {
    if n < 1 {
        return 1
    }
    return n * factorial(n-1)
```

```
    }
func main() {
    fmt.Println(factorial(11))      // "39916800"
}
```

For any integer n greater than one, `factorial` will call itself with a parameter of
n - 1. This can add up very quickly!

Defer

Go's `defer` keyword can be used to schedule the execution of a function call for
immediately before the surrounding function returns, and is commonly used to guarantee that resources are released or otherwise cleaned up.

For example, to defer printing the text "cruel world" to the end of a function call, we
insert the `defer` keyword immediately before it:

```
func main() {
    defer fmt.Println("cruel world")

    fmt.Println("goodbye")
}
```

When the previous snippet is run, it produces the following output, with the deferred
output printed last:

```
goodbye
cruel world
```

For a less trivial example, we'll create an empty file and attempt to write to it. A `close`
`File` function is provided to close the file when we're done with it. However, if we
simply call it at the end of `main`, an error could result in `closeFile` never being called
and the file being left in an open state. Therefore, we use a `defer` to ensure that the
`closeFile` function is called before the function returns, however it returns:

```
func main() {
    file, err := os.Create("/tmp/foo.txt")  // Create an empty file
    defer closeFile(file)                    // Ensure closeFile(file) is called
    if err != nil {
        return
    }

    _, err = fmt.Fprintln(file, "Your mother was a hamster")
    if err != nil {
        return
    }

    fmt.Println("File written to successfully")
}
```

```
func closeFile(f *os.File) {
    if err := f.Close(); err != nil {
        fmt.Println("Error closing file:", err.Error())
    } else {
        fmt.Println("File closed successfully")
    }
}
```

When you run this code, you should get the following output:

```
File written to successfully
File closed successfully
```

If multiple defer calls are used in a function, each is pushed onto a stack. When the surrounding function returns, the deferred calls are executed in last-in-first-out order. For example:

```
func main() {
    defer fmt.Println("world")
    defer fmt.Println("cruel")
    defer fmt.Println("goodbye")
}
```

This function, when run, will output the following:

```
goodbye
cruel
world
```

Defers are a very useful feature for ensuring that resources are cleaned up. If you're working with external resources, you'll want to make liberal use of them.

Pointers as parameters

Much of the power of pointers becomes evident when they're combined with functions. Typically, function parameters are *passed by value*: when a function is called it receives a copy of each parameter, and changes made to the copy by the function don't affect the caller. However, pointers contain a *reference* to a value, rather than the value itself, and can be used by a receiving function to indirectly modify the value passed to the function in a way that can affect the function caller.

The follow function demonstrates both scenarios:

```
func main() {
    x := 5

    zeroByValue(x)
    fmt.Println(x)              // "5"

    zeroByReference(&x)
    fmt.Println(x)              // "0"
}
```

```
func zeroByValue(x int) {
    x = 0
}

func zeroByReference(x *int) {
    *x = 0                          // Dereference x and set it to 0
}
```

This behavior isn't unique to pointers. In fact, under the hood, several data types are actually references to memory locations, including slices, maps, functions, and channels. Changes made to such *reference types* in a function can affect the caller, without needing to explicitly dereference them:

```
func update(m map[string]int) {
    m["c"] = 2
}

func main() {
    m := map[string]int{ "a" : 0, "b" : 1}

    fmt.Println(m)                  // "map[a:0 b:1]"

    update(m)

    fmt.Println(m)                  // "map[a:0 b:1 c:2]"
}
```

In this example, the map m has a length of two when it's passed to the update function, which adds the pair { "c" : 2 }. Because m is a reference type, it's passed to update as a reference to an underlying data structure instead of a copy of one, so the insertion is reflected in m in main after the update function returns.

Variadic Functions

A *variadic function* is one that may be called with zero or more trailing arguments. The most familiar example is the members of the fmt.Printf family of functions, which accept a single format specifier string and an arbitrary number of additional arguments.

This is the signature for the standard fmt.Printf function:

```
func Printf(format string, a ...interface{}) (n int, err error)
```

Note that it accepts a string, and zero or more interface{} values. If you're rusty on the interface{} syntax, we'll review it in "Interfaces" on page 59, but you can interpret interface{} to mean "some arbitrarily typed thing." What's most interesting here, however, is that the final argument contains an ellipsis (...). This is the *variadic operator*, which indicates that the function may be called with any number of arguments of this type. For example, you can call `fmt.Printf` with a format and two differently typed parameters:

```
const name, age = "Kim", 22
fmt.Printf("%s is %d years old.\n", name, age)
```

Within the variadic function, the variadic argument is a slice of the argument type. In the following example, the variadic `factors` parameter of the `product` method is of type `[]int` and may be ranged over accordingly:

```
func product(factors ...int) int {
    p := 1

    for _, n := range factors {
        p *= n
    }

    return p
}

func main() {
    fmt.Println(product(2, 2, 2))   // "8"
}
```

In this example, the call to `product` from `main` uses three parameters (though it could use any number of parameters it likes). In the `product` function, these are translated into an `[]int` slice with the value {2, 2, 2} that are iteratively multiplied to construct the final return value of 8.

Passing slices as variadic values

What if your value is already in slice form, and you still want to pass it to a variadic function? Do you need to split it into multiple individual parameters? Goodness no.

In this case, you can apply the variadic operator after the variable name when calling the variadic function:

```
m := []int{3, 3, 3}
fmt.Println(product(m...))   // "27"
```

Here, you have a variable `m` with the type `[]int`, which you want to pass to the variadic function `product`. Using the variadic operator when calling `product(m...)` makes this possible.

Anonymous Functions and Closures

In Go, functions are *first-class values* that can be operated upon in the same way as any other entity in the language: they have types, may be assigned to variables, and may even be passed to and returned by other functions.

The zero value of a function type is nil; calling a nil function value will cause a panic:

```go
func sum(x, y int) int     { return x + y }
func product(x, y int) int { return x * y }

func main() {
    var f func(int, int) int     // Function variables have types

    f = sum
    fmt.Println(f(3, 5))         // "8"

    f = product                  // Legal: product has same type as sum
    fmt.Println(f(3, 5))         // "15"
}
```

Functions may be created within other functions as *anonymous functions*, which may be called, passed, or otherwise treated like any other functions. A particularly powerful feature of Go is that anonymous functions have access to the state of their parent, and retain that access *even after* the parent function has executed. This is, in fact, the definition of a *closure*.

 A *closure* is a nested function that has access to the variables of its parent function, even after the parent has executed.

Take, for example, the following incrementor function. This function has state, in the form of the variable i, and returns an anonymous function that increments that value before returning it. The returned function can be said to *close over* the variable i, making it a true (if trivial) closure:

```go
func incrementer() func() int {
    i := 0

    return func() int {     // Return an anonymous function
        i++                 // "Closes over" parent function's i
        return i
    }
}
```

When we call incrementor, it creates its own new, local value of i, and returns a new anonymous function of type that will increment that value. Subsequent calls to incrementor will each receive their own copy of i. We can demonstrate that in the following:

```go
func main() {
    increment := incrementer()
    fmt.Println(increment())     // "1"
```

```
    fmt.Println(increment())      // "2"
    fmt.Println(increment())      // "3"

    newIncrement := incrementer()
    fmt.Println(newIncrement())   // "1"
}
```

As you can see, the `incrementer` provides a new function `increment`; each call to `increment` increments its internal counter by one. When `incrementer` is called again, though, it creates and returns an entirely new function, with its own brand new counter. Neither of these functions can influence the other.

Structs, Methods, and Interfaces

One of the biggest mental switches that people sometimes have to make when first coming to the Go language is that Go isn't a traditional object-oriented language. Not really. Sure, Go has types with methods, which kind of look like objects, but they don't have a prescribed inheritance hierarchy. Instead Go allows components to be assembled into a whole using *composition*.

For example, where a more strictly object-oriented language might have a `Car` class that extends an abstract `Vehicle` class; perhaps it would implement `Wheels` and `Engine`. This sounds fine in theory, but these relationships can grow to become convoluted and hard to manage.

Go's composition approach, on the other hand, allows components to be "put together" without having to define their ontological relationships. Extending the previous example, Go could have a `Car` struct, which could be have its various parts, such as `Wheels` and `Engine`, embedded within it. Furthermore, methods in Go can be defined for any sort of data; they're not just for structs anymore.

Structs

In Go, a *struct* is nothing more than an aggregation of zero or more fields as a single entity, where each field is a named value of an arbitrary type. A struct can be defined using the following `type Name struct` syntax. A struct is never `nil`: rather, the zero value of a struct is the zero value of all of its fields:

```
type Vertex struct {
    X, Y float64
}

func main() {
    var v Vertex           // Structs are never nil
    fmt.Println(v)         // "{0 0}"

    v = Vertex{}           // Explicitly define an empty struct
```

```
    fmt.Println(v)          // "{0 0}"

    v = Vertex{1.0, 2.0}    // Defining fields, in order
    fmt.Println(v)          // "{1 2}"

    v = Vertex{Y:2.5}       // Defining specific fields, by label
    fmt.Println(v)          // "{0 2.5}"
}
```

Struct fields can be accessed using the standard dot notation:

```
func main() {
    v := Vertex{X: 1.0, Y: 3.0}
    fmt.Println(v)                  // "{1 3}"

    v.X *= 1.5
    v.Y *= 2.5

    fmt.Println(v)                  // "{1.5 7.5}"
}
```

Structs are commonly created and manipulated by reference, so Go provides a little bit of syntactic sugar: members of structs can be accessed from a pointer to the struct using dot notation; the pointers are automatically dereferenced:

```
func main() {
    var v *Vertex = &Vertex{1, 3}
    fmt.Println(v)              // &{1 3}

    v.X, v.Y = v.Y, v.X
    fmt.Println(v)              // &{3 1}
}
```

In this example, v is a pointer to a Vertex whose X and Y member values you want to swap. If you had to dereference the pointer to do this, you'd have to do something like (*v).X, (*v).Y = (*v).Y, (*v).X, which is clearly terrible. Instead, automatic pointer dereferencing lets you do v.X, v.Y = v.Y, v.X, which is far less terrible.

Methods

In Go, *methods* are functions that are attached to types, including but not limited to structs. The declaration syntax for a method is very similar to that of a function, except that it includes an extra *receiver argument* before the function name that specifies the type that the method is attached to. When the method is called, the instance is accessible by the name specified in the receiver.

For example, our earlier Vertex type can be extended by attaching a Square method with a receiver named v of type *Vertex:

```
func (v *Vertex) Square() {      // Attach method to the *Vertex type
    v.X *= v.X
    v.Y *= v.Y
}

func main() {
    vert := &Vertex{3, 4}
    fmt.Println(vert)            // "&{3 4}"

    vert.Square()
    fmt.Println(vert)            // "&{9 16}"
}
```

 Receivers are type specific: methods attached to a pointer type can only be called on a pointer to that type.

In addition to structs, you can also claim standard composite types—structs, slices, or maps—as your own, and attach methods to them. For example, we declare a new type, MyMap, which is just a standard map[string]int, and attach a Length method to it:

```
type MyMap map[string]int

func (m MyMap) Length() int {
    return len(m)
}

func main() {
    mm := MyMap{"A":1, "B": 2}

    fmt.Println(mm)            // "map[A:1 B:2]"
    fmt.Println(mm["A"])       // "1"
    fmt.Println(mm.Length())   // "2"
}
```

The result is a new type, MyMap, which is (and can be used as) a map of strings to integers, map[string]int, but which also has a Length method that returns the map's length.

Interfaces

In Go, an *interface* is just a set of method signatures. As in other languages with a concept of an interface, they are used to describe the general behaviors of other types without being coupled to implementation details. An interface can thus be viewed as a *contract* that a type may satisfy, opening the door to powerful abstraction techniques.

For example, a `Shape` interface can be defined that includes an `Area` method signature. Any type that wants to be a `Shape` must have an `Area` method that returns a `float64`:

```
type Shape interface {
    Area() float64
}
```

Now we'll define two shapes, `Circle` and `Rectangle`, that satisfy the `Shape` interface by attaching an `Area` method to each one. Note that we don't have to explicitly declare that they satisfy the interface: if a type possesses all of its methods, it can *implicitly satisfy* an interface. This is particularly useful when you want to design interfaces that are satisfied by types that you don't own or control:

```
type Circle struct {
    Radius float64
}

func (c Circle) Area() float64 {
    return math.Pi * c.Radius * c.Radius
}

type Rectangle struct {
    Width, Height float64
}

func (r Rectangle) Area() float64 {
    return r.Width * r.Height
}
```

Because both `Circle` and `Rectangle` implicitly satisfy the `Shape` interface, we can pass them to any function that expects a `Shape`:

```
func PrintArea(s Shape) {
    fmt.Printf("%T's area is %0.2f\n", s, s.Area())
}

func main() {
    r := Rectangle{Width:5, Height:10}
    PrintArea(r)                        // "main.Rectangle's area is 50.00"

    c := Circle{Radius:5}
    PrintArea(c)                        // "main.Circle's area is 78.54"
}
```

Type assertions

A *type assertion* can be applied to an interface value to "assert" its identity as a concrete type. The syntax takes the general form of `x.(T)`, where `x` is an expression of an interface, and `T` is the asserted type.

Referring to the Shape interface and Circle struct we used previously:

```
var s Shape
s = Circle{}           // s is an expression of Shape
c := s.(Circle)        // Assert that s is a Circle
fmt.Printf("%T\n", c)  // "main.Circle"
```

The empty interface

One curious construct is the *empty interface*: interface{}. The empty interface specifies no methods. It carries no information; it says nothing.[7]

A variable of type interface{} can hold values of any type, which can be very useful when your code needs to handle values of any type. The fmt.Println method is a good example of a function using this strategy.

There are downsides, however. Working with the empty interface requires certain assumptions to be made, which have to be checked at runtime and result in code that's more fragile and less efficient.

Composition with Type Embedding

Go doesn't allow subclassing or inheritance in the traditional object-oriented sense. Instead it allows types to be *embedded* within one another, extending the functionalities of the embedded types into the embedding type.

This is a particularly useful feature of Go that allows functionalities to be reused via *composition*—combining the features of existing types to create new types—instead of inheritance, removing the need for the kinds of elaborate type hierarchies that can saddle traditional object-oriented programming projects.

Interface embedding

A popular example of embedding interfaces comes to us by way of the io package. Specifically, the widely used io.Reader and io.Writer interfaces, which are defined as follows:

```
type Reader interface {
    Read(p []byte) (n int, err error)
}

type Writer interface {
    Write(p []byte) (n int, err error)
}
```

---

7 Pike, Rob. "Go Proverbs." YouTube. 1 Dec. 2015. *https://oreil.ly/g8Rid*.

But what if you want an interface with the methods of both an io.Reader and io.Writer? Well, you *could* implement a third interface that copies the methods of both, but then you have to keep all of them in agreement. That doesn't just add unnecessary maintenance overhead: it's also a good way to accidentally introduce errors.

Rather than go the copy–paste route, Go allows you to embed the two existing interfaces into a third one that takes on the features of both. Syntactically, this is done by adding the embedded interfaces as anonymous fields, as demonstrated by the standard io.ReadWriter interface, shown here:

```
type ReadWriter interface {
    Reader
    Writer
}
```

The result of this composition is a new interface that has all of the methods of the interfaces embedded within it.

Only interfaces can be embedded within interfaces.

Struct embedding

Embedding isn't limited to interfaces: structs can also be embedded into other structs.

The struct equivalent to the io.Reader and io.Writer example in the previous section comes from the bufio package. Specifically, bufio.Reader (which implements io.Reader) and bufio.Writer (which implements io.Writer). Similarly, bufio also provides an implementation of io.ReadWriter, which is just a composition of the existing bufio.Reader and bufio.Writer types:

```
type ReadWriter struct {
    *Reader
    *Writer
}
```

As you can see, the syntax for embedding structs is identical to that of interfaces: adding the embedded types as unnamed fields. In the preceding case, the bufio.ReadWriter embeds bufio.Reader and bufio.Writer as pointer types.

Just like any pointers, embedded pointers to structs have a zero value of nil, and must be initialized to point to valid structs before they can be used.

Promotion

So, why would you use composition instead of just adding a struct field? The answer is that when a type is embedded, its exported properties and methods are *promoted* to the embedding type, allowing them to be directly invoked. For example, the Read method of a bufio.Reader is accessible directly from an instance of bufio.ReadWriter:

```
var rw *bufio.ReadWriter = GetReadWriter()
var bytes []byte = make([]byte, 1024)

n, err := rw.Read(bytes) {
    // Do something
}
```

You don't have to know or care that the Read method is actually attached to the embedded *bufio.Reader. It's important to know, though, that when a promoted method is invoked the method's receiver is still the embedded type, so the receiver of rw.Read is the ReadWriter's Reader field, not the ReadWriter.

Directly accessing embedded fields

Occasionally, you'll need to refer to an embedded field directly. To do this, you use the type name of the field as a field name. In the following (somewhat contrived) example, the UseReader function requires a *bufio.Reader, but what you have is a *bufio.ReadWriter instance:

```
func UseReader(r *bufio.Reader) {
    fmt.Printf("We got a %T\n", r)      // "We got a *bufio.Reader"
}

func main() {
    var rw *bufio.ReadWriter = GetReadWriter()
    UseReader(rw.Reader)
}
```

As you can see, this snippet uses the type name of the field you want to access (Reader) as the field name (rw.Reader) to retrieve the *bufio.Reader from rw. This can be handy for initialization as well:

```
rw := &bufio.ReadWriter{Reader: &bufio.Reader{}, Writer: &bufio.Writer{}}
```

If we'd just created rw as &bufio.ReadWriter{}, its embedded fields would be nil, but the snippet produces a *bufio.ReadWriter with fully defined *bufio.Reader and `*bufio.Writer` fields. While you wouldn't typically do this with a `&bufio.Read Writer`, this approach could be used to provide a useful mock in a pinch.

The Good Stuff: Concurrency

The intricacies of concurrent programming are many, and are well beyond the scope of this work. However, you can say that reasoning about concurrency is hard, and that the way concurrency is generally done makes it harder. In most languages, the usual approach to processes orchestration is to create some shared bit of memory, which is then wrapped in locks to restrict access to one process at a time, often introducing maddeningly difficult-to-debug errors such as race conditions or deadlocks.

Go, on the other hand, favors another strategy: it provides two concurrency primitives—goroutines and channels—that can be used together to elegantly structure concurrent software, that don't depend quite so much on locking. It encourages developers to limit sharing memory, and to instead allow processes to interact with one other entirely by passing messages.

Goroutines

One of Go's most powerful features is the go keyword. Any function call prepended with the go keyword will run as usual, but the caller can proceed uninterrupted rather than wait for the function to return. Under the hood, the function is executed as a lightweight, concurrently executing process called a *goroutine*.

The syntax is strikingly simple: a function `foo`, which may be executed sequentially as `foo()`, may be executed as a concurrent goroutine simply by adding the go keyword: `go foo()`:

```
foo()      // Call foo() and wait for it to return
go foo()   // Spawn a new goroutine that calls foo() concurrently
```

Goroutines can also be used to invoke a function literal:

```
func Log(w io.Writer, message string) {
    go func() {
        fmt.Fprintln(w, message)
    }() // Don't forget the trailing parentheses!
}
```

Channels

In Go, *channels* are typed primitives that allow communication between two goroutines. They act as pipes into which a value can be sent and then received by a goroutine on the other end.

Channels may be created using the make function. Each channel can transmit values of a specific type, called its *element type*. Channel types are written using the chan keyword followed by their element type. The following example declares and allocates an int channel:

```
var ch chan int = make(chan int)
```

The two primary operations supported by channels are *send* and *receive*, both of which use the <- operator, where the arrow indicates the direction of the data flow as demonstrated in the following:

```
ch <- val     // Sending on a channel
val = <-ch    // Receiving on a channel and assigning it to val
<-ch          // Receiving on a channel and discarding the result
```

Channel blocking

By default, a channel is *unbuffered*. Unbuffered channels have a very useful property: sends on them block until another goroutine receives on the channel, and receives block until another goroutine sends on the channel. This behavior can be exploited to synchronize two goroutines, as demonstrated in the following:

```
func main() {
    ch := make(chan string)   // Allocate a string channel

    go func() {
        message := <-ch       // Blocking receive; assigns to message
        fmt.Println(message)  // "ping"
        ch <- "pong"          // Blocking send
    }()

    ch <- "ping"              // Send "ping"
    fmt.Println(<-ch)         // "pong"
}
```

Although main and the anonymous goroutine run concurrently and could in theory run in any order, the blocking behavior of unbuffered channels guarantees that the output will always be "ping" followed by "pong."

Channel buffering

Go channels may be *buffered*, in which case they contain an internal value queue with a fixed *capacity* that's specified when the buffer is initialized. Sends to a buffered channel only block when the buffer is full; receives from a channel only block when the buffer is empty. Any other time, send and receive operations write to or read from the buffer, respectively, and exit immediately.

A buffered channel can be created by providing a second argument to the make function to indicate its capacity:

```
ch := make(chan string, 2)      // Buffered channel with capacity 2

ch <- "foo"                     // Two non-blocking sends
ch <- "bar"

fmt.Println(<-ch)               // Two non-blocking receives
fmt.Println(<-ch)

fmt.Println(<-ch)               // The third receive will block
```

Closing channels

The third available channel operation is *close*, which sets a flag to indicate that no more values will be sent on it. The built-in close function can be used to close a channel: close(ch).

 The channel close operation is just a flag to tell the receiver not to expect any more values. You don't *have to* explicitly close channels.

Trying to send on a closed channel will cause a panic. Receiving from a closed channel will retrieve any values sent on the channel prior to its closure; any subsequent receive operations will immediately yield the zero value of the channel's element type. Receivers may also test whether a channel has been closed (and its buffer is empty) by assigning a second bool parameter to the receive expression:

```
ch := make(chan string, 10)

ch <- "foo"

close(ch)                       // One value left in the buffer

msg, ok := <-ch
fmt.Printf("%q, %v\n", msg, ok)    // "foo", true

msg, ok = <-ch
fmt.Printf("%q, %v\n", msg, ok)    // "", false
```

 While either party may close a channel, in practice only the sender should do so. Inadvertently sending on a closed channel will cause a panic.

Looping over channels

The `range` keyword may be used to loop over channels that are open or contain buffered values. The loop will block until a value is available to be read or until the channel is closed. You can see how this works in the following:

```
ch := make(chan string, 3)

ch <- "foo"                 // Send three (buffered) values to the channel
ch <- "bar"
ch <- "baz"

close(ch)                   // Close the channel

for s := range ch {         // Range will continue to the "closed" flag
    fmt.Println(s)
}
```

In this example, the buffered channel ch is created, and three values are sent before being closed. Because the three values were sent to the channel before it was closed, looping over this channel will output all three lines before terminating.

Had the channel not been closed, the loop would stop and wait for the next value to be sent along the channel, potentially indefinitely.

Select

Go's `select` statements are a little like `switch` statements that provide a convenient mechanism for multiplexing communications with multiple channels. The syntax for `select` is very similar to `switch`, with some number of `case` statements that specify code to be executed upon a successful send or receive operation:

```
select {
case <-ch1:                    // Discard received value
    fmt.Println("Got something")

case x := <-ch2:               // Assign received value to x
    fmt.Println(x)

case ch3 <- y:                 // Send y to channel
    fmt.Println(y)

default:
    fmt.Println("None of the above")
}
```

In the preceding snippet, there are three primary cases specified with three different conditions. If the channel ch1 is ready to be read, then its value will be read (and discarded) and the text "Got something" will be printed. If ch2 is ready to be read, then its value will be read and assigned to the variable x before printing the value of x.

Finally, if ch3 is ready to be sent to, then the value y is sent to it before printing the value of y.

Finally, if no cases are ready, the default statements will be executed. If there's no default, then the select will block until one of its cases is ready, at which point it performs the associated communication and executes the associated statements. If multiple cases are ready, select will execute one at random.

Gotcha!

When using select, keep in mind that a closed channel never blocks and is always readable.

Implementing channel timeouts

The ability to use select to multiplex on channels can be very powerful, and can make otherwise very difficult or tedious tasks trivial. Take, for example, the implementation of a timeout on an arbitrary channel. In some languages this might require some awkward thread work, but a select with a call to time.After, which returns a channel that sends a message after a specified duration, makes short work of it:

```
var ch chan int

select {
case m := <-ch:                      // Read from ch; blocks forever
    fmt.Println(m)

case <-time.After(10 * time.Second):  // time.After returns a channel
    fmt.Println("Timed out")
}
```

Since there's no default statement, this select will block until one if its case conditions becomes true. If ch doesn't become available to read before the channel returned by time.After emits a message, then the second case will activate and the statement will time out.

Summary

What I covered in this chapter could easily have consumed an entire book, if I'd been able to drill down into the level of detail the subject really deserves. But space and time are limited (and that book's already been written[8]) so I have to remain content to have only this one chapter as a broad and shallow survey of the Go language (at least until the second edition comes out).

But learning Go's syntax and grammar will only get you so far. In Chapter 4 I'll be presenting a variety of Go programming patterns that I see come up pretty regularly in the "cloud native" context. So, if you thought this chapter was interesting, you're going to love the next one.

---

8 One last time, if you haven't read it yet, go read *The Go Programming Language* by Donovan and Kernighan (Addison-Wesley Professional).

Cloud Native Patterns

> Progress is possible only if we train ourselves to think about programs without think-
> ing of them as pieces of executable code.[1]
>
> —Edsger W. Dijkstra, *August 1979*

In 1991, while still at Sun Microsystems, L Peter Deutsch[2] formulated the *Fallacies of
Distributed Computing*, which lists some of the false assumptions that programmers
new (and not so new) to distributed applications often make:

- *The network is reliable*: switches fail, routers get misconfigured
- *Latency is zero*: it takes time to move data across a network
- *Bandwidth is infinite*: a network can only handle so much data at a time
- *The network is secure*: don't share secrets in plain text; encrypt everything
- *Topology doesn't change*: servers and services come and go
- *There is one administrator*: multiple admins lead to heterogeneous solutions
- *Transport cost is zero*: moving data around costs time and money
- *The network is homogeneous*: every network is (sometimes very) different

If I might be so audacious, I'd like to add a ninth one as well:

- *Services are reliable*: services that you depend on can fail at any time

---

1 Spoken August 1979. Attested to by Vicki Almstrum, Tony Hoare, Niklaus Wirth, Wim Feijen, and Rajeev
  Joshi. In Pursuit of Simplicity: A Symposium Honoring Professor Edsger Wybe Dijkstra, 12–13 May 2000.

2 L (yes, his legal name is L) is a brilliant and fascinating human being. Look him up some time.

In this chapter, I'll present a selection of idiomatic patterns—tested, proven development paradigms—designed to address one or more of the conditions described in Deutsch's Fallacies, and demonstrate how to implement them in Go. None of the patterns discussed in this book are original to this book—some have been around for as long as distributed applications have existed—but most haven't been previously published together in a single work. Many of them are unique to Go or have novel implementations in Go relative to other languages.

Unfortunately, this book won't cover infrastructure-level patterns like the Bulkhead (*https://oreil.ly/0hxmU*) or Gatekeeper (*https://oreil.ly/0v5Jc*) patterns. Largely, this is because our focus is on application-layer development in Go, and those patterns, while indispensable, function at an entirely different abstraction level. If you're interested in learning more, I recommend *Cloud Native Infrastructure* by Justin Garrison and Kris Nova (O'Reilly) and *Designing Distributed Systems* by Brendan Burns (O'Reilly).

The Context Package

Most of the code examples in this chapter make use of the `context` package, which was introduced in Go 1.7 to provide an idiomatic means of carrying deadlines, cancellation signals, and request-scoped values between processes. It contains a single interface, `context.Context`, whose methods are listed in the following:

```
type Context interface {
    // Done returns a channel that's closed when this Context is cancelled.
    Done() <-chan struct{}

    // Err indicates why this context was cancelled after the Done channel is
    // closed. If Done is not yet closed, Err returns nil.
    Err() error

    // Deadline returns the time when this Context should be cancelled; it
    // returns ok==false if no deadline is set.
    Deadline() (deadline time.Time, ok bool)

    // Value returns the value associated with this context for key, or nil
    // if no value is associated with key. Use with care.
    Value(key interface{}) interface{}
}
```

Three of these methods can be used to learn something about a `Context` value's cancellation status or behavior. The fourth, `Value`, can be used to retrieve a value associated with an arbitrary key. `Context`'s `Value` method is the focus of some controversy in the Go world, and will be discussed more in "Defining Request-Scoped Values" on page 75.

What Context Can Do for You

A `context.Context` value is used by passing it directly to a service request, which may in turn pass it to one or more subrequests. What makes this useful is that when the `Context` is cancelled, all functions holding it (or a derived `Context`; more on this in Figures 4-1, 4-2, and 4-3) will receive the signal, allowing them to coordinate their cancellation and reduce the amount of wasted effort.

Take, for example, a request from a user to a service, which in turn makes a request to a database. In an ideal scenario, the user, application, and database requests can be diagrammed as in Figure 4-1.

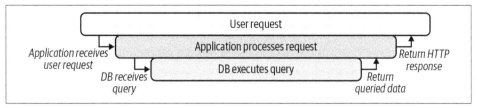

Figure 4-1. A successful request from a user, to a service, to a database

But what if the user terminates their request before it's fully completed? In most cases, oblivious to the overall context of the request, the processes will continue to live on anyway (Figure 4-2), consuming resources in order to provide a result that'll never be used.

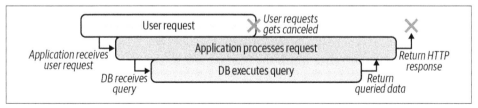

Figure 4-2. Subprocesses, unaware of a cancelled user request, will continue anyway

However, by sharing a `Context` to each subsequent request, all long-running processes can be sent a simultaneous "done" signal, allowing the cancellation signal to be coordinated among each of the processes (Figure 4-3).

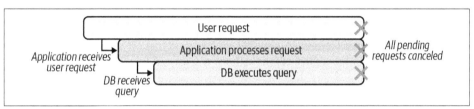

Figure 4-3. By sharing context, cancellation signals can be coordinated among processes

Importantly, Context values are also thread safe, i.e., they can be safely used by multiple concurrently executing goroutines without fear of unexpected behaviors.

Creating Context

A brand-new context.Context can be obtained using one of two functions:

func Background() Context
> Returns an empty Context that's never cancelled, has no values, and has no deadline. It is typically used by the main function, initialization, and tests, and as the top-level Context for incoming requests.

func TODO() Context
> Also provides an empty Context, but it's intended to be used as a placeholder when it's unclear which Context to use or when a parent Context is not yet available.

Defining Context Deadlines and Timeouts

The context package also includes a number of methods for creating *derived* Context values that allow you to direct cancellation behavior, either by applying a timeout or by a function hook that can explicitly trigger a cancellation.

func WithDeadline(Context, time.Time) (Context, CancelFunc)
> Accepts a specific time at which the Context will be cancelled and the Done channel will be closed.

func WithTimeout(Context, time.Duration) (Context, CancelFunc)
> Accepts a duration after which the Context will be cancelled and the Done channel will be closed.

func WithCancel(Context) (Context, CancelFunc)
> Unlike the previous functions, WithCancel accepts nothing, and only returns a function that can be called to explicitly cancel the Context.

All three of these functions return a derived Context that includes any requested decoration, and a context.CancelFunc, a zero-parameter function that can be called to explicitly cancel the Context and all of its derived values.

> When a Context is cancelled, all Contexts that are *derived from it* are also cancelled. Contexts that *it was derived from* are not.

Defining Request-Scoped Values

Finally, the context package includes a function that can be used to define an arbitrary *request-scoped* key-value pair that can be accessed from the returned Context—and all Context values derived from it—via the Value method.

```
func WithValue(parent Context, key, val interface{}) Context
```
   WithValue returns a derivation of parent in which key is associated with the value val.

On Context Values

The context.WithValue and context.Value functions provide convenient mechanisms for setting and getting arbitrary key-value pairs that can be used by consuming processes and APIs. However, it has been argued that this functionality is orthogonal to Context's function of orchestrating the cancellation of long-lived requests, obscures your program's flow, and can easily break compile-time coupling. For a more in-depth discussion, please see Dave Cheney's blog post *Context Is for Cancelation* (*https://oreil.ly/DaGN1*).

This functionality isn't used in any of the examples in this chapter (or this book). If you choose to make use of it, please take care to ensure that all of your values are scoped only to the request, don't alter the functioning of any processes, and don't break your processes if they happen to be absent.

Using a Context

When a service request is initiated, either by an incoming request or triggered by the main function, the top-level process will use the Background function to create a new Context value, possibly decorating it with one or more of the context.With* functions, before passing it along to any subrequests. Those subrequests then need only watch the Done channel for cancellation signals.

For example, take a look at the following Stream function:

```
func Stream(ctx context.Context, out chan<- Value) error {
    // Create a derived Context with a 10s timeout; dctx
    // will be cancelled upon timeout, but ctx will not.
    // cancel is a function that will explicitly cancel dctx.
    dctx, cancel := context.WithTimeout(ctx, time.Second * 10)

    // Release resources if SlowOperation completes before timeout
    defer cancel()

    res, err := SlowOperation(dctx)
    if err != nil {                       // True if dctx times out
```

```
        return err
    }

    for {
        select {
        case out <- res:              // Read from res; send to out

        case <-ctx.Done():            // Triggered if ctx is cancelled
            return ctx.Err()
        }
    }
}
```

Stream receives a ctx Context as an input parameter, which it sends to WithTimeout to create dctx, a derived Context with a 10-second timeout. Because of this decoration, the SlowOperation(dctx) call could possibly time out after ten seconds and return an error. Functions using the original ctx, however, will not have this timeout decoration, and will not time out.

Further down, the original ctx value is used in a for loop around a select statement to retrieve values from the res channel provided by the SlowOperation function. Note the case <-ctx.Done() statement, which is executed when the ctx.Done channel closes to return an appropriate error value.

Layout of this Chapter

The general presentation of each pattern in this chapter is loosely based on the one used in the famous "Gang of Four" *Design Patterns* book,[3] but simpler and less formal. Each pattern opens with a very brief description of its purpose and the reasons for using it, and is followed by the following sections:

Applicability
    Context and descriptions of where this pattern may be applied.

Participants
    A listing of the components of the pattern and their roles.

Implementation
    A discussion of the solution and its implementation.

Sample code
    A demonstration of how the code may be implemented in Go.

---

3 Erich Gamma et al. *Design Patterns: Elements of Reusable Object-Oriented Software*, 1st edition. Addison-Wesley Professional, 1994).

Stability Patterns

The stability patterns presented here address one or more of the assumptions called out by the Fallacies of Distributed Computing. They're generally intended to be applied by distributed applications to improve their own stability and the stability of the larger system they're a part of.

Circuit Breaker

Circuit Breaker automatically degrades service functions in response to a likely fault, preventing larger or cascading failures by eliminating recurring errors and providing reasonable error responses.

Applicability

If the *Fallacies of Distributed Computing* were to be distilled to one point, it would be that errors and failures are an undeniable fact of life for distributed, cloud native systems. Services become misconfigured, databases crash, networks partition. We can't prevent it; we can only accept and account for it.

Failing to do so can have some rather unpleasant consequences. We've all seen them, and they aren't pretty. Some services might keep futilely trying to do their job and returning nonsense to their client; others might fail catastrophically and maybe even fall into a crash/restart death spiral. It doesn't matter, because in the end they're all wasting resources, obscuring the source of original failure, and making cascading failures even more likely.

On the other hand, a service that's designed with the assumption that its dependencies can fail at any time can respond reasonably when they do. The Circuit Breaker allows a service to detect such failures and to "open the circuit" by temporarily ceasing to execute requests, instead providing clients with an error message consistent with the service's communication contract.

For example, imagine a service that (ideally) receives a request from a client, executes a database query, and returns a response. What if the database fails? The service might continue futilely trying to query it anyway, flooding the logs with error messages and eventually timing out or returning useless errors. Such a service can use a Circuit Breaker to "open the circuit" when the database fails, preventing the service from making any more doomed database requests (at least for a while), and allowing it to respond to the client immediately with a meaningful notification.

Participants

This pattern includes the following participants:

Circuit
    The function that interacts with the service.

Breaker
    A closure with the same function signature as *Circuit*.

Implementation

Essentially, the Circuit Breaker is just a specialized Adapter (*https://oreil.ly/bEeru*) pattern, with `Breaker` wrapping `Circuit` to add some additional error handling logic.

Like the electrical switch from which this pattern derives its name, `Breaker` has two possible states: *closed* and *open*. In the closed state everything is functioning normally. All requests received from the client by `Breaker` are forwarded unchanged to `Circuit`, and all responses from `Circuit` are forwarded back to the client. In the open state, `Breaker` doesn't forward requests to `Circuit`. Instead it "fails fast" by responding with an informative error message.

`Breaker` internally tracks the errors returned by `Circuit`; if the number of consecutive errors returned by `Circuit` returns exceeds a defined threshold, `Breaker` *trips* and its state switches to *open*.

Most implementations of Circuit Breaker include some logic to automatically close the circuit after some period of time. Keep in mind, though, that hammering an already malfunctioning service with lots of retries can cause its own problems, so it's standard to include some kind of *backoff*, logic that reduces the rate of retries over time. The subject of backoff is actually fairly nuanced, but it will be covered in detail in in "Play It Again: Retrying Requests" on page 275.

In a multinode service, this implementation may be extended to include some shared storage mechanism, such as a Memcached or Redis network cache, to track the circuit state.

Sample code

We begin by creating a `Circuit` type that specifies the signature of the function that's interacting with your database or other upstream service. In practice, this can take whatever form is appropriate for your functionality. It should include an `error` in its return list, however:

```
type Circuit func(context.Context) (string, error)
```

In this example, `Circuit` is a function that accepts a `Context` value, which was described in depth in "The Context Package" on page 72. Your implementation may vary.

The `Breaker` function accepts any function that conforms to the `Circuit` type definition, and an unsigned integer representing the number of consecutive failures allowed before the circuit automatically opens. In return it provides another function, which also conforms to the `Circuit` type definition:

```go
func Breaker(circuit Circuit, failureThreshold uint) Circuit {
    var consecutiveFailures int = 0
    var lastAttempt = time.Now()
    var m sync.RWMutex

    return func(ctx context.Context) (string, error) {
        m.RLock()                         // Establish a "read lock"

        d := consecutiveFailures - int(failureThreshold)

        if d >= 0 {
            shouldRetryAt := lastAttempt.Add(time.Second * 2 << d)
            if !time.Now().After(shouldRetryAt) {
                m.RUnlock()
                return "", errors.New("service unreachable")
            }
        }

        m.RUnlock()                       // Release read lock

        response, err := circuit(ctx)     // Issue request proper

        m.Lock()                          // Lock around shared resources
        defer m.Unlock()

        lastAttempt = time.Now()          // Record time of attempt

        if err != nil {                   // Circuit returned an error,
            consecutiveFailures++         // so we count the failure
            return response, err          // and return
        }

        consecutiveFailures = 0           // Reset failures counter

        return response, nil
    }
}
```

The `Breaker` function constructs another function, also of type `Circuit`, which wraps `circuit` to provide the desired functionality. You may recognize this from "Anonymous Functions and Closures" on page 55 as a closure: a nested function with access to the variables of its parent function. As you will see, all of the "stability" functions implemented for this chapter work this way.

The closure works by counting the number of consecutive errors returned by circuit. If that value meets the failure threshold, then it returns the error "service unreachable" without actually calling circuit. Any successful calls to circuit cause consecutiveFailures to reset to 0, and the cycle begins again.

The closure even includes an automatic reset mechanism that allows requests to call circuit again after several seconds, with an *exponential backoff* in which the durations of the delays between retries roughly doubles with each attempt. Though simple and quite common, this actually isn't the ideal backoff algorithm. We'll review exactly why in "Backoff Algorithms" on page 276.

Debounce

Debounce limits the frequency of a function invocation so that only the first or last in a cluster of calls is actually performed.

Applicability

Debounce is the second of our patterns to be labeled with an electrical circuit theme. Specifically, it's named after a phenomenon in which a switch's contacts "bounce" when they're opened or closed, causing the circuit to fluctuate a bit before settling down. It's usually no big deal, but this "contact bounce" can be a real problem in logic circuits where a series of on/off pulses can be interpreted as a data stream. The practice of eliminating contact bounce so that only one signal is transmitted by an opening or closing contact is called "debouncing."

In the world of services, we sometimes find ourselves performing a cluster of potentially slow or costly operations where only one would do. Using the Debounce pattern, a series of similar calls that are tightly clustered in time are restricted to only one call, typically the first or last in a batch.

This technique has been used in the JavaScript world for years to limit the number of operations that could slow the browser by taking only the first in a series of user events or to delay a call until a user is ready. You've probably seen an application of this technique in practice before. We're all familiar with the experience of using a search bar whose autocomplete pop-up doesn't display until after you pause typing, or spam-clicking a button only to see the clicks after the first ignored.

Those of us who specialize in backend services can learn a lot from our frontend brethren, who have been working for years to account for the reliability, latency, and bandwidth issues inherent to distributed systems. For example, this approach could be used to retrieve some slowly updating remote resource without bogging down, wasting both client and server time with wasteful requests.

This pattern is similar to "Throttle" on page 86, in that it limits how often a function can be called. But where Debounce restricts clusters of invocations, Throttle simply limits according to time period. For more on the difference between the Debounce and Throttle patterns, see "What's the Difference Between Throttle and Debounce?" on page 87.

Participants

This pattern includes the following participants:

Circuit
   The function to regulate.

Debounce
   A closure with the same function signature as *Circuit*.

Implementation

The Debounce implementation is actually very similar to the one for Circuit Breaker in that it wraps *Circuit* to provide the rate-limiting logic. That logic is actually quite straightforward: on each call of the outer function—regardless of its outcome—a time interval is set. Any subsequent call made before that time interval expires is ignored; any call made afterwards is passed along to the inner function. This implementation, in which the inner function is called once and subsequent calls are ignored, is called *function-first*, and is useful because it allows the initial response from the inner function to be cached and returned.

A *function-last* implementation will wait for a pause after a series of calls before calling the inner function. This variant is common in the JavaScript world when a programmer wants a certain amount of input before making a function call, such as when a search bar waits for a pause in typing before autocompleting. Function-last tends to be less common in backend services because it doesn't provide an immediate response, but it can be useful if your function doesn't need results right away.

Sample code

Just like in the Circuit Breaker implementation, we start by defining a function type with the signature of the function we want to limit. Also like Circuit Breaker, we call it `Circuit`; it's identical to the one declared in that example. Again, `Circuit` can take whatever form is appropriate for your functionality, but it should include an `error` in its returns:

```
type Circuit func(context.Context) (string, error)
```

The similarity with the Circuit Breaker implementation is quite intentional: their compatibility makes them "chainable," as demonstrated in the following:

```
func myFunction func(ctx context.Context) (string, error) { /* ... */ }

wrapped := Breaker(Debounce(myFunction))
response, err := wrapped(ctx)
```

The function-first implementation of Debounce—DebounceFirst—is very straight-forward compared to function-last because it only needs to track the last time it was called and return a cached result if it's called again less than d duration after:

```
func DebounceFirst(circuit Circuit, d time.Duration) Circuit {
    var threshold time.Time
    var result string
    var err error
    var m sync.Mutex

    return func(ctx context.Context) (string, error) {
        m.Lock()

        defer func() {
            threshold = time.Now().Add(d)
            m.Unlock()
        }()

        if time.Now().Before(threshold) {
            return result, err
        }

        result, err = circuit(ctx)

        return result, err
    }
}
```

This implementation of DebounceFirst takes pains to ensure thread safety by wrapping the entire function in a mutex. While this will force overlapping calls at the start of a cluster to have to wait until the result is cached, it also guarantees that circuit is called exactly once, at the very beginning of a cluster. A defer ensures that the value of threshold, representing the time when a cluster ends (if there are no further calls), is reset with every call.

Our function-last implementation is a bit more awkward because it involves the use of a time.Ticker to determine whether enough time has passed since the function was last called, and to call circuit when it has. Alternatively, we could create a new time.Ticker with every call, but that can get quite expensive if it's called frequently:

```go
type Circuit func(context.Context) (string, error)

func DebounceLast(circuit Circuit, d time.Duration) Circuit {
    var threshold time.Time = time.Now()
    var ticker *time.Ticker
    var result string
    var err error
    var once sync.Once
    var m sync.Mutex

    return func(ctx context.Context) (string, error) {
        m.Lock()
        defer m.Unlock()

        threshold = time.Now().Add(d)

        once.Do(func() {
            ticker = time.NewTicker(time.Millisecond * 100)

            go func() {
                defer func() {
                    m.Lock()
                    ticker.Stop()
                    once = sync.Once{}
                    m.Unlock()
                }()

                for {
                    select {
                    case <-ticker.C:
                        m.Lock()
                        if time.Now().After(threshold) {
                            result, err = circuit(ctx)
                            m.Unlock()
                            return
                        }
                        m.Unlock()
                    case <-ctx.Done():
                        m.Lock()
                        result, err = "", ctx.Err()
                        m.Unlock()
                        return
                    }
                }
            }()
        })

        return result, err
    }
}
```

Like DebounceFirst, DebounceLast uses a value called threshold to indicate the end of a cluster of calls (assuming there are no additional calls). The similarity largely ends there however.

You'll notice that almost the entire function is run inside of the Do method of a sync.Once value, which ensures that (as its name suggests) the contained function is run *exactly* once. Inside this block, a time.Ticker is used to check whether threshold has been passed and to call circuit if it has. Finally, the time.Ticker is stopped, the sync.Once is reset, and the cycle is primed to repeat.

Retry

Retry accounts for a possible transient fault in a distributed system by transparently retrying a failed operation.

Applicability

Transient errors are a fact of life when working with complex distributed systems. These can be caused by any number of (hopefully) temporary conditions, especially if the downstream service or network resource has protective strategies in place, such as throttling that temporarily rejects requests under high workload, or adaptive strategies like autoscaling that can add capacity when needed.

These faults typically resolve themselves after a bit of time, so repeating the request after a reasonable delay is likely (but not guaranteed) to be successful. Failing to account for transient faults can lead to a system that's unnecessarily brittle. On the other hand, implementing an automatic retry strategy can considerably improve the stability of the service that can benefit both it and its upstream consumers.

Participants

This pattern includes the following participants:

Effector
    The function that interacts with the service.

Retry
    A function that accepts *Effector* and returns a closure with the same function signature as *Effector*.

Implementation

This pattern works similarly to Circuit Breaker or Debounce in that there is a type, *Effector*, that defines a function signature. This signature can take whatever form is appropriate for your implementation, but when the function executing the potentially-failing operation is implemented, it must match the signature defined by *Effector*.

The *Retry* function accepts the user-defined *Effector* function and returns an *Effector* function that wraps the user-defined function to provide the retry logic. Along with the user-defined function, *Retry* also accepts an integer describing the maximum number of retry attempts that it will make, and a `time.Duration` that describes how long it'll wait between each retry attempt. If the `retries` parameter is 0, then the retry logic will effectively become a no-op.

 Although not included here, retry logic will typically include some kind of a backoff algorithm.

Sample code

The signature for function argument of the `Retry` function is `Effector`. It looks exactly like the function types for the previous patterns:

```
type Effector func(context.Context) (string, error)
```

The `Retry` function itself is relatively straightforward, at least when compared to the functions we've seen so far:

```
func Retry(effector Effector, retries int, delay time.Duration) Effector {
    return func(ctx context.Context) (string, error) {
        for r := 0; ; r++ {
            response, err := effector(ctx)
            if err == nil || r >= retries {
                return response, err
            }

            log.Printf("Attempt %d failed; retrying in %v", r + 1, delay)

            select {
            case <-time.After(delay):
            case <-ctx.Done():
                return "", ctx.Err()
            }
        }
    }
}
```

You may have already noticed what it is that keeps the `Retry` function so slender: although it returns a function, that function doesn't have any external state. This means we don't need any elaborate mechanisms to support concurrency.

To use Retry, we can implement the function that executes the potentially-failing operation and whose signature matches the Effector type; this role is played by EmulateTransientError in the following example:

```
var count int

func EmulateTransientError(ctx context.Context) (string, error) {
    count++

    if count <= 3 {
        return "intentional fail", errors.New("error")
    } else {
        return "success", nil
    }
}

func main() {
    r := Retry(EmulateTransientError, 5, 2*time.Second)

    res, err := r(context.Background())

    fmt.Println(res, err)
}
```

In the main function, the EmulateTransientError function is passed to Retry, providing the function variable r. When r is called, EmulateTransientError is called, and called again after a delay if it returns an error, according to the retry logic shown previously. Finally, after the fourth attempt, EmulateTransientError returns a nil error and exits.

Throttle

Throttle limits the frequency of a function call to some maximum number of invocations per unit of time.

Applicability

The Throttle pattern is named after a device used to manage the flow of a fluid, such as the amount of fuel going into a car engine. Like its namesake mechanism, Throttle restricts the number of times that a function can be called during over a period of time. For example:

- A user may only be allowed 10 service requests per second.
- A client may restrict itself to call a particular function once every 500 milliseconds.
- An account may only be allowed three failed login attempts in a 24-hour period.

Perhaps the most common reason to apply a Throttle is to account for sharp activity spikes that could saturate the system with a possibly unreasonable number of requests that may be expensive to satisfy, or lead to service degradation and eventually failure. While it may be possible for a system to scale up to add sufficient capacity to meet user demand, this takes time, and the system may not be able to react quickly enough.

What's the Difference Between Throttle and Debounce?

Conceptually, Debounce and Throttle seem fairly similar. After all, they're both about reducing the number of calls per unit of time. However, as illustrated in Figure 4-4, the precise timing of each differs quite a bit:

- *Throttle* works like the throttle in a car, limiting the amount of fuel going into the engine by capping the flow of fuel to some maximum rate. This is illustrated in Figure 4-4: no matter how many times the input function is called, Throttle only allows a fixed number of calls to proceed per unit of time.

- *Debounce* focuses on clusters of activity, making sure that a function is called only once during a cluster of requests, either at the start or the end of the cluster. A function-first debounce implementation is illustrated in Figure 4-4: for each of the two clusters of calls to the input function, Debounce only allows one call to proceed at the beginning of each cluster.

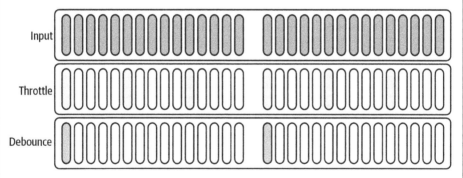

Figure 4-4. Throttle limits the event rate; debounce allows only one event in a cluster

Participants

This pattern includes the following participants:

Effector
    The function to regulate.

Throttle
    A function that accepts *Effector* and returns a closure with the same function signature as *Effector*.

Implementation

The Throttle pattern is similar to many of the other patterns described in this chapter: it's implemented as a function that accepts an effector function, and returns a `Throttle` closure with the same signature that provides the rate-limiting logic.

The most common algorithm for implementing rate-limiting behavior is the *token bucket* (*https://oreil.ly/5A5aP*), which uses the analogy of a bucket that can hold some maximum number of tokens. When a function is called, a token is taken from the bucket, which then refills at some fixed rate.

The way that a `Throttle` treats requests when there are insufficient tokens in the bucket to pay for it can vary depending according to the needs of the developer. Some common strategies are:

Return an error
    This is the most basic strategy and is common when you're only trying to restrict unreasonable or potentially abusive numbers of client requests. A RESTful service adopting this strategy might respond with a status 429 (Too Many Requests).

Replay the response of the last successful function call
    This strategy can be useful when a service or expensive function call is likely to provide an identical result if called too soon. It's commonly used in the JavaScript world.

Enqueue the request for execution when sufficient tokens are available
    This approach can be useful when you want to eventually handle all requests, but it's also more complex and may require care to be taken to ensure that memory isn't exhausted.

Sample code

The following example implements a very basic "token bucket" algorithm that uses the "error" strategy:

```
type Effector func(context.Context) (string, error)

func Throttle(e Effector, max uint, refill uint, d time.Duration) Effector {
    var tokens = max
    var once sync.Once

    return func(ctx context.Context) (string, error) {
        if ctx.Err() != nil {
            return "", ctx.Err()
        }

        once.Do(func() {
            ticker := time.NewTicker(d)

            go func() {
                defer ticker.Stop()

                for {
                    select {
                    case <-ctx.Done():
                        return

                    case <-ticker.C:
                        t := tokens + refill
                        if t > max {
                            t = max
                        }
                        tokens = t
                    }
                }
            }()
        })

        if tokens <= 0 {
            return "", fmt.Errorf("too many calls")
        }

        tokens--

        return e(ctx)
    }
}
```

This `Throttle` implementation is similar to our other examples in that it wraps an
effector function e with a closure that contains the rate-limiting logic. The bucket is
initially allocated max tokens; each time the closure is triggered it checks whether it
has any remaining tokens. If tokens are available, it decrements the token count by
one and triggers the effector function. If not, an error is returned. Tokens are added
at a rate of refill tokens every duration d.

Timeout

Timeout allows a process to stop waiting for an answer once it's clear that an answer may not be coming.

Applicability

The first of the Fallacies of Distributed Computing is that "the network is reliable," and it's first for a reason. Switches fail, routers and firewalls get misconfigured; packets get blackholed. Even if your network is working perfectly, not every service is thoughtful enough to guarantee a meaningful and timely response—or any response at all—if and when it malfunctions.

Timeout represents a common solution to this dilemma, and is so beautifully simple that it barely even qualifies as a pattern at all: given a service request or function call that's running for a longer-than-expected time, the caller simply…stops waiting.

However, don't mistake "simple" or "common" for "useless." On the contrary, the ubiquity of the timeout strategy is a testament to its usefulness. The judicious use of timeouts can provide a degree of fault isolation, preventing cascading failures and reducing the chance that a problem in a downstream resource becomes *your* problem.

Participants

This pattern includes the following participants:

Client
    The client who wants to execute *SlowFunction*.

SlowFunction
    The long-running function that implements the functionality desired by *Client*.

Timeout
    A wrapper function around *SlowFunction* that implements the timeout logic.

Implementation

There are several ways to implement a timeout in Go, but the idiomatic way is to use the functionality provided by the `context` package. See "The Context Package" on page 72 for more information.

In an ideal world, any possibly long-running function will accept a `context.Context` parameter directly. If so, your work is fairly straightforward: you need only pass it a `Context` value decorated with the `context.WithTimeout` function:

```
ctx := context.Background()
ctxt, cancel := context.WithTimeout(ctx, 10 * time.Second)
defer cancel()

result, err := SomeFunction(ctxt)
```

However, this isn't always the case, and with third party libraries you don't always have the option of refactoring to accept a Context value. In these cases, the best course of action may be to wrap the function call in such a way that it *does* respect your Context.

For example, imagine you have a potentially long-running function that not only doesn't accept a Context value, but comes from a package you don't control. If *Client* were to call *SlowFunction* directly it would be forced to wait until the function completes, if indeed it ever does. Now what?

Instead of calling *SlowFunction* directly, you can call it in a goroutine. In this way, you can capture the results it returns, if it returns them in an acceptable period of time. However, this also allows you to move on if it doesn't.

To do this, we can leverage a few tools that we've seen before: context.Context for timeouts, channels for communicating results, and select to catch whichever one acts first.

Sample code

The following example imagines the existence of the fictional function, Slow, whose execution may or may not complete in some reasonable amount of time, and whose signature conforms with the following type definition:

```
type SlowFunction func(string) (string, error)
```

Rather than calling Slow directly, we instead provide a Timeout function, which wraps a provided SlowFunction in a closure and returns a WithContext function, which adds a context.Context to the SlowFunction's parameter list:

```
type WithContext func(context.Context, string) (string, error)

func Timeout(f SlowFunction) WithContext {
    return func(ctx context.Context, arg string) (string, error) {
        chres := make(chan string)
        cherr := make(chan error)

        go func() {
            res, err := f(arg)
            chres <- res
            cherr <- err
        }()

        select {
```

```
            case res := <-chres:
                return res, <-cherr
            case <-ctx.Done():
                return "", ctx.Err()
            }
        }
    }
```

Within the function that Timeout constructs, Slow is run in a goroutine, with its
return values being sent into channels constructed for that purpose, if and when it
ever completes.

The following goroutine statement is a select block on two channels: the first of the
Slow function response channels, and the Context value's Done channel. If the former
completes first, the closure will return the Slow function's return values; otherwise it
returns the error provided by the Context.

Using the Timeout function isn't much more complicated than consuming Slow
directly, except that instead of one function call, we have two: the call to Timeout to
retrieve the closure, and the call to the closure itself:

```
func main() {
    ctx := context.Background()
    ctxt, cancel := context.WithTimeout(ctx, 1*time.Second)
    defer cancel()

    timeout := Timeout(Slow)
    res, err := timeout(ctxt, "some input")

    fmt.Println(res, err)
}
```

Finally, although it's usually preferred to implement service timeouts using
context.Context, channel timeouts *can* also be implemented using the channel provided by the time.After function. See "Implementing channel timeouts" on page 68
for an example of how this is done.

Concurrency Patterns

A cloud native service will often be called upon to efficiently juggle multiple processes and handle high (and highly variable) levels of load, ideally without having to
suffer the trouble and expense of scaling up. As such, it needs to be highly concurrent
and able to manage multiple simultaneous requests from multiple clients. While Go
is known for its concurrency support, bottlenecks can and do happen. Some of the
patterns that have been developed to prevent them are presented here.

Fan-In

Fan-in multiplexes multiple input channels onto one output channel.

Applicability

Services that have some number of workers that all generate output may find it useful to combine all of the workers' outputs to be processed as a single unified stream. For these scenarios we use the fan-in pattern, which can read from multiple input channels by multiplexing them onto a single destination channel.

Participants

This pattern includes the following participants:

Sources
> A set of one or more input channels with the same type. Accepted by *Funnel*.

Destination
> An output channel of the same type as *Sources*. Created and provided by *Funnel*.

Funnel
> Accepts *Sources* and immediately returns *Destination*. Any input from any *Sources* will be output by *Destination*.

Implementation

Funnel is implemented as a function that receives zero to N input channels (*Sources*). For each input channel in *Sources*, the *Funnel* function starts a separate goroutine to read values from its assigned channel and forward them to a single output channel shared by all of the goroutines (*Destination*).

Sample code

The Funnel function is a variadic function that receives sources: zero to N channels of some type (int in the following example):

```
func Funnel(sources ...<-chan int) <-chan int {
    dest := make(chan int)              // The shared output channel

    var wg sync.WaitGroup               // Used to automatically close dest
                                        // when all sources are closed

    wg.Add(len(sources))                // Set size of the WaitGroup

    for _, ch := range sources {        // Start a goroutine for each source
        go func(c <-chan int) {
            defer wg.Done()             // Notify WaitGroup when c closes
```

```go
        for n := range c {
            dest <- n
        }
    }(ch)
}

go func() {                          // Start a goroutine to close dest
    wg.Wait()                        // after all sources close
    close(dest)
}()

return dest
}
```

For each channel in the list of sources, Funnel starts a dedicated goroutine that reads values from its assigned channel and forwards them to dest, a single-output channel shared by all of the goroutines.

Note the use of a sync.WaitGroup to ensure that the destination channel is closed appropriately. Initially, a WaitGroup is created and set to the total number of source channels. If a channel is closed, its associated goroutine exits, calling wg.Done. When all of the channels are closed, the WaitGroup's counter reaches zero, the lock imposed by wg.Wait is released, and the dest channel is closed.

Using Funnel is reasonably straightforward: given N source channels (or a slice of N channels), pass the channels to Funnel. The returned destination channel may be read in the usual way, and will close when all source channels close:

```go
func main() {
    sources := make([]<-chan int, 0)     // Create an empty channel slice

    for i := 0; i < 3; i++ {
        ch := make(chan int)
        sources = append(sources, ch)    // Create a channel; add to sources

        go func() {                      // Run a toy goroutine for each
            defer close(ch)              // Close ch when the routine ends

            for i := 1; i <= 5; i++ {
                ch <- i
                time.Sleep(time.Second)
            }
        }()
    }

    dest := Funnel(sources...)
    for d := range dest {
        fmt.Println(d)
    }
}
```

This example creates a slice of three `int` channels, into which the values from 1 to 5 are sent before being closed. In a separate goroutine, the outputs of the single `dest` channel are printed. Running this will result in the appropriate 15 lines being printed before `dest` closes and the function ends.

Fan-Out

Fan-out evenly distributes messages from an input channel to multiple output channels.

Applicability

Fan-out receives messages from an input channel, distributing them evenly among output channels, and is a useful pattern for parallelizing CPU and I/O utilization.

For example, imagine that you have an input source, such as a `Reader` on an input stream, or a listener on a message broker, that provides the inputs for some resource-intensive unit of work. Rather than coupling the input and computation processes, which would confine the effort to a single serial process, you might prefer to parallelize the workload by distributing it among some number of concurrent worker processes.

Participants

This pattern includes the following participants:

Source
    An input channel. Accepted by *Split*.

Destinations
    An output channel of the same type as *Source*. Created and provided by *Split*.

Split
    A function that accepts *Source* and immediately returns *Destinations*. Any input from *Source* will be output to a *Destination*.

Implementation

Fan-out may be relatively conceptually straightforward, but the devil is in the details.

Typically, fan-out is implemented as a *Split* function, which accepts a single *Source* channel and integer representing the desired number of *Destination* channels. The *Split* function creates the *Destination* channels and executes some background process that retrieves values from *Source* channel and forwards them to one of the *Destinations*.

The implementation of the forwarding logic can be done in one of two ways:

- Using a single goroutine that reads values from *Source* and forwards them to the *Destinations* in a round-robin fashion. This has the virtue of requiring only one master goroutine, but if the next channel isn't ready to read yet, it'll slow the entire process.

- Using separate goroutines for each *Destination* that compete to read the next value from *Source* and forward it to their respective *Destination*. This requires slightly more resources, but is less likely to get bogged down by a single slow-running worker.

The next example uses the latter approach.

Sample code

In this example, the Split function accepts a single receive-only channel, source, and an integer describing the number of channels to split the input into, n. It returns a slice of n send-only channels with the same type as source.

Internally, Split creates the destination channels. For each channel created, it executes a goroutine that retrieves values from source in a for loop and forwards them to their assigned output channel. Effectively, each goroutine competes for reads from source; if several are trying to read, the "winner" will be randomly determined. If source is closed, all goroutines terminate and all of the destination channels are closed:

```
func Split(source <-chan int, n int) []<-chan int {
    dests := make([]<-chan int, 0)        // Create the dests slice

    for i := 0; i < n; i++ {              // Create n destination channels
        ch := make(chan int)
        dests = append(dests, ch)

        go func() {                        // Each channel gets a dedicated
            defer close(ch)                // goroutine that competes for reads

            for val := range source {
                ch <- val
            }
        }()
    }

    return dests
}
```

Given a channel of some specific type, the Split function will return a number of destination channels. Typically, each will be passed to a separate goroutine, as demonstrated in the following example:

```go
func main() {
    source := make(chan int)              // The input channel
    dests := Split(source, 5)             // Retrieve 5 output channels

    go func() {                           // Send the number 1..10 to source
        for i := 1; i <= 10; i++ {        // and close it when we're done
            source <- i
        }

        close(source)
    }()

    var wg sync.WaitGroup                 // Use WaitGroup to wait until
    wg.Add(len(dests))                    // the output channels all close

    for i, ch := range dests {
        go func(i int, d <-chan int) {
            defer wg.Done()

            for val := range d {
                fmt.Printf("#%d got %d\n", i, val)
            }
        }(i, ch)
    }

    wg.Wait()
}
```

This example creates an input channel, source, which it passes to Split to receive its output channels. Concurrently it passes the values 1 to 10 into source in a goroutine, while receiving values from dests in five others. When the inputs are complete, the source channel is closed, which triggers closures in the output channels, which ends the read loops, which causes wg.Done to be called by each of the read goroutines, which releases the lock on wg.Wait, and allows the function to end.

Future

Future provides a placeholder for a value that's not yet known.

Applicability

Futures (also known as Promises or Delays[4]) are a synchronization construct that provide a placeholder for a value that's still being generated by an asynchronous process.

---

4 While these terms are often used interchangeably, they can also have shades of meaning depending on their
   context. I know. Please don't write me any angry letters about this.

This pattern isn't used as frequently in Go as in some other languages because channels can be often used in a similar way. For example, the long-running blocking function `BlockingInverse` (not shown) can be executed in a goroutine that returns the result (when it arrives) along a channel. The `ConcurrentInverse` function does exactly that, returning a channel that can be read when a result is available:

```go
func ConcurrentInverse(m Matrix) <-chan Matrix {
    out := make(chan Matrix)

    go func() {
        out <- BlockingInverse(m)
        close(out)
    }()

    return out
}
```

Using `ConcurrentInverse`, one could then build a function to calculate the inverse product of two matrices:

```go
func InverseProduct(a, b Matrix) Matrix {
    inva := ConcurrentInverse(a)
    invb := ConcurrentInverse(b)

    return Product(<-inva, <-invb)
}
```

This doesn't seem so bad, but it comes with some baggage that makes it undesirable for something like a public API. First, the caller has be careful to call `ConcurrentInverse` with the correct timing. To see what I mean, take a close look at the following:

```go
return Product(<-ConcurrentInverse(a), <-ConcurrentInverse(b))
```

See the problem? Since the computation isn't started until `ConcurrentInverse` is actually called, this construct would be effectively executed serially, requiring twice the runtime.

What's more, when using channels in this way, functions with more than one return value will usually assign a dedicated channel to each member of the return list, which can become awkward as the return list grows or when the values need to be read by more than one goroutine.

The Future pattern contains this complexity by encapsulating it in an API that provides the consumer with a simple interface whose method can be called normally, blocking all calling routines until all of its results are resolved. The interface that the value satisfies doesn't even have to be constructed specially for that purpose; any interface that's convenient for the consumer can be used.

Participants

This pattern includes the following participants:

Future
> The interface that is received by the consumer to retrieve the eventual result.

SlowFunction
> A wrapper function around some function to be asynchronously executed; provides *Future*.

InnerFuture
> Satisfies the *Future* interface; includes an attached method that contains the result access logic.

Implementation

The API presented to the consumer is fairly straightforward: the programmer calls *SlowFunction*, which returns a value that satisfies the *Future* interface. *Future* may be a bespoke interface, as in the following example, or it may be something more like an io.Reader that can be passed to its own functions.

In actuality, when *SlowFunction* is called, it executes the core function of interest as a goroutine. In doing so, it defines channels to capture the core function's output, which it wraps in *InnerFuture*.

InnerFuture has one or more methods that satisfy the *Future* interface, which retrieve the values returned by the core function from the channels, cache them, and return them. If the values aren't available on the channel, the request blocks. If they have already been retrieved, the cached values are returned.

Sample code

In this example, we use a Future interface that the InnerFuture will satisfy:

```
type Future interface {
    Result() (string, error)
}
```

The InnerFuture struct is used internally to provide the concurrent functionality. In this example, it satisfies the Future interface, but could just as easily choose to satisfy something like io.Reader by attaching a Read method, for example:

```
type InnerFuture struct {
    once sync.Once
    wg   sync.WaitGroup

    res   string
    err   error
    resCh <-chan string
```

```
    errCh <-chan error
}

func (f *InnerFuture) Result() (string, error) {
    f.once.Do(func() {
        f.wg.Add(1)
        defer f.wg.Done()
        f.res = <-f.resCh
        f.err = <-f.errCh
    })

    f.wg.Wait()

    return f.res, f.err
}
```

In this implementation, the struct itself contains a channel and a variable for each value returned by the Result method. When Result is first called, it attempts to read the results from the channels and send them back to the InnerFuture struct so that subsequent calls to Result can immediately return the cached values.

Note the use of sync.Once and sync.WaitGroup. The former does what it says on the tin: it ensures that the function that's passed to it is called exactly once. The WaitGroup is used to make this function call thread safe: any calls after the first will be blocked at wg.Wait until the channel reads are complete.

SlowFunction is a wrapper around the core functionality that you want to run concurrently. It has the job of creating the results channels, running the core function in a goroutine, and creating and returning the Future implementation (InnerFuture, in this example):

```
func SlowFunction(ctx context.Context) Future {
    resCh := make(chan string)
    errCh := make(chan error)

    go func() {
        select {
        case <-time.After(time.Second * 2):
            resCh <- "I slept for 2 seconds"
            errCh <- nil
        case <-ctx.Done():
            resCh <- ""
            errCh <- ctx.Err()
        }
    }()

    return &InnerFuture{resCh: resCh, errCh: errCh}
}
```

To make use of this pattern, you need only call the SlowFunction and use the returned Future as you would any other value:

```
func main() {
    ctx := context.Background()
    future := SlowFunction(ctx)

    res, err := future.Result()
    if err != nil {
        fmt.Println("error:", err)
        return
    }

    fmt.Println(res)
}
```

This approach provides a reasonably good user experience. The programmer can create a Future and access it as they wish, and can even apply timeouts or deadlines with a Context.

Sharding

Sharding splits a large data structure into multiple partitions to localize the effects of read/write locks.

Applicability

The term *sharding* is typically used in the context of distributed state to describe data that is partitioned between server instances. This kind of *horizontal sharding* is commonly used by databases and other data stores to distribute load and provide redundancy.

A slightly different issue can sometimes affect highly concurrent services that have a shared data structure with a locking mechanism to protect it from conflicting writes. In this scenario, the locks that serve to ensure the fidelity of the data can also create a bottleneck when processes start to spend more time waiting for locks than they do doing their jobs. This unfortunate phenomenon is called *lock contention*.

While this might be resolved in some cases by scaling the number of instances, this also increases complexity and latency, because distributed locks need to be established, and writes need to establish consistency. An alternative strategy for reducing lock contention around shared data structures within an instance of a service is *vertical sharding*, in which a large data structure is partitioned into two or more structures, each representing a part of the whole. Using this strategy, only a portion of the overall structure needs to be locked at a time, decreasing overall lock contention.

Participants

This pattern includes the following participants:

ShardedMap
> An abstraction around one or more *Shards* providing read and write access as if the *Shards* were a single map.

Shard
> An individually lockable collection representing a single data partition.

Implementation

While idiomatic Go strongly prefers the use of memory sharing via channels (*https://oreil.ly/BipeP*) over using locks to protect shared resources,[5] this isn't always possible. Maps are particularly unsafe for concurrent use, making the use of locks as a synchronization mechanism a necessary evil. Fortunately, Go provides `sync.RWMutex` for precisely this purpose.

`RWMutex` provides methods to establish both read and write locks, as demonstrated in the following. Using this method, any number of processes can establish simultaneous read locks as long as there are no open write locks; a process can establish a write lock only when there are no existing read or write locks. Attempts to establish additional locks will block until any locks ahead of it are released:

```
var items = struct{                  // Struct with a map and a
    sync.RWMutex                     // composed sync.RWMutex
    m map[string]int
}{m: make(map[string]int)}

func ThreadSafeRead(key string) int {
```

---

5 See the article, "Share Memory By Communicating," on *The Go Blog*.

```
    items.RLock()                                    // Establish read lock
    value := items.m[key]
    items.RUnlock()                                  // Release read lock
    return value
}

func ThreadSafeWrite(key string, value int) {
    items.Lock()                                     // Establish write lock
    items.m[key] = value
    items.Unlock()                                   // Release write lock
}
```

This strategy generally works perfectly fine. However, because locks allow access to only one process at a time, the average amount of time spent waiting for locks to clear in a read/write intensive application can increase dramatically with the number of concurrent processes acting on the resource. The resulting lock contention can potentially bottleneck key functionality.

Vertical sharding reduces lock contention by splitting the underlying data structure —usually a map—into several individually lockable maps. An abstraction layer provides access to the underlying shards as if they were a single structure (see Figure 4-5).

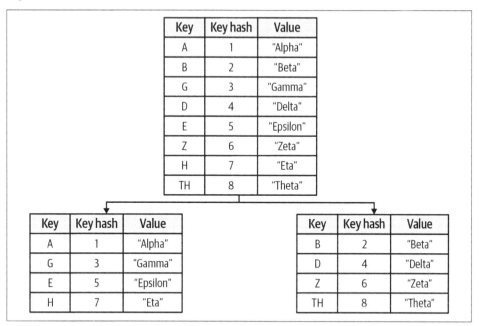

Figure 4-5. Vertically sharding a map by key hash

Internally, this is accomplished by creating an abstraction layer around what is essentially a map of maps. Whenever a value is read or written to the map abstraction, a hash value is calculated for the key, which is then modded by the number of shards to generate a shard index. This allows the map abstraction to isolate the necessary locking to only the shard at that index.

Sample code

In the following example, we use the standard sync and crypto/sha1 packages to implement a basic sharded map: ShardedMap.

Internally, ShardedMap is just a slice of pointers to some number of Shard values, but we define it as a type so we can attach methods to it. Each Shard includes a map[string]interface{} that contains that shard's data, and a composed sync.RWMutex so that it can be individually locked:

```go
type Shard struct {
    sync.RWMutex                    // Compose from sync.RWMutex
    m map[string]interface{}        // m contains the shard's data
}

type ShardedMap []*Shard           // ShardedMap is a *Shards slice
```

Go doesn't have any concept of constructors, so we provide a NewShardedMap function to retrieve a new ShardedMap:

```go
func NewShardedMap(nshards int) ShardedMap {
    shards := make([]*Shard, nshards)       // Initialize a *Shards slice

    for i := 0; i < nshards; i++ {
        shard := make(map[string]interface{})
        shards[i] = &Shard{m: shard}
    }

    return shards                           // A ShardedMap IS a *Shards slice!
}
```

ShardedMap has two unexported methods, getShardIndex and getShard, which are used to calculate a key's shard index and retrieve a key's correct shard, respectively. These could be easily combined into a single method, but slitting them this way makes them easier to test:

```go
func (m ShardedMap) getShardIndex(key string) int {
    checksum := sha1.Sum([]byte(key))   // Use Sum from "crypto/sha1"
    hash := int(checksum[17])           // Pick an arbitrary byte as the hash
    return hash % len(m)                // Mod by len(m) to get index
}

func (m ShardedMap) getShard(key string) *Shard {
    index := m.getShardIndex(key)
    return m[index]
}
```

Note that the previous example has an obvious weakness: because it's effectively using a byte-sized value as the hash value, it can only handle up to 255 shards. If for some reason you want more than that, you can sprinkle some binary arithmetic on it: hash := int(sum[13]) << 8 | int(sum[17]).

Finally, we add methods to ShardedMap to allow a user to read and write values. Obviously these don't demonstrate all of the functionality a map might need. The source for this example is in the GitHub repository associated with this book, however, so please feel free to implement them as an exercise. A Delete and a Contains method would be nice:

```
func (m ShardedMap) Get(key string) interface{} {
    shard := m.getShard(key)
    shard.RLock()
    defer shard.RUnlock()

    return shard.m[key]
}

func (m ShardedMap) Set(key string, value interface{}) {
    shard := m.getShard(key)
    shard.Lock()
    defer shard.Unlock()

    shard.m[key] = value
}
```

When you do need to establish locks on all of the tables, it's generally best to do so concurrently. In the following, we implement a Keys function using goroutines and our old friend sync.WaitGroup:

```
func (m ShardedMap) Keys() []string {
    keys := make([]string, 0)          // Create an empty keys slice

    mutex := sync.Mutex{}              // Mutex for write safety to keys

    wg := sync.WaitGroup{}             // Create a wait group and add a
    wg.Add(len(m))                     // wait value for each slice

    for _, shard := range m {          // Run a goroutine for each slice
        go func(s *Shard) {
            s.RLock()                  // Establish a read lock on s

            for key := range s.m {     // Get the slice's keys
                mutex.Lock()
                keys = append(keys, key)
                mutex.Unlock()
            }

            s.RUnlock()                // Release the read lock
            wg.Done()                  // Tell the WaitGroup it's done
```

```
        }(shard)
    }

    wg.Wait()                      // Block until all reads are done

    return keys                    // Return combined keys slice
}
```

Using `ShardedMap` isn't quite like using a standard map unfortunately, but while it's different, it's no more complicated:

```
func main() {
    shardedMap := NewShardedMap(5)

    shardedMap.Set("alpha", 1)
    shardedMap.Set("beta", 2)
    shardedMap.Set("gamma", 3)

    fmt.Println(shardedMap.Get("alpha"))
    fmt.Println(shardedMap.Get("beta"))
    fmt.Println(shardedMap.Get("gamma"))

    keys := shardedMap.Keys()
    for _, k := range keys {
        fmt.Println(k)
    }
}
```

Perhaps the greatest downside of the `ShardedMap` (besides its complexity, of course) is the loss of type safety associated with the use of `interface{}`, and the subsequent requirement of type assertions. Hopefully, with the impending release of generics for Go, this will soon be (or perhaps already is, depending on when you read this) a problem of the past!

Summary

This chapter covered quite a few very interesting—and useful—idioms. There are probably many more,[6] but these are the ones I felt were most important, either because they're somehow practical in a directly applicable way, or because they showcase some interesting feature of the Go language. Often both.

In Chapter 5 we'll move on to the next level, taking some of the things we discussed in Chapters 3 and 4, and putting them into practice by building a simple key-value store from scratch!

---

6 Did I leave out your favorite? Let me know, and I'll try to include it in the next edition!

Building a Cloud Native Service

Life was simple before World War II. After that, we had systems.[1]

—Grace Hopper, *OCLC Newsletter (1987)*

In this chapter, our real work finally begins.

We'll weave together many of the materials discussed throughout Part II to create a service that will serve as the jumping-off point for the remainder of the book. As we go forward, we'll iterate on what we begin here, adding layers of functionality with each chapter until, at the conclusion, we have ourselves a true cloud native application.

Naturally, it won't be "production ready"—it will be missing important security features, for example—but it will provide a solid foundation for us to build upon.

But what do we build?

Let's Build a Service!

Okay. So. We need something to build.

It should be conceptually simple, straightforward enough to implement in its most basic form, but non-trivial and amenable to scaling and distributing. Something that we can iteratively refine over the remainder of the book. I put a lot of thought into this, considering different ideas for what our application would be, but in the end the answer was obvious.

We'll build ourselves a distributed key-value store.

---

1 Schieber, Philip. "The Wit and Wisdom of Grace Hopper." *OCLC Newsletter*, March/April, 1987, No. 167.

What's a Key-Value Store?

A key-value store is a kind of nonrelational database that stores data as a collection of key-value pairs. They're very different from the better-known relational databases, like Microsoft SQL Server or PostgreSQL, that we know and love.[2] Where relational databases structure their data among fixed tables with well-defined data types, key-value stores are far simpler, allowing users to associate a unique identifier (the key) with an arbitrary value.

In other words, at its heart, a key-value store is really just a map with a service endpoint, as shown in Figure 5-1. They're the simplest possible database.

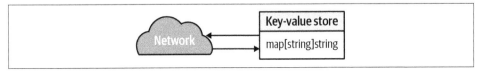

Figure 5-1. A key-value store is essentially a map with a service endpoint

Requirements

By the end of this chapter, we're going to have built a simple, nondistributed key-value store that can do all of the things that a (monolithic) key-value store should do.

- It must be able to store arbitrary key-value pairs.
- It must provide service endpoints that allow a user to put, get, and delete key-value pairs.
- It must be able to persistently store its data in some fashion.

Finally, we'd like the service to be idempotent. But why?

What Is Idempotence and Why Does It Matter?

The concept of *idempotence* has its origins in algebra, where it describes particular properties of certain mathematical operations. Fortunately, this isn't a math book. We're not going to talk about that (except in the sidebar at the end of this section).

In the programming world, an operation (such as a method or service call) is idempotent if calling it once has the same effect as calling it multiple times. For example, the assignment operation x=1 is idempotent, because x will always be 1 no matter how many times you assign it. Similarly, an HTTP PUT method is idempotent because PUT-ting a resource in a place multiple times won't change anything: it won't get any

---

2 For some definition of "love."

more PUT the second time.[3] The operation x+=1, however, is not idempotent, because every time that it's called, a new state is produced.

Less discussed, but also important, is the related property of *nullipotence*, in which a function or operation has no side effect at all. For example, the x=1 assignment and an HTTP PUT are idempotent but not nullipotent because they trigger state changes. Assigning a value to itself, such as x=x, is nullipotent because no state has changed as a result of it. Similarly, simply reading data, as with an HTTP GET, usually has no side effects, so it's also nullipotent.

Of course, that's all very nice in theory, but why should we care in the real world? Well, as it turns out, designing your service methods to be idempotent provides a number of very real benefits:

Idempotent operations are safer
> What if you make a request to a service, but get no response? You'll probably try again. But what if it heard you the first time?[4] If the service method is idempotent, then no harm done. But if it's not, you could have a problem. This scenario is more common than you think. Networks are unreliable. Responses can be delayed; packets can get dropped.

Idempotent operations are often simpler
> Idempotent operations are more self-contained and easier to implement. Compare, for example, an idempotent PUT method that simply adds a key-value pair into a backing data store, and a similar but nonidempotent CREATE method that returns an error if the data store already contains the key. The PUT logic is simple: receive request, set value. The CREATE, on the other hand, requires additional layers of error checking and handling, and possibly even distributed locking and coordination among any service replicas, making its service harder to scale.

Idempotent operations are more declarative
> Building an idempotent API encourages the designer to focus on end-states, encouraging the production of methods that are more *declarative*: they allow users to tell a service *what needs to be done*, instead of telling it *how to do it*. This may seem to be a fine point, but declarative methods—as opposed to *imperative methods*—free users from having to deal with low-level constructs, allowing them to focus on their goals and minimizing potential side-effects.

In fact, idempotence provides such an advantage, particularly in a cloud native context, that some very smart people have even gone so far as to assert that it's a

---

3 If it does, something is very wrong.

4 Or, like my son, was only *pretending* not to hear you.

synonym for "cloud native."[5] I don't think that I'd go quite that far, but I *would* say that if your service aims to be cloud native, accepting any less than idempotence is asking for trouble.

The Mathematical Definition of Idempotence

The origin of idempotence is in mathematics, where it describes an operation that can be applied multiple times without changing the result beyond the initial application.

In purely mathematical terms: a function is idempotent if $f(f(x)) = f(x)$ for all x.

For example, taking the absolute value $abs(x)$ of an integer number x is an idempotent function because $abs(x) = abs(abs(x))$ is true for each real number x.

The Eventual Goal

These requirements are quite a lot to chew on, but they represent the absolute minimum for our key-value store to be usable. Later on we'll add some important basic functionality, like support for multiple users and data encryption in transit. More importantly, though, we'll introduce techniques and technologies that make the service more scalable, resilient, and generally capable of surviving and thriving in a cruel, uncertain universe.

Generation 0: The Core Functionality

Okay, let's get started. First things first. Without worrying about user requests and persistence, let's first build the core functions, which can be called later from whatever web framework we decide to use.

Storing arbitrary key-value pairs
> For now, we can implement this with a simple map, but what kind? For the sake of simplicity, we'll limit ourselves to keys and values that are simple strings, though we may choose to allow arbitrary types later. We'll just use a simple `map[string]string` as our core data structure.

Allow put, get, and delete of key-value pairs
> In this initial iteration, we'll create a simple Go API that we can call to perform the basic modification operations. Partitioning the functionality in this way will make it easier to test and easier to update in future iterations.

---

5 "Cloud native is not a synonym for microservices... if cloud native has to be a synonym for anything, it would be idempotent, which definitely needs a synonym." —Holly Cummins (Cloud Native London 2018).

Your Super Simple API

The first thing that we need to do is to create our map. The heart of our key-value store:

```
var store = make(map[string]string)
```

Isn't it a beauty? So simple. Don't worry, we'll make it more complicated later.

The first function that we'll create is, appropriately, PUT, which will be used to add records to the store. It does exactly what its name suggests: it accepts key and value strings, and puts them into store. PUT's function signature includes an error return, which we'll need later:

```
func Put(key string, value string) error {
    store[key] = value

    return nil
}
```

Because we're making the conscious choice to create an idempotent service, Put doesn't check to see whether an existing key-value pair is being overwritten, so it will happily do so if asked. Multiple executions of Put with the same parameters will have the same result, regardless of any current state.

Now that we've established a basic pattern, writing the Get and Delete operations is just a matter of following through:

```
var ErrorNoSuchKey = errors.New("no such key")

func Get(key string) (string, error) {
    value, ok := store[key]

    if !ok {
        return "", ErrorNoSuchKey
    }

    return value, nil
}

func Delete(key string) error {
    delete(store, key)

    return nil
}
```

But look carefully: see how when Get returns an error, it doesn't use errors.New? Instead it returns the prebuilt ErrorNoSuchKey error value. But why? This is an example of a *sentinel error*, which allows the consuming service to determine exactly what type of error it's receiving and to respond accordingly. For example, it might do something like this:

```
    if errors.Is(err, ErrorNoSuchKey) {
        http.Error(w, err.Error(), http.StatusNotFound)
        return
    }
```

Now that you have your absolute minimal function set (really, really minimal), don't forget to write tests. We're not going to do that here, but if you're feeling anxious to move forward (or lazy—lazy works too) you can grab the code from the GitHub repository created for this book (*https://oreil.ly/ois1B*).

Generation 1: The Monolith

Now that we have a minimally functional key-value API, we can begin building a service around it. We have a few different options for how to do this. We could use something like GraphQL. There are some decent third-party packages out there that we could use, but we don't have the kind of complex data landscape to necessitate it. We could also use remote procedure call (RPC), which is supported by the standard net/rpc package, or even gRPC, but these require additional overhead for the client, and again our data just isn't complex enough to warrant it.

That leaves us with representational state transfer (REST). REST isn't a lot of people's favorite, but it *is* simple, and it's perfectly adequate for our needs.

Building an HTTP Server with net/http

Go doesn't have any web frameworks that are as sophisticated or historied as something like Django or Flask. What it does have, however, is a strong set of standard libraries that are perfectly adequate for 80% of use cases. Even better: they're designed to be extensible, so there *are* a number of Go web frameworks that extend them.

For now, let's take a look at the standard HTTP handler idiom in Go, in the form of a "Hello World" as implemented with net/http:

```
package main

import (
    "log"
    "net/http"
)

func helloGoHandler(w http.ResponseWriter, r *http.Request) {
    w.Write([]byte("Hello net/http!\n"))
}

func main() {
    http.HandleFunc("/", helloGoHandler)

    log.Fatal(http.ListenAndServe(":8080", nil))
}
```

In the previous example, we define a method, helloGoHandler, which satisfies the definition of a http.HandlerFunc:

```
type HandlerFunc func(http.ResponseWriter, *http.Request)
```

The http.ResponseWriter and a *http.Request parameters can be used to construct the HTTP response and retrieve the request, respectively. You can use the http.HandleFunc function to register helloGoHandler as the handler function for any request that matches a given pattern (the root path, in this example).

Once you've registered our handlers, you can call ListenAndServe, which listens on the address addr. It also accepts a second parameter, set to nil in our example.

You'll notice that ListenAndServe is also wrapped in a log.Fatal call. This is because ListenAndServe always stops the execution flow, only returning in the event of an error. Therefore, it always returns a non-nil error, which we always want to log.

The previous example is a complete program that can be compiled and run using go run:

```
$ go run .
```

Congratulations! You're now running the world's tiniest web service. Now go ahead and test it with curl or your favorite web browser:

```
$ curl http://localhost:8080
Hello net/http!
```

ListenAndServe, Handlers, and HTTP Request Multiplexers

The http.ListenAndServe function starts an HTTP server with a given address and handler. If the handler is nil, which it usually is when you're using only the standard net/http library, the DefaultServeMux value is used. But what's a handler? What is DefaultServeMux? *What's a "mux"?*

A Handler is any type that satisfies the Handler interface by providing a ServeHTTP method, defined in the following:

```
type Handler interface {
    ServeHTTP(ResponseWriter, *Request)
}
```

Most handler implementations, including the default handler, act as a "mux"—short for "multiplexer"—that can direct incoming signals to one of several possible outputs. When a request is received by a service that's been started by ListenAndServe, it's the job of a mux to compare the requested URL to the registered patterns and call the handler function associated with the one that matches most closely.

> DefaultServeMux is a global value of type ServeMux, which implements the default HTTP multiplexer logic.

Building an HTTP Server with gorilla/mux

For many web services the net/http and DefaultServeMux will be perfectly sufficient. However, sometimes you'll need the additional functionality provided by a third-party web toolkit. A popular choice is Gorilla (*https://oreil.ly/15sGK*), which, while being relatively new and less fully developed and resource-rich than something like Django or Flask, does build on Go's standard net/http package to provide some excellent enhancements.

The gorilla/mux package—one of several packages provided as part of the Gorilla web toolkit—provides an HTTP request router and dispatcher that can fully replace DefaultServeMux, Go's default service handler, to add several very useful enhancements to request routing and handling. We're not going to make use of these features just yet, but they will come in handy going forward. If you're curious and/or impatient, however, you can take a look at the gorilla/mux documentation (*https://oreil.ly/qfIph*) for more information.

Creating a minimal service

Once you've done so, making use of the minimal gorilla/mux router is a matter of adding an import and one line of code: the initialization of a new router, which can be passed to the handler parameter of ListenAndServe:

```
package main

import (
    "log"
    "net/http"

    "github.com/gorilla/mux"
)

func helloMuxHandler(w http.ResponseWriter, r *http.Request) {
    w.Write([]byte("Hello gorilla/mux!\n"))
}

func main() {
    r := mux.NewRouter()

    r.HandleFunc("/", helloMuxHandler)

    log.Fatal(http.ListenAndServe(":8080", r))
}
```

So you should be able to just run this now with `go run`, right? Give it a try:

```
$ go run .
main.go:7:5: cannot find package "github.com/gorilla/mux" in any of:
        /go/1.15.8/libexec/src/github.com/gorilla/mux (from $GOROOT)
        /go/src/github.com/gorilla/mux (from $GOPATH)
```

It turns out that you can't (yet). Since you're now using a third-party package—a package that lives outside the standard library—you're going to have to use Go modules.

Initializing your project with Go modules

Using a package from outside the standard library requires that you make use of Go modules (*https://oreil.ly/QJzOi*), which were introduced in Go 1.12 to replace an essentially nonexistent dependency management system with one that's explicit and actually quite painless to use. All of the operations that you'll use for managing your dependencies will use one of a small handful of `go mod` commands.

The first thing you're going to have to do is initialize your project. Start by creating a new, empty directory, `cd` into it, and create (or move) the Go file for your service there. Your directory should now contain only a single Go file.

Next, use the `go mod init` command to initialize the project. Typically, if a project will be imported by other projects, it'll have to be initialized with its import path. This is less important for a standalone service like ours, though, so you can be a little more lax about the name you choose. I'll just use `example.com/gorilla`; you can use whatever you like:

```
$ go mod init example.com/gorilla
go: creating new go.mod: module example.com/gorilla
```

You'll now have an (almost) empty module file, `go.mod`, in your directory:[6]

```
$ cat go.mod
module example.com/gorilla

go 1.15
```

Next, we'll want to add our dependencies, which can be done automatically using `go mod tidy`:

```
$ go mod tidy
go: finding module for package github.com/gorilla/mux
go: found github.com/gorilla/mux in github.com/gorilla/mux v1.8.0
```

---

6 Isn't this exciting?

If you check your `go.mod` file, you'll see that the dependency (and a version number) have been added:

```
$ cat go.mod
module example.com/gorilla

go 1.15

require github.com/gorilla/mux v1.8.0
```

Believe it or not, that's all you need. If your required dependencies change in the future you need only run `go mod tidy` again to rebuild the file. Now try again to start your service:

```
$ go run .
```

Since the service runs in the foreground, your terminal should pause. Calling the endpoint with `curl` from another terminal or browsing to it with a browser should provide the expected response:

```
$ curl http://localhost:8080
Hello gorilla/mux!
```

Success! But surely you want your service to do more than print a simple string, right? Of course you do. Read on!

Variables in URI paths

The Gorilla web toolkit provides a wealth of additional functionality over the standard `net/http` package, but one feature is particularly interesting right now: the ability to create paths with variable segments, which can even optionally contain a regular expression pattern. Using the `gorilla/mux` package, a programmer can define variables using the format {name} or {name:pattern}, as follows:

```
r := mux.NewRouter()
r.HandleFunc("/products/{key}", ProductHandler)
r.HandleFunc("/articles/{category}/", ArticlesCategoryHandler)
r.HandleFunc("/articles/{category}/{id:[0-9]+}", ArticleHandler)
```

The `mux.Vars` function conveniently allows the handler function to retrieve the variable names and values as a `map[string]string`:

```
vars := mux.Vars(request)
category := vars["category"]
```

In the next section we'll use this ability to allow clients to perform operations on arbitrary keys.

So many matchers

Another feature provided by `gorilla/mux` is that it allows a variety of *matchers* to be added to routes that let the programmer add a variety of additional matching request criteria. These include (but aren't limited to) specific domains or subdomains, path prefixes, schemes, headers, and even custom matching functions of your own creation.

Matchers can be applied by calling the appropriate function on the `*Route` value that's returned by Gorilla's `HandleFunc` implementation. Each matcher function returns the affected `*Route`, so they can be chained. For example:

```
r := mux.NewRouter()

r.HandleFunc("/products", ProductsHandler).
    Host("www.example.com").          // Only match a specific domain
    Methods("GET", "PUT").            // Only match GET+PUT methods
    Schemes("http")                   // Only match the http scheme
```

See the `gorilla/mux` documentation (*https://oreil.ly/6ztZe*) for an exhaustive list of available matcher functions.

Building a RESTful Service

Now that you know how to use Go's standard HTTP library, you can use it to create a RESTful service that a client can interact with to execute call to the API you built in "Your Super Simple API" on page 111. Once you've done this you'll have implemented the absolute minimal viable key-value store.

Your RESTful methods

We're going to do our best to follow RESTful conventions, so our API will consider every key-value pair to be a distinct resource with a distinct URI that can be operated upon using the various HTTP methods. Each of our three basic operations—Put, Get, and Delete—will be requested using a different HTTP method that we summarize in Table 5-1.

The URI for your key-value pair resources will have the form `/v1/key/{key}`, where `{key}` is the unique key string. The `v1` segment indicates the API version. This convention is often used to manage API changes, and while this practice is by no means required or universal, it can be helpful for managing the impact of future changes that could break existing client integrations.

Table 5-1. Your RESTful methods

Functionality	Method	Possible Statuses
Put a key-value pair into the store	PUT	201 (Created)
Read a key-value pair from the store	GET	200 (OK), 404 (Not Found)
Delete a key-value pair	DELETE	200 (OK)

In "Variables in URI paths" on page 116, we discussed how to use the gorilla/mux package to register paths that contain variable segments, which will allow you to define a single variable path that handles *all* keys, mercifully freeing you from having to register every key independently. Then, in "So many matchers" on page 117, we discussed how to use route matchers to direct requests to specific handler functions based on various nonpath criteria, which you can use to create a separate handler function for each of the five HTTP methods that you'll be supporting.

Implementing the create function

Okay, you now have everything you need to get started! So, let's go ahead and implement the handler function for the creation of key-value pairs. This function has to be sure to satisfy several requirements:

- It must only match PUT requests for /v1/key/{key}.
- It must call the Put method from "Your Super Simple API" on page 111.
- It must respond with a 201 (Created) when a key-value pair is created.
- It must respond to unexpected errors with a 500 (Internal Server Error).

All of the previous requirements are implemented in the keyValuePutHandler function. Note how the key's value is retrieved from the request body:

```go
// keyValuePutHandler expects to be called with a PUT request for
// the "/v1/key/{key}" resource.
func keyValuePutHandler(w http.ResponseWriter, r *http.Request) {
    vars := mux.Vars(r)                        // Retrieve "key" from the request
    key := vars["key"]

    value, err := io.ReadAll(r.Body)           // The request body has our value
    defer r.Body.Close()

    if err != nil {                            // If we have an error, report it
        http.Error(w,
            err.Error(),
            http.StatusInternalServerError)
        return
    }
```

```
        err = Put(key, string(value))          // Store the value as a string
        if err != nil {                         // If we have an error, report it
            http.Error(w,
                err.Error(),
                http.StatusInternalServerError)
            return
        }

        w.WriteHeader(http.StatusCreated)       // All good! Return StatusCreated
    }
```

Now that you have your "key-value create" handler function, you can register it with your Gorilla request router for the desired path and method:

```
func main() {
    r := mux.NewRouter()

    // Register keyValuePutHandler as the handler function for PUT
    // requests matching "/v1/{key}"
    r.HandleFunc("/v1/{key}", keyValuePutHandler).Methods("PUT")

    log.Fatal(http.ListenAndServe(":8080", r))
}
```

Now that you have your service put together, you can run it using go run . from the project root. Do that now, and send it some requests to see how it responds.

First, use our old friend curl to send a PUT containing a short snippet of text to the /v1/key-a endpoint to create a key named key-a with a value of Hello, key-value store!:

```
$ curl -X PUT -d 'Hello, key-value store!' -v http://localhost:8080/v1/key-a
```

Executing this command provides the following output. The complete output was quite wordy, so I've selected the relevant bits for readability:

```
> PUT /v1/key-a HTTP/1.1
< HTTP/1.1 201 Created
```

The first portion, prefixed with a greater-than symbol (>), shows some details about the request. The last portion, prefixed with a less-than symbol (<), gives details about the server response.

In this output you can see that you did in fact transmit a PUT to the /v1/key-a endpoint, and that the server responded with a 201 Created—as expected.

What if you hit the /v1/key-a endpoint with an unsupported GET method? Assuming that the matcher function is working correctly, you should receive an error message:

```
$ curl -X GET -v http://localhost:8080/v1/key-a
> GET /v1/key-a HTTP/1.1
< HTTP/1.1 405 Method Not Allowed
```

Indeed, the server responds with a `405 Method Not Allowed` error. Everything seems to be working correctly.

Implementing the read function

Now that your service has a fully functioning `Put` method, it sure would be nice if you could read your data back! For our next trick, we're going to implement the `Get` functionality, which has the following requirements:

- It must only match GET requests for `/v1/key/{key}`.
- It must call the `Get` method from "Your Super Simple API" on page 111.
- It must respond with a `404` (`Not Found`) when a requested key doesn't exist.
- It must respond with the requested value and a status `200` if the key exists.
- It must respond to unexpected errors with a `500` (`Internal Server Error`).

All of the previous requirements are implemented in the `keyValueGetHandler` function. Note how the value is written to `w`—the handler function's `http.Response Writer` parameter—after it's retrieved from the key-value API:

```
func keyValueGetHandler(w http.ResponseWriter, r *http.Request) {
    vars := mux.Vars(r)                    // Retrieve "key" from the request
    key := vars["key"]

    value, err := Get(key)                 // Get value for key
    if errors.Is(err, ErrorNoSuchKey) {
        http.Error(w,err.Error(), http.StatusNotFound)
        return
    }
    if err != nil {
        http.Error(w, err.Error(), http.StatusInternalServerError)
        return
    }

    w.Write([]byte(value))                 // Write the value to the response
}
```

And now that you have the "get" handler function, you can register it with the request router alongside the "put" handler:

```
func main() {
    r := mux.NewRouter()

    r.HandleFunc("/v1/{key}", keyValuePutHandler).Methods("PUT")
    r.HandleFunc("/v1/{key}", keyValueGetHandler).Methods("GET")

    log.Fatal(http.ListenAndServe(":8080", r))
}
```

Now let's fire up your newly improved service and see if it works:

```
$ curl -X PUT -d 'Hello, key-value store!' -v http://localhost:8080/v1/key-a
> PUT /v1/key-a HTTP/1.1
< HTTP/1.1 201 Created

$ curl -v http://localhost:8080/v1/key-a
> GET /v1/key-a HTTP/1.1
< HTTP/1.1 200 OK
Hello, key-value store!
```

It works! Now that you can get your values back, you're able to test for idempotence as well. Let's repeat the requests and make sure that you get the same results:

```
$ curl -X PUT -d 'Hello, key-value store!' -v http://localhost:8080/v1/key-a
> PUT /v1/key-a HTTP/1.1
< HTTP/1.1 201 Created

$ curl -v http://localhost:8080/v1/key-a
> GET /v1/key-a HTTP/1.1
< HTTP/1.1 200 OK
Hello, key-value store!
```

You do! But what if you want to overwrite the key with a new value? Will the subsequent GET have the new value? You can test that by changing the value sent by your curl slightly to be Hello, again, key-value store!:

```
$ curl -X PUT -d 'Hello, again, key-value store!' \
    -v http://localhost:8080/v1/key-a
> PUT /v1/key-a HTTP/1.1
< HTTP/1.1 201 Created

$ curl -v http://localhost:8080/v1/key-a
> GET /v1/key-a HTTP/1.1
< HTTP/1.1 200 OK
Hello, again, key-value store!
```

As expected, the GET responds back with a 200 status and your new value.

Finally, to complete your method set you'll just need to create a handler for the DELETE method. I'll leave that as an exercise, though. Enjoy!

Making Your Data Structure Concurrency-Safe

Maps in Go are not atomic and are not safe for concurrent use. Unfortunately, you now have a service designed to handle concurrent requests that's wrapped around exactly such a map.

So what do you do? Well, typically when a programmer has a data structure that needs to be read from and written to by concurrently executing goroutines, they'll use something like a mutex—also known as a lock—to act as a synchronization mechanism. By using a mutex in this way, you can ensure that exactly one process has exclusive access to a particular resource.

Fortunately, you don't need to implement this yourself:[7] Go's sync package provides exactly what you need in the form of sync.RWMutex. The following statement uses the magic of composition to create an *anonymous struct* that contains your map and an embedded sync.RWMutex:

```go
var myMap = struct{
    sync.RWMutex
    m map[string]string
}{m: make(map[string]string)}
```

The myMap struct has all of the methods from the embedded sync.RWMutex, allowing you to use the Lock method to take the write lock when you want to write to the myMap map:

```go
myMap.Lock()                            // Take a write lock
myMap.m["some_key"] = "some_value"
myMap.Unlock()                          // Release the write lock
```

If another process has either a read or write lock, then Lock will block until that lock is released.

Similarly, to read from the map, you use the RLock method to take the read lock:

```go
myMap.RLock()                           // Take a read lock
value := myMap.m["some_key"]
myMap.RUnlock()                         // Release the read lock

fmt.Println("some_key:", value)
```

Read locks are less restrictive than write locks in that any number of processes can simultaneously take read locks. However, RLock will block until any open write locks are released.

Integrating a read-write mutex into your application

Now that you know how to use a sync.RWMutex to implement a basic read-write mutex, you can go back and work it into the code you created for "Your Super Simple API" on page 111.

First, you'll want to refactor the store map.[8] You can construct it like myMap, i.e., as an anonymous struct that contains the map and an embedded sync.RWMutex:

---

7 It's a good thing too. Mutexes can be pretty tedious to implement correctly!

8 Didn't I tell you that we'd make it more complicated?

```
var store = struct{
    sync.RWMutex
    m map[string]string
}{m: make(map[string]string)}
```

Now that you have your store struct, you can update the Get and Put functions to establish the appropriate locks. Because Get only needs to *read* the store map, it'll use RLock to take a read lock only. Put, on the other hand, needs to *modify* the map, so it'll need to use Lock to take a write lock:

```
func Get(key string) (string, error) {
    store.RLock()
    value, ok := store.m[key]
    store.RUnlock()

    if !ok {
        return "", ErrorNoSuchKey
    }

    return value, nil
}

func Put(key string, value string) error {
    store.Lock()
    store.m[key] = value
    store.Unlock()

    return nil
}
```

The pattern here is clear: if a function needs to modify the map (Put, Delete), it'll use Lock to take a write lock. If it only needs to read existing data (Get), it'll use RLock to take a read lock. We leave the creation of the Delete function as an exercise for the reader.

Don't forget to release your locks, and make sure you're releasing the correct lock type!

Generation 2: Persisting Resource State

One of the stickiest challenges with distributed cloud native applications is how to handle state.

There are various techniques for distributing the state of application resources between multiple service instances, but for now we're just going to concern ourselves with the minimum viable product and consider two ways of maintaining the state of our application:

- In "Storing State in a Transaction Log File" on page 126, you'll use a file-based *transaction log* to maintain a record of every time a resource is modified. If a service crashes, is restarted, or otherwise finds itself in an inconsistent state, a transaction log allows a service to reconstruct original state simply by replaying the transactions.

- In "Storing State in an External Database" on page 137, you'll use an external database instead of a file to store a transaction log. It might seem redundant to use a database given the nature of the application you're building, but externalizing data into another service designed specifically for that purpose is a common means of sharing state between service replicas and providing resilience.

You may be wondering why you're using a transaction log strategy to record the events when you could just use the database to store the values themselves. This makes sense when you intend to store your data in memory most of the time, only accessing your persistence mechanism in the background and at startup time.

This also affords you another opportunity: given that you're creating two different implementations of a similar functionality—a transaction log written both to a file and to a database—you can describe your functionality with an interface that both implementations can satisfy. This could come in quite handy, especially if you want to be able to choose the implementation according to your needs.

Application State Versus Resource State

The term "stateless" is used a lot in the context of cloud native architecture, and state is often regarded as a Very Bad Thing. But what is state, exactly, and why is it so bad? Does an application have to be completely devoid of any kind of state to be "cloud native"? The answer is… well, it's complicated.

First, it's important to draw a distinction between *application state* and *resource state*. These are very different things, but they're easily confused.

Application state
> Server-side data about the application or how it's being used by a client. A common example is client session tracking, such as to associate them with their access credentials or some other application context.

Resource state
> The current state of a resource within a service at any point of time. It's the same for every client, and has nothing to do with the interaction between client and server.

Any state introduces technical challenges, but application state is particularly problematic because it forces services to depend on *server affinity*—sending each of a user's requests to the same server where their session was initiated—resulting in a more complex application and making it hard to destroy or replace service replicas.

State and statelessness will be discussed in quite a bit more detail in "State and Statelessness" on page 195.

What's a Transaction Log?

In its simplest form, a *transaction log* is just a log file that maintains a history of mutating changes executed by the data store. If a service crashes, is restarted, or otherwise finds itself in an inconsistent state, a transaction log makes it possible to replay the transactions to reconstruct the service's functional state.

Transaction logs are commonly used by database management systems to provide a degree of data resilience against crashes or hardware failures. However, while this technique can get quite sophisticated, we'll be keeping ours pretty straightforward.

Your transaction log format

Before we get to the code, let's decide what the transaction log should contain.

We'll assume that your transaction log will be read only when your service is restarted or otherwise needs to recover its state, and that it'll be read from top to bottom, sequentially replaying each event. It follows that your transaction log will consist of an ordered list of mutating events. For speed and simplicity, a transaction log is also generally append-only, so when a record is deleted from your key-value store, for example, a delete is recorded in the log.

Given everything we've discussed so far, each recorded transaction event will need to include the following attributes:

Sequence number
    A unique record ID, in monotonically increasing order.

Event type
    A descriptor of the type of action taken; this can be PUT or DELETE.

Key
    A string containing the key affected by this transaction.

Value
    If the event is a PUT, the value of the transaction.

Nice and simple. Hopefully we can keep it that way.

Your transaction logger interface

The first thing we're going to do is define a `TransactionLogger` interface. For now, we're only going to define two methods: `WritePut` and `WriteDelete`, which will be used to write `PUT` and `DELETE` events, respectively, to a transaction log:

```
type TransactionLogger interface {
    WriteDelete(key string)
    WritePut(key, value string)
}
```

You'll no doubt want to add other methods later, but we'll cross that bridge when we come to it. For now, let's focus on the first implementation and add additional methods to the interface as we come across them.

Storing State in a Transaction Log File

The first approach we'll take is to use the most basic (and most common) form of transaction log, which is just an append-only log file that maintains a history of mutating changes executed by the data store. This file-based implementation has some tempting pros, but some pretty significant cons as well:

Pros:

No downstream dependency
> There's no dependency on an external service that could fail or that we can lose access to.

Technically straightforward
> The logic isn't especially sophisticated. We can be up and running quickly.

Cons:

Harder to scale
> You'll need some additional way to distribute your state between nodes when you want to scale.

Uncontrolled growth
> These logs have to be stored on disk, so you can't let them grow forever. You'll need some way of compacting them.

Prototyping your transaction logger

Before we get to the code, let's make some design decisions. First, for simplicity, the log will be written in plain text; a binary, compressed format might be more time- and space-efficient, but we can always optimize later. Second, each entry will be written on its own line; this will make it much easier to read the data later.

Finally, each transaction will include the four fields listed in "Your transaction log format" on page 125, delimited by tabs. Once again, these are:

Sequence number
> A unique record ID, in monotonically increasing order.

Event type
> A descriptor of the type of action taken; this can be PUT or DELETE.

Key
> A string containing the key affected by this transaction.

Value
> If the event is a PUT, the value of the transaction.

Now that we've established these fundamentals, let's go ahead and define a type, `FileTransactionLogger`, which will implicitly implement the `TransactionLogger` interface described in "Your transaction logger interface" on page 126 by defining `WritePut` and `WriteDelete` methods for writing PUT and DELETE events, respectively, to the transaction log:

```
type FileTransactionLogger struct {
    // Something, something, fields
}

func (l *FileTransactionLogger) WritePut(key, value string) {
    // Something, something, logic
}

func (l *FileTransactionLogger) WriteDelete(key string) {
    // Something, something, logic
}
```

Clearly these methods are a little light on detail, but we'll flesh them out soon!

Defining the event type

Thinking ahead, we probably want the `WritePut` and `WriteDelete` methods to operate asynchronously. You could implement that using some kind of `events` channel that some concurrent goroutine could read from and perform the log writes. That sounds like a nice idea, but if you're going to do that you'll need some kind of internal representation of an "event."

That shouldn't give you too much trouble. Incorporating all of the fields that we listed in "Your transaction log format" on page 125 gives something like the `Event` struct, in the following:

```
type Event struct {
    Sequence  uint64        // A unique record ID
    EventType EventType     // The action taken
```

```
    Key       string          // The key affected by this transaction
    Value     string          // The value of a PUT the transaction
}
```

Seems straightforward, right? Sequence is the sequence number, and Key and Value are self-explanatory. But…what's an EventType? Well, it's whatever we say it is, and we're going to say that it's a constant that we can use to refer to the different types of events, which we've already established will include one each for PUT and DELETE events.

One way to do this might be to just assign some constant byte values, like this:

```
const (
    EventDelete byte = 1
    EventPut    byte = 2
)
```

Sure, this would work, but Go actually provides a better (and more idiomatic) way: iota. iota is a predefined value that can be used in a constant declaration to construct a series of related constant values.

Declaring Constants with Iota

When used in a constant declaration, iota represents successive untyped integer constants that can be used to construct a set of related constants. Its value restarts at zero in each constant declaration and increments with each constant assignment (whether or not the iota identifier is actually referenced).

An iota can also be operated upon. We demonstrate this in the following by using in multiplication, left binary shift, and division operations:

```
const (
    a = 42 * iota        // iota == 0; a == 0
    b = 1 << iota        // iota == 1; b == 2
    c = 3                // iota == 2; c == 3 (iota increments anyway!)
    d = iota / 2         // iota == 3; d == 1
)
```

Because iota is itself an untyped number, you can use it to make typed assignments without explicit type casts. You can even assign iota to a float64 value:

```
const (
    u         = iota * 42  // iota == 0; u == 0 (untyped integer constant)
    v float64 = iota * 42  // iota == 1; v == 42.0 (float64 constant)
)
```

The iota keyword allows implicit repetition, which makes it trivial to create arbitrarily long sets of related constants, like we do in the following with the numbers of bytes in various digital units:

```
type ByteSize uint64

const (
    _              = iota        // iota == 0; ignore the zero value
    KB ByteSize = 1 << (10 * iota)  // iota == 1; KB == 2^10
    MB                           // iota == 2; MB == 2^20
    GB                           // iota == 3; GB == 2^30
    TB                           // iota == 4; TB == 2^40
    PB                           // iota == 5; PB == 2^50
)
```

Using the `iota` technique, you don't have to manually assign values to constants. Instead, you can do something like the following:

```
type EventType byte

const (
    _                        = iota  // iota == 0; ignore the zero value
    EventDelete EventType = iota     // iota == 1
    EventPut                         // iota == 2; implicitly repeat
)
```

This might not be a big deal when you only have two constants like we have here, but it can come in handy when you have a number of related constants and don't want to be bothered manually keeping track of which value is assigned to what.

 If you're using `iota` as enumerations in serializations (as we are here), take care to only *append* to the list, and don't reorder or insert values in the middle, or you won't be able to deserialize later.

We now have an idea of what the `TransactionLogger` will look like, as well as the two primary write methods. We've also defined a struct that describes a single event, and created a new `EventType` type and used `iota` to define its legal values. Now we're finally ready to get started.

Implementing your FileTransactionLogger

We've made some progress. We know we want a `TransactionLogger` implementation with methods for writing events, and we've created a description of an event in code. But what about the `FileTransactionLogger` itself?

The service will want to keep track of the physical location of the transaction log, so it makes sense to have an `os.File` attribute representing that. It'll also need to remember the last sequence number that was assigned so it can correctly set each event's sequence number; that can be kept as an unsigned 64-bit integer attribute. That's great, but how will the FileTransactionLogger actually write the events?

One possible approach would be to keep an io.Writer that the WritePut and Write Delete methods can operate on directly, but that would be a single-threaded approach, so unless you explicitly execute them in goroutines, you may find yourself spending more time in I/O than you'd like. Alternatively, you could create a buffer from a slice of Event values that are processed by a separate goroutine. Definitely warmer, but too complicated.

After all, why go through all of that work when we can just use standard buffered channels? Taking our own advice, we end up with a FileTransactionLogger and Write methods that look like the following:

```go
type FileTransactionLogger struct {
    events       chan<- Event      // Write-only channel for sending events
    errors       <-chan error      // Read-only channel for receiving errors
    lastSequence uint64            // The last used event sequence number
    file         *os.File          // The location of the transaction log
}

func (l *FileTransactionLogger) WritePut(key, value string) {
    l.events <- Event{EventType: EventPut, Key: key, Value: value}
}

func (l *FileTransactionLogger) WriteDelete(key string) {
    l.events <- Event{EventType: EventDelete, Key: key}
}

func (l *FileTransactionLogger) Err() <-chan error {
    return l.errors
}
```

You now have your FileTransactionLogger, which has a uint64 value that's used to track the last-used event sequence number, a write-only channel that receives Event values, and WritePut and WriteDelete methods that send Event values into that channel.

But it looks like there might be a part left over: there's an Err method there that returns a receive-only error channel. There's a good reason for that. We've already mentioned that writes to the transaction log will be done concurrently by a goroutine that receives events from the events channel. While that makes for a more efficient write, it also means that WritePut and WriteDelete can't simply return an error when they encounter a problem, so we provide a dedicated error channel to communicate errors instead.

Creating a new FileTransactionLogger

If you've followed along so far you may have noticed that none of the attributes in the FileTransactionLogger have been initialized. If you don't fix this issue, it's going to cause some problems. Go doesn't have constructors, though, so to solve this you need to define a construction function, which you'll call, for lack of a better name,[9] NewFileTransactionLogger:

```
func NewFileTransactionLogger(filename string) (TransactionLogger, error) {
    file, err := os.OpenFile(filename, os.O_RDWR|os.O_APPEND|os.O_CREATE, 0755)
    if err != nil {
        return nil, fmt.Errorf("cannot open transaction log file: %w", err)
    }

    return &FileTransactionLogger{file: file}, nil
}
```

 See how NewFileTransactionLogger returns a pointer type, but its return list specifies the decidedly nonpointy TransactionLogger interface type?

The reason for this is tricksy: while Go allows pointer types to implement an interface, it doesn't allow pointers to interface types.

NewFileTransactionLogger calls the os.OpenFile function to open the file specified by the filename parameter. You'll notice it accepts several flags that have been binary OR-ed together to set its behavior:

os.O_RDWR
> Opens the file in read/write mode.

os.O_APPEND
> Any writes to this file will append, not overwrite.

os.O_CREATE
> If the file doesn't exist, creates it.

There are quite a few of these flags besides the three we use here. Take a look at the os package documentation (*https://pkg.go.dev/os*) for a full listing.

We now have a construction function that ensures that the transaction log file is correctly created. But what about the channels? We *could* create the channels and spawn a goroutine with NewFileTransactionLogger, but that feels like we'd be adding too much mysterious functionality. Instead, we'll create a Run method.

---

9 That's a lie. There are probably lots of better names.

Appending entries to the transaction log

As of yet, there's nothing reading from the events channel, which is less than ideal. What's worse, the channels aren't even initialized. Let's change this by creating a Run method, shown in the following:

```go
func (l *FileTransactionLogger) Run() {
    events := make(chan Event, 16)          // Make an events channel
    l.events = events

    errors := make(chan error, 1)           // Make an errors channel
    l.errors = errors

    go func() {
        for e := range events {             // Retrieve the next Event

            l.lastSequence++                // Increment sequence number

            _, err := fmt.Fprintf(          // Write the event to the log
                l.file,
                "%d\t%d\t%s\t%s\n",
                l.lastSequence, e.EventType, e.Key, e.Value)

            if err != nil {
                errors <- err
                return
            }
        }
    }()
}
```

 This implementation is incredibly basic. It won't even correctly handle entries with whitespace or multiple lines!

The Run function does several important things.

First, it creates a buffered events channel. Using a buffered channel in our Transac tionLogger means that calls to WritePut and WriteDelete won't block as long as the buffer isn't full. This lets the consuming service handle short bursts of events without being slowed by disk I/O. If the buffer does fill up, then the write methods will block until the log writing goroutine catches up.

Second, it creates an errors channel, which is also buffered, that we'll use to signal any errors that arise in the goroutine that's responsible for concurrently writing events to the transaction log. The buffer value of 1 allows us to send an error in a nonblocking manner.

Finally, it starts a goroutine that retrieves Event values from our events channel and uses the fmt.Fprintf function to write them to the transaction log. If fmt.Fprintf returns an error, the goroutine sends the error to the errors channel and halts.

Using a bufio.Scanner to play back file transaction logs

Even the best transaction log is useless if it's never read.[10] But how do we do that?

You'll need to read the log from the beginning and parse each line; io.ReadString and fmt.Sscanf let you do this with minimal fuss.

Channels, our dependable friends, will let your service stream the results to a consumer as it retrieves them. This might be starting to feel routine, but stop for a second to appreciate it. In most other languages the path of least resistance here would be to read in the entire file, stash it in an array, and finally loop over that array to replay the events. Go's convenient concurrency primitives make it almost trivially easy to stream the data to the consumer in a much more space- and memory-efficient way.

The ReadEvents method[11] demonstrates this:

```go
func (l *FileTransactionLogger) ReadEvents() (<-chan Event, <-chan error) {
    scanner := bufio.NewScanner(l.file)   // Create a Scanner for l.file
    outEvent := make(chan Event)          // An unbuffered Event channel
    outError := make(chan error, 1)       // A buffered error channel

    go func() {
        var e Event

        defer close(outEvent)             // Close the channels when the
        defer close(outError)             // goroutine ends

        for scanner.Scan() {
            line := scanner.Text()

            if err := fmt.Sscanf(line, "%d\t%d\t%s\t%s",
                &e.Sequence, &e.EventType, &e.Key, &e.Value); err != nil {

                outError <- fmt.Errorf("input parse error: %w", err)
                return
            }

            // Sanity check! Are the sequence numbers in increasing order?
            if l.lastSequence >= e.Sequence {
                outError <- fmt.Errorf("transaction numbers out of sequence")
```

---

10 What makes a transaction log "good" anyway?

11 Naming is hard.

```
                return
            }

            l.lastSequence = e.Sequence      // Update last used sequence #

            outEvent <- e                    // Send the event along
        }

        if err := scanner.Err(); err != nil {
            outError <- fmt.Errorf("transaction log read failure: %w", err)
            return
        }
    }()

    return outEvent, outError
}
```

The ReadEvents method can really be said to be two functions in one: the outer function initializes the file reader, and creates and returns the event and error channels. The inner function runs concurrently to ingest the file contents line by line and send the results to the channels.

Interestingly, the file attribute of TransactionLogger is of type *os.File, which has a Read method that satisfies the io.Reader interface. Read is fairly low-level, but, if you wanted to, you could actually use it to retrieve the data. The bufio package, however, gives us a better way: the Scanner interface, which provides a convenient means for reading newline-delimited lines of text. We can get a new Scanner value by passing an io.Reader—an os.File in this case—to bufio.NewScanner.

Each call to the scanner.Scan method advances it to the next line, returning false if there aren't any lines left. A subsequent call to scanner.Text returns the line.

Note the defer statements in the inner anonymous goroutine. These ensure that the output channels are always closed. Because defer is scoped to the function they're declared in, these get called at the end of the goroutine, not ReadEvents.

You may recall from "Formatting I/O in Go" on page 34 that the fmt.Sscanf function provides a simple (but sometimes simplistic) means of parsing simple strings. Like the other methods in the fmt package, the expected format is specified using a format string with various "verbs" embedded: two digits (%d) and two strings (%s), separated by tab characters (\t). Conveniently, fmt.Sscanf lets you pass in pointers to the target values for each verb, which it can update directly.[12]

---

12 After all this time, I still think that's pretty neat.

Go's format strings have a long history dating back to C's `printf` and `scanf`, but they've been adopted by many other languages over the years, including C++, Java, Perl, PHP, Ruby, and Scala. You may already be familiar with them, but if you're not, take a break now to look at the `fmt` package documentation (*https://pkg.go.dev/ fmt*).

At the end of each loop the last-used sequence number is updated to the value that was just read, and the event is sent on its merry way. A minor point: note how the same `Event` value is reused on each iteration rather than creating a new one. This is possible because the `outEvent` channel is sending struct values, not *pointers* to struct values, so it already provides copies of whatever value we send into it.

Finally, the function checks for `Scanner` errors. The `Scan` method returns only a single boolean value, which is really convenient for looping. Instead, when it encounters an error, `Scan` returns `false` and exposes the error via the `Err` method.

Your transaction logger interface (redux)

Now that you've implemented a fully functional `FileTransactionLogger`, it's time to look back and see which of the new methods we can use to incorporate into the `TransactionLogger` interface. It actually looks like there are quite few we might like to keep in any implementation, leaving us with the following final form for the `TransactionLogger` interface:

```
type TransactionLogger interface {
    WriteDelete(key string)
    WritePut(key, value string)
    Err() <-chan error

    ReadEvents() (<-chan Event, <-chan error)

    Run()
}
```

Now that that's settled, you can finally start integrating the transaction log into your key-value service.

Initializing the FileTransactionLogger in your web service

The `FileTransactionLogger` is now complete! All that's left to do now is to integrate it with your web service. The first step of this is to add a new function that can create a new `TransactionLogger` value, read in and replay any existing events, and call `Run`.

First, let's add a `TransactionLogger` reference to our `service.go`. You can call it `logger` because naming is hard:

```
var logger TransactionLogger
```

Now that you have that detail out of the way, you can define your initialization method, which can look like the following:

```go
func initializeTransactionLog() error {
    var err error

    logger, err = NewFileTransactionLogger("transaction.log")
    if err != nil {
        return fmt.Errorf("failed to create event logger: %w", err)
    }

    events, errors := logger.ReadEvents()
    e, ok := Event{}, true

    for ok && err == nil {
        select {
        case err, ok = <-errors:                // Retrieve any errors
        case e, ok = <-events:
            switch e.EventType {
            case EventDelete:                    // Got a DELETE event!
                err = Delete(e.Key)
            case EventPut:                       // Got a PUT event!
                err = Put(e.Key, e.Value)
            }
        }
    }

    logger.Run()

    return err
}
```

This function starts as you'd expect: it calls NewFileTransactionLogger and assigns it to logger.

The next part is more interesting: it calls logger.ReadEvents, and replays the results based on the Event values received from it. This is done by looping over a select with cases for both the events and errors channels. Note how the cases in the select use the format case foo, ok = <-ch. The bool returned by a channel read in this way will be false if the channel in question has been closed, setting the value of ok and terminating the for loop.

If we get an Event value from the events channel, we call either Delete or Put as appropriate; if we get an error from the errors channel, err will be set to a non-nil value and the for loop will be terminated.

Integrating FileTransactionLogger with your web service

Now that the initialization logic is put together, all that's left to do to complete the integration of the TransactionLogger is add exactly three function calls into the web

---

service. This is fairly straightforward, so we won't walk through it here. But, briefly, you'll need to add the following:

- `initializeTransactionLog` to the `main` method
- `logger.WriteDelete` to `keyValueDeleteHandler`
- `logger.WritePut` to `keyValuePutHandler`

We'll leave the actual integration as an exercise for the reader.[13]

Future improvements

We may have completed a minimal viable implementation of our transaction logger, but it still has plenty of issues and opportunities for improvement, such as:

- There aren't any tests.
- There's no `Close` method to gracefully close the file.
- The service can close with events still in the write buffer: events can get lost.
- Keys and values aren't encoded in the transaction log: multiple lines or whitespace will fail to parse correctly.
- The sizes of keys and values are unbound: huge keys or values can be added, filling the disk.
- The transaction log is written in plain text: it will take up more disk space than it probably needs to.
- The log retains records of deleted values forever: it will grow indefinitely.

All of these would be impediments in production. I encourage you to take the time to consider—or even implement—solutions to one or more of these points.

Storing State in an External Database

Databases, and data, are at the core of many, if not most, business and web applications, so it makes perfect sense that Go includes a standard interface for SQL (or SQL-like) databases in its core libraries (*https://oreil.ly/NosgK*).

But does it make sense to use a SQL database to back our key-value store? After all, isn't it redundant for our data store to just depend on another data store? Yes, certainly. But externalizing a service's data into another service designed specifically for that purpose—a database—is a common pattern that allows state to be shared

---

13 You're welcome.

between service replicas and provides data resilience. Besides, the point is to show how you might interact with a database, not to design the perfect application.

In this section, you'll be implementing a transaction log backed by an external database and satisfying the `TransactionLogger` interface, just as you did in "Storing State in a Transaction Log File" on page 126. This would certainly work, and even have some benefits as mentioned previously, but it comes with some tradeoffs:

Pros:

Externalizes application state
    Less need to worry about distributed state and closer to "cloud native."

Easier to scale
    Not having to share data between replicas makes scaling out *easier* (but not *easy*).

Cons:

Introduces a bottleneck
    What if you had to scale way up? What if all replicas had to read from the database at once?

Introduces an upstream dependency
    Creates a dependency on another resource that might fail.

Requires initialization
    What if the `Transactions` table doesn't exist?

Increases complexity
    Yet another thing to manage and configure.

Working with databases in Go

Databases, particularly SQL and SQL-like databases, are everywhere. You can try to avoid them, but if you're building applications with some kind of data component, you will at some point have to interact with one.

Fortunately for us, the creators of the Go standard library provided the `database/sql` package (*https://oreil.ly/YKPZ6*), which provides an idiomatic and lightweight interface around SQL (and SQL-like) databases. In this section we'll briefly demonstrate how to use this package, and point out some of the gotchas along the way.

Among the most ubiquitous members of the `database/sql` package is `sql.DB`: Go's primary database abstraction and entry point for creating statements and transactions, executing queries, and fetching results. While it doesn't, as its name might suggest, map to any particular concept of a database or schema, it does do quite a lot of things for you, including, but not limited to, negotiating connections with your database and managing a database connection pool.

We'll get into how you create your `sql.DB` in a bit. But first, we have to talk about database drivers.

Importing a database driver

While the `sql.DB` type provides a common interface for interacting with a SQL database, it depends on database drivers to implement the specifics for particular database types. At the time of this writing there are 45 drivers listed in the Go repository (*https://oreil.ly/QDQIe*).

In the following section we'll be working with a Postgres database, so we'll use the third-party `lib/pq` Postgres driver implementation (*https://oreil.ly/hYW8r*).

To load a database driver, anonymously import the driver package by aliasing its package qualifier to _. This triggers any initializers the package might have while also informing the compiler that you have no intention of directly using it:

```
import (
    "database/sql"
    _ "github.com/lib/pq"        // Anonymously import the driver package
)
```

Now that you've done this, you're finally ready to create your `sql.DB` value and access the database.

Implementing your PostgresTransactionLogger

Previously, we presented the `TransactionLogger` interface, which provides a standard definition for a generic transaction log. You might recall that it defined methods for starting the logger, as well as reading and writing events to the log, as detailed here:

```
type TransactionLogger interface {
    WriteDelete(key string)
    WritePut(key, value string)
    Err() <-chan error

    ReadEvents() (<-chan Event, <-chan error)

    Run()
}
```

Our goal now is to create a database-backed implementation of `TransactionLogger`. Fortunately, much of our work is already done for us. Looking back at "Implementing your FileTransactionLogger" on page 129 for guidance, it looks like we can create a `PostgresTransactionLogger` using very similar logic.

Starting with the `WritePut`, `WriteDelete`, and `Err` methods, you can do something like the following:

```
type PostgresTransactionLogger struct {
    events      chan<- Event        // Write-only channel for sending events
    errors      <-chan error        // Read-only channel for receiving errors
    db          *sql.DB             // The database access interface
}

func (l *PostgresTransactionLogger) WritePut(key, value string) {
    l.events <- Event{EventType: EventPut, Key: key, Value: value}
}

func (l *PostgresTransactionLogger) WriteDelete(key string) {
    l.events <- Event{EventType: EventDelete, Key: key}
}

func (l *PostgresTransactionLogger) Err() <-chan error {
    return l.errors
}
```

If you compare this to the `FileTransactionLogger` it's clear that the code is nearly identical. All we've really changed is:

- Renaming (obviously) the type to `PostgresTransactionLogger`
- Swapping the `*os.File` for a `*sql.DB`
- Removing `lastSequence`; you can let the database handle the sequencing

Creating a new PostgresTransactionLogger

That's all well and good, but we still haven't talked about how we create the `sql.DB`. I know how you must feel. The suspense is definitely killing me, too.

Much like we did in the `NewFileTransactionLogger` function, we're going to create a construction function for our `PostgresTransactionLogger`, which we'll call (quite predictably) `NewPostgresTransactionLogger`. However, instead of opening a file like `NewFileTransactionLogger`, it'll establish a connection with the database, returning an `error` if it fails.

There's a little bit of a wrinkle, though. Namely, that the setup for a Postgres connection takes a lot of parameters. At the bare minimum we need to know the host where the database lives, the name of the database, and the user name and password. One way to deal with this would be to create a function like the following, which simply accepts a bunch of string parameters:

```
func NewPostgresTransactionLogger(host, dbName, user, password string)
    (TransactionLogger, error) { ... }
```

This approach is pretty ugly, though. Plus, what if you wanted an additional parameter? Do you chunk it onto the end of the parameter list, breaking any code that's already using this function? Maybe worse, the parameter order isn't clear without looking at the documentation.

There has to be a better way. So, instead of this potential horror show, you can create a small helper struct:

```
type PostgresDBParams struct {
    dbName   string
    host     string
    user     string
    password string
}
```

Unlike the big-bag-of-strings approach, this struct is small, readable, and easily extended. To use it, you can create a PostgresDBParams variable and pass it to your construction function. Here's what that looks like:

```
logger, err = NewPostgresTransactionLogger(PostgresDBParams{
    host:     "localhost",
    dbName:   "kvs",
    user:     "test",
    password: "hunter2"
})
```

The new construction function looks something like the following:

```
func NewPostgresTransactionLogger(config PostgresDBParams) (TransactionLogger,
    error) {

    connStr := fmt.Sprintf("host=%s dbname=%s user=%s password=%s",
        config.host, config.dbName, config.user, config.password)

    db, err := sql.Open("postgres", connStr)
    if err != nil {
        return nil, fmt.Errorf("failed to open db: %w", err)
    }

    err = db.Ping()                    // Test the database connection
    if err != nil {
        return nil, fmt.Errorf("failed to open db connection: %w", err)
    }

    logger := &PostgresTransactionLogger{db: db}

    exists, err := logger.verifyTableExists()
    if err != nil {
        return nil, fmt.Errorf("failed to verify table exists: %w", err)
    }
    if !exists {
        if err = logger.createTable(); err != nil {
            return nil, fmt.Errorf("failed to create table: %w", err)
        }
    }
```

```
    return logger, nil
}
```

This does quite a few things, but fundamentally it is not very different from `NewFileTransactionLogger`.

The first thing it does is to use `sql.Open` to retrieve a `*sql.DB` value. You'll note that the connection string passed to `sql.Open` contains several parameters; the `lib/pq` package supports many more than the ones listed here. See the package documentation (*https://oreil.ly/uIgyN*) for a complete listing.

Many drivers, including `lib/pq`, don't actually create a connection to the database immediately, so it uses `db.Ping` to force the driver to establish and test a connection.

Finally, it creates the `PostgresTransactionLogger` and uses that to verify that the `transactions` table exists, creating it if necessary. Without this step, the `PostgresTransactionLogger` will essentially assume that the table already exists, and will fail if it doesn't.

You may have noticed that the `verifyTableExists` and `createTable` methods aren't implemented here. This is entirely intentional. As an exercise, you're encouraged to dive into the `database/sql` docs (*https://oreil.ly/xuFlE*) and think about how you might go about doing that. If you'd prefer not to, you can find an implementation in the GitHub repository (*https://oreil.ly/1MEIr*) that comes with this book.

You now have a construction function that establishes a connection to the database and returns a newly created `TransactionLogger`. But, once again, you need to get things started. For that, you need to implement the Run method that will create the `events` and `errors` channels and spawn the event ingestion goroutine.

Using db.Exec to execute a SQL INSERT

For the `FileTransactionLogger`, you implemented a Run method that initialized the channels and created the go function responsible for writing to the transaction log.

The `PostgresTransactionLogger` is very similar. However, instead of appending a line to a file, the new logger uses `db.Exec` to execute an SQL INSERT to accomplish the same result:

```go
func (l *PostgresTransactionLogger) Run() {
    events := make(chan Event, 16)          // Make an events channel
    l.events = events

    errors := make(chan error, 1)           // Make an errors channel
    l.errors = errors

    go func() {                             // The INSERT query
        query := `INSERT INTO transactions
```

```
                (event_type, key, value)
                VALUES ($1, $2, $3)`

        for e := range events {                    // Retrieve the next Event

            _, err := l.db.Exec(                    // Execute the INSERT query
                query,
                e.EventType, e.Key, e.Value)

            if err != nil {
                errors <- err
            }
        }
    }()
}
```

This implementation of the Run method does almost exactly what its FileTransac
tionLogger equivalent does: it creates the buffered events and errors channels, and
it starts a goroutine that retrieves Event values from our events channel and writes
them to the transaction log.

Unlike the FileTransactionLogger, which appends to a file, this goroutine uses
db.Exec to execute a SQL query that appends a row to the transactions table. The
numbered arguments ($1, $2, $3) in the query are placeholder query parameters,
which must be satisfied when the db.Exec function is called.

Using db.Query to play back postgres transaction logs

In "Using a bufio.Scanner to play back file transaction logs" on page 133, you used a
bufio.Scanner to read previously written transaction log entries.

The Postgres implementation won't be *quite* as straightforward, but the principle is
the same: you point at the top of your data source and read until you hit the bottom:

```
func (l *PostgresTransactionLogger) ReadEvents() (<-chan Event, <-chan error) {
    outEvent := make(chan Event)              // An unbuffered events channel
    outError := make(chan error, 1)           // A buffered errors channel

    go func() {
        defer close(outEvent)                 // Close the channels when the
        defer close(outError)                 // goroutine ends

        query := `SELECT sequence, event_type, key, value FROM transactions
                ORDER BY sequence`

        rows, err := db.Query(query)          // Run query; get result set
        if err != nil {
            outError <- fmt.Errorf("sql query error: %w", err)
            return
        }
```

```
        defer rows.Close()                       // This is important!

        e := Event{}                             // Create an empty Event

        for rows.Next() {                        // Iterate over the rows

            err = rows.Scan(                     // Read the values from the
                &e.Sequence, &e.EventType,       // row into the Event.
                &e.Key, &e.Value)

            if err != nil {
                outError <- fmt.Errorf("error reading row: %w", err)
                return
            }

            outEvent <- e                        // Send e to the channel
        }

        err = rows.Err()
        if err != nil {
            outError <- fmt.Errorf("transaction log read failure: %w", err)
        }
    }()

    return outEvent, outError
}
```

All of the interesting (or at least new) bits are happening in the goroutine. Let's break them down:

- query is a string that contains the SQL query. The query in this code requests four columns: sequence, event_type, key, and value.

- db.Query sends query to the database, and returns values of type *sql.Rows and error.

- We defer a call to rows.Close. Failing to do so can lead to connection leakage!

- rows.Next lets us iterate over the rows; it returns false if there are no more rows or if there's an error.

- rows.Scan copies the columns in the current row into the values we pointed at in the call.

- We send event e to the output channel.

- Err returns the error, if any, that may have caused rows.Next to return false.

Initializing the PostgresTransactionLogger in your web service

The PostgresTransactionLogger is pretty much complete. Now let's go ahead and integrate it into the web service.

Fortunately, since we already had the `FileTransactionLogger` in place, we only need to change one line:

```
logger, err = NewFileTransactionLogger("transaction.log")
```

which becomes…

```
logger, err = NewPostgresTransactionLogger("localhost")
```

Yup. That's it. Really.

Because this represents a complete implementation of the `TransactionLogger` interface, everything else stays exactly the same. You can interact with the `PostgresTransactionLogger` using exactly the same methods as before.

Future improvements

As with the `FileTransactionLogger`, the `PostgresTransactionLogger` represents a minimal viable implementation of a transaction logger and has lots of room for improvement. Some of the areas for improvement include, but are certainly not limited to:

- We assume that the database and table exist, and we'll get errors if they don't.
- The connection string is hard-coded. Even the password.
- There's still no `Close` method to clean up open connections.
- The service can close with events still in the write buffer: events can get lost.
- The log retains records of deleted values forever: it will grow indefinitely.

All of these would be (major) impediments in production. I encourage you to take the time to consider—or even implement—solutions to one or more of these points.

Generation 3: Implementing Transport Layer Security

Security. Love it or hate it, the simple fact is that security is a critical feature of *any* application, cloud native or otherwise. Sadly, security is often treated as an afterthought, with potentially catastrophic consequences.

There are rich tools and established security best practices for traditional environments, but this is less true of cloud native applications, which tend to take the form of several small, often ephemeral, microservices. While this architecture provides significant flexibility and scalability benefits, it also creates a distinct opportunity for would-be attackers: every communication between services is transmitted across a network, opening it up to eavesdropping and manipulation.

The subject of security can take up an entire book of its own,[14] so we'll focus on one common technique: encryption. Encrypting data "in transit" (or "on the wire") is commonly used to guard against eavesdropping and message manipulation, and any language worth its salt—including, and especially, Go—will make it relatively low-lift to implement.

Transport Layer Security

Transport Layer Security (TLS) is a cryptographic protocol that's designed to provide communications security over a computer network. Its use is ubiquitous and widespread, being applicable to virtually any Internet communications. You're most likely familiar with it (and perhaps using it right now) in the form of HTTPS—also known as HTTP over TLS—which uses TLS to encrypt exchanges over HTTP.

TLS encrypts messages using *public-key cryptography*, in which both parties possess their own *key pair*, which includes a *public key* that's freely given out, and a *private key* that's known only to its owner, illustrated in Figure 5-2. Anybody can use a public key to encrypt a message, but it can only be decrypted with the corresponding private key. Using this protocol, two parties that wish to communicate privately can exchange their public keys, which can then be used to secure all subsequent communications in a way that can only be read by the owner of the intended recipient, who holds the corresponding private key.[15]

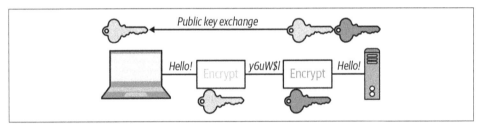

Figure 5-2. One half of a public key exchange

Certificates, certificate authorities, and trust

If TLS had a motto, it would be "trust but verify." Actually, scratch the trust part. Verify everything.

It's not enough for a service to simply provide a public key.[16] Instead, every public key is associated with a *digital certificate*, an electronic document used to prove the key's

---

14 Ideally written by somebody who knows more than I do about security.

15 This is a gross over-simplification, but it'll do for our purposes. I encourage you to learn more about this and correct me, though.

16 You don't know where that key has been.

ownership. A certificate shows that the owner of the public key is, in fact, the named subject (owner) of the certificate, and describes how the key may be used. This allows the recipient to compare the certificate against various "trusts" to decide whether it will accept it as valid.

First, the certificate must be digitally signed and authenticated by a *certificate authority*, a trusted entity that issues digital certificates.

Second, the subject of the certificate has to match the domain name of the service the client is trying to connect to. Among other things, this helps to ensure that the certificates you're receiving are valid and haven't been swapped out by a man-in-the-middle.

Only then will your conversation proceed.

Web browsers or other tools will usually allow you to choose to proceed if a certificate can't be validated. If you're using self-signed certificates for development, for example, that might make sense. But generally speaking, heed the warnings.

Private Key and Certificate Files

TLS (and its predecessor, SSL) has been around long enough[17] that you'd think that we'd have settled on a single key container format, but you'd be wrong. Web searches for "key file format" will return a virtual zoo of file extensions: *.csr*, *.key*, *.pkcs12*, *.der*, and *.pem* just to name a few.

Of these, however, *.pem* seems to be the most common. It also happens to be the format that's most easily supported by Go's `net/http` package, so that's what we'll be using.

Privacy enhanced mail (PEM) file format

Privacy enhanced mail (PEM) is a common certificate container format, usually stored in *.pem* files, but *.cer* or *.crt* (for certificates) and *.key* (for public or private keys) are common too. Conveniently, PEM is also base64 encoded and therefore viewable in a text editor, and even safe to paste into (for example) the body of an email message.[18]

---

17 SSL 2.0 was released in 1995 and TLS 1.0 was released in 1999. Interestingly, SSL 1.0 had some pretty profound security flaws and was never publicly released.

18 Public keys only, please.

Often, *.pem* files will come in a pair, representing a complete key pair:

cert.pem
> The server certificate (including the CA-signed public key).

key.pem
> A private key, not to be shared.

Going forward, we'll assume that your keys are in this configuration. If you don't yet have any keys and need to generate some for development purposes, instructions are available in multiple places online. If you already have a key file in some other format, converting it is beyond the scope of this book. However, the Internet is a magical place, and there are plenty of tutorials online for converting between common key formats.

Securing Your Web Service with HTTPS

So, now that we've established that security should be taken seriously, and that communication via TLS is a bare-minimum first step towards securing our communications, how do we go about doing that?

One way might be to put a reverse proxy in front of our service that can handle HTTPS requests and forward them to our key-value service as HTTP, but unless the two are co-located on the same server, we're still sending unencrypted messages over a network. Plus, the additional service adds some architectural complexity that we might prefer to avoid. Perhaps we can have our key-value service serve HTTPS?

Actually, we can. Going all the way back to "Building an HTTP Server with net/http" on page 112, you might recall that the `net/http` package contains a function, `ListenAndServe`, which, in its most basic form, looks something like the following:

```
func main() {
    http.HandleFunc("/", helloGoHandler)          // Add a root path handler

    http.ListenAndServe(":8080", nil)             // Start the HTTP server
}
```

In this example, we call `HandleFunc` to add a handler function for the root path, followed by `ListenAndServe` to start the service listening and serving. For the sake of simplicity, we ignore any errors returned by `ListenAndServe`.

There aren't a lot of moving parts here, which is kind of nice. In keeping with that philosophy, the designers of `net/http` kindly provided a TLS-enabled variant of the `ListenAndServe` function that we're familiar with:

```
func ListenAndServeTLS(addr, certFile, keyFile string, handler Handler) error
```

As you can see, `ListenAndServeTLS` looks and feels almost exactly like `ListenAndServe` except that it has two extra parameters: `certFile` and `keyFile`. If you happen to have certificate and private key PEM files, then service HTTPS-encrypted connections is just a matter of passing the names of those files to `ListenAndServeTLS`:

```
http.ListenAndServeTLS(":8080", "cert.pem", "key.pem", nil)
```

This sure looks super convenient, but does it work? Let's fire up our service (using self-signed certificates) and find out.

Dusting off our old friend `curl`, let's try inserting a key/value pair. Note that we use the `https` scheme in our URL instead of `http`:

```
$ curl -X PUT -d 'Hello, key-value store!' -v https://localhost:8080/v1/key-a
* SSL certificate problem: self signed certificate
curl: (60) SSL certificate problem: self signed certificate
```

Well, that didn't go as planned. As we mentioned in "Certificates, certificate authorities, and trust" on page 146, TLS expects any certificates to be signed by a certificate authority. It doesn't like self-signed certificates.

Fortunately, we can turn this safety check off in `curl` with the appropriately named `--insecure` flag:

```
$ curl -X PUT -d 'Hello, key-value store!' --insecure -v \
    https://localhost:8080/v1/key-a
* SSL certificate verify result: self signed certificate (18), continuing anyway.
> PUT /v1/key-a HTTP/2
< HTTP/2 201
```

We got a sternly worded warning, but it worked!

Transport Layer Summary

We've covered quite a lot in just a few pages. The topic of security is vast, and there's no way we're going to do it justice, but we were able to at least introduce TLS, and how it can serve as one relatively low-cost, high-return component of a larger security strategy.

We were also able to demonstrate how to implement TLS in an Go `net/http` web service, and saw how—as long as we have valid certificates—to secure a service's communications without a great deal of effort.

Containerizing Your Key-Value Store

A *container* is a lightweight operating-system-level virtualization[19] abstraction that provides processes with a degree of isolation, both from their host and from other containers. The concept of the container has been around since at least 2000, but it was the introduction of Docker in 2013 that made containers accessible to the masses and brought containerization into the mainstream.

Importantly, containers are not virtual machines:[20] they don't use hypervisors, and they share the host's kernel rather than carrying their own guest operating system. Instead, their isolation is provided by a clever application of several Linux kernel features, including chroot, cgroups, and kernel namespaces. In fact, it can be reasonably argued that containers are nothing more than a convenient abstraction, and that there's actually no such thing as a container.

Even though they're not virtual machines,[21] containers do provide some virtual-machine-like benefits. The most obvious of which is that they allow an application, its dependencies, and much of its environment to be packaged within a single distributable artifact—a container image—that can be executed on any suitable host.

The benefits don't stop there, however. In case you need them, here's a few more:

Agility
Unlike virtual machines that are saddled with an entire operating system and a colossal memory footprint, containers boast image sizes in the megabyte range and startup times that measure in milliseconds. This is particularly true of Go applications, whose binaries have few, if any, dependencies.

Isolation
This was hinted at previously, but bears repeating. Containers virtualize CPU, memory, storage, and network resources at the operating-system-level, providing developers with a sandboxed view of the OS that is logically isolated from other applications.

Standardization and productivity
Containers let you package an application alongside its dependencies, such as specific versions of language runtimes and libraries, as a single distributable binary, making your deployments reproducible, predictable, and versionable.

---

19 Containers are not virtual machines. They virtualize the operating system instead of hardware.

20 Repetition intended. This is an important point.

21 Yup. I said it. Again.

Orchestration

Sophisticated container orchestration systems like Kubernetes provide a huge number of benefits. By containerizing your application(s) you're taking the first step towards being able to take advantage of them.

There are just four (very) motivating arguments.[22] In other words, containerization is super, super useful.

For this book, we'll be using Docker to build our container images. Alternative build tools exist, but Docker is the most common containerization tool in use today, and the syntax for its build file—termed a *Dockerfile*—lets you use familiar shell scripting commands and utilities.

That being said, this isn't a book about Docker or containerization, so our discussion will mostly be limited to the bare basics of using Docker with Go. If you're interested in learning more, I suggest picking up a copy of *Docker: Up & Running: Shipping Reliable Containers in Production* by Sean P. Kane and Karl Matthias (O'Reilly).

Docker (Absolute) Basics

Before we continue, it's important to draw a distinction between container images and the containers themselves. A *container image* is essentially an executable binary that contains your application runtime and its dependencies. When an image is run, the resulting process is the *container*. An image can be run many times to create multiple (essentially) identical containers.

Over the next few pages we'll create a simple Dockerfile and build and execute an image. If you haven't already, please take a moment and install the Docker Community Edition (CE) (*https://oreil.ly/yYwKL*).

The Dockerfile

Dockerfiles are essentially build files that describe the steps required to build an image. A very minimal—but complete—example is demonstrated in the following:

```
# The parent image. At build time, this image will be pulled and
# subsequent instructions run against it.
FROM ubuntu:20.04

# Update apt cache and install nginx without an approval prompt.
RUN apt-get update && apt-get install --yes nginx

# Tell Docker this image's containers will use port 80.
EXPOSE 80
```

---

22 The initial draft had several more, but this chapter is already pretty lengthy.

```
# Run Nginx in the foreground. This is important: without a
# foreground process the container will automatically stop.
CMD ["nginx", "-g", "daemon off;"]
```

As you can see, this Dockerfile includes four different commands:

FROM

> Specifies a *base image* that this build will extend, and will typically be a common Linux distribution, such as `ubuntu` or `alpine`. At build time this image is pulled and run, and the subsequent commands applied to it.

RUN

> Will execute any commands on top of the current image. The result will be used for the next step in the Dockerfile.

EXPOSE

> Tells Docker which port(s) the container will use. See "What's the Difference Between Exposing and Publishing Ports?" on page 154 for more information on exposing ports.

CMD

> The command to execute when the container is executed. There can only be one `CMD` in a Dockerfile.

These are four of the most common Dockerfile instructions of many available. For a complete listing see the official Dockerfile reference (*https://oreil.ly/8LGdP*).

As you may have inferred, the previous example starts with an existing Linux distribution image (Ubuntu 20.04) and installs Nginx, which is executed when the container is started.

By convention, the file name of a Dockerfile is *Dockerfile*. Go ahead and create a new file named *Dockerfile* and paste the previous example into it.

Building your container image

Now that you have a simple Dockerfile, you can build it! Make sure that you're in the same directory as your Dockerfile and enter the following:

```
$ docker build --tag my-nginx .
```

This will instruct Docker to begin the build process. If everything works correctly (and why wouldn't it?) you'll see the output as Docker downloads the parent image, and runs the `apt` commands. This will probably take a minute or two the first time you run it.

At the end, you'll see a line that looks something like the following: `Successfully tagged my-nginx:latest`.

If you do, you can use the `docker images` command to verify that your image is now present. You should see something like the following:

```
$ docker images
REPOSITORY      TAG       IMAGE ID       CREATED          SIZE
my-nginx        latest    64ea3e21a388   29 seconds ago   159MB
ubuntu          20.04     f63181f19b2f   3 weeks ago      72.9MB
```

If all has gone as planned, you'll see at least two images listed: our parent image `ubuntu:20.04`, and your own `my-nginx:latest` image. Next step: running the service container!

What Does latest Mean?

Note the name of the image. What's `latest`? That's a simple question with a complicated answer. Docker images have two name components: a `repository` and a `tag`.

The repository name component can include the domain name of a host where the image is stored (or will be stored). For example, the repository name for an image hosted by FooCorp may be named something like `docker.foo.com/ubuntu`. If no repository URL is evident, then the image is either 100% local (like the image we just built) or lives in the Docker Hub (*https://hub.docker.com*).

The `tag` component is intended as a unique label for a particular version of an image, and often takes the form of a version number. The `latest` tag is a default tag name that's added by many `docker` operations if no tag is specified.

Using `latest` in production is generally considered a bad practice, however, because its contents can change—sometimes significantly—with unfortunate consequences.

Running your container image

Now that you've built your image, you can run it. For that, you'll use the `docker run` command:

```
$ docker run --detach --publish 8080:80 --name nginx my-nginx
61bb4d01017236f6261ede5749b421e4f65d43cb67e8e7aa8439dc0f06afe0f3
```

This instructs Docker to run a container using your `my-nginx` image. The `--detach` flag will cause the container to be run in the background. Using `--publish 8080:80` instructs Docker to publish port 8080 on the host bridged to port 80 in the container, so any connections to `localhost:8080` will be forwarded to the container's port 80. Finally, the `--name nginx` flag specifies a name for the container; without this, a randomly generated name will be assigned instead.

You'll notice that running this command presents us with a very cryptic line containing 65 very cryptic hexadecimal characters. This is the *container ID*, which can be used to refer to the container in lieu of its name.

What's the Difference Between Exposing and Publishing Ports?

The difference between "exposing" and "publishing" container ports can be confusing, but there's actually an important distinction:

- *Exposing* ports is a way of clearly documenting—both to users and to Docker—which ports a container uses. It does not map or open any ports on the host. Ports can be exposed using the EXPOSE keyword in the Dockerfile or the --expose flag to docker run.

- *Publishing* ports tells Docker which ports to open on the container's network interface. Ports can be published using the --publish or --publish-all flag to docker run, which create firewall rules that map a container port to a port on the host.

Running your container image

To verify that your container is running and is doing what you expect, you can use the docker ps command to list all running containers. This should look something like the following:

```
$ docker ps
CONTAINER ID    IMAGE      STATUS         PORTS                   NAMES
4cce9201f484    my-nginx   Up 4 minutes   0.0.0.0:8080->80/tcp    nginx
```

The preceding output has been edited for brevity (you may notice that it's missing the COMMAND and CREATED columns). Your output should include seven columns:

CONTAINER ID
> The first 12 characters of the container ID. You'll notice it matches the output of your docker run.

IMAGE
> The name (and tag, if specified) of this container's source image. No tag implies latest.

COMMAND *(not shown)*
> The command running inside the container. Unless overridden in the docker run this will be the same as the CMD instruction in the Dockerfile. In our case this will be nginx -g 'daemon off;'.

CREATED *(not shown)*

How long ago the container was created.

STATUS

The current state of the container (up, exited, restarting, etc) and how long it's been in that state. If the state changed, then the time will differ from CREATED.

PORTS

Lists all exposed and published ports (see "What's the Difference Between Exposing and Publishing Ports?" on page 154). In our case, we've published 0.0.0.0:8080 on the host and mapped it to 80 on the container, so that all requests to host port 8080 are forwarded to container port 80.

NAMES

The name of the container. Docker will randomly set this if it's not explicitly defined. Two containers with the same name, regardless of state, cannot exist on the same host at the same time. To reuse a name, you'll first have to delete the unwanted container.

Issuing a request to a published container port

If you've gotten this far, then your docker ps output should show a container named nginx that appears to have port 8080 published and forwarding to the container's port 80. If so, then you're ready to send a request to your running container. But which port should you query?

Well, the Nginx container is listening on port 80. Can you reach that? Actually, no. That port won't be accessible because it wasn't published to any network interface during the docker run. Any attempt to connect to an unpublished container port is doomed to failure:

```
$ curl localhost:80
curl: (7) Failed to connect to localhost port 80: Connection refused
```

You haven't published to port 80, but you *have* published port 8080 and forwarded it to the container's port 80. You can verify this with our old friend curl or by browsing to localhost:8080. If everything is working correctly you'll be greeted with the familiar Nginx "Welcome" page illustrated in Figure 5-3.

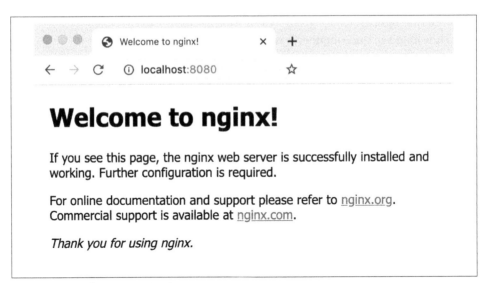

Figure 5-3. Welcome to nginx!

Running multiple containers

One of the "killer features" of containerization is this: because all of the containers on a host are isolated from one another, it's possible to run quite a lot of them—even ones that contain different technologies and stacks—on the same host, with each listening on a different published port. For example, if you wanted to run an `httpd` container alongside your already-running `my-nginx` container, you could do exactly that.

"But," you might say, "both of those containers expose port 80! Won't they collide?"

Great question, to which the answer is, happily, no. In fact, you can actually have as many containers as you want that *expose* the same port—even multiple instances of the same image—as long as they don't attempt to *publish* the same port on the same network interface.

For example, if you want to run the stock `httpd` image, you can run it by using the `docker run` command again, as long as you take care to publish to a different port (8081, in this case):

```
$ docker run --detach --publish 8081:80 --name httpd httpd
```

If all goes as planned, this will spawn a new container listening on the host at port 8081. Go ahead: use `docker ps` and `curl` to test:

```
$ curl localhost:8081
<html><body><h1>It works!</h1></body></html>
```

Stopping and deleting your containers

Now you've successfully run your container, you'll probably need to stop and delete it at some point, particularly if you want to rerun a new container using the same name.

To stop a running container, you can use the `docker stop` command, passing it either the container name or the first few characters of its container ID (how many characters doesn't matter, as long they can be used to uniquely identify the desired container). Using the container ID to stop our `nginx` container looks like this:

```
$ docker stop 4cce      # "docker stop nginx" will work too
4cce
```

The output of a successful `docker stop` is just the name or ID that we passed into the command. You can verify that your container has actually been stopped using `docker ps --all`, which will show *all* containers, not just the running ones:

```
$ docker ps
CONTAINER ID    IMAGE      STATUS                    PORTS    NAMES
4cce9201f484    my-nginx   Exited (0) 3 minutes ago           nginx
```

If you ran the `httpd` container, it will also be displayed with a status of Up. You will probably want to stop it as well.

As you can see, the status of our `nginx` container has changed to `Exited`, followed by its exit code—an exit status of 0 indicates that we were able to execute a graceful shutdown—and how long ago the container entered its current status.

Now that you've stopped your container you can freely delete it.

 You can't delete a running container or an image that's used by a running container.

To do this, you use the `docker rm` (or the newer `docker container rm`) command to remove your container, again passing it either the container name or the first few characters of the ID of the container you want to delete:

```
$ docker rm 4cce          # "docker rm nginx" will work too
4cce
```

As before, the output name or ID indicates success. If you were to go ahead and run `docker ps --all` again, you shouldn't see the container listed anymore.

Building Your Key-Value Store Container

Now that you have the basics down, you can start applying them to containerizing our key-value service.

Fortunately, Go's ability to compile into statically linked binaries makes it especially well suited for containerization. While most other languages have to be built into a parent image that contains the language runtime, like the 486MB openjdk:15 for Java or the 885MB python:3.9 for Python,[23] Go binaries need no runtime at all. They can be placed into a "scratch" image: an image, with no parent at all.

Iteration 1: adding your binary to a FROM scratch image

To do this, you'll need a Dockerfile. The following example is a pretty typical example of a Dockerfile for a containerized Go binary:

```
# We use a "scratch" image, which contains no distribution files. The
# resulting image and containers will have only the service binary.
FROM scratch

# Copy the existing binary from the host.
COPY kvs .

# Copy in your PEM files.
COPY *.pem .

# Tell Docker we'll be using port 8080.
EXPOSE 8080

# Tell Docker to execute this command on a `docker run`.
CMD ["/kvs"]
```

This Dockerfile is fairly similar to the previous one, except that instead of using apt to install an application from a repository, it uses COPY to retrieve a compiled binary from the filesystem it's being built on. In this case, it assumes the presence of a binary named kvs. For this to work, we'll need to build the binary first.

In order for your binary to be usable inside a container, it has to meet a few criteria:

- It has to be compiled (or cross-compiled) for Linux.
- It has to be statically linked.
- It has to be named kvs (because that's what the Dockerfile is expecting).

We can do all of these things in one command, as follows:

---

23 To be fair, these images are "only" 240MB and 337MB compressed, respectively.

```
$ CGO_ENABLED=0 GOOS=linux go build -a -o kvs
```

Let's walk through what this does:

- `CGO_ENABLED=0` tells the compiler to disable `cgo` and statically link any C bindings. We won't go into what this is, other than that it enforces static linking, but I encourage you to look at the `cgo` documentation (*https://oreil.ly/XUI8H*) if you're curious.

- `GOOS=linux` instructs the compiler to generate a Linux binary, cross-compiling if necessary.

- `-a` forces the compiler to rebuild any packages that are already up to date.

- `-o kvs` specifies that the binary will be named `kvs`.

Executing the command should yield a statically linked Linux binary. This can be verified using the `file` command:

```
$ file kvs
kvs: ELF 64-bit LSB executable, x86-64, version 1 (SYSV), statically linked,
not stripped
```

 Linux binaries will run in a Linux container, even one running in Docker for MacOS or Windows, but won't run on MacOS or Windows otherwise.

Great! Now let's build the container image, and see what comes out:

```
$ docker build --tag kvs .
...output omitted.

$ docker images
REPOSITORY    TAG      IMAGE ID       CREATED            SIZE
kvs           latest   7b1fb6fa93e3   About a minute ago 6.88MB
node          15       ebcfbb59a4bd   7 days ago         936MB
python        3.9      2a93c239d591   8 days ago         885MB
openjdk       15       7666c92f41b0   2 weeks ago        486MB
```

Less than 7MB! That's roughly two orders of magnitude smaller than the relatively massive images for other languages' runtimes. This can come in quite handy when you're operating at scale and have to pull your image onto a couple hundred nodes a few times a day.

But does it run? Let's find out:

```
$ docker run --detach --publish 8080:8080 kvs
4a05617539125f7f28357d3310759c2ef388f456b07ea0763350a78da661afd3
```

```
$ curl -X PUT -d 'Hello, key-value store!' -v http://localhost:8080/v1/key-a
> PUT /v1/key-a HTTP/1.1
< HTTP/1.1 201 Created

$ curl http://localhost:8080/v1/key-a
Hello, key-value store!
```

Looks like it works!

So now you have a nice, simple Dockerfile that builds an image using a precompiled binary. Unfortunately, that means that you have to make sure that you (or your CI system) rebuilds the binary fresh for each Docker build. That's not *too* terrible, but it does mean that you need to have Go installed on your build workers. Again, not terrible, but we can certainly do better.

Iteration 2: using a multi-stage build

In the last section, you created a simple Dockerfile that would take an existing Linux binary and wrap it in a bare-bones "scratch" image. But what if you could perform the *entire* image build—Go compilation and all—in Docker?

One approach might be to use the `golang` image as our parent image. If you did that, your Dockerfile could compile your Go code and run the resulting binary at deploy time. This could build on hosts that don't have the Go compiler installed, but the resulting image would be saddled with an additional 862MB (the size of the `golang: 1.16` image) of entirely unnecessary build machinery.

Another approach might be to use two Dockerfiles: one for building the binary, and another that containerizes the output of the first build. This is a lot closer to where you want to be, but it requires two distinct Dockerfiles that need be sequentially built or managed by a separate script.

A better way became available with the introduction of multistage Docker builds, which allow multiple distinct builds—even with entirely different base images—to be chained together so that artifacts from one stage can be selectively copied into another, leaving behind everything you don't want in the final image. To use this approach, you define a build with two stages: a "build" stage that generates the Go binary, and an "image" stage that uses that binary to produce the final image.

To do this, you use multiple `FROM` statements in our Dockerfile, each defining the start of a new stage. Each stage can be arbitrarily named. For example, you might name your build stage `build`, as follows:

```
FROM golang:1.16 as build
```

Once you have stages with names, you can use the `COPY` instruction in your Dockerfile to copy any artifact *from any previous stage*. Your final stage might have an instruction like the following, which copies the file /src/kvs from the build stage to the current working directory:

```
COPY --from=build /src/kvs .
```

Putting these things together yields a complete, two-stage Dockerfile:

```
# Stage 1: Compile the binary in a containerized Golang environment
#
FROM golang:1.16 as build

# Copy the source files from the host
COPY . /src

# Set the working directory to the same place we copied the code
WORKDIR /src

# Build the binary!
RUN CGO_ENABLED=0 GOOS=linux go build -o kvs


# Stage 2: Build the Key-Value Store image proper
#
# Use a "scratch" image, which contains no distribution files
FROM scratch

# Copy the binary from the build container
COPY --from=build /src/kvs .

# If you're using TLS, copy the .pem files too
COPY --from=build /src/*.pem .

# Tell Docker we'll be using port 8080
EXPOSE 8080

# Tell Docker to execute this command on a "docker run"
CMD ["/kvs"]
```

Now that you have your complete Dockerfile, you can build it in precisely the same way as before. We'll tag it as multipart this time, though, so that you can compare the two images:

```
$ docker build --tag kvs:multipart .
...output omitted.

$ docker images
REPOSITORY     TAG         IMAGE ID       CREATED         SIZE
kvs            latest      7b1fb6fa93e3   2 hours ago     6.88MB
kvs            multipart   b83b9e479ae7   4 minutes ago   6.56MB
```

This is encouraging! You now have a single Dockerfile that can compile your Go code—regardless of whether or not the Go compiler is even installed on the build worker—and that drops the resulting statically linked executable binary into a

`FROM scratch` base to produce a very, very small image containing nothing except your key-value store service.

You don't need to stop there, though. If you wanted to, you could add other stages as well, such as a `test` stage that runs any unit tests prior to the build step. We won't go through that exercise now, however, since it's more of the same thing, but I encourage you to try it for yourself.

Externalizing Container Data

Containers are intended to be ephemeral, and any container should be designed and run with the understanding that it can (and will) be destroyed and recreated at any time, taking all of its data with it. To be clear, this is a feature, and is very intentional, but sometimes you might *want* your data to outlive your containers.

For example, the ability to mount externally managed files directly into the filesystem of an otherwise general-purpose container can decouple configurations from images so you don't have to rebuild them whenever just to change their settings. This is a very powerful strategy, and is probably the most common use-case for container data externalization. So common in fact that Kubernetes even provides a resource type— `ConfigMap`—dedicated to it.

Similarly, you might want data generated in a container to exist beyond the lifetime of the container. Storing data on the host can be an excellent strategy for warming caches, for example. It's important to keep in mind, however, one of the realities of cloud native infrastructure: nothing is permanent, not even servers. Don't store anything on the host that you don't mind possibly losing forever.

Fortunately, while "pure" Docker limits you to externalizing data directly onto local disk,[24] container orchestration systems like Kubernetes provides various abstractions (*https://oreil.ly/vBXfA*) that allows data to survive the loss of a host.

Unfortunately, this is supposed to be a book about Go, so we really can't cover Kubernetes in detail here. But if you haven't already, I strongly encourage you to take a long look at the excellent Kubernetes documentation (*https://oreil.ly/wxImg*), and equally excellent *Kubernetes: Up and Running* by Brendan Burns, Joe Beda, and Kelsey Hightower (O'Reilly).

---

24 I'm intentionally ignoring solutions like Amazon's Elastic Block Store, which can help, but have issues of their own.

Summary

This was a long chapter, and we touched on a lot of different topics. Consider how much we've accomplished!

- Starting from first principles, we designed and implemented a simple monolithic key-value store, using `net/http` and `gorilla/mux` to build a RESTful service around functionality provided by a small, independent, and easily testable Go library.

- We leveraged Go's powerful interface capabilities to produce two completely different transaction logger implementations, one based on local files and using `os.File` and the `fmt` and `bufio` packages; the other backed by a Postgres database and using the `database/sql` and `github.com/lib/pq` Postgres driver packages.

- We discussed the importance of security in general, covered some of the basics of TLS as one part of a larger security strategy, and implemented HTTPS in our service.

- Finally, we covered containerization, one of the core cloud native technologies, including how to build images and how to run and manage containers. We even containerized not only our application, but we even containerized its build process.

Going forward, we'll be extending on our key-value service in various ways when we introduce new concepts, so stay tuned. Things are about to get even more interesting.

## PART III

The Cloud Native Attributes

## CHAPTER 6

It's All About Dependability

The most important property of a program is whether it accomplishes the intention of its user.[1]

—C.A.R. Hoare, *Communications of the ACM (October 1969)*

Professor Sir Charles Antony Richard (Tony) Hoare is a brilliant guy. He invented quicksort, authored Hoare Logic for reasoning about the correctness of computer programs, and created the formal language "communicating sequential processes" (CSP) that inspired Go's beloved concurrency model. Oh, and he developed the structured programming paradigm[2] that forms the foundation of all modern programming languages in common use today. He also invented the null reference. Please don't hold that against him, though. He publicly apologized[3] for it in 2009, calling it his "billion-dollar mistake."

Tony Hoare literally invented programming as we know it. So when he says that the single most important property of a program is whether it accomplishes the intention of its user, you can take that on some authority. Think about this for a second: Hoare specifically (and quite rightly) points out that it's the intention of a program's *users*— not its *creators*—that dictates whether a program is performing correctly. How inconvenient that the intentions of a program's users aren't always the same as those of its creator!

---

1 Hoare, C.A.R. "An Axiomatic Basis for Computer Programming.". *Communications of the ACM*, vol. 12, no. 10, October 1969, pp. 576–583. *https://oreil.ly/jOwO9*.

2 When Edsger W. Dijkstra coined the expression "GOTO considered harmful," he was referencing Hoare's work in structured programming.

3 Hoare, Tony. "Null References: The Billion Dollar Mistake." *InfoQ.com*. 25 August 2009. *https://oreil.ly/4QWS8*.

Given this assertion, it stands to reason that a user's first expectation about a program is that *the program works*. But when is a program "working"? This is actually a pretty big question, one that lies at the heart of cloud native design. The first goal of this chapter is to explore that very idea, and in the process, introduce concepts like "dependability" and "reliability" that we can use to better describe (and meet) user expectations. Finally, we'll briefly review a number of practices commonly used in cloud native development to ensure that services meet the expectations of its users. We'll discuss each of these in-depth throughout the remainder of this book.

What's the Point of Cloud Native?

In Chapter 1 we spent a few pages defining "cloud native," starting with the Cloud Native Computing Foundation's definition and working forward to the properties of an ideal cloud native service. We spent a few more pages talking about the pressures that have driven cloud native to be a thing in the first place.

What we didn't spend so much time on, however, was the *why* of cloud native. Why does the concept of cloud native even exist? Why would we even want our systems to be cloud native? What's its purpose? What makes it so special? Why should I care?

So, why *does* cloud native exist? The answer is actually pretty straightforward: it's all about dependability. In the first part of this chapter, we'll dig into the concept of dependability, what it is, why it's important, and how it underlies all the patterns and techniques that we call cloud native.

It's All About Dependability

Holly Cummins, the worldwide development community practice lead for the IBM Garage, famously said that "if cloud native has to be a synonym for anything, it would be idempotent."[4] Cummins is absolutely brilliant, and has said a lot of absolutely brilliant things,[5] but I think she only has half of the picture on this one. I think that idempotence is very important—perhaps even necessary for cloud native—but not sufficient. I'll elaborate.

The history of software, particularly the network-based kind, has been one of struggling to meet the expectations of increasingly sophisticated users. Long gone are the days when a service could go down at night "for maintenance." Users today rely heavily on the services they use, and they expect those services to be available and to respond promptly to their requests. Remember the last time you tried to start a Netflix movie and it took the longest five seconds of your life? Yeah, that.

---

4 *Cloud Native Is About Culture, Not Containers*. Cummins, Holly. Cloud Native London 2018.

5 If you ever have a chance to see her speak, I strongly recommend you take it.

Users don't care that your services have to be maintained. They won't wait patiently while you hunt down that mysterious source of latency. They just want to finish binge-watching the second season of Breaking Bad.[6]

All of the patterns and techniques that we associate with cloud native—*every single one*—exist to allow services to be deployed, operated, and maintained at scale in unreliable environments, driven by the need to produce dependable services that keep users happy.

In other words, I think that if "cloud native" has to be a synonym for anything, it would be "dependability."

What Is Dependability and Why Is It So Important?

I didn't choose the word "dependability" arbitrarily. It's actually a core concept in the field of *systems engineering*, which is full of some very smart people who say some very smart things about the design and management of complex systems. The concept of dependability in a computing context was first rigorously defined by Jean-Claude Laprie about 35 years ago,[7] who defined a system's dependability according to the expectations of its users. Laprie's original definition has been tweaked and extended over the years by various authors, but here's my favorite:

> The dependability of a computer system is its ability to avoid failures that are more frequent or more severe, and outage durations that are longer, than is acceptable to the user(s).[8]
>
> —Fundamental Concepts of Computer System Dependability (2001)

In other words, a dependable system consistently does what its users expect and can be quickly fixed when it doesn't.

By this definition, a system is dependable only when it can *justifiably* be trusted. Obviously, a system can't be considered dependable if it falls over any time one of its components glitch, or if it requires hours to recover from a failure. Even if it's been running for months without interruption, an undependable system may still be one bad day away from catastrophe: lucky isn't dependable.

Unfortunately, it's hard to objectively gauge "user expectations." For this reason, as illustrated in Figure 6-1, dependability is an umbrella concept encompassing several

---

6 Remember what Walt did to Jane that time? That was so messed up.

7 Laprie, J-C. "Dependable Computing and Fault Tolerance: Concepts and Terminology." *FTCS-15 The 15th Int'l Symposium on Fault-Tolerant Computing*, June 1985, pp. 2–11. *https://oreil.ly/UZFFY*.

8 A. Avižienis, J. Laprie, and B. Randell. "Fundamental Concepts of Computer System Dependability." *Research Report No. 1145, LAAS-CNRS*, April 2001. *https://oreil.ly/4YXd1*.

more specific and quantifiable attributes—availability, reliability, and maintainability—all of which are subject to similar threats that may be overcome by similar means.

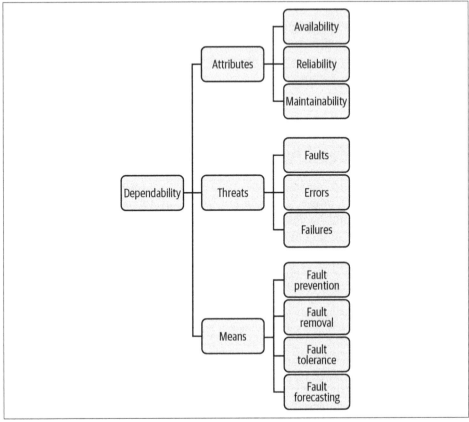

Figure 6-1. The system attributes and means that contribute to dependability

So while the concept of "dependability" alone might be a little squishy and subjective, the attributes that contribute to it are quantitative and measurable enough to be useful:

Availability
> The ability of a system to perform its intended function at a random moment in time. This is usually expressed as the probability that a request made of the system will be successful, defined as uptime divided by total time.

Reliability
> The ability of a system to perform its intended function for a given time interval. This is often expressed as either the mean time between failures (MTBF: total time divided by the number of failures) or failure rate (number of failures divided by total time).

Maintainability

The ability of a system to undergo modifications and repairs. There are a variety of indirect measures for maintainability, ranging from calculations of cyclomatic complexity to tracking the amount of time required to change a system's behavior to meet new requirements or to restore it to a functional state.

 Later authors extended Laprie's definition of dependability to include several security-related properties, including safety, confidentiality, and integrity. I've reluctantly omitted these, not because security isn't important (it's *SO* important!), but for brevity. A worthy discussion of security would require an entire book of its own.

Dependability Is Not Reliability

If you've read any of O'Reilly's Site Reliability Engineering (SRE) books[9] you've already heard quite a lot about reliability. However, as illustrated in Figure 6-1, reliability is just one property that contributes to overall dependability.

If that's true, though, then why has reliability become the standard metric for service functionality? Why are there "site reliability engineers" but no "site dependability engineers"?

There are probably several answers to these questions, but perhaps the most definitive is that the definition of "dependability" is purely qualitative. There's no measure for it, and when you can't measure something it's very hard to construct a set of rules around it.

Reliability, on the other hand, is quantitative. Given a robust definition[10] for what it means for a system to provide "correct" service, it becomes relatively straightforward to calculate that system's "reliability," making it a powerful (if indirect) measure of user experience.

Dependability: It's Not Just for Ops Anymore

Since the introduction of networked services, it's been the job of developers to build services, and of systems administrators ("operations") to deploy those services onto servers and keep them running. This worked well enough for a time, but it had the unfortunate side-effect of incentivizing developers to prioritize feature development at the expense of stability and operations.

---

9 If you haven't, start with *Site Reliability Engineering: How Google Runs Production Systems* (*https://oreil.ly/OJn99*). It really is very good.

10 Many organizations use service-level objectives (SLOs) for precisely this purpose.

Fortunately, over the past decade or so—coinciding with the DevOps movement—a new wave of technologies has become available with the potential to completely change the way technologists of all kinds do their jobs.

On the operations side, with the availability of infrastructure and platforms as a service (IaaS/PaaS) and tools like Terraform and Ansible, working with infrastructure has never been more like writing software.

On the development side, the popularization of technologies like containers and serverless functions has given developers an entire new set of "operations-like" capabilities, particularly around virtualization and deployment.

As a result, the once-stark line between software and infrastructure is getting increasingly blurry. One could even argue that with the growing advancement and adoption of infrastructure abstractions like virtualization, container orchestration frameworks like Kubernetes, and software-defined behavior like service meshes, we may even be at the point where they could be said to have merged. Everything is software now.

The ever-increasing demand for service dependability has driven the creation of a whole new generation of cloud native technologies. The effects of these new technologies and the capabilities they provide has been considerable, and the traditional developer and operations roles are changing to suit them. At long last, the silos are crumbling, and, increasingly, the rapid production of dependable, high-quality services is a fully collaborative effort of all of its designers, implementors, and maintainers.

Achieving Dependability

This is where the rubber meets the road. If you've made it this far, congratulations.

So far we've discussed Laprie's definition of "dependability," which can be (very) loosely paraphrased as "happy users," and we've discussed the attributes—availability, reliability, and maintainability—that contribute to it. This is all well and good, but without actionable advice for how to achieve dependability the entire discussion is purely academic.

Laprie thought so too, and defined four broad categories of techniques that can be used together to improve a system's dependability (or which, by their absence, can reduce it):

Fault prevention
Fault prevention techniques are used during system construction to prevent the occurrence or introduction of faults.

Fault tolerance

Fault tolerance techniques are used during system design and implementation to prevent service failures in the presence of faults.

Fault removal

Fault removal techniques are used to reduce the number and severity of faults.

Fault forecasting

Fault forecasting techniques are used to identify the presence, the creation, and the consequences of faults.

Interestingly, as illustrated in Figure 6-2, these four categories correspond surprisingly well to the five cloud native attributes that we introduced all the way back in Chapter 1.

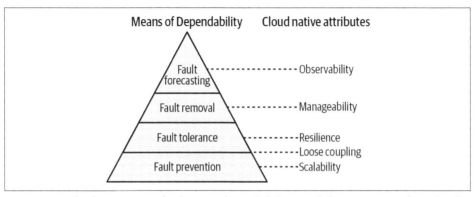

Figure 6-2. The four means of achieving dependability, and their corresponding cloud native attributes

Fault prevention and fault tolerance make up the bottom two layers of the pyramid, corresponding with scalability, loose coupling, and resilience. Designing a system for scalability prevents a variety of faults common among cloud native applications, and resiliency techniques allow a system to tolerate faults when they do inevitably arise. Techniques for loose coupling can be said to fall into both categories, preventing and enhancing a service's fault tolerance. Together these can be said to contribute to what Laprie terms *dependability procurement*: the means by which a system is provided with the ability to perform its designated function.

Techniques and designs that contribute to manageability are intended to produce a system that can be easily modified, simplifying the process of removing faults when they're identified. Similarly, observability naturally contributes to the ability to forecast faults in a system. Together fault removal and forecasting techniques contribute to what Laprie termed *dependability validation*: the means by which confidence is gained in a system's ability to perform its designated function.

Consider the implications of this relationship: what was a purely academic exercise 35 years ago has essentially been rediscovered—apparently independently—as a natural consequence of years of accumulated experience building reliable production systems. Dependability has come full-circle.

In the subsequent sections we'll explore these relationships more fully and preview later chapters, in which we discuss exactly how these two apparently disparate systems actually correspond quite closely.

Fault Prevention

At the base of our "Means of Dependability" pyramid are techniques that focus on preventing the occurrence or introduction of faults. As veteran programmers can attest, many—if not most—classes of errors and faults can be predicted and prevented during the earliest phases of development. As such, many fault prevention techniques come into play during the design and implementation of a service.

Good programming practices

Fault prevention is one of the primary goals of software engineering in general, and is the explicit goal of any development methodology, from pair programming to test-driven development and code review practices. Many such techniques can really be grouped into what might be considered to be "good programming practice," about which innumerable excellent books and articles have already been written, so we won't explicitly cover it here.

Language features

Your choice of language can also greatly affect your ability to prevent or fix faults. Many language features that some programmers have sometimes come to expect, such as dynamic typing, pointer arithmetic, manual memory management, and thrown exceptions (to name a few) can easily introduce unintended behaviors that are difficult to find and fix, and may even be maliciously exploitable.

These kinds of features strongly motivated many of the design decisions for Go, resulting in the strongly typed garbage-collected language we have today. For a refresher for why Go is particularly well suited for the development of cloud native services, take a look back at Chapter 2.

Scalability

We briefly introduced the concept of scalability way back in Chapter 1, where it was defined as the ability of a system to continue to provide correct service in the face of significant changes in demand.

In that section we introduced two different approaches to scaling—vertical scaling (scaling up) by resizing existing resources, and horizontal scaling (scaling out) by adding (or removing) service instances—and some of the pros and cons of each.

We'll go quite a bit deeper into each of these in Chapter 7, especially into the gotchas and downsides. We'll also talk a lot about the problems posed by state.[11] For now, though, it'll suffice to say that having to scale your service adds quite a bit of over-head, including but not limited to cost, complexity, and debugging.

While scaling resources is eventually often inevitable, it's often better (and cheaper!) to resist the temptation to throw hardware at the problem and postpone scaling events as long as possible by considering runtime efficiency and algorithmic scaling. As such, we'll cover a number of Go features and tooling that allow us to identify and fix common problems like memory leaks and lock contention that tend to plague systems at scale.

Loose coupling

Loose coupling, which we first defined in "Loose Coupling" on page 7, is the system property and design strategy of ensuring that a system's components have as little knowledge of other components as possible. The degree of coupling between services can have an enormous—and too often under-appreciated—impact on a system's ability to scale and to isolate and tolerate failures.

Since the beginning of microservices there have been dissenters who point to the dif-ficulty of deploying and maintaining microservice-based systems as evidence that such architectures are just too complex to be viable. I don't agree, but I can see where they're coming from, given how incredibly easy it is to build a *distributed monolith*. The hallmark of a distributed monolith is the tight coupling between its components, which results in an application saddled with all of the complexity of microservices plus the all of the tangled dependencies of the typical monolith. If you have to deploy most of your services together, or if a failed health check sends cascading failures through your entire system, you probably have a distributed monolith.

Building a loosely coupled system is easier said than done, but is possible with a little discipline and reasonable boundaries. In Chapter 8 we'll cover how to use data exchange contracts to establish those boundaries, and different synchronous and asynchronous communication models and architectural patterns and packages used to implement them and avoid the dreaded distributed monolith.

---

11 Application state is hard, and when done wrong it's poison to scalability.

Fault Tolerance

Fault tolerance has a number of synonyms—self-repair, self-healing, resilience—that all describe a system's ability to detect errors and prevent them from cascading into a full-blown failure. Typically, this consists of two parts: *error detection*, in which an error is discovered during normal service, and *recovery*, in which the system is returned to a state where it can be activated again.

Perhaps the most common strategy for providing resilience is redundancy: the duplication of critical components (having multiple service replicas) or functions (retrying service requests). This is a broad and very interesting field with a number of subtle gotchas that we'll dig into in Chapter 9.

Fault Removal

Fault removal, the third of the four dependability means, is the process of reducing the number and severity of faults—latent software flaws that can cause errors—before they manifest as errors.

Even under ideal conditions, there are plenty of ways that a system can error or otherwise misbehave. It might fail to perform an expected action, or perform the wrong action entirely, perhaps maliciously. Just to make things even more complicated, conditions aren't always—or often—ideal.

Many faults can be identified by testing, which allows you to verify that the system (or at least its components) behaves as expected under known test conditions.

But what about unknown conditions? Requirements change, and the real world doesn't care about your test conditions. Fortunately, with effort, a system can be designed to be manageable enough that its behavior can often be adjusted to keep it secure, running smoothly, and compliant with changing requirements.

We'll briefly discuss these next.

Verification and testing

There are exactly four ways of finding latent software faults in your code: testing, testing, testing, and bad luck.

Yes, I joke, but that's not so far from the truth: if you don't find your software faults, your users will. If you're lucky. If you're not, then they'll be found by bad actors seeking to take advantage of them.

Bad jokes aside, there are two common approaches to finding software faults in development:

Static analysis

Automated, rule-based code analysis performed without actually executing programs. Static analysis is useful for providing early feedback, enforcing consistent practices, and finding common errors and security holes without depending on human knowledge or effort.

Dynamic analysis

Verifying the correctness of a system or subsystem by executing it under controlled conditions and evaluating its behavior. More commonly referred to simply as "testing."

Key to software testing is having software that's *designed for testability* by minimizing the *degrees of freedom*—the range of possible states—of its components. Highly testable functions have a single purpose, with well-defined inputs and outputs and few or no *side effects*; that is, they don't modify variables outside of their scope. If you'll forgive the nerdiness, this approach minimizes the *search space*—the set of all possible solutions—of each function.

Testing is a critical step in software development that's all too often neglected. The Go creators understood this and baked unit testing and benchmarking into the language itself in the form of the `go test` command and the testing package (*https:// oreil.ly/PrhXq*). Unfortunately, a deep dive into testing theory is well beyond the scope of this book, but we'll do our best to scratch the surface in Chapter 9.

Manageability

Faults exist when your system doesn't behave according to requirements. But what happens when those requirements change?

Designing for *manageability*, first introduced back in "Manageability" on page 10, allows a system's behavior to be adjusted without code changes. A manageable system essentially has "knobs" that allow real-time control to keep your system secure, running smoothly, and compliant with changing requirements.

Manageability can take a variety of forms, including (but not limited to!) adjusting and configuring resource consumption, applying on-the-fly security remediations, *feature flags* that can turn features on or off, or even loading plug-in-defined behaviors.

Clearly, manageability is a broad topic. We'll review a few of the mechanisms Go provides for it in Chapter 10.

Fault Forecasting

At the peak of our "Means of Dependability" pyramid (Figure 6-2) is *fault forecasting*, which builds on the knowledge gained and solutions implemented in the levels below it to attempt to estimate the present number, the future incidence, and the likely consequence of faults.

Too often this consists of guesswork and gut feelings instead, generally resulting in unexpected failures when a starting assumption stops being true. More systematic approaches include Failure Mode and Effects Analysis (*https://oreil.ly/sNe6P*) and stress testing, which are very useful for understanding a system's possible failure modes.

In a system designed for *observability*, which we'll discuss in depth in Chapter 11, failure mode indicators can be tracked so that they can be forecast and corrected before they manifest as errors. Furthermore, when unexpected failures occur—as they inevitably will—observable systems allow the underlying faults to be quickly identified, isolated, and corrected.

The Continuing Relevance of the Twelve-Factor App

In the early 2010s, developers at Heroku, a platform as a service (PaaS) company and early cloud pioneer, realized that they were seeing web applications being developed again and again with the same fundamental flaws.

Motivated by what they felt were systemic problems in modern application development, they drafted *The Twelve-Factor App*. This was a set of twelve rules and guidelines constituting a development methodology for building web applications, and by extension, cloud native applications (although "cloud native" wasn't a commonly used term at the time). The methodology was for building web applications that: [12]

- Use declarative formats for setup automation, to minimize time and cost for new developers joining the project
- Have a clean contract with the underlying operating system, offering maximum portability between execution environments
- Are suitable for deployment on modern cloud platforms, obviating the need for servers and systems administration

---

12 Wiggins, Adam. *The Twelve-Factor App.* 2011. *https://12factor.net.*

- Minimize divergence between development and production, enabling continuous deployment for maximum agility
- Can scale up without significant changes to tooling, architecture, or development practices

While not fully appreciated when it was first published in 2011, as the complexities of cloud native development have become more widely understood (and felt), *The Twelve Factor App* and the properties it advocates have started to be cited as the bare minimum for any service to be cloud native.

I. Codebase

One codebase tracked in revision control, many deploys.

—The Twelve-Factor App

For any given service, there should be exactly one codebase that's used to produce any number of immutable releases for multiple deployments to multiple environments. These environments typically include a production site, and one or more staging and development sites.

Having multiple services sharing the same code tends to lead to a blurring of the lines between modules, trending in time to something like a monolith, making it harder to make changes in one part of the service without affecting another part (or another service!) in unexpected ways. Instead, shared code should be refactored into libraries that can be individually versioned and included through a dependency manager.

Having a single service spread across multiple repositories, however, makes it nearly impossible to automatically apply the build and deploy phases of your service's life cycle.

II. Dependencies

Explicitly declare and isolate (code) dependencies.

—The Twelve-Factor App

For any given version of the codebase, `go build`, `go test`, and `go run` should be deterministic: they should have the same result, however they're run, and the product should always respond the same way to the same inputs.

But what if a dependency—an imported code package or installed system tool beyond the programmer's control—changes in such a way that it breaks the build, introduces a bug, or becomes incompatible with the service?

Most programming languages offer a packaging system for distributing support libraries, and Go is no different.[13] By using Go modules (*https://oreil.ly/68ds1*) to declare all dependencies, completely and exactly, you can ensure that imported packages won't change out from under you and break your build in unexpected ways.

To extend this somewhat, services should generally try to avoid using the `os/exec` package's `Command` function to shell out to external tools like ImageMagick or `curl`.

Yes, your target tool might be available on all (or most) systems, but there's no way to *guarantee* that they both exist and are fully compatible with the service everywhere that it might run in the present or future. Ideally, if your service requires an external tool, that tool should be *vendored* into the service by including it in the service's repository.

III. Configuration

> Store configuration in the environment.
>
> —The Twelve-Factor App

Configuration—anything that's likely to vary between environments (staging, production, developer environments, etc)—should always be cleanly separated from the code. Under no circumstances should an application's configuration be baked into the code.

Configuration items may include, but certainly aren't limited to:

- URLs or other resource handles to a database or other upstream service dependencies—even if it's not likely to change any time soon.
- Secrets of *any* kind, such as passwords or credentials for external services.
- Per-environment values, such as the canonical hostname for the deploy.

A common means of extracting configuration from code is by *externalizing* them into some configuration file—often YAML[14]—which may or may not be checked into the repository alongside the code. This is certainly an improvement over configuration-in-code, but it's also less than ideal.

First, if your configuration file lives outside of the repository, it's all too easy to accidentally check it in. What's more, such files tend to proliferate, with different versions for different environments living in different places, making it hard to see and manage configurations with any consistency.

---

13 Although it was for too long!

14 The world's worst configuration language (except for all the other ones).

Alternatively, you *could* have different versions of your configurations for each environment in the repository, but this can be unwieldy and tends to lead to some awkward repository acrobatics.

There Are No Partially Compromised Secrets

It's worth emphasizing that while configuration values should never be in code, passwords or other sensitive secrets should *absolutely, never ever* be in code. It's all too easy for those secrets, in a moment of forgetfulness, to get shared with the whole world.

Once a secret is out, it's out. There are no partially compromised secrets.

Always treat your repository—and the code it contains—as if it can be made public at any time. Which, of course, it can.

Instead of configurations as code or even as external configurations, *The Twelve Factor App* recommends that configurations be stored as *environment variables*. Using environment variables in this way actually has a lot of advantages:

- They are standard and largely OS and language agnostic.
- That are easy to change between deploys without changing any code.
- They're very easy to inject into containers.

Go has several tools for doing this.

The first—and most basic—is the os package, which provides the os.Getenv function for this purpose:

```
name := os.Getenv("NAME")
place := os.Getenv("CITY")

fmt.Printf("%s lives in %s.\n", name, place)
```

For more sophisticated configuration options, there are several excellent packages available. Of these, spf13/viper (*https://oreil.ly/8giE4*) seems to be particularly popular. A snippet of Viper in action might look like the following:

```
viper.BindEnv("id")            // Will be uppercased automatically
viper.SetDefault("id", "13")   // Default value is "13"

id1 := viper.GetInt("id")
fmt.Println(id1)               // 13

os.Setenv("ID", "50")          // Typically done outside of the app!
```

```
id2 := viper.GetInt("id")
fmt.Println(id2)                    // 50
```

Additionally, Viper provides a number of features that the standard packages do not, such as default values, typed variables, and reading from command-line flags, variously formatted configuration files, and even remote configuration systems like etcd and Consul.

We'll dive more deeply into Viper and other configuration topics in Chapter 10.

IV. Backing Services

> Treat backing services as attached resources.
>
> —The Twelve-Factor App

A backing service is any downstream dependency that a service consumes across the network as part of its normal operation (see "Upstream and Downstream Dependencies" on page 5). A service should make no distinction between backing services of the same type. Whether it's an internal service that's managed within the same organization or a remote service managed by a third party should make no difference.

To the service, each distinct upstream service should be treated as just another resource, each addressable by a configurable URL or some other resource handle, as illustrated oi Figure 6-3. All resources should be treated as equally subject to the *Fallacies of Distributed Computing* (see Chapter 4 for a refresher, if necessary).

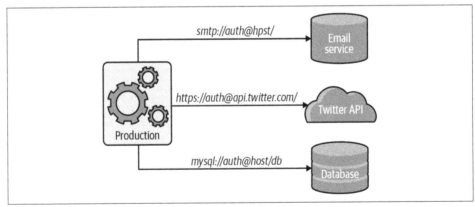

Figure 6-3. Each upstream service should be treated as just another resource, each addressable by a configurable URL or some other resource handle, each equally subject to the Fallacies of Distributed Computing

In other words, a MySQL database run by your own team's sysadmins should be treated no differently than an AWS-managed RDS instance. The same goes for *any*

---

upstream service, whether it's running in a data center in another hemisphere or in a Docker container on the same server.

A service that's able to swap out any resource at will with another one of the same kind—internally managed or otherwise—just by changing a configuration value can be more easily deployed to different environments, can be more easily tested, and more easily maintained.

V. Build, Release, Run

Strictly separate build and run stages.

—The Twelve-Factor App

Each (nondevelopment) deployment—the union of a specific version of the built code and a configuration—should be immutable and uniquely labeled. It should be possible, if necessary, to precisely recreate a deployment if (heaven forbid) it is necessary to roll a deployment back to an earlier version.

Typically, this is accomplished in three distinct stages, illustrated in Figure 6-4 and described in the following:

Build

In the build stage, an automated process retrieves a specific version of the code, fetches dependencies, and compiles an executable artifact we call a *build*. Every build should always have a unique identifier, typically a timestamp or an incrementing build number.

Release

In the release stage, a specific build is combined with a configuration specific to the target deployment. The resulting *release* is ready for immediate execution in the execution environment. Like builds, releases should also have a unique identifier. Importantly, producing releases with same version of a build shouldn't involve a rebuild of the code: to ensure environment parity, each environment-specific configuration should use the same build artifact.

Run

In the run stage, the release is delivered to the deployment environment and executed by launching the service's processes.

Ideally, a new versioned build will be automatically produced whenever new code is deployed.

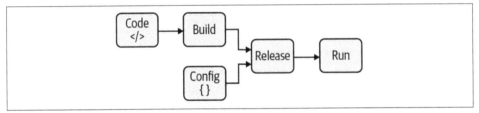

Figure 6-4. The process of deploying a codebase to a (nondevelopment) environment should be performed in distinct build, release, and run stages

VI. Processes

> Execute the app as one or more stateless processes.
>
> —The Twelve-Factor App

Service processes should be stateless and share nothing. Any data that has to be persisted should be stored in a stateful backing service, typically a database or external cache.

We've already spent some time talking about statelessness—and we'll spend more in the next chapter—so we won't dive into this point any further.

However, if you're interested in reading ahead, feel free to take a look at "State and Statelessness" on page 195.

VII. Data Isolation

> Each service manages its own data.
>
> —Cloud Native, *Data Isolation*

Each service should be entirely *self-contained*. That is, it should manage its own data, and make its data accessible only via an API designed for that purpose. If this sounds familiar to you, good! This is actually one of the core principles of microservices, which we'll discuss more in "The Microservices System Architecture" on page 211.

Very often this will be implemented as a request-response service like a RESTful API or RPC protocol that's exported by listening to requests coming in on a port, but this can also take the form of an asynchronous, event-based service using a publish-subscribe messaging pattern. Both of these patterns will be described in more detail in Chapter 8.

> ## Historical Note
>
> The actual title of the seventh section of *The Twelve Factor App* is "Port Binding," and is summarized as "export services via port binding."[15]
>
> At the time, this advice certainly made sense, but this title obscures its main point: that a service should encapsulate and manage its own data, and only share that data via an API.
>
> While many (or even most) web applications do, in fact, expose their APIs via ports, the increasing popularity of functions as a service (FaaS) and event-driven architectures means this is no longer necessarily always the case.
>
> So, instead of the original text, I've decided to use the more up-to-date (and true-to-intent) summary provided by Boris Scholl, Trent Swanson, and Peter Jausovec in *Cloud Native: Using Containers, Functions, and Data to Build Next-Generation Applications* (O'Reilly).

And finally, although this is something you don't see in the Go world, some languages and frameworks allow the runtime injection of an application server into the execution environment to create a web-facing service. This practice limits testability and portability by breaking data isolation and environment agnosticism, and is *very strongly* discouraged.

VIII. Scalability

> Scale out via the process model.
>
> —The Twelve-Factor App

Services should be able to scale horizontally by adding more instances.

We talk about scalability quite a bit in this book. We even dedicated all of Chapter 7 to it. With good reason: the importance of scalability can't be understated.

Sure, it's certainly convenient to just beef up the one server your service is running on —and that's fine in the (very) short term—but vertical scaling is a losing strategy in the long run. If you're lucky, you'll eventually hit a point where you simply can't scale up any more. It's more likely that your single server will either suffer load spikes faster than you can scale up, or just die without warning and without a redundant failover.[16] Both scenarios end with a lot of unhappy users. We'll discuss scalability quite a bit more in Chapter 7.

---

15 Wiggins, Adam. "Port Binding." *The Twelve-Factor App.* 2011. *https://oreil.ly/bp8lC.*

16 Probably at three in the morning.

IX. Disposability

> Maximize robustness with fast startup and graceful shutdown.
>
> —The Twelve-Factor App

Cloud environments are fickle: provisioned servers have a funny way of disappearing at odd times. Services should account for this by being *disposable*: service instances should be able to be started or stopped—intentionally or not—at any time.

Services should strive to minimize the time it takes to start up to reduce the time it takes for the service to be deployed (or redeployed) to elastically scale. Go, having no virtual machine or other significant overhead, is especially good at this.

Containers provide fast startup time and are also very useful for this, but care must be taken to keep image sizes small to minimize the data transfer overhead incurred with each initial deploy of a new image. This is another area in which Go excels: its self-sufficient binaries can generally be installed into SCRATCH images, without requiring an external language runtime or other external dependencies. We demonstrated this in the previous chapter, in "Containerizing Your Key-Value Store" on page 150.

Services should also be capable of shutting down when they receive a SIGTERM signal by saving all data that needs to be saved, closing open network connections, or finishing any in-progress work that's left or by returning the current job to the work queue.

X. Development/Production Parity

> Keep development, staging, and production as similar as possible.
>
> —The Twelve-Factor App

Any possible differences between development and production should be kept as small as possible. This includes code differences, of course, but it extends well beyond that:

Code divergence
: Development branches should be small and short-lived, and should be tested and deployed into production as quickly as possible. This minimizes functional differences between environments and reduces the risk of both deploys and rollbacks.

Stack divergence
: Rather than having different components for development and production (say, SQLite on OS X versus MySQL on Linux), environments should remain as similar as possible. Lightweight containers are an excellent tool for this. This minimizes the possibility that inconvenient differences between almost-but-not-quite-the-same implementations will emerge to ruin your day.

Personnel divergence

Once it was common to have programmers who wrote code and operators who deployed code, but that arrangement created conflicting incentives and counterproductive adversarial relationships. Keeping code authors involved in deploying their work and responsible for its behavior in production helps break down development/operations silos and aligns incentives around stability and velocity.

Taken together, these approaches help to keep the gap between development and production small, which in turn encourages rapid, automated, continuous deployment.

XI. Logs

Treat logs as event streams.

—The Twelve-Factor App

Logs—a service's never-ending stream of consciousness—are incredibly useful things, particularly in a distributed environment. By providing visibility into the behavior of a running application, good logging can greatly simplify the task of locating and diagnosing misbehavior.

Traditionally, services wrote log events to a file on the local disk. At cloud scale, however, this just makes valuable information awkward to find, inconvenient to access, and impossible to aggregate. In dynamic, ephemeral environments like Kubernetes your service instances (and their log files) may not even exist by the time you get around to viewing them.

Instead, a cloud native service should treat log information as nothing more than a stream of events, writing each event, unbuffered, directly to `stdout`. It shouldn't concern itself with implementation trivialities like routing or storage of its log events, and allow the executor to decide what happens to them.

Though seemingly simple (and perhaps somewhat counterintuitive), this small change provides a great deal of freedom.

During local development, a programmer can watch the event stream in a terminal to observe the service's behavior. In deployment, the output stream can be captured by the execution environment and forwarded to one or more destinations, such as a log indexing system like Elasticsearch, Logstash, and Kibana (ELK) or Splunk for review and analysis, or a data warehouse for long-term storage.

We'll discuss logs and logging, in the context of observability, in more detail in Chapter 11.

XII. Administrative Processes

> Run administrative/management tasks as one-off processes.
>
> —The Twelve-Factor App

Of all of the original Twelve Factors, this is the one that most shows its age. For one thing, it explicitly advocates shelling into an environment to manually execute tasks.

To be clear: *making manual changes to a server instance creates snowflakes. This is a bad thing.* See "Special Snowflakes" on page 188.

Assuming you even have an environment that you can shell into, you should assume that it can (and eventually will) be destroyed and re-created any moment.

Ignoring all of that for a moment, let's distill the point to its original intent: administrative and management tasks should be run as one-off processes. This could be interpreted in two ways, each requiring its own approach:

- If your task is an administrative process, like a data repair job or database migration, it should be run as a short-lived process. Containers and functions are excellent vehicles for such purposes.
- If your change is an update to your service or execution environment, you should instead modify your service or environment construction/configuration scripts, respectively.

Special Snowflakes

Keeping servers healthy can be a challenge. At 3 a.m., when things aren't working quite right, it's really tempting to make a quick change and go back to bed. Congratulations, you've just created a *snowflake*: a special server instance with manual changes that give it unique, usually undocumented, behaviors.

Even minor, seemingly harmless changes can lead to significant problems. Even if the changes are documented—which is rarely the case—snowflake servers are hard to reproduce exactly, particularly if you need to keep an entire cluster in sync. This can lead to a bad time when you have to redeploy your service onto new hardware and can't figure out why it's not working.

Furthermore, because your testing environment no longer matches production, you can no longer trust your development environments to reliably reproduce your production deployment.

Instead, servers and containers should be treated as *immutable*. If something needs to be updated, fixed, or modified in any way, changes should be made by updating the

---

appropriate build scripts, baking[17] a new common image, and provisioning new server or container instances to replace the old ones.

As the expression goes, instances should be treated as "cattle, not pets."

Summary

In this chapter we considered the question "what's the point of cloud native?" The common answer is "a computer system that works in the cloud." But "work" can mean anything. Surely we can do better.

So we went back to thinkers like Tony Hoare and J-C Laprie, who provided the first part of the answer: *dependability*. That is, to paraphrase, computer systems that behave in ways that users find acceptable, despite living in a fundamentally unreliable environment.

Obviously, that's more easily said than done, so we reviewed three schools of thought regarding how to achieve it:

- Laprie's academic "means of dependability," which include preventing, tolerating, removing, and forecasting faults
- Adam Wiggins' *Twelve Factor App*, which took a more prescriptive (and slightly dated, in spots) approach
- Our own "cloud native attributes," based on the Cloud Native Computing Foundation's definition of "cloud native," that we introduced in Chapter 1 and organized this entire book around

Although this chapter was essentially a short survey of theory, there's a lot of important, foundational information here that describes the motivations and means used to achieve what we call "cloud native."

---

17 "Baking" is a term sometimes used to refer to the process of creating a new container or server image.

## CHAPTER 7

Scalability

> Some of the best programming is done on paper, really. Putting it into the computer is just a minor detail.[1]

—Max Kanat-Alexander, *Code Simplicity: The Fundamentals of Software*

In the summer of 2016, I joined a small company that digitized the kind of forms and miscellaneous paperwork that state and local governments are known and loved for. The state of their core application was pretty typical of early-stage startups, so we got to work and, by that fall, had managed to containerize it, describe its infrastructure in code, and fully automate its deployment.

One of our clients was a small coastal city in southeastern Virginia, so when Hurricane Matthew—the first Category 5 Atlantic hurricane in nearly a decade—was forecast to make landfall not far from there, the local officials dutifully declared a state of emergency and used our system to create the necessary paperwork for citizens to fill out. Then they posted it to social media, and half a million people all logged in at the same time.

When the pager went off, the on-call checked the metrics and found that aggregated CPU for the servers was pegged at 100%, and that hundreds of thousands of requests were timing out.

So, we added a zero to the desired server count, created a "to-do" task to implement autoscaling, and went back to our day. Within 24 hours, the rush had passed, so we scaled the servers in.

What did we learn from this, other than the benefits of autoscaling?[2]

---

1 Kanat-Alexander, Max. *Code Simplicity: The Science of Software Design*. O'Reilly Media, 23 March 2012.

2 Honestly, if we had autoscaling in place I probably wouldn't even remember that this happened.

First of all, it underscored the fact that without the ability to scale, our system would have certainly suffered extended downtime. But being able to add resources on demand meant that we could serve our users even under load far beyond what we had ever anticipated. As an added benefit, if any one server failed, its work could have been divided among the survivors.

Second, having far more resources than necessary isn't just wasteful, it's expensive. The ability to scale our instances back in when demand ebbed meant that we were only paying for the resources that we needed. A major plus for a startup on a budget.

Unfortunately, because unscalable services can seem to function perfectly well under initial conditions, scalability isn't always a consideration during service design. While this might be perfectly adequate in the short term, services that aren't capable of growing much beyond their original expectations also have a limited lifetime value. What's more, it's often fiendishly difficult to refactor a service for scalability, so building with it in mind can save both time and money in the long run.

First and foremost, this is meant to be a Go book, or at least more of a Go book than an infrastructure or architecture book. While we will discuss things like scalable architecture and messaging patterns, much of this chapter will focus on demonstrating how Go can be used to produce services that lean on the other (non-infrastructure) part of the scalability equation: efficiency.[3]

What Is Scalability?

You may recall that concept of scalability was first introduced way back in Chapter 1, where it was defined as the ability of a system to continue to provide correct service in the face of significant changes in demand. By this definition, a system can be considered to be scalable if it doesn't need to be redesigned to perform its intended function during steep increases in load.

Note that this definition[4] doesn't actually say anything at all about adding physical resources. Rather, it calls out a system's ability to handle large swings in demand. The thing being "scaled" here is the magnitude of the demand. While adding resources is one perfectly acceptable means of achieving scalability, it isn't exactly the same as being scalable. To make things just a little more confusing, the word "scaling" can also be applied to a system, in which case it *does* mean a change in the amount of dedicated resources.

---

3 If you want to know more about cloud native infrastructure and architecture, a bunch of excellent books on the subject have already been written. I particularly recommend *Cloud Native Infrastructure* by Justin Garrison and Kris Nova, and *Cloud Native Transformation* by Pini Reznik, Jamie Dobson, and Michelle Gienow (both O'Reilly Media).

4 This is my definition. I acknowledge that it diverges from other common definitions.

So how do we handle high demand without adding resources? As we'll discuss in "Scaling Postponed: Efficiency" on page 197, systems built with *efficiency* in mind are inherently more scalable by virtue of their ability to gracefully absorb high levels of demand, without immediately having to resort to adding hardware in response to every dramatic swing in demand, and without having to massively over-provision "just in case."

Different Forms of Scaling

Unfortunately, even the most efficient of efficiency strategies has its limit, and eventually you'll find yourself needing to scale your service to provide additional resources. There are two different ways that this can be done (see Figure 7-1), each with its own associated pros and cons:

Vertical scaling
> A system can be *vertically scaled* (or *scaled up*) by increasing its resource allocations. In a public cloud, an existing server can be vertically scaled fairly easily just by changing its instance size, but only until you run out of larger instance types (or money).

Horizontal scaling
> A system can be *horizontally scaled* (or *scaled out*) by duplicating the system or service to limit the burden on any individual server. Systems using this strategy can typically scale to handle greater amounts of load, but as you'll see in "State and Statelessness" on page 195, the presence of state can make this strategy difficult or impossible for some systems.

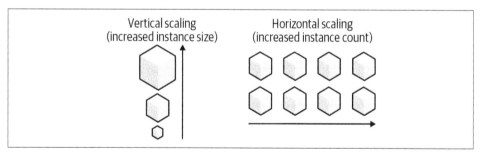

Figure 7-1. Vertical scaling can be an effective short-term solution; horizontal scaling is more technically challenging but may be a better long-term strategy

These two terms are used to describe the most common way of thinking about scaling: taking an entire system, and just making *more* of it. There are a variety of other scaling strategies in use, however.

Perhaps the most common of these is *functional partitioning*, which you're no doubt already familiar with, if not by name. Functional partitioning involves decomposing complex systems into smaller functional units that can be independently optimized, managed, and scaled. You might recognize this as a generalization of a number of best practices ranging from basic program design to advanced distributed systems design.

Another approach common in systems with large amounts of data—particularly databases—is *sharding*. Systems that use this strategy distribute load by dividing their data into partitions called *shards*, each of which holds a specific subset of the larger dataset. A basic example of this is presented in "Minimizing locking with sharding" on page 205.

The Four Common Bottlenecks

As the demands on a system increase, there will inevitably come a point at which one resource just isn't able to keep pace, effectively stalling any further efforts to scale. That resource has become a *bottleneck*.

Returning the system to operable performance levels requires identifying and addressing the bottleneck. This can be done in the short-term by increasing the bottlenecked component—vertically scaling—by adding more memory or up-sizing the CPU, for instance. As you might recall from the discussion in "Different Forms of Scaling" on page 193, this approach isn't always possible (or cost-effective), and it can never be relied upon forever.

However, it's often possible to address a bottleneck by enhancing or reducing the burden on the affected component by utilizing another resource that the system still has in abundance. A database might avoid disk I/O bottlenecking by caching data in RAM; conversely a memory-hungry service could page data to disk. Horizontally scaling doesn't make a system immune: adding more instances can mean more communication overhead, which puts additional strain on the network. Even highly-concurrent systems can become victims of their own inner workings as the demand on them increases, and phenomena like lock contention come into play. Using resources effectively often means making tradeoffs.

Of course, fixing a bottleneck requires that you first identify the constrained component, and while there are many different resources that can emerge as targets for scaling efforts—whether by actually scaling the resource or by using it more efficiently—such efforts tend to focus on just four resources:

CPU

The number of operations per unit of time that can be performed by a system's central processor and a common bottleneck for many systems. Scaling strategies for CPU include caching the results of expensive deterministic operations (at the expense of memory), or simply increasing the size or number of processors (at the expense of network I/O if scaling out).

Memory

The amount of data that can be stored in main memory. While today's systems can store incredible amounts of data on the order of tens or hundreds of gigabytes, even this can fall short, particularly for data-intensive systems that lean on memory to circumvent disk I/O speed limits. Scaling strategies include offloading data from memory to disk (at the expense of disk I/O) or an external dedicated cache (at the expense of network I/O), or simply increasing the amount of available memory.

Disk I/O

The speed at which data can be read from and written to a hard disk or other persistent storage medium. Disk I/O is a common bottleneck on highly parallel systems that read and write heavily to disk, such as databases. Scaling strategies include caching data in RAM (at the expense of memory) or using an external dedicated cache (at the expense of network I/O).

Network I/O

The speed at which data can be sent across a network, either from a particular point or in aggregate. Network I/O translates directly into *how much* data the network can transmit per unit of time. Scaling strategies for network I/O are often limited,[5] but network I/O is particularly amenable to various optimization strategies that we'll discuss shortly.

As the demand on a system increases, it'll almost certainly find itself bottlenecked by one of these, and while there are efficiency strategies that can be applied, those tend to come at the expense of one or more other resources, so you'll eventually find your system being bottlenecked *again* by another resource.

State and Statelessness

We briefly touched on statelessness in "Application State Versus Resource State" on page 124, where we described application state—server-side data about the application or how it's being used by a client—as something to be avoided if at all possible. But this time, let's spend a little more time discussing what state is, why it can be problematic, and what we can do about it.

It turns out that "state" is strangely difficult to define, so I'll do my best on my own. For the purposes of this book I'll define state as the set of an application's variables which, if changed, affect the behavior of the application.[6]

---

5 Some cloud providers impose lower network I/O limits on smaller instances. Increasing the size of the instance may increase these limits in some cases.

6 If you have a better definition, let me know. I'm already thinking about the second edition.

Application State Versus Resource State

Most applications have some form of state, but not all state is created equal. It comes in two kinds, one of which is far less desirable than the other.

First, there's *application state*, which exists any time an application needs to remember an event locally. Whenever somebody talks about a *stateful* application, they're usually talking about an application that's designed to use this kind of local state. "Local" is an operative word here.

Second, there's *resource state*, which is the same for every client and which has nothing to do with the actions of clients, like data stored in external data store or managed by configuration management. It's misleading, but saying that an application is *stateless* doesn't mean that it doesn't have any data, just that it's been designed in such a way that it's free of any local persistent data. Its only state is resource state, often because all of its state is stored in some external data store.

To illustrate the difference between the two, imagine an application that tracks client sessions, associating them with some application context. If users' session data was maintained locally by the application, that would be considered "application state." But if the data was stored in an external database, then it could be treated as a remote resource, and it would be "resource state."

Application state is something of the "anti-scalability." Multiple instances of a stateful service will quickly find their individual states diverging due to different inputs being received by each replica. Server affinity provides a workaround to this specific condition by ensuring that each of a client's requests are made to the same server, but this strategy poses a considerable data risk, since the failure of any single server is likely to result in a loss of data.

Advantages of Statelessness

So far, we've discussed the differences between application state and resource state, and we've even suggested—without much evidence (yet)—that application state is bad. However, statelessness provides some very noticeable advantages:

Scalability

The most visible and most often cited benefit is that stateless applications can handle each request or interaction independent of previous requests. This means that any service replica can handle any request, allowing applications to grow, shrink, or be restarted without losing data required to handle any in-flight sessions or requests. This is especially important when autoscaling your service, because the instances, nodes, or pods hosting the service can (and usually will) be created and destroyed unexpectedly.

Durability

Data that lives in exactly one place (such as a single service replica) can (and, at some point, *will*) get lost when that replica goes away for any reason. Remember: everything in "the cloud" evaporates eventually.

Simplicity

Without any application state, stateless services are freed from the need to... well... manage their state.[7] Not being burdened with having to maintain service-side state synchronization, consistency, and recovery logic[8] makes stateless APIs less complex, and therefore easier to design, build, and maintain.

Cacheability

APIs provided by stateless services are relatively easy to design for cacheability. If a service knows that the result of a particular request will always be the same, regardless of who's making it or when, the result can be safely set aside for easy retrieval later, increasing efficiency and reducing response time.

These might seem like four different things, but there's overlap with respect to what they provide. Specifically, statelessness makes services both simpler and safer to build, deploy, and maintain.

Scaling Postponed: Efficiency

In the context of cloud computing, we usually think of scalability in terms of the ability of a system to add network and computing resources. Often neglected, however, is the role of *efficiency* in scalability. Specifically, the ability for a system to handle changes in demand *without* having to add (or greatly over-provision) dedicated resources.

While it can be argued that most people don't care about program efficiency most of the time, this starts to become less true as demand on a service increases. If a language has a relatively high per-process concurrency overhead—often the case with dynamically typed languages—it will consume all available memory or compute resources much more quickly than a lighter-weight language, and consequently require resources and more scaling events to support the same demand.

This was a major consideration in the design of Go's concurrency model, whose goroutines aren't threads at all but lightweight routines multiplexed onto multiple OS threads. Each costs little more than the allocation of stack space, allowing potentially millions of concurrently executing routines to be created.

---

7 I know I said the word "state" a bunch of times there. Writing is hard.

8 See also: idempotence.

As such, in this section we'll cover a selection of Go features and tooling that allow us to avoid common scaling problems, such as memory leaks and lock contention, and to identify and fix them when they do arise.

Efficient Caching Using an LRU Cache

Caching to memory is a very flexible efficiency strategy that can be used to relieve pressure on anything from CPU to disk I/O or network I/O, or even just to reduce latency associated with remote or otherwise slow-running operations.

The concept of caching certainly *seems* straightforward. You have something you want to remember the value of—like the result of an expensive (but deterministic) calculation—and you put it in a map for later. Right?

Well, you could do that, but you'll soon start running into problems. What happens as the number of cores and goroutines increases? Since you didn't consider concurrency, you'll soon find your modifications stepping on one another, leading to some unpleasant results. Also, since we forgot to remove anything from our map, it'll continue growing indefinitely until it consumes all of our memory.

What we need is a cache that:

- Supports concurrent read, write, and delete operations
- Scales well as the number of cores and goroutines increase
- Won't grow without limit to consume all available memory

One common solution to this dilemma is an LRU (Least Recently Used) cache: a particularly lovely data structure that tracks how recently each of its keys have been "used" (read or written). When a value is added to the cache such that it exceeds a predefined capacity, the cache is able to "evict" (delete) its least recently used value.

A detailed discussion of how to implement an LRU cache is beyond the scope of this book, but I will say that it's quite clever. As illustrated on Figure 7-2, an LRU cache contains a doubly linked list (which actually contains the values), and a map that associates each key to a node in the linked list. Whenever a key is read or written, the appropriate node is moved to the bottom of the list, such that the least recently used node is always at the top.

There are a couple of Go LRU cache implementations available, though none in the core libraries (yet). Perhaps the most common can be found as part of the golang/groupcache (*https://oreil.ly/Q5pzk*) library. However, I prefer HashiCorp's open source extension to groupcache, `hashicorp/golang-lru` (*https://oreil.ly/25ESk*), which is better documented and includes `sync.RWMutexes` for concurrency safety.

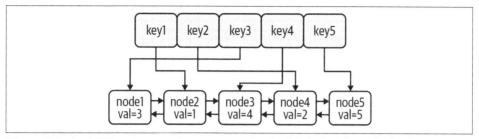

Figure 7-2. An LRU cache contains a map and a doubly linked list, which allows it to discard stale items when it exceeds its capacity

HashiCorp's library contains two construction functions, each of which returns a pointer of type *Cache and an error:

```
// New creates an LRU cache with the given capacity.
func New(size int) (*Cache, error)

// NewWithEvict creates an LRU cache with the given capacity, and also accepts
// an "eviction callback" function that's called when an eviction occurs.
func NewWithEvict(size int,
    onEvicted func(key interface{}, value interface{})) (*Cache, error)
```

The *Cache struct has a number of attached methods, the most useful of which are as follows:

```
// Add adds a value to the cache and returns true if an eviction occurred.
func (c *Cache) Add(key, value interface{}) (evicted bool)

// Check if a key is in the cache (without updating the recent-ness).
func (c *Cache) Contains(key interface{}) bool

// Get looks up a key's value and returns (value, true) if it exists.
// If the value doesn't exist, it returns (nil, false).
func (c *Cache) Get(key interface{}) (value interface{}, ok bool)

// Len returns the number of items in the cache.
func (c *Cache) Len() int

// Remove removes the provided key from the cache.
func (c *Cache) Remove(key interface{}) (present bool)
```

There are several other methods as well. Take a look at the GoDocs (*https://oreil.ly/ODcff*) for a complete list.

In the following example, we create and use an LRU cache with a capacity of two. To better highlight evictions, we include a callback function that prints some output to stdout whenever an eviction occurs. Note that we've decided to initialize the cache variable in an init function, a special function that's automatically called before the main function and after the variable declarations have evaluated their initializers:

```go
package main

import (
    "fmt"
    lru "github.com/hashicorp/golang-lru"
)

var cache *lru.Cache

func init() {
    cache, _ = lru.NewWithEvict(2,
        func(key interface{}, value interface{}) {
            fmt.Printf("Evicted: key=%v value=%v\n", key, value)
        },
    )
}

func main() {
    cache.Add(1, "a")           // adds 1
    cache.Add(2, "b")           // adds 2; cache is now at capacity

    fmt.Println(cache.Get(1))   // "a true"; 1 now most recently used

    cache.Add(3, "c")           // adds 3, evicts key 2

    fmt.Println(cache.Get(2))   // "<nil> false" (not found)
}
```

In the preceding program, we create a cache with a capacity of two, which means that the addition of a third value will force the eviction of the least recently used value.

After adding the values {1:"a"} and {2:"b"} to the cache, we call cache.Get(1), which makes {1:"a"} more recently used than {2:"b"}. So, when we add {3:"c"} in the next step, {2:"b"} is evicted, so the next cache.Get(2) shouldn't return a value.

If we run this program we'll be able to see this in action. We'll expect the following output:

```
$ go run lru.go
a true
Evicted: key=2 value=b
<nil> false
```

The LRU cache is an excellent data structure to use as a global cache for most use cases, but it does have a limitation: at very high levels of concurrency—on the order of several million operations per second—it will start to experience some contention.

Unfortunately, at the time of this writing, Go still doesn't seem to have a *very* high throughput cache implementation.[9]

Efficient Synchronization

A commonly repeated Go proverb is "don't communicate by sharing memory; share memory by communicating." In other words, channels are generally preferred over shared data structures.

This is a pretty powerful concept. After all, Go's concurrency primitives—goroutines and channels—provide a powerful and expressive synchronization mechanism, such that a set of goroutines using channels to exchange references to data structures can often allow locks to be dispensed with altogether.

(If you're a bit fuzzy on the details of channels and goroutines, don't stress. Take a moment to flip back to "Goroutines" on page 64. It's okay. I'll wait.)

That being said, Go *does* provide more traditional locking mechanisms by way of the sync package. But if channels are so great, why would we want to use something like a sync.Mutex, and when would we use it?

Well, as it turns out, channels *are* spectacularly useful, but they're not the solution to every problem. Channels shine when you're working with many discrete values, and are the better choice for passing ownership of data, distributing units of work, or communicating asynchronous results. Mutexes, on the other hand, are ideal for synchronizing access to caches or other large stateful structures.

At the end of the day, no tool solves every problem. Ultimately, the best option is to use whichever is most expressive and/or most simple.

Share memory by communicating

Threading is easy; locking is hard.

In this section we're going to use a classic example—originally presented in Andrew Gerrand's classic *Go Blog* article "Share Memory By Communicating"[10]—to demonstrate this truism and show how Go channels can make concurrency safer and easier to reason about.

---

9 However, if you're interested in learning more about high-performance caching in Go, take a look at Manish Rai Jain's excellent post on the subject, "The State of Caching in Go," on the *Dgraph Blog* (*https://oreil.ly/N6lrh*).

10 Gerrand, Andrew. "Share Memory By Communicating." *The Go Blog*, 13 July 2010. *https://oreil.ly/GTURp* Portions of this section are modifications based on work created and shared by Google (*https://oreil.ly/D8ntT*) and used according to terms described in the Creative Commons 4.0 Attribution License (*https://oreil.ly/la3YW*).

Imagine, if you will, a hypothetical program that polls a list of URLs by sending it a GET request and waiting for the response. The catch is that each request can spend quite a bit of time waiting for the service to respond: anywhere from milliseconds to seconds (or more), depending on the service. Exactly the kind of operation that can benefit from a bit of concurrency, isn't it?

In a traditional threading environment that depends on locking for synchronization you might structure its data something like the following:

```
type Resource struct {
    url        string
    polling    bool
    lastPolled int64
}

type Resources struct {
    data []*Resource
    lock *sync.Mutex
}
```

As you can see, instead of having a slice of URL strings, we have two structs— Resource and Resources—each of which is already saddled with a number of synchronization structures beyond the URL strings we really care about.

To multithread the polling process in the traditional way, you might have a `Poller` function like the following running in multiple threads:

```
func Poller(res *Resources) {
    for {
        // Get the least recently polled Resource and mark it as being polled
        res.lock.Lock()

        var r *Resource

        for _, v := range res.data {
            if v.polling {
                continue
            }
            if r == nil || v.lastPolled < r.lastPolled {
                r = v
            }
        }

        if r != nil {
            r.polling = true
        }

        res.lock.Unlock()

        if r == nil {
            continue
```

```
        }

        // Poll the URL

        // Update the Resource's polling and lastPolled
        res.lock.Lock()
        r.polling = false
        r.lastPolled = time.Nanoseconds()
        res.lock.Unlock()
    }
}
```

This does the job, but it has a lot of room for improvement. It's about a page long, hard to read, hard to reason about, and doesn't even include the URL polling logic or gracefully handle exhaustion of the `Resources` pool.

Now let's take a look at the same functionality implemented using Go channels. In this example, `Resource` has been reduced to its essential component (the URL string), and `Poller` is a function that receives `Resource` values from an input channel, and sends them to an output channel when they're done:

```
type Resource string

func Poller(in, out chan *Resource) {
    for r := range in {
        // Poll the URL

        // Send the processed Resource to out
        out <- r
    }
}
```

It's so...simple. We've completely shed the clockwork locking logic in `Poller`, and our `Resource` data structure no longer contains bookkeeping data. In fact, all that's left are the important parts.

But what if we wanted more than one `Poller` process? Isn't that what we were trying to do in the first place? The answer is, once again, gloriously simple: goroutines. Take a look at the following:

```
for i := 0; i < numPollers; i++ {
    go Poller(in, out)
}
```

By executing `numPollers` goroutines, we're creating `numPollers` concurrent processes, each reading from and writing to the same channels.

A lot has been omitted from the previous examples to highlight the relevant bits. For a walkthrough of a complete, idiomatic Go program that uses these ideas, see the "Share Memory By Communicating" (*https://oreil.ly/HF1Ay*) Codewalk.

Reduce blocking with buffered channels

At some point in this chapter you've probably thought to yourself, "sure, channels are great, but writing to channels still blocks." After all, every send operation on a channel blocks until there's a corresponding receive, right? Well, as it turns out, this is only *mostly* true. At least, it's true of default, unbuffered channels.

However, as we first describe in "Channel buffering" on page 65, it's possible to create channels that have an internal message buffer. Send operations on such buffered channels only block when the buffer is full and receives from a channel only block when the buffer is empty.

You may recall that buffered channels can be created by passing an additional capacity parameter to the make function to specify the size of the buffer:

```
ch := make(chan type, capacity)
```

Buffered channels are especially useful for handling "bursty" loads. In fact, we already used this strategy in Chapter 5 when we initialized our FileTransactionLogger. Distilling some of the logic that's spread through that chapter produces something like the following:

```
type FileTransactionLogger struct {
    events       chan<- Event    // Write-only channel for sending events
    lastSequence uint64          // The last used event sequence number
}

func (l *FileTransactionLogger) WritePut(key, value string) {
    l.events <- Event{EventType: EventPut, Key: key, Value: value}
}

func (l *FileTransactionLogger) Run() {
    l.events = make(chan Event, 16)          // Make an events channel

    go func() {
        for e := range events {              // Retrieve the next Event
            l.lastSequence++                 // Increment sequence number
        }
    }()
}
```

In this segment, we have a WritePut function that can be called to send a message to an events channel, which is received in the for loop inside the goroutine created in the Run function. If events was a standard channel, each send would block until the anonymous goroutine completed a receive operation. That might be fine most of the time, but if several writes came in faster than the goroutine could process them, the upstream client would be blocked.

By using a buffered channel we made it possible for this code to handle small bursts of up to 16 closely clustered write requests. Importantly, however, the 17th write *would* block.

It's also important to consider that using buffered channels like this creates a risk of data loss should the program terminate before any consuming goroutines are able to clear the buffer.

Minimizing locking with sharding

As lovely as channels are, as we mentioned in "Efficient Synchronization" on page 201 they don't solve *every* problem. A common example of this is a large, central data structure, such as a cache, that can't be easily decomposed into discrete units of work.[11]

When shared data structures have to be concurrently accessed, it's standard to use a locking mechanism, such as the mutexes provided by the sync package, as we do in "Making Your Data Structure Concurrency-Safe" on page 121. For example, we might create a struct that contains a map and an embedded sync.RWMutex:

```
var cache = struct {
    sync.RWMutex
    data map[string]string
}{data: make(map[string]string)}
```

When a routine wants to write to the cache, it would carefully use cache.Lock to establish the write lock, and cache.Unlock to release the lock when it's done. We might even want to wrap it in a convenience function as follows:

```
func ThreadSafeWrite(key, value string) {
    cache.Lock()                              // Establish write lock
    cache.data[key] = value
    cache.Unlock()                            // Release write lock
}
```

By design, this restricts write access to whichever routine happens to have the lock. This pattern generally works just fine. However, as we discussed in Chapter 4, as the number of concurrent processes acting on the data increases, the average amount of time that processes spend waiting for locks to be released also increases. You may remember the name for this unfortunate condition: lock contention.

While this might be resolved in some cases by scaling the number of instances, this also increases complexity and latency, as distributed locks need to be established and writes need to establish consistency. An alternative strategy for reducing lock

---

11 You could probably shoehorn channels into a solution for interacting with a cache, but you might find it difficult to make it simpler than locking.

contention around shared data structures within an instance of a service is *vertical sharding*, in which a large data structure is partitioned into two or more structures, each representing a part of the whole. Using this strategy, only a portion of the overall structure needs to be locked at a time, decreasing overall lock contention.

You may recall that we discussed vertical sharding in some detail in "Sharding" on page 101. If you're unclear on vertical sharding theory or implementation, feel free to take some time to go back and review that section.

Memory Leaks Can…fatal error: runtime: out of memory

Memory leaks are a class of bugs in which memory is not released even after it's no longer needed. These bugs can be quite subtle and often plague languages like C++ in which memory is manually managed. But while garbage collection certainly helps by attempting to reclaim memory occupied by objects that are no longer in use by the program, garbage-collected languages like Go aren't immune to memory leaks. Data structures can still grow unbounded, unresolved goroutines can still accumulate, and even unstopped `time.Ticker` values can get away from you.

In this section we'll review a few common causes of memory leaks particular to Go, and how to resolve them.

Leaking goroutines

I'm not aware of any actual data on the subject,[12] but based purely on my own personal experience, I strongly suspect that goroutines are the single largest source of memory leaks in Go.

Whenever a goroutine is executed, it's initially allocated a small memory stack—2048 bytes—that can be dynamically adjusted up or down as it runs to suit the needs of the process. The precise maximum stack size depends on a lot of things,[13] but it's essentially reflective of the amount of available physical memory.

Normally, when a goroutine returns, its stack is either deallocated or set aside for recycling.[14] Whether by design or by accident, however, not every goroutine actually returns. For example:

---

12 If you are, let me know!

13 Dave Cheney wrote an excellent article on this topic called *Why is a Goroutine's stack infinite?* (*https://oreil.ly/PUCLF*) that I recommend you take a look at if you're interested in the dynamics of goroutine memory allocation.

14 There's a very good article by Vincent Blanchon on the subject of goroutine recycling entitled *How Does Go Recycle Goroutines?* (*https://oreil.ly/GnoV2*)

```go
func leaky() {
    ch := make(chan string)

    go func() {
        s := <-ch
        fmt.Println("Message:", s)
    }()
}
```

In the previous example, the leaky function creates a channel and executes a goroutine that reads from that channel. The leaky function returns without error, but if you look closely you'll see that no values are ever sent to ch, so the goroutine will never return and its stack will never be deallocated. There's even collateral damage: because the goroutine references ch, that value can't be cleaned up by the garbage collector.

So we now have a bona fide memory leak. If such a function is called regularly the total amount of memory consumed will slowly increase over time until it's completely exhausted.

This is a contrived example, but there are good reasons why a programmer might want to create long-running goroutines, so it's usually quite hard to know whether such a process was created intentionally.

So what do we do about this? Dave Cheney offers some excellent advice here: "You should never start a goroutine without knowing how it will stop....Every time you use the go keyword in your program to launch a goroutine, you must know how, and when, that goroutine will exit. If you don't know the answer, that's a potential memory leak."[15]

This may seem like obvious, even trivial advice, but it's incredibly important. It's all too easy to write functions that leak goroutines, and those leaks can be a pain to identify and find.

Forever ticking tickers

Very often you'll want to add some kind of time dimension to your Go code, to execute it at some point in the future or repeatedly at some interval, for example.

The time package provides two useful tools to add such a time dimension to Go code execution: time.Timer, which fires at some point in the future, and time.Ticker, which fires repeatedly at some specified interval.

---

15 Cheney, Dave. "Never Start a Goroutine without Knowing How It Will Stop." dave.cheney.net, 22 Dec. 2016. *https://oreil.ly/VUlrY*.

However, where time.Timer has a finite useful life with a defined start and end, time.Ticker has no such limitation. A time.Ticker can live forever. Maybe you can see where this is going.

Both Timers and Tickers use a similar mechanism: each provides a channel that's sent a value whenever it fires. The following example uses both:

```
func timely() {
    timer := time.NewTimer(5 * time.Second)
    ticker := time.NewTicker(1 * time.Second)

    done := make(chan bool)

    go func() {
        for {
            select {
            case <-ticker.C:
                fmt.Println("Tick!")
            case <-done:
                return
            }
        }
    }()

    <-timer.C
    fmt.Println("It's time!")
    close(done)
}
```

The timely function executes a goroutine that loops at regular intervals by listening for signals from ticker—which occur every second—or from a done channel that returns the goroutine. The line <-timer.C blocks until the 5-second timer fires, allowing done to be closed, triggering the case <-done condition and ending the loop.

The timely function completes as expected, and the goroutine has a defined return, so you could be forgiven for thinking that everything's fine. There's a particularly sneaky bug here though: running time.Ticker values contain an active goroutine that can't be cleaned up. Because we never stopped the timer, timely contains a memory leak.

The solution: always be sure to stop your timers. A defer works quite nicely for this purpose:

```
func timelyFixed() {
    timer := time.NewTimer(5 * time.Second)
    ticker := time.NewTicker(1 * time.Second)
    defer ticker.Stop()                            // Be sure to stop the ticker!

    done := make(chan bool)
```

```go
go func() {
    for {
        select {
        case <-ticker.C:
            fmt.Println("Tick!")
        case <-done:
            return
        }
    }
}()

<-timer.C
fmt.Println("It's time!")
close(done)
}
```

By calling `ticker.Stop()`, we shut down the underlying `Ticker`, allowing it to be recovered by the garbage collector and preventing a leak.

On Efficiency

In this section, we covered a number of common methods for improving the efficiency of your programs, ranging from using an LRU cache rather than a map to constrain your cache's memory footprint, to approaches for effectively synchronizing your processes, to preventing memory leaks. While these sections might not seem particularly closely connected, they're all important for building programs that scale.

Of course, there are countless other methods that I would have liked to include as well, but wasn't able to given the fundamental limits imposed by time and space.

In the next section, we'll change themes once again to cover some common service architectures and their effects on scalability. These might be a little less focused on Go specifically, but they're critical for a study of scalability, especially in a cloud native context.

Service Architectures

The concept of the *microservice* first appeared in the early 2010s as a refinement and simplification of the earlier service-oriented architecture (SOA) and a response to the *monoliths*—server-side applications contained within a single large executable—that were then the most common architectural model of choice.[16]

At the time, the idea of the microservice architecture—a single application composed of multiple small services, each running in its own process and communicating with

---

16 Not that they've gone away.

lightweight mechanisms—was revolutionary. Unlike monoliths, which require the entire application to be rebuilt and deployed for any change to the system, microservices were independently deployable by fully automated deployment mechanisms. This sounds small, even trivial, but its implications were (and are) vast.

If you ask most programmers to compare monoliths to microservices, most of the answers you get will probably be something about how monoliths are slow, sluggish, and bloated, while microservices are small, agile, and the new hotness. Sweeping generalizations are always wrong, though, so let's take a moment to ask ourselves whether this is true, and whether monoliths might sometimes be the right choice.

We will begin by defining what we mean when we talk about monoliths and microservices.

The Monolith System Architecture

In a *monolith architecture*, all of the functionally distinguishable aspects of a service are coupled together in one place. A common example is a web application whose user interface, data layer, and business logic are all intermingled, often on a single server.

Traditionally, enterprise applications have been built in three main parts, as illustrated in Figure 7-3: a client-side interface running on the user's machine, a relational database where all of the application's data lives, and a server-side application that handles all user input, executes all business logic, and reads and writes data to the database.

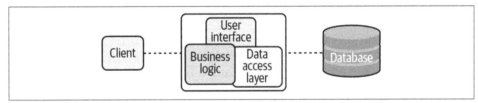

Figure 7-3. In a monolith architecture, all of the functionally distinguishable aspects of a service are coupled together in one place

At the time, this pattern made sense. All the business logic ran in a single process, making development easier, and you could even scale by running more monoliths behind a load balancer, usually using sticky sessions to maintain server affinity. Things were *perfectly fine*, and for many years this was by far the most common way of building web applications.

Even today, for relatively small or simple applications (for some definition of "small" and "simple") this works perfectly well (though I still strongly recommend statelessness over server affinity).

However, as the number of features and general complexity of a monolith increases, difficulties start to arise:

- Monoliths are usually deployed as a single artifact, so making even a small change generally requires a new version of the entire monolith to be built, tested, and deployed.

- Despite even the best of intentions and efforts, monolith code tends to decrease in modularity over time, making it harder to make changes in one part of the service without affecting another part in unexpected ways.

- Scaling the application means creating replicas of the entire application, not just the parts that need it.

The larger and more complex the monolith gets, the more pronounced these effects tend to become. By the early- to mid-2000s, these issues were well known, leading frustrated programmers to experiment with breaking their big, complex services into smaller, independently deployable and scalable components. By 2012, this pattern even had a name: microservices architecture.

The Microservices System Architecture

The defining characteristic of a *microservices architecture* is a service whose functional components have been divided into a set of discrete sub-services that can be independently built, tested, deployed, and scaled.

This is illustrated in Figure 7-4, in which a user interface service—perhaps an HTML-serving web application or a public API—interacts with clients, but rather than handling the business logic locally, it makes secondary requests of one or more component services to handle some specific functionality. Those services might in turn even make further requests of yet more services.

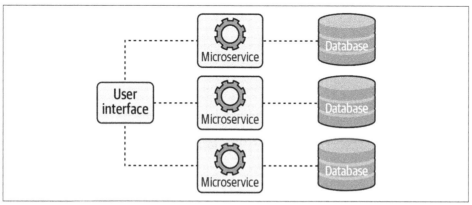

Figure 7-4. In a microservices architecture, functional components are divided into discrete subservices

While the microservices architecture has a number of advantages over the monolith, there are significant costs to consider. On one hand, microservices provide some significant benefits:

- A clearly-defined separation of concerns supports and reinforces modularity, which can be very useful for larger or multiple teams.
- Microservices should be independently deployable, making them easier to manage and making it possible to isolate errors and failures.
- In a microservices system, it's possible for different services to use the technology —language, development framework, data storage, etc—that's most appropriate to its function.

These benefits shouldn't be underestimated: the increased modularity and functional isolation of microservices tends to produce components that are themselves generally far more maintainable than a monolith with the same functionality. The resulting system isn't just easier to deploy and manage, but easier to understand, reason about, and extend for a larger number of programmers and teams.

 Mixing different technologies may sound appealing in theory, but use restraint. Each adds new requirements for tooling and expertise. The pros and cons of adopting a new technology—any new technology[17]—should always be carefully considered.

The discrete nature of microservices makes them far easier to maintain, deploy, and scale than monoliths. However, while these are real benefits that can pay real dividends, there are some downsides as well:

- The distributed nature of microservices makes them subject to the Fallacies of Distributed Computing (see Chapter 4), which makes them significantly harder to program and debug.
- Sharing any kind of state between your services can often be extremely difficult.
- Deploying and managing multiple services can be quite complex and tends to demand a high level of operational maturity.

So given these, which do you choose? The relative simplicity of the monolith, or the flexibility and scalability of microservices? You might have noticed that most of the benefits of microservices pay off as the application gets larger or the number of teams

---

17 Yes, even Go.

working on it increases. For this reason many authors advocate starting with a monolith and decomposing it later.

On a personal note, I'll mention that I've never seen any organization successfully break apart a large monolith, but I've seen many try. That's not to say it's impossible, just that it's hard. I can't tell you whether you should start your system as microservices, or with a monolith and break it up later. I'd certainly get a lot of angry emails if I tried. But please, whatever you do, stay stateless.

Serverless Architectures

Serverless computing is a pretty popular topic in web application architecture, and a lot of (digital) ink has been spilled about it. Much of this hype has been driven by the major cloud providers, which have invested heavily in serverlessness, but not all of it.

But what is serverless computing, really?

Well, as is often the case, it depends on who you ask. For the purposes of this book, however, we're defining it as a form of utility computing in which some server-side logic, written by a programmer, is transparently executed in a managed ephemeral environment in response to some predefined trigger. This is also sometimes referred to as "functions as a service," or "FaaS." All of the major cloud providers offer FaaS implementations, such as AWS's Lambda or GCP's Cloud Functions.

Such functions are quite flexible and can be usefully incorporated into many architectures. In fact, as we'll discuss shortly, entire *serverless architectures* can even be built that don't use traditional services at all, but are instead built entirely from FaaS resources and third-party managed services.

Be Suspicious of Hype

I may sound like a grizzled old dinosaur here, but I've learned to be wary of new technologies that nobody really understands claiming to solve all of our problems.

According to the research and advisory firm Gartner, which specializes in studying IT and technology trends, serverless infrastructure is hovering at or near the "Peak of Inflated Expectations"[18] of its "hype cycle" (*https://oreil.ly/fNuG8*). This is eventually, but inevitably, followed by the "Trough of Disillusionment."

In time, people start to figure out what the technology is really useful for (not *everything*) and when to use it (not *always*), and it enters the "Slope of Enlightenment" and

---

18 Bowers, Daniel, et al. "Hype Cycle for Compute Infrastructure, 2019." *Gartner*, Gartner Research, 26 July 2019, *https://oreil.ly/3gkJh*.

> "Plateau of Productivity." I've learned the hard way that it's usually best to wait until a technology has entered these two later phases before investing heavily in its use.
>
> That being said: serverless computing *is* intriguing, and it *does* seem appropriate for some use-cases.

The pros and cons of serverlessness

As with any other architectural decision, the choice to go with a partially or entirely serverless architecture should be carefully weighed against all available options. While serverlessness provides some clear benefits—some obvious (no servers to manage!), others less so (cost and energy savings)—it's very different from traditional architectures, and carries its own set of downsides.

That being said, let's start weighing. Let's start with the advantages:

Operational management
Perhaps the most obvious benefit of serverless architectures is that there's considerably less operational overhead.[19] There are no servers to provision and maintain, no licenses to buy, and no software to install.

Scalability
When using serverless functions, it's the provider—not the user—who's responsible for scaling capacity to meet demand. As such, the implementor can spend less time and effort considering and implementing scaling rules.

Reduced costs
FaaS providers typically use a "pay-as-you-go" model, charging only for the time and memory allocated when the function is run. This can be considerably more cost-effective than deploying traditional services to (likely underutilized) servers.

Productivity
In a FaaS model, the unit of work is an event-driven function. This model tends to encourage a "function first" mindset, resulting in code that's often simpler, more readable, and easier to test.

It's not all roses, though. There are very some real downsides to serverless architectures that need to be taken into consideration as well:

Startup latency
When a function is first called, it has to be "spun up" by the cloud provider. This typically takes less than a second, but in some cases can add 10 or more seconds to the initial requests. This is known as the *cold start* delay. What's more, if the

---

19 It's *right in the name!*

function isn't called for several minutes—the exact time varies between providers
—it's "spun down" by the provider so that it has to endure another cold start
when it's called again. This usually isn't a problem if your function doesn't have
enough idle time to get spun down, but can be a significant issue if your load is
particularly "bursty."

Observability

While most of the cloud vendors provide some basic monitoring for their FaaS
offerings, it's usually quite rudimentary. While third-party providers have been
working to fill the void, the quality and quantity of data available from your
ephemeral functions is often less than desired.

Testing

While unit testing tends to be pretty straightforward for serverless functions,
integration testing is quite hard. It's often difficult or impossible to simulate the
serverless environment, and mocks are approximations at best.

Cost

Although the "pay-as-you-go" model can be considerably cheaper when demand
is lower, there is a point at which this is no longer true. In fact, very high levels of
load can grow to be quite expensive.

Clearly, there's quite a lot to consider—on both sides—and while there *is* a great deal
of hype around serverless at the moment, to some degree I think it's merited. However, while serverlessness promises (and largely delivers) scalability and reduced
costs, it does have quite a few gotchas, including, but not limited to, testing and
debugging challenges. Not to mention the increased burden on operations around
observability![20]

Finally, as we'll see in the next section, serverless architectures also require quite a lot
more up-front planning than traditional architectures. While some people might call
this a positive feature, it can add significant complexity.

Serverless services

As mentioned previously, functions as a service (FaaS) are flexible enough to serve as
the foundation of entire serverless architectures that don't use traditional services
at all, but are instead built entirely from FaaS resources and third-party managed
services.

---

20 Sorry, there's no such thing as NoOps.

Let's take, as an example, the familiar three-tier system in which a client issues a request to a service, which in turn interacts with a database. A good example is the key-value store we started in Chapter 5, whose (admittedly primitive) monolithic architecture might look something like what's shown in Figure 7-5.

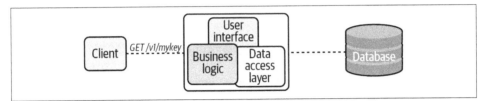

Figure 7-5. The monolithic architecture of our primitive key/value store

To convert this monolith into a serverless architecture, we'll need to use an *API gateway*: a managed service that's configured to expose specific HTTP endpoints and to direct requests to each endpoint to a specific resource—typically a FaaS functions—that handles requests and issue responses. Using this architecture, our key/value store might look something like what's shown in Figure 7-6.

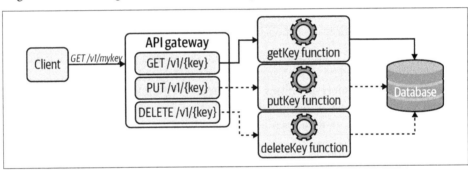

Figure 7-6. An API gateway routes HTTP calls to serverless handler functions

In this example, we've replaced the monolith with an API gateway that supports three endpoints: GET /v1/{key}, PUT /v1/{key}, and DELETE /v1/{key} (the {key} component indicates that this path will match any string, and refer to the value as key).

The API gateway is configured so that requests to each of its three endpoints are directed to a different handler function—getKey, putKey, and deleteKey, respectively—which performs all of the logic for handling that request and interacting with the backing database.

Granted, this is an incredibly simple application and doesn't account for things like authentication (which can be provided by a number of excellent third-party services like Auth0 or Okta), but some things are immediately evident.

First, there are a greater number of moving parts that you have to get your head around, which necessitates quite a bit more up-front planning and testing. For example, what happens if there's an error in a handler function? What happens to the request? Does it get forwarded to some other destination, or is it perhaps sent to a dead-letter queue for further processing?

Do not underestimate the significance of this increase in complexity! Replacing in-process interactions with distributed, fully managed components tends to introduce a variety of problems and failure cases that simply don't exist in the former. You may well have turned a relatively simple problem into an enormously complex one. Complexity kills; simplicity scales.

Second, with all of these different components, there's a need for more sophisticated distributed monitoring than you'd need with a monolith or small microservices system. Due to the fact that FaaS relies heavily on the cloud provider, this may be challenging or, at least, awkward.

Finally, the ephemeral nature of FaaS means that ALL state, even short-lived optimizations like caches, has to be externalized to a database, an external cache (like Redis), or network file/object store (like S3). Again, this can be argued to be a Good Thing, but it does add to up-front complexity.

Summary

This was a very difficult chapter to write, not because there isn't much to say, but because scalability is such a huge topic with so many different things I could have drilled down into. Every one of these battled in my brain for weeks.

I even ended up throwing away some perfectly good architecture content that, in retrospect, simply wasn't appropriate for this book. Fortunately, I was able to salvage a whole other chunk of work about messaging that ended up getting moved into Chapter 8. I think it's happier there anyway.

In those weeks, I spent a lot of time thinking about what scalability really is, and about the role that efficiency plays in it. Ultimately, I think that the decision to spend so much time on programmatic—rather than infrastructural—solutions to scaling problems was the right one.

All told, I think the end result is a good one. We certainly covered a lot of ground:

- We reviewed the different axes of scaling, and how scaling out is often the best long-term strategy.
- We discussed state and statelessness, and why application state is essentially "anti-scalability."

- We learned a few strategies for efficient in-memory caching and for avoiding memory leaks.
- We compared and contrasted monolithic, microservice, and serverless architectures.

That's quite a lot, and although I wish I'd been able to drill down in some more detail, I'm pleased to have been able to touch on the things I did.

## CHAPTER 8

Loose Coupling

We build our computers the way we build our cities—over time, without a plan, on top of ruins.[1]

—Ellen Ullman, *The Dumbing-down of Programming (May 1998)*

Coupling is one of those fascinating topics that seem straightforward in theory but are actually quite challenging in practice. As we'll discuss, there are lots of ways in which coupling can be introduced in a system, which means it's also a *big* subject. As you might imagine, this chapter is an ambitious one, and we cover a lot of ground.

First, we'll introduce the subject, diving more deeply into the concept of "coupling," and discussing the relative merits of "loose" versus "tight" coupling. We'll present some of the most common coupling mechanisms, and how some kinds of tight coupling can lead to the dreaded "distributed monolith."

Next, we'll talk about inter-service communications, and how fragile exchange protocols are a very common way of introducing tight coupling to distributed systems. We'll cover some of the common protocols in use today to minimize the degree of coupling between two services.

In the third part, we'll change direction for a bit, away from distributed systems and into the implementations of the services themselves. We'll talk about services as code artifacts, subject to coupling resulting from mingling implementations and violating separation of concerns, and present the use of plug-ins as a way to dynamically add implementations.

Finally, we'll close with a discussion of hexagonal architecture, an architectural pattern that makes loose coupling the central pillar of its design philosophy.

---

1 Ullman, Ellen. "The Dumbing-down of Programming." *Salon*, 12 May 1998. *https://oreil.ly/Eib3K*.

Throughout the chapter, we'll do our best to balance theory, architecture, and implementation. Most of the chapter will be spent on the fun stuff: discussing a variety of different strategies for managing coupling, particularly (but not exclusively) in the distributed context, and demonstrating by extending our example key/value store.

Tight Coupling

"Coupling" is a somewhat romantic term describing the degree of direct knowledge between components. For example, a client that sends requests to a service is by definition coupled to that service. The degree of that coupling can vary considerably, however, falling anywhere between two extremes.

"Tightly coupled" components have a great deal of knowledge about another component. Perhaps both require the same version of a shared library to communicate, or maybe the client needs an understanding of the server's architecture or database schema. It's easy to build tightly coupled systems when optimizing for the short term, but they have a huge downside: the more tightly coupled two components are, the more likely that a change to one component will necessitate corresponding changes to the other. As a result, tightly coupled systems lose many of the benefits of a microservice architecture.

In contrast, "loosely coupled" components have minimal direct knowledge of one another. They're relatively independent, typically interacting via a change-robust abstraction. Systems designed for loose coupling require more up-front planning, but they can be more freely upgraded, redeployed, or even entirely rewritten without greatly affecting the systems that depend on them.

Put simply, if you want to know how tightly coupled your system is, ask how many and what kind of changes can be made to one component without adversely affecting another.

 Some amount of coupling isn't necessarily a bad thing, especially early in a system's development. It can be temping to over-abstract and over-complicate, but premature optimization is *still* the root of all evil.

Coupling in Different Computing Contexts

The term "coupling" in the computing context predates microservices and service-oriented architecture by quite a bit, and has been used for many years to describe the degree of knowledge that one component has about another.

In programming, code can be tightly coupled when a dependent class directly references a concrete implementation instead of an abstraction (such as an interface; see

---

"Interfaces" on page 59). In Go this might be a function that requires an `os.File` when an `io.Reader` would do.

Multiprocessor systems that communicate by sharing memory can be said to be tightly coupled. In a loosely coupled system, components are connected through a MTS (Message Transfer System) (see "Efficient Synchronization" on page 201 for a refresher on how Go solves this problem with channels).

It's important to note that there might, on occasion, be good reason to tightly couple certain components. Eliminating abstractions and other intermediate layers can reduce overhead, which can be a useful optimization if speed is a critical system requirement.

Since this book is largely about distributed architectures, we'll focus on coupling between services that communicate across a network, but keep in mind that there are other ways that software can be tightly coupled to resources in its environment.

Tight Coupling Takes Many Forms

There's no limit to the ways components in a distributed system can find themselves tightly coupled. However, while these all share one fundamental flaw—they all depend on some property of another component that they wrongly assume won't change—most can be grouped into a few broad classes according to the resource that they're coupled to.

Fragile exchange protocols

Remember SOAP (simple object access protocol)? Statistically speaking, probably not.[2] SOAP was a messaging protocol developed in the late 1990s that was designed for extensibility and implementation neutrality. SOAP services provided a *contract* that clients could follow to format their requests.[3] The concept of the contract was something of a breakthrough at the time, but SOAP's implementation was exceedingly fragile: if the contract changed in any way, the clients had to be updated along with it. This requirement meant that SOAP clients were tightly coupled to their services.

It didn't take long for people to realize that this was a problem, and SOAP quickly lost its shine. It's since been largely replaced by REST, which, while a considerable improvement, can often introduce its own tight coupling. In 2016, Google released

---

2 Get off my lawn.

3 In XML, no less. We didn't know any better at the time.

gRPC (gRPC Remote Procedure Calls[4]), an open source framework with a number of useful features, including, importantly, allowing loose coupling between components.

We'll discuss some of these more contemporary options in "Communications Between Services" on page 224, where we'll see how to use Go's net/http package to build a REST/HTTP client and extend our key/value store with a gRPC frontend.

Shared dependencies

In 2016, Facebook's Ben Christensen gave a talk (*https://oreil.ly/ZX2Oe*) at the Microservices Practitioner Summit where he spoke about another increasingly common mechanism for tightly coupling distributed services, introducing the term "distributed monolith" in the process.

Ben described an anti-pattern in which services were *required* to use specific libraries —and versions of libraries—in order to launch and interact with one another. Such systems find themselves saddled with a fleet-wide dependency, such that upgrading these shared libraries can force all services to have to upgrade in lockstep. This shared dependency has tightly coupled all of the services in the fleet.

Distributed Monoliths

In Chapter 7 we made the case that monoliths, at least for complex systems with multiple distinct functions, are (generally) less desirable, and microservices are (generally) the way to go.[5] Of course, that's easier said than done, in large part because it's so easy to accidentally create a *distributed monolith*: a microservice-based system containing tightly coupled services.

In a distributed monolith, even small changes to one service can necessitate changes to others, often triggering unintended consequences. Services often can't be deployed independently, so deployments have to be carefully orchestrated, and errors in one component can send faults rippling through the entire system. Rollbacks are functionally impossible.

In other words, a distributed monolith is a "worst of all worlds" system that pairs the management and complexity overhead of multiple services with the dependencies and entanglements of a monolith, losing many of the benefits of microservices in the process. Avoid at all costs.

---

4 At Google, even the acronyms are recursive.

5 This is actually a pretty nuanced discussion. See "Service Architectures" on page 209.

Shared point-in-time

Often systems are designed in such a way that clients expect an immediate response from services. Systems using this *request-response messaging* pattern implicitly assume that a service is present and ready to promptly respond. But if it's not, the request will fail. It can be said that they're *coupled in time*.

Coupling in time isn't necessarily bad practice, though. It might even be preferable, particularly when there's a human waiting for a timely response. We even detail how to construct such a client in the section "Request-Response Messaging" on page 224.

But if the response isn't necessarily time-constrained, then a safer approach may be to send messages to an intermediate queue that recipients can retrieve from when they're ready, a messaging pattern commonly referred to as *publish-subscribe messaging* ("pub-sub" for short).

Fixed addresses

It's the nature of microservices that they need to talk to one another. But to do that, they first have to find each other. This process of locating services on a network is called *service discovery*.

Traditionally, services lived at relatively fixed, well-known network locations that could be discovered by referencing some centralized registry. Initially this took the form of manually maintained `hosts.txt` files, but as networks scaled up so did the adoption of DNS and URLs.

Traditional DNS works well for long-lived services whose locations on the network rarely change, but the increased popularity of ephemeral, microservice-based applications has ushered in a world in which the lifespans of service instances is often measurable in seconds or minutes rather than months or years. In such dynamic environments, URLs and traditional DNS become just another form of tight coupling.

This need for dynamic, fluid service discovery has driven the adoption of entirely new strategies like the *service mesh*, a dedicated layer for facilitating service-to-service communications between resources in a distributed system.

Unfortunately, we won't be able to cover the fascinating and fast-developing topics of service discovery or service meshes in this book. But the service mesh field is rich, with a number of mature open source projects with active communities—such as Envoy (*https://oreil.ly/woDEQ*), Linkerd (*https://linkerd.io*), and Istio (*https://oreil.ly/zggyu*)—and even commercial offerings like Hashicorp's Consul (*https://consul.io*).

Communications Between Services

Communication and message passing is a critical function of distributed systems, and all distributed systems depend on some form of messaging to receive instructions and directions, exchange information, and provide results and updates. Of course, a message is useless if the recipient can't understand it.

In order for services to communicate, they must first establish an implicit or explicit *contract* that defines how messages will be structured. While such a contract is necessary, it also effectively couples the components that depend on it.

It's actually very easy to introduce tight coupling in this way, the degree of which is reflected in the protocol's ability to change safely. Does it allow backward- and forward-compatible changes, like protocol buffers and gRPC, or do minor changes to the contract effectively break communications, as is the case with SOAP?

Of course, the data exchange protocol and its contract isn't the only variable in inter-service communications. There are, in fact, two broad classes of messaging patterns:

Request-response (synchronous)
> A two-way message exchange in which a requester (the client) issues a request of a receiver (the service) and waits for a response. A textbook example is HTML.

Publish-subscribe (asynchronous)
> A one-way message exchange in which a requester (the publisher) issues a message to an event bus or message exchange, rather than directly to a specific receiver. Messages can be retrieved asynchronously and acted upon by one or more services (subscribers).

Each of these patterns has a variety of implementations and particular use-cases, each with their own pros and cons. While we won't be able to cover every possible nuance, we'll do our best to provide a usable survey and some direction about how they may be implemented in Go.

Request-Response Messaging

As its name suggests, systems using a *request-response*, or *synchronous*, messaging pattern communicate using a series of coordinated requests and responses, in which a requester (or client) submits a request to a receiver (or service) and waits until the receiver responds (hopefully) with the requested the data or service (see Figure 8-1).

The most obvious example of this pattern might be HTTP, which is so ubiquitous and well-established that it's been extended beyond its original purpose, and now underlies common messaging protocols like REST and GraphQL.

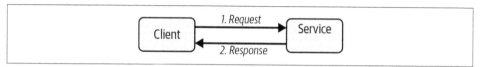

Figure 8-1. Systems using a request-response messaging pattern communicate using a series of coordinated requests and responses

The request-response pattern has the advantages of being relatively easy to reason about and straightforward to implement, and has long been considered the default messaging pattern, particularly for public-facing services. However, it's also "point-to-point," involving exactly one requester and receiver, and requires the requesting process to pause until it receives a response.

Together, these properties make the request-response pattern a good choice for straightforward exchanges between two endpoints where a response can be expected in a reasonably short amount of time, but less than ideal when a message has to be sent to multiple receivers or when a response might take longer than a requester might want to wait.

Common Request-Response Implementations

Over the years, a multitude of bespoke request-response protocols have been developed for any number of purposes. Over time, this has largely settled down, giving way to three major implementations.

REST

You're likely already very familiar with REST, which we discussed in some detail in "Building an HTTP Server with net/http" on page 112. REST has some things going for it. It's human-readable and easy to implement, making it a good choice for outward-facing services (which is why we chose it in Chapter 5). We'll discuss a little more in "Issuing HTTP Requests with net/http" on page 226.

Remote procedure calls (RPC)

Remote procedure call (RPC) frameworks allow programs to execute procedures in a different address space, often on another computer. Go provides a standard Go-specific RPC implementation in the form of net/rpc. There are also two big language-agnostic RPC players: Apache Thrift and gRPC. While similar in design and usage goals, gRPC seems to have taken the lead with respect to adoption and community support. We'll discuss gRPC in much more detail in "Remote Procedure Calls with gRPC" on page 230.

GraphQL

A relative newcomer on the scene, GraphQL is a query and manipulation language generally considered an alternative to REST, and is particularly powerful when working with complex datasets. We don't discuss GraphQL in much detail in this book, but I encourage you to look into it (*https://graphql.org*) the next time you're designing an outward-facing API.

Issuing HTTP Requests with net/http

HTTP is perhaps the most common request-response protocol, particularly for public-facing services, underlying popular API formats like REST and GraphQL. If you're interacting with an HTTP service, you'll need some way to programmatically issue requests to the service and retrieve the response.

Fortunately, the Go standard library comes with excellent HTTP client and server implementations in the form of the net/http package. You may remember net/http from "Building an HTTP Server with net/http" on page 112, where we used it to build the first iteration of our key/value store.

The net/http includes, among other things, convenience functions for GET, HEAD, and POST methods. The signatures for the first of these, http.Get and http.Head, are shown in the following:

```
// Get issues a GET to the specified URL
func Get(url string) (*http.Response, error)

// Head issues a HEAD to the specified URL
func Head(url string) (*http.Response, error)
```

The previous functions are very straightforward and are both used similarly: each accepts a string that represents the URL of interest, and each returns an error value and a pointer to an http.Response struct.

The http.Response struct is particularly useful because it contains all kinds of useful information about the service's response to our request, including the returned status code and the response body.

A small selection of the http.Response struct is in the following:

```
type Response struct {
    Status     string  // e.g. "200 OK"
    StatusCode int     // e.g. 200

    // Header maps header keys to values.
    Header Header

    // Body represents the response body.
    Body io.ReadCloser

    // ContentLength records the length of the associated content. The
    // value -1 indicates that the length is unknown.
    ContentLength int64

    // Request is the request that was sent to obtain this Response.
```

```
    Request *Request
}
```

There are some useful things in there! Of particular interest is the Body field, which provides access to the HTTP response body. It's a ReadCloser interface, which tells us two things: that the response body is streamed on demand as it's read, and that it has a Close method that we're expected to call.

In the following, we demonstrate several things: how to use the Get convenience function, how to close the response body, and how to use io.ReadAll to read the *entire* response body as a string (if you're into that kind of thing):

```
package main

import (
    "fmt"
    "io"
    "net/http"
)

func main() {
    resp, err := http.Get("http://example.com")      // Send an HTTP GET
    if err != nil {
        panic(err)
    }
    defer resp.Body.Close()                          // Close your response!

    body, err := io.ReadAll(resp.Body)               // Read body as []byte
    if err != nil {
        panic(err)
    }

    fmt.Println(string(body))
}
```

In the last example, we use the http.Get function to issue a GET to the URL http://example.com, which returns a pointer to a http.Response struct and an error value.

As we mentioned previously, access to the HTTP response body is provided via the resp.Body variable, which implements io.ReadCloser. Note how we defer the call resp.Body.Close(). This is very important: failing to close your response body can sometimes lead to some unfortunate memory leaks.

Because Body implements io.Reader, we have many different standard means to retrieve its data. In this case we use the very reliable io.ReadAll, which conveniently returns the entire response body as a []byte slice, which we simply print.

Always remember to use `Close()` to close your response body! Not doing so can lead to some unfortunate memory leaks.

We've already seen the `Get` and `Head` functions, but how do we issue POSTs? Fortunately, similar convenience functions exist for them too. Two, in fact: `http.Post` and `http.PostForm`. The signatures for each of these are shown in the following:

```
// Post issues a POST to the specified URL
func Post(url, contentType string, body io.Reader) (*Response, error)

// PostForm issues a POST to the specified URL, with data's keys
// and values URL-encoded as the request body
func PostForm(url string, data url.Values) (*Response, error)
```

The first of these, `Post`, expects an `io.Reader` that provides the body—such as a file of a JSON object—of the post. We demonstrate how to upload JSON text in a POST in the following code:

```
package main

import (
    "fmt"
    "io"
    "net/http"
    "strings"
)

const json = `{ "name":"Matt", "age":44 }`        // This is our JSON

func main() {
    in := strings.NewReader(json)                 // Wrap JSON with an io.Reader

    // Issue HTTP POST, declaring our content-type as "text/json"
    resp, err := http.Post("http://example.com/upload", "text/json", in)
    if err != nil {
        panic(err)
    }
    defer resp.Body.Close()                       // Close your response!

    message, err := io.ReadAll(resp.Body)
    if err != nil {
        panic(err)
    }

    fmt.Printf(string(message))
}
```

A Possible Pitfall of Convenience Functions

We've been referring to the Get, Head, Post, and PostForm functions as "convenience functions," but what does that mean?

It turns out that, under the hood, each is actually calling a method on a default *http.Client value, a concurrency-safe type that Go uses to manage the internals of communicating over HTTP.

The code for the Get convenience function, for example, is actually a call to the default client's http.Client.Get method:

```
func Get(url string) (resp *Response, err error) {
    return DefaultClient.Get(url)
}
```

As you can see, when you use http.Get, you're actually using http.DefaultClient. Because http.Client is concurrency safe, it's possible to have only one of these, predefined as a package variable.

The source code for the creation of DefaultClient itself is somewhat plain, creating a zero-value http.Client:

```
var DefaultClient = &Client{}
```

Generally, this is perfectly fine. However, there's a potential issue here, and it involves timeouts. The http.Client methods are capable of asserting timeouts that terminate long-running requests. This is super useful. Unfortunately, the default timeout value is 0, which Go interprets as "no timeout."

Okay, so Go's default HTTP client will never time out. Is that a problem? *Usually* not, but what if it connects to a server that doesn't respond and doesn't close the connection? The result would be an especially nasty and nondeterministic memory leak.

But how do we fix this? Well, as it turns out, http.Client *does* support timeouts; we just have to enable that functionality by creating a custom Client and setting a timeout:

```
var client = &http.Client{
    Timeout: time.Second * 10,
}
response, err := client.Get(url)
```

Take a look at the net/http package documentation (*https://oreil.ly/91haC*) for more information about http.Client and its available settings.

Remote Procedure Calls with gRPC

gRPC is an efficient, polyglot data exchange framework that was originally developed by Google as the successor to *Stubby*, a general-purpose RPC framework that had been in use internally at Google for over a decade. It was open sourced in 2015 under the name gRPC, and taken over by the Cloud Native Computing Foundation in 2017.

Unlike REST, which is essentially a set of unenforced best practices, gRPC is a fully-featured data exchange framework, which, like other RPC frameworks such as SOAP, Apache Thrift, Java RMI, and CORBA (to name a few) allows a client to execute specific methods implemented on different systems as if they were local functions.

This approach has a number of advantages over REST, including but not limited to:

Conciseness
Its messages are more compact, consuming less network I/O.

Speed
Its binary exchange format is much faster to marshal and unmarshal.

Strong-typing
It's natively strongly typed, eliminating a lot of boilerplate and removing a common source of errors.

Feature-rich
It has a number of built-in features like authentication, encryption, timeout, and compression (to name a few) that you would otherwise have to implement yourself.

That's not to say that gRPC is always the best choice. Compared to REST:

Contract-driven
gRPC's contracts make it less suitable for external-facing services.

Binary format
gRPC data isn't human-readable, making it harder to inspect and debug.

 gRPC is a very large and rich subject that this modest section can't fully do justice to. If you're interested in learning more I recommend the official "Introduction to gRPC" (*https://oreil.ly/10q7G*) and the excellent *gRPC: Up and Running* (*https://oreil.ly/Dxhjo*) by Kasun Indrasiri and Danesh Kuruppu (O'Reilly Media).

Interface definition with protocol buffers

As is the case with most RPC frameworks, gRPC requires you to define a *service interface*. By default, gRPC uses *protocol buffers* (*https://oreil.ly/JKoyj*) for this purpose, though it's possible to use an alternative Interface Definition Language (IDL) like JSON if you want.

To define a service interface, the author uses the protocol buffers schema to describe the service methods that can be called remotely by a client in a .proto file. This is then *compiled* into a language-specific interface (Go code, in our case).

As illustrated in Figure 8-2, gRPC servers implement the resulting source code to handle client calls, while the client has a stub that provides the same methods as the server.

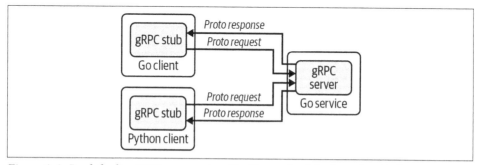

Figure 8-2. By default, gRPC uses protocol buffers as both its Interface Definition Language and its underlying message interchange format; servers and clients can be written in any supported language (https://oreil.ly/N0uWc)

Yes, this seems very hand-wavey and abstract right now. Keep reading for some more details!

Installing the protocol compiler

Before we proceed, we'll first need to install the protocol buffer compiler, protoc, and the Go protocol buffers plug-in. We'll use these to compile .proto files into Go service interface code.

1. If you're using Linux or MacOS, the simplest and easiest way to install protoc is to use a package manager. To install it on a Debian-flavored Linux you can use apt or apt-get:

   ```
   $ apt install -y protobuf-compiler
   $ protoc --version
   ```

The easiest way to install `protoc` on MacOS is to use Homebrew:

```
$ brew install protobuf
$ protoc --version
```

2. Run the following command to install the Go protocol buffers plug-in:

```
$ go install google.golang.org/protobuf/cmd/protoc-gen-go
```

The compiler plug-in `protoc-gen-go` will be installed in `$GOBIN`, defaulting to `$GOPATH/bin`. It must be in your `$PATH` for `protoc` to find it.

 This book uses protocol buffers version 3. Be sure to check your version of `protoc` after installation to make sure that it's version 3 or higher.

If you're using another OS, your chosen package manager has an old version, or if you just want to make sure you have the latest and greatest, you can find the instructions for installing the precompiled binaries on gRPC's Protocol Buffer Compiler Installation page (*https://oreil.ly/b6RAD*).

The message definition structure

Protocol buffers are a language-neutral mechanism for serializing structured data. You can think of it as a binary version of XML.[6] Protocol buffer data is structured as *messages*, where each message is a small record of information containing a series of name-value pairs called *fields*.

The first step when working with protocol buffers is to define the message structure by defining it in a `.proto` file. A basic example is presented in the following:

Example 8-1. An example `.proto` file. The `message` definitions define remote procedure payloads.

```
syntax = "proto3";

option go_package = "github.com/cloud-native-go/ch08/point";

// Point represents a labeled position on a 2-dimensional surface
message Point {
  int32 x = 1;
  int32 y = 2;
  string label = 3;
```

---

6 If you're into that kind of thing.

```
}

// Line contains start and end Points
message Line {
  Point start = 1;
  Point end = 2;
  string label = 3;
}

// Polyline contains any number (including zero) of Points
message Polyline {
  repeated Point point = 1;
  string label = 2;
}
```

You may have noticed that the protocol buffer syntax is reminiscent of C/C++, complete with its semicolon and commenting syntax.

The first line of the file specifies that you're using proto3 syntax: if you don't do this, the protocol buffer compiler will assume you are using proto2. This must be the first nonempty, noncomment line of the file.

The second line uses the option keyword to specify the full import path of the Go package that will contain the generated code.

Finally, we have three message definitions, which describe the structure of the payload messages. In this example, we have three messages of increasing complexity:

- Point, which contains x and y integer values, and a label string
- Line, which contains exactly two Point values
- Polyline, which uses the repeated keyword to indicate that it can contain any number of Point values

Each message contains zero or more fields that have a name and a type. Note that each field in a message definition has a *field number* that is unique for that message type. These are used to identify fields in the message binary format, and should not be changed once your message type is in use.

If this raises a "tight coupling" red flag in your mind, you get a gold star for paying attention. For this reason, protocol buffers provide explicit support for updating message types (*https://oreil.ly/IeyL2*), including marking a field as reserved (*https:// oreil.ly/I1Jiu*) so that it can't be accidentally reused.

This example is incredibly simple, but don't let that fool you: protocol buffers are capable of some very sophisticated encodings. See the Protocol Buffers Language Guide (*https://oreil.ly/UDl65*) for more information.

The key-value message structure

So how do we make use of protocol buffers and gRPC to extend the example key-value store that we started in Chapter 5?

Let's say that we want to implement gRPC equivalents to the Get, Put, and Delete functions we are already exposing via RESTful methods. The message formats for that might look something like the following .proto file:

Example 8-2. keyvalue.proto—the messages that will be passed to and from our key-value service procedures

```
syntax = "proto3";

option go_package = "github.com/cloud-native-go/ch08/keyvalue";

// GetRequest represents a request to the key-value store for the
// value associated with a particular key
message GetRequest {
  string key = 1;
}

// GetResponse represents a response from the key-value store for a
// particular value
message GetResponse {
  string value = 1;
}

// PutRequest represents a request to the key-value store for the
// value associated with a particular key
message PutRequest {
  string key = 1;
  string value = 2;
}

// PutResponse represents a response from the key-value store for a
// Put action.
message PutResponse {}

// DeleteRequest represents a request to the key-value store to delete
// the record associated with a key
message DeleteRequest {
  string key = 1;
}

// DeleteResponse represents a response from the key-value store for a
// Delete action.
message DeleteResponse {}
```

Don't let the names of the message definitions confuse you: they represent *messages* (nouns) that will be passed to and from functions (verbs) that we'll define in the next section.

In the *.proto* file, which we'll call *keyvalue.proto*, we have three `Request` message definitions describing messages that will be sent from the client to the server, and three `Response` message definitions describing the server's response messages.

You may have noticed that we don't include `error` or `status` values in the message response definitions. As you'll see in "Implementing the gRPC client" on page 239, these are unnecessary because they're included in the return values of the gRPC client functions.

Defining our service methods

So now that we've completed our message definitions, we'll need to describe the methods that'll use them.

To do that, we extend our *keyvalue.proto* file, using the `rpc` keyword to define our service interfaces. Compiling the modified *.proto* file will generate Go code that includes the service interface code and client stubs.

Example 8-3. `keyvalue.proto`—the procedures for our key-value service.

```
service KeyValue {
  rpc Get(GetRequest) returns (GetResponse);

  rpc Put(PutRequest) returns (PutResponse);

  rpc Delete(DeleteRequest) returns (DeleteResponse);
}
```

In contrast to the messages defined in Example 8-2, the `rpc` definitions represent functions (verbs) which will send and receive messages (nouns).

In this example, we add three methods to our service:

- `Get`, which accepts a `GetRequest` and returns a `GetResponse`
- `Put`, which accepts a `PutRequest` and returns a `PutResponse`
- `Delete`, which accepts a `DeleteRequest` and returns a `DeleteResponse`

Note that we don't actually implement the functionality here. We do that later.

The previous methods are all examples of *unary RPC* definitions, in which a client sends a single request to the server and gets a single response back. This is the simplest of the four service methods types. Various streaming modes are also supported, but these are beyond the scope of this simple primer. The gRPC documentation (*https://oreil.ly/rs3dN*) discusses these in more detail.

Compiling your protocol buffers

Now that you have a *.proto* file complete with message and service definitions, the next thing you need to do is generate the classes you'll need to read and write messages. To do this, you need to run the protocol buffer compiler `protoc` on our *keyvalue.proto*.

If you haven't installed the `protoc` compiler and Go protocol buffers plug-in, follow the directions in "Installing the protocol compiler" on page 231 to do so.

Now you can run the compiler, specifying the source directory ($SOURCE_DIR) where your application's source code lives (which defaults to the the current directory), the destination directory ($DEST_DIR; often the same as $SOURCE_DIR), and the path to your *keystore.proto*. Because we want Go code, you use the `--go_out` option. `protoc` provides equivalent options to generate code for other supported languages as well.

In this case, we would invoke:

```
$ protoc --proto_path=$SOURCE_DIR \
    --go_out=$DEST_DIR --go_opt=paths=source_relative \
    --go-grpc_out=$DEST_DIR --go-grpc_opt=paths=source_relative \
    $SOURCE_DIR/keyvalue.proto
```

The `go_opt` and `go-grpc_opt` flags tell `protoc` to place the output files in the same relative directory as the input file. Our *keyvalue.proto* file results in two files, named *keyvalue.pb.go* and *keyvalue_grpc.pb.go*.

Without these flags, the output files are placed in a directory named after the Go package's import path. Our *keyvalue.proto* file, for example, would result in a file named `github.com/cloud-native-go/ch08/keyvalue/keyvalue.pb.go`.

Implementing the gRPC service

To implement our gRPC server, we'll need to implement the generated service interface, which defines the server API for our key-value service. It can be found in *keyvalue_grpc.pb.go* as `KeyValueServer`:

```
type KeyValueServer interface {
    Get(context.Context, *GetRequest) (*GetResponse, error)
    Put(context.Context, *PutRequest) (*PutResponse, error)
```

```
        Delete(context.Context, *DeleteRequest) (*PutResponse, error)
}
```

As you can see, the KeyValueServer interface specifies our Get, Put, and Delete methods: each accepts a context.Context and a request pointer, and returns a response pointer and an error.

 As a side effect of its simplicity, it's dead easy to mock requests to, and responses from, a gRPC server implementation.

To implement our server, we'll make use of a generated struct that provides a default implementation for the KeyValueServer interface, which, in our case, is named UnimplementedKeyValueServer. It's so named because it includes default "unimplemented" versions of all of our client methods attached, which look something like the following:

```
type UnimplementedKeyValueServer struct {}

func (*UnimplementedKeyValueServer) Get(context.Context, *GetRequest)
        (*GetResponse, error) {

    return nil, status.Errorf(codes.Unimplemented, "method not implemented")
}
```

By embedding the UnimplementedKeyValueServer, we're able to implement our key-value gRPC server. This is demonstrated with the following code, in which we implement the Get method. The Put and Delete methods are omitted for brevity:

```
package main

import (
    "context"
    "log"
    "net"

    pb "github.com/cloud-native-go/ch08/keyvalue"
    "google.golang.org/grpc"
)

// server is used to implement KeyValueServer. It MUST embed the generated
// struct pb.UnimplementedKeyValueServer
type server struct {
    pb.UnimplementedKeyValueServer
}

func (s *server) Get(ctx context.Context, r *pb.GetRequest)
        (*pb.GetResponse, error) {
```

```
        log.Printf("Received GET key=%v", r.Key)

        // The local Get function is implemented back in Chapter 5
        value, err := Get(r.Key)

        // Return expects a GetResponse pointer and an err
        return &pb.GetResponse{Value: value}, err
    }

    func main() {
        // Create a gRPC server and register our KeyValueServer with it
        s := grpc.NewServer()
        pb.RegisterKeyValueServer(s, &server{})

        // Open a listening port on 50051
        lis, err := net.Listen("tcp", ":50051")
        if err != nil {
            log.Fatalf("failed to listen: %v", err)
        }

        // Start accepting connections on the listening port
        if err := s.Serve(lis); err != nil {
            log.Fatalf("failed to serve: %v", err)
        }
    }
```

In the previous code, we implement and start our service in four steps:

1. *Create the server struct.* Our `server` struct embeds `pb.UnimplementedKeyValue
   Server`. This is not optional: gRPC requires your server struct to similarly embed
   its generated `UnimplementedXXXServer`.

2. *Implement the service methods.* We implement the service methods defined in the
   generated `pb.KeyValueServer` interface. Interestingly, because the `pb.Unimple
   mentedKeyValueServer` includes stubs for all of these service methods, we don't
   have to implement them all right away.

3. *Register our gRPC server.* In the `main` function, we create a new instance of the
   `server` struct and register it with the gRPC framework. This is similar to how we
   registered handler functions in "Building an HTTP Server with net/http" on page
   112, except we register an entire instance rather than individual functions.

4. *Start accepting connections.* Finally, we open a listening port[7] using `net.Listen`,
   which we pass to the gRPC framework via `s.Serve` to begin listening.

---

7 If you wanted to be creative, this could be a `FileListener` (*https://oreil.ly/mViL3*), or even a `stdio` stream.

It could be argued that gRPC provides the best of both worlds by providing the freedom to implement any desired functionality without having to be concerned with building many of the tests and checks usually associated with a RESTful service.

Implementing the gRPC client

Because all of the client code is generated, making use of a gRPC client is fairly straightforward.

The generated client interface will be named XXXClient, which in our case will be KeyValueClient, shown in the following:

```
type KeyValueClient interface {
    Get(ctx context.Context, in *GetRequest, opts ...grpc.CallOption)
        (*GetResponse, error)

    Put(ctx context.Context, in *PutRequest, opts ...grpc.CallOption)
        (*PutResponse, error)

    Delete(ctx context.Context, in *DeleteRequest, opts ...grpc.CallOption)
        (*PutResponse, error)
}
```

All of the methods described in our source .proto file are specified here, each accepting a request type pointer, and returning a response type pointer and an error.

Additionally, each of the methods accepts a context.Context (if you're rusty on what this is or how it's used, take a look at "The Context Package" on page 72), and zero or more instances of grpc.CallOption. CallOption is used to modify the behavior of the client when it executes its calls. More detail can be found in the gRPC API documentation (*https://oreil.ly/t8fEz*).

I demonstrate how to create and use a gRPC client in the following:

```
package main

import (
    "context"
    "log"
    "os"
    "strings"
    "time"

    pb "github.com/cloud-native-go/ch08/keyvalue"
    "google.golang.org/grpc"
)

func main() {
    // Set up a connection to the gRPC server
    conn, err := grpc.Dial("localhost:50051",
        grpc.WithInsecure(), grpc.WithBlock(), grpc.WithTimeout(time.Second))
```

```
    if err != nil {
        log.Fatalf("did not connect: %v", err)
    }
    defer conn.Close()

    // Get a new instance of our client
    client := pb.NewKeyValueClient(conn)

    var action, key, value string

    // Expect something like "set foo bar"
    if len(os.Args) > 2 {
        action, key = os.Args[1], os.Args[2]
        value = strings.Join(os.Args[3:], " ")
    }

    // Use context to establish a 1-second timeout.
    ctx, cancel := context.WithTimeout(context.Background(), time.Second)
    defer cancel()

    // Call client.Get() or client.Put() as appropriate.
    switch action {
    case "get":
        r, err := client.Get(ctx, &pb.GetRequest{Key: key})
        if err != nil {
            log.Fatalf("could not get value for key %s: %v\n", key, err)
        }
        log.Printf("Get %s returns: %s", key, r.Value)

    case "put":
        _, err := client.Put(ctx, &pb.PutRequest{Key: key, Value: value})
        if err != nil {
            log.Fatalf("could not put key %s: %v\n", key, err)
        }
        log.Printf("Put %s", key)

    default:
        log.Fatalf("Syntax: go run [get|put] KEY VALUE...")
    }
}
```

The preceding example parses command-line values to determine whether it should do a Get or a Put operation.

First, it establishes a connection with the gRPC server using the grpc.Dial function, which takes a target address string, and one or more grpc.DialOption arguments that configure how the connection gets set up. In our case we use:

- `WithInsecure`, which disables transport security for this `ClientConn`. *Don't use insecure connections in production.*

- `WithBlock`, which makes `Dial` a block until a connection is established, otherwise the connection will occur in the background.

- `WithTimeout`, which makes a blocking `Dial` throw an error if it takes longer than the specified amount of time.

Next, it uses `NewKeyValueClient` to get a new `KeyValueClient`, and gets the various command-line arguments.

Finally, based on the `action` value, we call either `client.Get` or `client.Put`, both of which return an appropriate return type and an error.

Once again, these functions look and feel exactly like local function calls. No checking status codes, hand-building our own clients, or any other funny business.

Loose Coupling Local Resources with Plug-ins

At first glance, the topic of loose coupling of local—as opposed to remote or distributed—resources might seem mostly irrelevant to a discussion of "cloud native" technologies. But you might be surprised how often such patterns come in handy.

For example, it's often useful to build services or tools that can accept data from different kinds of input sources (such as REST interface, a gRPC interface, and a chatbot interface) or generate different kinds of outputs (such as generating different kinds of logging or metric formats). As an added bonus, designs that support such modularity can also make mocking resources for testing dead simple.

As we'll see in "Hexagonal Architecture" on page 255, entire software architectures have even been built around this concept.

No discussion of loose coupling would be complete without a review of plug-in technologies.

In-Process Plug-ins with the plugin Package

Go provides a native plug-in system in the form of the standard `plugin` package (*https://oreil.ly/zxt9W*). This package is used to open and access Go plug-ins, but it's not necessary to actually build the plug-ins themselves.

As we'll demonstrate in the following, the requirements for building and using a Go plug-in are pretty minimal. It doesn't have to even know it's a plug-in or even import the `plugin` package. A Go plug-in has three real requirements: it must be in the `main` package, it must export one or more functions or variables, and it must be compiled using the `-buildmode=plugin` build flag. That's it, really.

Go Plug-in Caveats

Before we get too deep into the subject of Go plug-ins, it's important to mention some caveats up front.

1. As of Go version 1.16.1, Go plug-ins are only supported on Linux, FreeBSD, and MacOS.
2. The version of Go used to build a plug-in must match the program that's using it *exactly*. Plug-ins built with Go 1.16.0 won't work with Go 1.16.1.
3. Similarly, the versions of any packages used by both the plug-in and program must also match *exactly*.
4. Finally, building plug-ins forces `CGO_ENABLED`, making cross-compiling more complicated.

These conditions make Go plug-ins most appropriate when you're building plug-ins for use within the same codebase, but it adds considerable obstacles for creating distributable plug-ins.

Plug-in vocabulary

Before we continue, we need to define a few terms that are particular to plug-ins. Each of the following describes a specific plug-in concept, and each has a corresponding type or function implementation in the `plugin` package. We'll go into all of these in more detail in our example.

Plug-in
> A *plug-in* is a Go `main` package with one or more exported functions and variables that has been built with the `-buildmode=plugin` build flag. It's represented in the `plugin` package by the `Plugin` type.

Open
> *Opening* a plug-in is the process of loading it into memory, validating it, and discovering its exposed symbols. A plug-in at a known location in the file system can be opened using the `Open` function, which returns a `*Plugin` value:
> ```
> func Open(path string) (*Plugin, error)
> ```

Symbol
> A plug-in *symbol* is any variable or function that's exported by the plug-in's package. Symbols can be retrieved by "looking them up," and are represented in the `plugin` package by the `Symbol` type:
> ```
> type Symbol interface{}
> ```

Look up

> *Looking up* describes the process of searching for and retrieving a symbol exposed by a plug-in. The `plugin` package's `Lookup` method provides that functionality, and returns a `Symbol` value:

```
func (p *Plugin) Lookup(symName string) (Symbol, error)
```

In the next section, we present a toy example that demonstrates how these resources are used, and dig into a little detail in the process.

A toy plug-in example

You can only learn so much from a review of the API, even one as minimal as the `plugin` package. So, let's build ourselves a toy example: a program that tells you about various animals,[8] as implemented by plug-ins.

For this example, we'll be creating three independent packages with the following package structure:

```
~/cloud-native-go/ch08/go-plugin
├── duck
│   └── duck.go
├── frog
│   └── frog.go
└── main
    └── main.go
```

The duck/duck.go and frog/frog.go files each contain the source code for one plug-in. The main/main.go file contains our example's `main` function, which will load and use the plug-ins we'll generate by building frog.go and duck.go.

The complete source code for this example is available in this book's companion Git-Hub repository (*https://oreil.ly/9jRyU*).

The Sayer interface

In order for a plug-in to be useful, the functions that access it need to know what symbols to look up and what contract those symbols conform to.

One convenient—but by no means required—way to do this is to use an interface that a symbol can be expected to satisfy. In our particular implementation our plug-ins will expose just one symbol—`Animal`—which we'll expect to conform to the following `Sayer` interface:

---

8 Yes, I know the animal thing has been done before. Sue me.

```
type Sayer interface {
    Says() string
}
```

This interface describes only one method, `Says`, which returns a string that says what an animal says.

The Go plugin code

We have source for two separate plug-ins in `duck/duck.go` and `frog/frog.go`. In the following snippet, the first of these, `duck/duck.go`, is shown in its entirety and displays all of the requirements of a plug-in implementation:

```
package main

type duck struct{}

func (d duck) Says() string {
    return "quack!"
}

// Animal is exported as a symbol.
var Animal duck
```

As described in the introduction to this section, the requirements for Go plug-in are really, really minimal: it just has to be a `main` package that exports one or more variables or functions.

The previous plug-in code describes and exports just one feature—`Animal`—that satisfies the preceding `Sayer` interface. Recall that exported package variables and symbols are exposed on the plug-in as shared library symbols that can be looked up later. In this case, our code will have to look specifically for the exported `Animal` symbol.

In this example we have only one symbol, but there's no explicit limit to the number of symbols we can have. We could have exported many more features, if we wanted to.

We won't show the `frog/frog.go` file here because it's essentially the same. But it's important to know that the internals of a plug-in don't matter as long as it satisfies the expectations of its consumer. These expectations are that:

- The plug-in exposes a symbol named `Animal`.
- The `Animal` symbol adheres to the contract defined by the `Sayer` interface.

Building the plug-ins

Building a Go plug-in is very similar to building any other Go `main` package, except that you have to include the `-buildmode=plugin` build parameter.

To build our duck/duck.go plug-in code, we do the following:

```
$ go build -buildmode=plugin -o duck/duck.so duck/duck.go
```

The result is a shared object (.so) file in ELF (Executable Linkable Format) format:

```
$ file duck/duck.so
duck/duck.so: Mach-O 64-bit dynamically linked shared library x86_64
```

ELF files are commonly used for plug-ins because once they're loaded into memory by the kernel they expose symbols in a way that allows for easy discovery and access.

Using our go plug-ins

Now that we've built our plug-ins, which are patiently sitting there with their `.so` extensions, we need to write some code that'll load and use them.

Note that even though we have our plug-ins fully built and in place, we haven't had to reach for the `plugin` package yet. However, now that we want to actually use our plug-ins, we get to change that now.

The process of finding, opening, and consuming a plug-in requires several steps, which I demonstrate next.

Import the plugin package. First things first: we have to import the `plugin` package, which will provide us the tools we need to open and access our plug-ins.

In this example, we import four packages: `fmt`, `log`, `os`, and most relevant to this example, `plugin`:

```
import (
    "fmt"
    "log"
    "os"
    "plugin"
)
```

Find our plug-in. To load a plug-in, we have to find its relative or absolute file path. For this reason, plug-in binaries are usually named according to some pattern and placed somewhere where they can be easily discovered, like the user's command path or other standard fixed location.

For simplicity, our implementation assumes that our plug-in has the same name as the user's chosen animal and lives in a path relative to the execution location:

```
if len(os.Args) != 2 {
    log.Fatal("usage: run main/main.go animal")
}

// Get the animal name, and build the path where we expect to
// find the corresponding shared object (.so) file.
```

```
name := os.Args[1]
module := fmt.Sprintf("./%s/%s.so", name, name)
```

Importantly, this approach means that our plug-in doesn't need to be known—or even exist—at compile time. In this manner, we're able to implement whatever plug-ins we want at any time, and load and access them dynamically as we see fit.

Open our plug-in. Now that we think we know our plug-in's path we can use the Open function to "open" it, loading it into memory and discovering its available symbols. The Open function returns a *Plugin value that can then be used to look up any symbols exposed by the plug-in:

```
// Open our plugin and get a *plugin.Plugin.
p, err := plugin.Open(module)
if err != nil {
    log.Fatal(err)
}
```

When a plug-in is first opened by the Open function, the init functions of all packages that aren't already part of the program are called. The package's main function is *not* run.

When a plug-in is opened, a single canonical *Plugin value representation of it is loaded into memory. If a particular path has already been opened, subsequent calls to Open will return the same *Plugin value.

A plug-in can't be loaded more than once, and can't be closed.

Look up your symbol. To retrieve a variable or function exported by our package—and therefore exposed as a symbol by the plug-in—we have to use the Lookup method to find it. Unfortunately, the plugin package doesn't provide any way to list all of the symbols exposed by a plug-in, so you we to know the name of our symbol ahead of time:

```
// Lookup searches for a symbol named "Animal" in plug-in p.
symbol, err := p.Lookup("Animal")
if err != nil {
    log.Fatal(err)
}
```

If the symbol exists in the plug-in p, then Lookup returns a Symbol value. If the symbol doesn't exist in p, then a non-nil error is returned instead.

Assert and use your symbol. Now that we have our Symbol, we can convert it into the form we need and use it however we want. To make things nice and easy for us, the Symbol type is essentially a rebranded interface{} value. From the plugin source code:

```
type Symbol interface{}
```

This means that as long as we know what our symbol's type is, we can use type assertion to coerce it into a concrete type value that can be used however we see fit:

```
// Asserts that the symbol interface holds a Sayer.
animal, ok := symbol.(Sayer)
if !ok {
    log.Fatal("that's not a Sayer")
}

// Now we can use our loaded plug-in!
fmt.Printf("A %s says: %q\n", name, animal.Says())
```

In the previous code, we assert that the symbol value satisfies the Sayer interface. If it does, we print what our animal says. If it doesn't we're able to exit gracefully.

Executing our example

Now that we've written our main code that attempts to open and access the plug-in, we can run it like any other Go main package, passing the animal name in the arguments:

```
$ go run main/main.go duck
A duck says: "quack!"

$ go run main/main.go frog
A frog says: "ribbit!"
```

We can even implement arbitrary plug-ins later without changing our main source code:

```
$ go run main/main.go fox
A fox says: "ring-ding-ding-ding-dingeringeding!"
```

HashiCorp's Go Plug-in System over RPC

HashiCorp's Go plugin system (*https://oreil.ly/owKQp*) has been in wide use—both internally to HashiCorp and elsewhere—since at least 2016, predating the release of Go's standard plugin package by about a year.

Unlike Go plug-ins, which use shared libraries, HashiCorp's plug-ins are standalone processes that are executed by using exec.Command, which has some obvious benefits over shared libraries:

They can't crash your host process
    Because they're separate processes, a panic in a plug-in doesn't automatically crash the plug-in consumer.

They're more version-flexible

Go plug-ins are famously version-specific. HashiCorp plug-ins are far less so, expecting only that plug-ins adhere to a contract. It also supports explicit protocol versioning.

They're relatively secure

HashiCorp plug-ins only have access to the interfaces and parameters passed to them, as opposed to the entire memory space of the consuming process.

They do have a couple of downsides, though:

More verbose

HashiCorp plug-ins require more boilerplate than Go plug-ins.

Lower performance

Because all data exchange with HashiCorp plug-ins occurs over RPC, communication with Go plug-ins is generally more performant.

That being said, let's take a look at what it takes to assemble a simple plug-in.

Another toy plug-in example

So we can compare apples to apples, we're going to work through a toy example that's functionally identical to the one for the standard `plugin` package in "A toy plug-in example" on page 243: a program that tells you what various animals say.

As before, we'll be creating several independent packages with the following structure:

```
~/cloud-native-go/ch08/hashicorp-plugin
├── commons
│   └── commons.go
├── duck
│   └── duck.go
└── main
    └── main.go
```

As before, the duck/duck.go file contains the source code for a plug-in, and the main/main.go file contains our example's `main` function that loads and uses the plug-in. Because both of these are independently compiled to produce executable binaries, both files are in the `main` package.

The `commons` package is new. It contains some resources that are shared by the plug-in and the consumer, including the service interface and some RPC boilerplate.

As before, the complete source code for this example is available in this book's companion GitHub repository (*https://oreil.ly/9jRyU*).

Common code

The commons package contains some resources that are shared by both the plug-in and the consumer, so in our example it's imported by both the plug-in and client code.

It contains the RPC stubs that are used by the underlying net/rpc machinery to define the service abstraction for the host and allow the plug-ins to construct their service implementations.

The Sayer interface. The first of these is the Sayer interface. This is our service interface, which provides the service contract that the plug-in service implementations must conform to and that the host can expect.

It's identical to the interface that we used in "The Sayer interface" on page 243:

```
type Sayer interface {
    Says() string
}
```

The Sayer interface only describes one method: Says. Although this code is shared, as long as this interface doesn't change, the shared contract will be satisfied and the degree of coupling is kept fairly low.

The SayerPlugin struct. The more complex of the common resources is the SayerPlugin struct, shown in the following. It's an implementation of plugin.Plugin, the primary plug-in interface from the github.com/hashicorp/go-plugin package.

> The package declaration inside the *github.com/hashicorp/go-plugin* repository is plugin, not go-plugin, as its path might suggest. Adjust your imports accordingly!

The Client and Server methods are used to describe our service according to the expectations of Go's standard net/rpc package. We won't cover that package in this book, but if you're interested, you can find a wealth of information in the Go documentation (*https://oreil.ly/uoe8k*):

```
type SayerPlugin struct {
    Impl Sayer
}

func (SayerPlugin) Client(b *plugin.MuxBroker, c *rpc.Client)
        (interface{}, error) {

    return &SayerRPC{client: c}, nil
}
```

```
func (p *SayerPlugin) Server(*plugin.MuxBroker) (interface{}, error) {
    return &SayerRPCServer{Impl: p.Impl}, nil
}
```

Both methods accept a plugin.MuxBroker, which is used to create multiplexed streams on a plug-in connection. While very useful, this is a more advanced use case that we won't have time to cover in this book.

The SayerRPC client implementation. SayerPlugin's Client method provides an implementation of our Sayer interface that communicates over an RPC client—the appropriately named SayerRPC struct—shown in the following:

```
type SayerRPC struct{ client *rpc.Client }

func (g *SayerRPC) Says() string {
    var resp string

    err := g.client.Call("Plugin.Says", new(interface{}), &resp)
    if err != nil {
        panic(err)
    }

    return resp
}
```

SayerRPC uses Go's RPC framework to remotely call the Says method implemented in the plug-in. It invokes the Call method attached to the *rpc.Client, passing in any parameters (Says doesn't have any parameters, so we pass an empty interface{}) and retrieves the response, which it puts it into the resp string.

The handshake configuration. HandshakeConfig is used by both the plug-in and host to do a basic handshake between the host and the plug-in. If the handshake fails—if the plug-in was compiled with a different protocol version, for example—a user-friendly error is shown. This prevents users from executing bad plug-ins or executing a plug-in directly. Importantly, this is a UX feature, not a security feature:

```
var HandshakeConfig = plugin.HandshakeConfig{
    ProtocolVersion:  1,
    MagicCookieKey:   "BASIC_PLUGIN",
    MagicCookieValue: "hello",
}
```

The SayerRPCServer server implementation. SayerPlugin's Server method provides a definition of an RPC server—the SayerRPCServer struct—to serve the actual methods in a way that's consistent with net/rpc:

```
type SayerRPCServer struct {
    Impl Sayer    // Impl contains our actual implementation
```

```
    }

    func (s *SayerRPCServer) Says(args interface{}, resp *string) error {
        *resp = s.Impl.Says()
        return nil
    }
```

SayerRPCServer doesn't implement the Sayer service. Instead, its Says method calls into a Sayer implementation—Impl—that we'll provide when we use this to build our plug-in.

Our plug-in implementation

Now that we've assembled the code that's common between the host and plug-ins—the Sayer interface and the RPC stubs—we can build our plug-in code. The code in this section represents the entirety of our main/main.go file.

Just like standard Go plug-ins, HashiCorp plug-ins are compiled into standalone executable binaries, so they must be in the main package. Effectively, every HashiCorp plug-in is a small, self-contained RPC server:

```
    package main
```

We have to import our commons package, as well as the hashicorp/go-plugin package, whose contents we'll reference as plugin:

```
    import (
        "github.com/cloud-native-go/ch08/hashicorp-plugin/commons"
        "github.com/hashicorp/go-plugin"
    )
```

In our plug-ins we get to build our real implementations. We can build it however we want,[9] as long as it conforms to the Sayer interface that we define in the commons package:

```
    type Duck struct{}

    func (g *Duck) Says() string {
        return "Quack!"
    }
```

Finally, we get to our main function. It's somewhat "boilerplate-y" but it's essential:

```
    func main() {
        // Create and initialize our service implementation.
        sayer := &Duck{}

        // pluginMap is the map of plug-ins we can dispense.
```

---

9 So, naturally, we're building a duck. Obviously.

```
    var pluginMap = map[string]plugin.Plugin{
        "sayer": &commons.SayerPlugin{Impl: sayer},
    }

    plugin.Serve(&plugin.ServeConfig{
        HandshakeConfig: handshakeConfig,
        Plugins:         pluginMap,
    })
}
```

The main function does three things. First, it creates and initializes our service implementation, a *Duck value, in this case.

Next, it maps the service implementation to the name "sayer" in the pluginMap. If we wanted to, we could actually implement several plug-ins, listing them all here with different names.

Finally, we call plugin.Serve, which starts the RPC server that will handle any connections from the host process, allowing the handshake with the host to proceed and the service's methods to be executed as the host sees fit.

Our host process

We now have our host process; the main command that acts as a client that finds, loads, and executes the plug-in processes.

As you'll see, using HashiCorp plug-ins isn't all that different from the steps that described for Go plug-ins in "Using our go plug-ins" on page 245.

Import the hashicorp/go-plugin and commons packages.   As usual, we start with our package declaration and imports. The imports mostly aren't interesting, and their necessity should be clear from examination of the code.

The two that *are* interesting (but not surprising) are github.com/hashicorp/go-plugin, which we, once again, have to reference as plugin, and our commons package, which contains the interface and handshake configuration, both of which must be agreed upon by the host and the plug-ins:

```
package main

import (
    "fmt"
    "log"
    "os"
    "os/exec"

    "github.com/cloud-native-go/ch08/hashicorp-plugin/commons"
    "github.com/hashicorp/go-plugin"
)
```

Find our plug-in. Since our plug-in is an external file, we have to find it. Again, for simplicity, our implementation assumes that our plug-in has the same name as the user's chosen animal and lives in a path relative to the execution location:

```go
func main() {
    if len(os.Args) != 2 {
        log.Fatal("usage: run main/main.go animal")
    }

    // Get the animal name, and build the path where we expect to
    // find the corresponding executable file.
    name := os.Args[1]
    module := fmt.Sprintf("./%s/%s", name, name)

    // Does the file exist?
    _, err := os.Stat(module)
    if os.IsNotExist(err) {
        log.Fatal("can't find an animal named", name)
    }
}
```

It bears repeating that the value of this approach is that our plug-in—and its implementation—doesn't need to be known, or even exist, at compile time. We're able to implement whatever plug-ins we want at any time, and use then dynamically as we see fit.

Create our plug-in client. The first way that a HashiCorp RPC plug-in differs from a Go plug-in is the way that it retrieves the implementation. Where Go plug-ins have to be "opened" and their symbol "looked up," HashiCorp plug-ins are built on RPC, and therefore require an RPC client.

This actually requires two steps, and two clients: a `*plugin.Client` that manages the lifecycle of the plug-in subprocess, and a protocol client—a `plugin.ClientProtocol` implementation—that can communicate with the plug-in subprocess.

This awkward API is mostly historical, but is used to split the client that deals with subprocess management and the client that does RPC management:

```go
// pluginMap is the map of plug-ins we can dispense.
var pluginMap = map[string]plugin.Plugin{
    "sayer": &commons.SayerPlugin{},
}

// Launch the plugin process!
client := plugin.NewClient(&plugin.ClientConfig{
    HandshakeConfig: commons.HandshakeConfig,
    Plugins:         pluginMap,
    Cmd:             exec.Command(module),
})
defer client.Kill()
```

```
// Connect to the plugin via RPC
rpcClient, err := client.Client()
if err != nil {
    log.Fatal(err)
}
```

Most of this snippet consists of defining the parameters of the plug-in that we want in the form of a `plugin.ClientConfig`. The complete list of available client configurations (*https://oreil.ly/z29Ys*) is lengthy. This example uses only three:

HandshakeConfig
> The handshake configuration. This has to match the plug-in's own handshake configuration or we'll get an error in the next step.

Plugins
> A map that specifies the name and type of the plug-in we want.

Cmd
> An `*exec.Cmd` value that represents the command for starting the plug-in subprocess.

With all of the configuration stuff out of the way, we can first use `plugin.NewClient` to retrieve a `*plugin.Client` value, which we call `client`.

Once we have that, we can use `client.Client` to request a protocol client. We call this `rpcClient` because it knows how to use RPC to communicate with the plug-in subprocess.

Connect to our plug-in and dispense our Sayer. Now that we have our protocol client, we can use it to dispense our `Sayer` implementation:

```
// Request the plug-in from the client
raw, err := rpcClient.Dispense("sayer")
if err != nil {
    log.Fatal(err)
}

// We should have a Sayer now! This feels like a normal interface
// implementation, but is actually over an RPC connection.
sayer := raw.(commons.Sayer)

// Now we can use our loaded plug-in!
fmt.Printf("A %s says: %q\n", name, sayer.Says())
}
```

Using the protocol client's `Dispense` function, we're able to finally retrieve our `Sayer` implementation as an `interface{}`, which we can assert as a `commons.Sayer` value and immediately use exactly like using a local value.

Under the covers, our `sayer` is in fact a `SayerRPC` value, and calls to its functions trigger RPC calls that are executed in our plug-in's address space.

In the next section, we'll introduce the hexagonal architecture, an architectural pattern built around the entire concept of loose coupling by using easily exchangeable "ports and adapters" to connect to its environment.

Hexagonal Architecture

Hexagonal architecture—also known as the "ports and adapters" pattern—is an architectural pattern that uses loose coupling and *inversion of control* as its central design philosophy to establish clear boundaries between business and peripheral logic.

In a hexagonal application, the core application doesn't know any details at all about the outside world, operating entirely through loosely coupled *ports* and technology-specific *adapters*.

This approach allows the application to, for example, expose different APIs (REST, gRPC, a test harness, etc.) or use different data sources (database, message queues, local files, etc.) without impacting its core logic or requiring major code changes.

 It took me an embarrassingly long time to realize that the name "hexagonal architecture" doesn't actually mean anything. Alistair Cockburn, the author of hexagonal architecture (*https://oreil.ly/ sx5io*), chose the shape because it gave him enough room to illustrate the design.

The Architecture

As illustrated in Figure 8-3, hexagonal architecture is composed of three components conceptually arranged in and around a central hexagon:

The core application
> The application proper, represented by the hexagon. This contains all of the business logic but has no direct reference to any technology, framework, or real world device. The business logic shouldn't depend on whether it exposes a REST or a gRPC API, or whether it gets data from a database or a *.csv* file. Its only view of the world should be through ports.

Ports and adapters
> The ports and adapters are represented on the edge of the hexagon. Ports allow different kinds of actors to "plug in" and interact with the core service. Adapters can "plug into" a port and translate signals between the core application and an actor.

For example, your application might have a "data port" into which a "data adapter" might plug. One data adapter might write to a database, while another might use an in-memory datastore or automated test harness.

Actors

The actors can be anything in the environment that interacts with the core application (users, upstream services, etc.) or that the core application interacts with (storage devices, downstream services, etc.). They exist outside the hexagon.

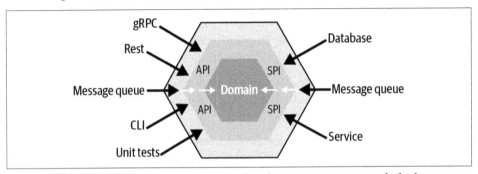

Figure 8-3. All dependencies in the hexagonal architecture point inward; the hexagons represent the core application's domain and API layers, and the ports and adapters are represented as arrows on the edge of the hexagon, each of which interfaces with a particular actor

In a traditional layered architecture, all of the dependencies point in the same direction, with each layer depending on the one below it.

In a hexagonal architecture, however, all dependencies point inward: the core business logic doesn't know any details about the outer world, the adapters know how to ferry information to and from the core, and the adapters in the outer world know how to interact with the actors.

Implementing a Hexagonal Service

To illustrate this, we're going to refactor our old friend the key-value store.

If you'll recall from Chapter 5, the core application of our key-value store reads and writes to a in-memory map, which can be accessed via a RESTful (or gRPC) frontend. Later in the same chapter, we implemented a transaction logger, which knows how to write all transactions to *somewhere* and read them all back when the system restarts.

We'll reproduce important snippets of the service here, but if you want a refresher on what we did, go back and do so now.

By this point in the book, we've accumulated a couple of different implementations for a couple of different components of our service that seem like good candidates for ports and adapters in a hexagonal architecture:

The frontend

Back in "Generation 1: The Monolith" on page 112 we implemented a REST frontend, and then in "Remote Procedure Calls with gRPC" on page 230 we implemented a separate gRPC frontend. We can describe these with a single "driver" port into which we'll be able to plug either (or both!) as adapters.

The transaction logger

In "What's a Transaction Log?" on page 125 we created two implementations of a transaction log. These seem like a natural choice for a "driven" port and adapters.

While all the logic for all of these already exists, we'll need to do some refactoring to make this architecture "hexagonal":

1. Our original core application—originally described in "Generation 0: The Core Functionality" on page 110—uses exclusively public functions. We'll refactor those into struct methods to make it easier to use in a "ports and adapters" format.

2. Both the RESTful and gRPC frontends are already consistent with hexagonal architecture, since the core application doesn't know or care about them, but they're constructed in a `main` function. We'll convert these into `FrontEnd` adapters into which we can pass our core application. This pattern is typical of a "driver" port.

3. The transaction loggers themselves won't need much refactoring, but they're currently embedded in the frontend logic. When we refactor the core application, we'll add a transaction logger port so that the adapter can be passed into the core logic. This pattern is typical of a "driven" port.

In the next section, we'll begin taking the existing components and refactoring them in accordance with hexagonal principles.

Our refactored components

For the sake of this example, all of our components live under the `github.com/cloud-native-go/examples/ch08/hexarch` package:

```
~/cloud-native-go/ch08/hexarch/
├── core
│   └── core.go
├── frontend
│   ├── grpc.go
│   └── rest.go
```

```
├── main.go
└── transact
    ├── filelogger.go
    └── pglogger.go
```

core
> The core key-value application logic. Importantly, it has no dependencies outside of the Go standard libraries.

frontend
> Contains the REST and gRPC frontend driver adapters. These have a dependency on core.

transact
> Contains the file and PostgreSQL transaction logger driven adapters. These also have a dependency on core.

main.go
> Makes the core application instance, into which it passes the driven components, and which it passes to the driver adapters.

The complete source code is also available in the companion GitHub repository (*https://oreil.ly/SsujV*).

Now that we have our very high-level structure, let's go ahead and implement our first plug.

Our first plug

You may remember that we also implemented a *transaction log* to maintain a record of every time a resource is modified so that if our service crashes, is restarted, or otherwise finds itself in an inconsistent state, it can reconstruct its complete state by replaying the transactions.

In "Your transaction logger interface" on page 126, we represented a generic transaction logger with the TransactionLogger:

```
type TransactionLogger interface {
    WriteDelete(key string)
    WritePut(key, value string)
}
```

For brevity, we only define the WriteDelete and WritePut methods.

A common aspect of "driven" adapters is that the core logic acts *on them*, so the core application has to know about the port. As such, this code lives in the core package.

Our core application

In our original implementation in "Your Super Simple API" on page 111, the transaction logger was used by the frontend. In a hexagonal architecture we move the port—in the form of the `TransactionLogger` interface—into the core application:

```go
package core

import (
    "errors"
    "log"
    "sync"
)

type KeyValueStore struct {
    m        map[string]string
    transact TransactionLogger
}

func NewKeyValueStore(tl TransactionLogger) *KeyValueStore {
    return &KeyValueStore{
        m:        make(map[string]string),
        transact: tl,
    }
}

func (store *KeyValueStore) Delete(key string) error {
    delete(store.m, key)
    store.transact.WriteDelete(key)
    return nil
}

func (store *KeyValueStore) Put(key string, value string) error {
    store.m[key] = value
    store.transact.WritePut(key, value)
    return nil
}
```

Comparing the previous code with the original form in "Generation 0: The Core Functionality" on page 110, you'll see some significant changes.

First, `Put` and `Delete` aren't pure functions anymore: they're now methods on a new `KeyValueStore` struct, which also has the map data structure. We've also added a `New KeyValueStore` function that initializes and returns a new `KeyValueStore` pointer value.

Finally, `KeyValueStore` now has a `TransactionLogger`, which `Put` and `Delete` act upon appropriately. This is our port.

Our TransactionLogger adapters

In Chapter 5 we created two `TransactionLogger` implementations:

- In "Implementing your FileTransactionLogger" on page 129, we describe a file-based implementation.
- In "Implementing your PostgresTransactionLogger" on page 139, we describe a PostgreSQL-backed implementation.

Both of these have been moved to the `transact` package. They hardly have to change at all, except to account for the fact that the `TransactionLogger` interface and `Event` struct now live in the `core` package.

But how do we determine which one to load? Well, Go doesn't have annotations or any fancy dependency injection features,[10] but there are still a couple of ways you can do this.

The first option is to use plug-ins of some kind (this is actually a primary use case for Go plug-ins). This might make sense if you want changing adapters to require *zero* code changes.

More commonly, you'll see some kind of "factory" function[11] that's used by the initializing function. While this still requires code changes to add adapters, they're isolated to a single, easily modified location. A more sophisticated approach might accept a parameter or configuration value to choose which adapter to use.

An example of a `TransactionLogger` factory function might look like the following:

```
func NewTransactionLogger(logger string) (core.TransactionLogger, error) {
    switch logger {
    case "file":
        return NewFileTransactionLogger(os.Getenv("TLOG_FILENAME"))

    case "postgres":
        return NewPostgresTransactionLogger(
            PostgresDbParams{
                dbName:   os.Getenv("TLOG_DB_HOST"),
                host:     os.Getenv("TLOG_DB_DATABASE"),
                user:     os.Getenv("TLOG_DB_USERNAME"),
                password: os.Getenv("TLOG_DB_PASSWORD"),
            }
        )

    case "":
```

---

10 Good riddance.

11 I'm sorry.

```
        return nil, fmt.Errorf("transaction logger type not defined")

    default:
        return nil, fmt.Errorf("no such transaction logger %s", s)
    }
}
```

In this example, the NewTransactionLogger function accepts a string that specifies the desired implementation, returning either one of our implementations or an error. We use the os.Getenv function to retrieve the appropriate parameters from environment variables.

Our FrontEnd port

But what about our frontends? If you will recall, we now have two frontend implementations:

- In "Generation 1: The Monolith" on page 112 in Chapter 5, we built a RESTful interface using net/http and gorilla/mux.
- In "Remote Procedure Calls with gRPC" on page 230, earlier in this chapter, we built an RPC interface with gRPC.

Both of these implementations include a main function where we configure and start the service to listen for connections.

Since they're "driver" ports, we need to pass the core application to them, so let's refactor both frontends into structs according to the following interface:

```
package frontend

type FrontEnd interface {
    Start(kv *core.KeyValueStore) error
}
```

The FrontEnd interface serves as our "frontend port," which all frontend implementations are expected to satisfy. The Start method accepts the core application API in the form of a *core.KeyValueStore, and will also include the setup logic that formerly lived in a main function.

Now that we have this, we can refactor both frontends so that they comply with the FrontEnd interface, starting with the RESTful frontend. As usual, the complete source code for this and the gRPC service refactor are available in this book's companion GitHub repository (*https://oreil.ly/9jRyU*):

```
package frontend

import (
    "net/http"

    "github.com/cloud-native-go/examples/ch08/hexarch/core"
    "github.com/gorilla/mux"
)

// restFrontEnd contains a reference to the core application logic,
// and complies with the contract defined by the FrontEnd interface.
type restFrontEnd struct {
    store *core.KeyValueStore
}

// keyValueDeleteHandler handles the logic for the DELETE HTTP method.
func (f *restFrontEnd) keyValueDeleteHandler(w http.ResponseWriter,
        r *http.Request) {

    vars := mux.Vars(r)
    key := vars["key"]

    err := f.store.Delete(key)
    if err != nil {
        http.Error(w, err.Error(), http.StatusInternalServerError)
        return
    }
}

// ...other handler functions omitted for brevity.

// Start includes the setup and start logic that previously
// lived in a main function.
func (f *restFrontEnd) Start(store *core.KeyValueStore) error {
    // Remember our core application reference.
    f.store = store

    r := mux.NewRouter()

    r.HandleFunc("/v1/{key}", f.keyValueGetHandler).Methods("GET")
    r.HandleFunc("/v1/{key}", f.keyValuePutHandler).Methods("PUT")
    r.HandleFunc("/v1/{key}", f.keyValueDeleteHandler).Methods("DELETE")

    return http.ListenAndServe(":8080", r)
}
```

Comparing the previous code to the code we produced in "Generation 1: The Monolith" on page 112, some differences stand out:

- All functions are now methods attached to a `restFrontEnd` struct.

- All calls to the core application go through the `store` value that lives in the `rest FrontEnd` struct.

- Creating the router, defining the handlers, and starting the server now live in the `Start` method.

Similar changes will have been made for our gRPC frontend implementation to make it consistent with the `FrontEnd` port.

This new arrangement makes it easier for a consumer to choose and plug in a "front-end adapter," as demonstrated in the following.

Putting it all together

Here, we have our `main` function, in which we plug all of the components into our application:

```
package main

import (
    "log"

    "github.com/cloud-native-go/examples/ch08/hexarch/core"
    "github.com/cloud-native-go/examples/ch08/hexarch/frontend"
    "github.com/cloud-native-go/examples/ch08/hexarch/transact"
)

func main() {
    // Create our TransactionLogger. This is an adapter that will plug
    // into the core application's TransactionLogger port.
    tl, err := transact.NewTransactionLogger(os.Getenv("TLOG_TYPE"))
    if err != nil {
        log.Fatal(err)
    }

    // Create Core and tell it which TransactionLogger to use.
    // This is an example of a "driven agent"
    store := core.NewKeyValueStore(tl)
    store.Restore()

    // Create the frontend.
    // This is an example of a "driving agent."
    fe, err := frontend.NewFrontEnd(os.Getenv("FRONTEND_TYPE"))
    if err != nil {
        log.Fatal(err)
    }

    log.Fatal(fe.Start(store))
}
```

First, we then create a transaction logger according to the environment `TLOG_TYPE`. We do this first because the "transaction logger port" is "driven," so we'll need to provide it to the application to plug it in.

We then create our `KeyValueStore` value, which represents our core application functions and provides an API for ports to interact with, and provide it with any driven adapters.

Next, we create any "driver" adapters. Since these act on the core application API, we provide the API to the adapter instead of the other way around as we would with a "driven" adapter. This means we could also create multiple frontends here, if we wanted, by creating a new adapter and passing it the `KeyValueStore` that exposes the core application API.

Finally, we call `Start` on our frontend, which instructs it to start listening for connections. At last, we have a complete hexagonal service!

Summary

We covered a lot of ground in this chapter, but really only scratched the surface of all the different ways that components can find themselves tightly coupled and all the different ways of managing each of those tightly coupled components.

In the first half of the chapter, we focused on the coupling that can result from how services communicate. We talked about the problems caused by fragile exchange protocols like SOAP, and demonstrated REST and gRPC, which are less fragile because they can be changed to some degree without necessarily forcing client upgrades. We also touched on coupling "in time," in which one service implicitly expects a timely response from another, and how publish-subscribe messaging might be used to relieve this.

In the second half we addressed some of the ways that systems can minimize coupling to local resources. After all, even distributed services are just programs, subject to the same limitations of the architectures and implementations as any program. Plug-ins implementations and hexagonal architectures are two ways of doing this by enforcing separation of concerns and inversion of control.

Unfortunately, we didn't get to drill down into some other fascinating topics like service discovery, but, sadly, I had to draw a line somewhere before this subject got away from me!

## CHAPTER 9

Resilience

> A distributed system is one in which the failure of a computer you didn't even know
> about can render your own computer unusable.[1]
>
> —Leslie Lamport, *DEC SRC Bulletin Board (May 1987)*

Late one September night, at just after two in the morning, a portion of Amazon's internal network quietly stopped working.[2] This event was brief, and not particularly interesting, except that it happened to affect a sizable number of the servers that supported the DynamoDB service.

Most days, this wouldn't be such a big deal. Any affected servers would just try to reconnect to the cluster by retrieving their membership data from a dedicated metadata service. If that failed, they would temporarily take themselves offline and try again.

But this time, when the network was restored, a small army of storage servers simultaneously requested their membership data from the metadata service, overwhelming it so that requests—even ones from previously unaffected servers—started to time out. Storage servers dutifully responded to the timeouts by taking themselves offline and retrying (again), further stressing the metadata service, causing even more servers to go offline, and so on. Within minutes, the outage had spread to the entire cluster. The service was effectively down, taking a number of dependent services down with it.

---

1 Lamport, Leslie. *DEC SRC Bulletin Board*, 28 May 1987. *https://oreil.ly/nD85V*.

2 Summary of the Amazon DynamoDB Service Disruption and Related Impacts in the US-East Region. Amazon AWS, September 2015. *https://oreil.ly/Y1P5S*.

To make matters worse, the sheer volume of retry attempts—a "retry storm"—put such a burden on the metadata service that it even became entirely unresponsive to requests to add capacity. The on-call engineers were forced to explicitly block requests to the metadata service just to relieve enough pressure to allow them to manually scale up.

Finally, nearly five hours after the initial network hiccup that triggered the incident, normal operations resumed, putting an end to what must have been a long night for all involved.

Keeping on Ticking: Why Resilience Matters

So, what was the root cause of Amazon's outage? Was it the network disruption? Was it the storage servers' enthusiastic retry behavior? Was it the metadata service's response time, or maybe its limited capacity?

Clearly, what happened that early morning didn't have a single root cause. Failures in complex systems never do.[3] Rather, the system failed as complex systems do: with a failure in a subsystem, which triggered a latent fault in another subsystem causing *it* to fail, followed by another, and another, until eventually the entire system went down. What's interesting, though, is that if any of the components in our story—the network, the storage servers, the metadata service—had been able to isolate and recover from failures elsewhere in the system, the overall system likely would have recovered without human intervention.

Unfortunately, this is just one example of a common pattern. Complex systems fail in complex (and often surprising) ways, but they don't fail all at once: they fail one subsystem at a time. For this reason, resilience patterns in complex systems take the form of bulwarks and safety valves that work to isolate failures at component boundaries. Frequently, a failure contained is a failure avoided.

This property, the measure of a system's ability to withstand and recover from errors and failures, is its *resilience*. A system can be considered *resilient* if it can continue operating correctly—possibly at a reduced level—rather than failing completely when one of its subsystems fails.

---

3 Cook, Richard I. "How Complex Systems Fail." 1998. *https://oreil.ly/WyJ4Q*.

What Does It Mean for a System to Fail?

> For want of a nail the shoe was lost,
> for want of a shoe the horse was lost;
> for want of a horse the rider was lost;
> all for want of care about a horse-shoe nail.
>
> —Benjamin Franklin, *The Way to Wealth (1758)*

If we want to know what it means for a system to fail, we first have to ask what a "system" is.

This is important. Bear with me.

By definition, a *system* is a set of components that work together to accomplish an overall goal. So far, so good. But here's the important part: each component of a system—a *subsystem*—is also a complete system unto itself, that in turn is composed of still smaller subsystems, and so on, and so on.

Take a car, for example. Its engine is one of dozens of subsystems, but it—like all the others—is also a very complex system with a number of subsystems of its own, including a cooling subsystem, which includes a thermostat, which includes a temperature switch, and so on. That's just some of thousands of components and subcomponents and sub-subcomponents. It's enough to make the mind spin: so many things that can fail. But what happens when they do?

As we mentioned earlier—and discussed in some depth in Chapter 6—failures of complex systems don't just happen all at once. They unravel in predictable steps:

---

4 If you're interested in a complete academic treatment, I highly recommend *Reliability and Availability Engineering* (*https://oreil.ly/tfKr1*) by Kishor S. Trivedi and Andrea Bobbio (Cambridge University Press).

1. All systems contain *faults*, which we lovingly refer to as "bugs" in the software world. A tendency for a temperature switch in a car engine to stick would be a fault. So would the metadata service's limited capacity and the storage server's retry behavior in the DynamoDB case study.[5] Under the right conditions, a fault can be exercised to produce an *error*.

2. An *error* is any discrepancy between the system's intended and actual behavior. Many errors can be caught and handled appropriately, but if they're not they can —singly or in accumulation—give rise to a *failure*. A stuck temperature switch in a car engine's thermostat is an error.

3. Finally, a system can be said to be experiencing a *failure* when it's no longer able to provide correct service.[6] A temperature switch that no longer responds to high temperatures can be said to have failed. A failure at the subsystem level becomes a fault at the system level.

This last bit bears repeating: *a failure at the subsystem level becomes a fault at the system level.* A stuck temperature switch causes a thermostat to fail, preventing coolant from flowing through the radiator, raising the temperature of the engine, causing it to stall and the car to stop.[7]

That's how systems fail. It starts with the failure of one component—one subsystem —which causes an error in one or more components that interact with it, and ones that interact with that, and so on, propagating upward until the entire system fails.

This isn't just academic. Knowing how complex systems fail—one component at a time—makes the means of resisting failures clearer: if a fault can be contained before it propagates all the way to the system level, the system may be able to recover (or at least fail on its own terms).

Building for Resilience

In a perfect world it would be possible to rid a system of every possible fault, but this isn't realistic, and it's wasteful and unproductive to try. By instead assuming that all components are destined to fail eventually—which they absolutely are—and designing them to respond gracefully to errors when they do occur, you can produce a system that's functionally healthy even when some of its components are not.

There are lots of ways to increase the resiliency of a system. Redundancy, such as deploying multiple components of the same type, is probably the most common

---

5 Importantly, many faults are only evident in retrospect.

6 See? We eventually got there.

7 Go on, ask me how I know this.

approach. Specialized logic like circuit breakers and request throttles can be used to isolate specific kinds of errors, preventing them from propagating. Faulty components can even be reaped—or intentionally allowed to fail—to benefit the health of the larger system.

Resilience is a particularly rich subject. We'll explore several of these approaches—and more—over the remainder of the chapter.

Cascading Failures

The reason the DynamoDB case study is so appropriate is that it demonstrates so many different ways that things that can go wrong at scale.

Take, for example, how the failure of a group of storage servers caused requests to the metadata service to time out, which in turn caused more storage servers to fail, which increased the pressure on the metadata service, and so on. This is an excellent example of a particular—and particularly common—failure mode known as a *cascading failure*. Once a cascading failure has begun, it tends to spread very quickly, often on the order of a few minutes.

The mechanisms of cascading failures can vary a bit, but one thing they share is some kind of positive feedback mechanism. One part of a system experiences a local failure —a reduction in capacity, an increase in latency, etc.—that causes other components to attempt to compensate for the failed component in a way that exacerbates the problem, eventually leading to the failure of the entire system.

The classic cause of cascading failures is overload, illustrated in Figure 9-1. This occurs when one or more nodes in a set fails, causing the load to be catastrophically redistributed to the survivors. The increase in load overloads the remaining nodes, causing them to fail from resource exhaustion, taking the entire system down.

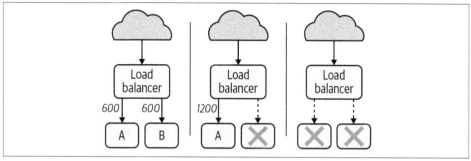

Figure 9-1. Server overload is a common cause of cascade failures; each server handles 600 requests per second, so when server B fails, server A is overloaded and also fails

The nature of positive feedback often makes it very difficult to scale your way out of a cascading failure by adding more capacity. New nodes can be overwhelmed as quickly as they come online, often contributing the feedback that took the system down in the first place. Sometimes, the only fix is to take your entire service down—perhaps by explicitly blocking the problematic traffic—in order to recover, and then slowly reintroduce load.

But how do you prevent cascading failures in the first place? This will be the subject of the next section (and, to some extent, most of this chapter).

Preventing Overload

Every service, however well-designed and implemented, has its functional limitations. This is particularly evident in services intended to handle and respond to client requests.[8] For any such service there exists some request frequency, a threshold beyond which bad things will start to happen. So, how do we keep a large number of requests from accidentally (or intentionally!) bringing our service down?

Ultimately, a service that finds itself in such a situation has no choice but to reject—partially or entirely—some number of requests. There are two main strategies for doing this:

Throttling
> Throttling is a relatively straightforward strategy that kicks in when requests come in faster than some predetermined frequency, typically, by just refusing to handle them. This is often used as a preventative measure by ensuring that no particular user consumes more resources than they would reasonably require.

Load shedding
> Load shedding is a little more adaptive. Services using this strategy intentionally drop ("shed") some proportion of load as they approach overload conditions by either refusing requests or falling back into a degraded mode.

These strategies aren't mutually exclusive; a service may choose to employ either or both of them, according to its needs.

Throttling

As we discussed in Chapter 4, a throttle pattern works a lot like the throttle in a car, except that instead of limiting the amount of fuel entering an engine, it limits the number of requests that a user (human or otherwise) can make to a service in a set period of time.

---

8 Especially if the service is available on the open sewer that is the public internet.

The general-purpose throttle example that we provided in "Throttle" on page 86 was relatively simple, and effectively global, at least as written. However, throttles are also frequently applied on a per-user basis to provide something like a usage quota, so that no one caller can consume too much of a service's resources.

In the following, we demonstrate a throttle implementation that, while still using a token bucket,[9] is otherwise quite different in several ways.

First, instead of having a single bucket that's used to gate all incoming requests, the following implementation throttles on a per-user basis, returning a function that accepts a "key" parameter, that's meant to represent a username or some other unique identifier.

Second, rather than attempting to "replay" a cached value when imposing a throttle limit, the returned function returns a Boolean that indicates when a throttle has been imposed. Note that the throttle doesn't return an error when it's activated: throttling isn't an error condition, so we don't treat it as one.

Finally, and perhaps most interestingly, it doesn't actually use a timer (a time.Ticker) to explicitly add tokens to buckets on some regular cadence. Rather, it refills buckets on demand, based on the time elapsed between requests. This strategy means that we don't have to dedicate background processes to filling buckets until they're actually used, which will scale much more effectively:

```go
// Effector is the function that you want to subject to throttling.
type Effector func(context.Context) (string, error)

// Throttled wraps an Effector. It accepts the same parameters, plus a
// "UID" string that represents a caller identity. It returns the same,
// plus a bool that's true if the call is not throttled.
type Throttled func(context.Context, string) (bool, string, error)

// A bucket tracks the requests associated with a UID.
type bucket struct {
    tokens uint
    time   time.Time
}

// Throttle accepts an Effector function, and returns a Throttled
// function with a per-UID token bucket with a capacity of max
// that refills at a rate of refill tokens every d.
func Throttle(e Effector, max uint, refill uint, d time.Duration) Throttled {
    // buckets maps UIDs to specific buckets
    buckets := map[string]*bucket{}
```

---

9 Wikipedia contributors. "Token bucket." *Wikipedia, The Free Encyclopedia*, 5 Jun. 2019. *https://oreil.ly/ vkOov*.

```go
    return func(ctx context.Context, uid string) (bool, string, error) {
        b := buckets[uid]

        // This is a new entry! It passes. Assumes that capacity >= 1.
        if b == nil {
            buckets[uid] = &bucket{tokens: max - 1, time: time.Now()}

            str, err := e(ctx)
            return true, str, err
        }

        // Calculate how many tokens we now have based on the time
        // passed since the previous request.
        refillInterval := uint(time.Since(b.time) / d)
        tokensAdded := refill * refillInterval
        currentTokens := b.tokens + tokensAdded

        // We don't have enough tokens. Return false.
        if currentTokens < 1 {
            return false, "", nil
        }

        // If we've refilled our bucket, we can restart the clock.
        // Otherwise, we figure out when the most recent tokens were added.
        if currentTokens > max {
            b.time = time.Now()
            b.tokens = max - 1
        } else {
            deltaTokens := currentTokens - b.tokens
            deltaRefills := deltaTokens / refill
            deltaTime := time.Duration(deltaRefills) * d

            b.time = b.time.Add(deltaTime)
            b.tokens = currentTokens - 1
        }

        str, err := e(ctx)

        return true, str, err
    }
}
```

Like the example in "Throttle" on page 86, this Throttle function accepts a function literal that conforms to the Effector contract, plus some values that define the size and refill rate of the underlying token bucket.

Instead of returning another Effector, however, it returns a Throttled function, which in addition to wrapping the effector with the throttling logic adds a "key" input parameter, which represents a unique user identifier, and a Boolean return value, which indicates whether the function has been throttled (and therefore not executed).

As interesting as you may (or may not) find the Throttle code, it's still not production ready. First of all, it's not entirely safe for concurrent use. A production implementation will probably want to lock on the record values, and possibly the bucket map. Second, there's no way to purge old records. In production, we'd probably want to use something like an LRU cache, like the one we described in "Efficient Caching Using an LRU Cache" on page 198, instead.

In the following, we show a toy example of how Throttle might be used in a RESTful web service:

```
var throttled = Throttle(getHostname, 1, 1, time.Second)

func getHostname(ctx context.Context) (string, error) {
    if ctx.Err() != nil {
        return "", ctx.Err()
    }

    return os.Hostname()
}

func throttledHandler(w http.ResponseWriter, r *http.Request) {
    ok, hostname, err := throttled(r.Context(), r.RemoteAddr)

    if err != nil {
        http.Error(w, err.Error(), http.StatusInternalServerError)
        return
    }

    if !ok {
        http.Error(w, "Too many requests", http.StatusTooManyRequests)
        return
    }

    w.WriteHeader(http.StatusOK)
    w.Write([]byte(hostname))
}

func main() {
    r := mux.NewRouter()
    r.HandleFunc("/hostname", throttledHandler)
    log.Fatal(http.ListenAndServe(":8080", r))
}
```

The previous code creates a small web service with a single (somewhat contrived) endpoint at /hostname that returns the service's hostname. When the program is run, the throttled var is created by wrapping the getHostname function—which provides the actual service logic—by passing it to Throttle, which we defined previously.

When the router receives a request for the /hostname endpoint, the request is forwarded to the throttledHandler function, which performs the calls to throttled, receiving a bool indicating throttling status, the hostname string, and an error value. A defined error causes us to return a 500 Internal Server Error, and a throttled request gets a 429 Too Many Requests. If all else goes well, we return the hostname and a status 200 OK.

Note that the bucket values are stored locally, so this implementation can't really be considered production-ready either. If you want this to scale out, you might want to store the record values in an external cache of some kind so that multiple service replicas can share them.

Load shedding

It's an unavoidable fact of life that, as load on a server increases beyond what it can handle, something eventually has to give.

Load shedding is a technique used to predict when a server is approaching that saturation point and then mitigating the saturation by dropping some proportion of traffic in a controlled fashion. Ideally, this will prevent the server from overloading and failing health checks, serving with high latency, or just collapsing in a graceless, uncontrolled failure.

Unlike quota-based throttling, load shedding is reactive, typically engaging in response to depletion of a resource like CPU, memory, or request-queue depth.

Perhaps the most straightforward form of load shedding is a per-task throttling that drops requests when one or more resources exceed a particular threshold. For example, if your service provides a RESTful endpoint, you might choose to to return an HTTP 503 (service unavailable). The gorilla/mux web toolkit, which we found very effective in Chapter 5 in the section "Building an HTTP Server with gorilla/mux" on page 114, makes this fairly straightforward by supporting "middleware" handler functions (*https://oreil.ly/GTxes*) that are called on every request:

```
const MaxQueueDepth = 1000

// Middleware function, which will be called for each request.
// If queue depth is exceeded, it returns HTTP 503 (service unavailable).
func loadSheddingMiddleware(next http.Handler) http.Handler {
    return http.HandlerFunc(func(w http.ResponseWriter, r *http.Request) {
        // CurrentQueueDepth is fictional and for example purposes only.
        if CurrentQueueDepth() > MaxQueueDepth {
            log.Println("load shedding engaged")

            http.Error(w,
                err.Error(),
                http.StatusServiceUnavailable)
            return
        }

        next.ServeHTTP(w, r)
```

```
        })
    }

    func main() {
        r := mux.NewRouter()

        // Register middleware
        r.Use(loadSheddingMiddleware)

        log.Fatal(http.ListenAndServe(":8080", r))
    }
```

Gorilla Mux middlewares are called on every request, each taking a request, doing something with it, and passing it down to another middleware or the final handler. This makes them perfect for implementing general request logging, header manipulation, `ResponseWriter` hijacking, or in our case, resource-reactive load shedding.

Our middleware uses the fictional `CurrentQueueDepth()` (your actual function will depend on your implementation) to check the current queue depth, and rejects requests with an HTTP 503 (service unavailable) if the value is too high. More sophisticated implementations might even be smarter about choosing which work is dropped by prioritizing particularly important requests.

Graceful service degradation

Resource-sensitive load shedding works well, but in some applications it's possible to act a little more gracefully by significantly decreasing the quality of responses when the service is approaching overload. Such *graceful degradation* takes the concept of load shedding one step further by strategically reducing the amount of work needed to satisfy each request instead of just rejecting requests.

There are as many ways of doing this as there are services, and not every service can be degraded in a reasonable manner, but common approaches include falling back on cached data or less expensive—if less precise—algorithms.

Play It Again: Retrying Requests

When a request receives an error response, or doesn't receive a response at all, it should just try again, right? Well, kinda. Retrying makes sense, but it's a lot more nuanced than that.

Take this snippet for example, a version of which I've found in a production system:

```
res, err := SendRequest()
for err != nil {
    res, err = SendRequest()
}
```

It seems seductively straightforward, doesn't it? It *will* repeat failed requests, but that's also *exactly* what it will do. So when this logic was deployed to a few hundred servers and the service to which it was issuing requests went down, the entire system went with it. A review of the service metrics, shown in Figure 9-2, revealed this.

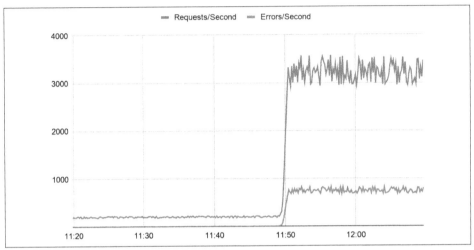

Figure 9-2. The anatomy of a "retry storm"

It seems that when the downstream service failed, our service—every single instance of it—entered its retry loop, making *thousands* of requests per second and bringing the network to its knees so severely that we were forced to essentially restart the entire system.

This is actually a very common kind of cascading failure known as a *retry storm*. In a retry storm, well-meaning logic intended to add resilience to a component, acts against the larger system. Very often, even when the conditions that caused the downstream service to go down are resolved, it can't come back up because it's instantly brought under too much load.

But, retries are a good thing, right?

Yes, but whenever you implement retry logic, you should always include a *backoff algorithm*, which we'll conveniently discuss in the next section.

Backoff Algorithms

When a request to a downstream service fails for any reason, "best" practice is to retry the request. But how long should you wait? If you wait too long, important work may be delayed. Too little and you risk overwhelming the target, the network, or both.

The common solution is to implement a backoff algorithm that introduces a delay between retries to reduce the frequency of attempts to a safe and acceptable rate.

There are a variety of backoff algorithms available, the simplest of which is to include a short, fixed-duration pause between retries, as follows:

```
res, err := SendRequest()
for err != nil {
    time.Sleep(2 * time.Second)
    res, err = SendRequest()
}
```

In the previous snippet, SendRequest is used to issue a request, returning string and error values. However, if err isn't nil, the code enters a loop, sleeping for two seconds before retrying, repeating indefinitely until it receives a nonerror response.

In Figure 9-3, we illustrate the number of requests generated by 1,000 simulated instances using this method.[10] As you can see, while the fixed-delay approach might reduce the request count compared to having no backoff at all, the overall number of requests is still quite consistently high.

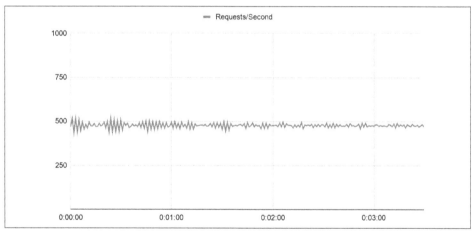

Figure 9-3. Requests/second of 1,000 simulated instances using a two-second retry delay

A fixed-duration backoff delay might work fine if you have a very small number of retrying instances, but it doesn't scale very well, since a sufficient number of requestors can still overwhelm the network.

However, we can't always assume that any given service will have a small enough number of instances not to overwhelm the network with retries, or that our service

---

10 The code used to simulate all data in this section is available in the associated GitHub repository (*https://oreil.ly/m61X7*).

will even be the only one retrying. For this reason, many backoff algorithms implement an *exponential backoff*, in which the durations of the delays between retries roughly doubles with each attempt up to some fixed maximum.

A very common (but flawed, as you'll soon see) exponential backoff implementation might look something like the following:

```
res, err := SendRequest()
base, cap := time.Second, time.Minute

for backoff := base; err != nil; backoff <<= 1 {
    if backoff > cap {
        backoff = cap
    }
    time.Sleep(backoff)
    res, err = SendRequest()
}
```

In this snippet, we specify a starting duration, base, and a fixed maximum duration, cap. In the loop, the value of backoff starts at base and doubles each iteration to a maximum value of cap.

You would think that this logic would help to mitigate the network load and retry request burden on downstream services. Simulating this implementation for 1,000 nodes, however, tells another story, illustrated in Figure 9-4.

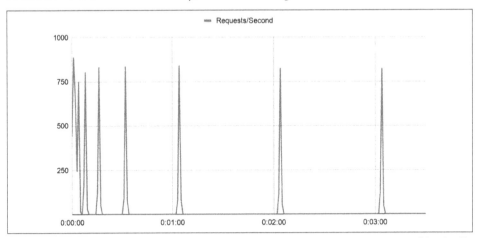

Figure 9-4. Requests/second of 1,000 simulated instances using an exponential backoff

It would seem that having 1,000 nodes with exactly the same retry schedule still isn't optimal, since the retries are now clustering, possibly generating enough load in the process to cause problems. So, in practice, pure exponential backoff doesn't necessarily help as much we'd like.

It would seem that we need some way to spread the spikes out so that the retries occur at a roughly constant rate. The solution is to include an element of randomness, called *jitter*. Adding jitter to our previous backoff function results in something like the snippet here:

```
res, err := SendRequest()
base, cap := time.Second, time.Minute

for backoff := base; err != nil; backoff <<= 1 {
    if backoff > cap {
        backoff = cap
    }

    jitter := rand.Int63n(int64(backoff * 3))
    sleep := base + time.Duration(jitter)
    time.Sleep(sleep)
    res, err = SendRequest()
}
```

Simulating running this code on 1,000 nodes produces the pattern presented in Figure 9-5.

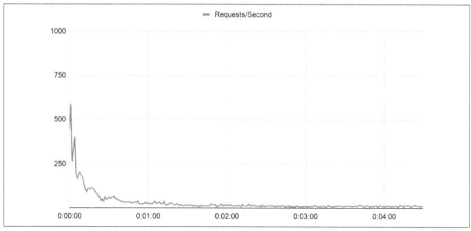

Figure 9-5. Requests/second of 1,000 simulated instances using an exponential backoff with jitter

 The rand package's top-level functions produce a deterministic sequence of values each time the program is run. If you don't use the rand.Seed function to provide a new seed value, they behave as if seeded by rand.Seed(1) and always produce the same "random" sequence of numbers.

When we use exponential backoff with jitter, the number of retries decreases over a short interval—so as not to overstress services that are trying to come up—and spreads them out over time so that they occur at an approximately constant rate.

Who would have thought there was more to retrying requests than retrying requests?

Circuit Breaking

We first introduced the Circuit Breaker pattern in Chapter 4 as a function that degrades potentially failing method calls as a way to prevent larger or cascading failures. That definition still holds, and because we're not going to extend or change it much, we won't dig into it in *too* much detail here.

To review, the Circuit Breaker pattern tracks the number of consecutive failed requests made to a downstream component. If the failure count passes a certain threshold, the circuit is "opened," and all attempts to issue additional requests fail immediately (or return some defined fallback). After a waiting period, the circuit automatically "closes," resuming its normal state and allowing requests to be made normally.

Not all resilience patterns are defensive.

Sometimes it pays to be a good neighbor.

A properly applied Circuit Breaker pattern can make the difference between system recovery and cascading failure. In addition to the obvious benefits of not wasting resources or clogging the network with doomed requests, a circuit breaker (particularly one with a backoff function) can give a malfunctioning service enough room to recover, allowing it to come back up and restore correct service.

What's the Difference Between Circuit Breaker and Throttle?

At a quick glance, the Circuit Breaker pattern might seem to resemble a Throttle—after all they're both resilience patterns that rate requests—but they really are two quite different things:

- *Circuit Breaker* is generally applied only to *outgoing* requests. It usually doesn't care one bit about the request rate: it's only concerned with the number of failed requests, and only if they're consecutive.

- *Throttle* works like the throttle in a car by limiting a number of requests—regardless of success or failure—to some maximum rate. It's *typically* applied to incoming traffic, but there's no rule that says it has to be.

The Circuit Breaker pattern was covered in some detail in Chapter 4, so that's all we're going to say about it here. Take a look at "Circuit Breaker" on page 77 for more background and code examples. The addition of jitter to the example's backoff function is left as an exercise for the reader.[11]

Timeouts

The importance of timeouts isn't always appreciated. However, the ability for a client to recognize when a request is unlikely to be satisfied allows the client to release resources that it—and any upstream requestors it might be acting on behalf of— might otherwise hold on to. This holds just as true for a service, which may find itself holding onto requests until long after a client has given up.

For example, imagine a basic service that queries a database. If that database should suddenly slow so that queries take a few seconds to complete, requests to the service —each holding onto a database connection—could accumulate, eventually depleting the connection pool. If the database is shared, it could even cause other services to fail, resulting in a cascading failure.

If the service had timed out instead of holding on to the database, it could have degraded service instead of failing outright.

In other words, if you think you're going to fail, fail fast.

Using Context for service-side timeouts

We first introduced `context.Context` back in Chapter 4 as Go's idiomatic means of carrying deadlines and cancellation signals between processes.[12] If you'd like a refresher, or just want to put yourself in the right frame of mind before continuing, go ahead and take a look at "The Context Package" on page 72.

You might also recall that later in the same chapter, in "Timeout" on page 90, we covered the *Timeout* pattern, which uses `Context` to not only allow a process to stop waiting for an answer once it's clear that a result may not be coming, but to also notify other functions with derived `Contexts` to stop working and release any resources that they might also be holding on to.

This ability to cancel not just local functions, but subfunctions, is so powerful that it's generally considered good form for functions to accept a `Context` value if they have the potential to run longer than a caller might want to wait, which is almost always true if the call traverses a network.

---

11 Doing that here felt redundant, but I'll admit that I may have gotten a bit lazy.

12 And, technically, request-scoped values, but the correctness of this functionality is debatable.

For this reason, there are many excellent samples of Context-accepting functions scattered throughout Go's standard library. Many of these can be found in the sql package, which includes Context-accepting versions of many of its functions. For example, the DB struct's QueryRow method has an equivalent QueryRowContext that accepts a Context value.

A function that uses this technique to provide the username of a user based on an ID value might look something like the following:

```go
func UserName(ctx context.Context, id int) (string, error) {
    const query = "SELECT username FROM users WHERE id=?"

    dctx, cancel := context.WithTimeout(ctx, 15*time.Second)
    defer cancel()

    var username string
    err := db.QueryRowContext(dctx, query, id).Scan(&username)

    return username, err
}
```

The UserName function accepts a context.Context and an id integer, but it also creates its own derived Context with a rather long timeout. This approach provides a default timeout that automatically releases any open connections after 15 seconds—longer than many clients are likely to be willing to wait—while also being responsive to cancellation signals from the caller.

The responsiveness to outside cancellation signals can be quite useful. The http framework provides yet another excellent example of this, as demonstrated in the following UserGetHandler HTTP handler function:

```go
func UserGetHandler(w http.ResponseWriter, r *http.Request) {
    vars := mux.Vars(r)
    id := vars["id"]

    // Get the request's context. This context is canceled when
    // the client's connection closes, the request is canceled
    // (with HTTP/2), or when the ServeHTTP method returns.
    rctx := r.Context()

    ctx, cancel := context.WithTimeout(rctx, 10*time.Second)
    defer cancel()

    username, err := UserName(ctx, id)

    switch {
    case errors.Is(err, sql.ErrNoRows):
        http.Error(w, "no such user", http.StatusNotFound)
    case errors.Is(err, context.DeadlineExceeded):
        http.Error(w, "database timeout", http.StatusGatewayTimeout)
```

```
        case err != nil:
            http.Error(w, err.Error(), http.StatusInternalServerError)
        default:
            w.Write([]byte(username))
        }
    }
```

In `UserGetHandler`, the first thing we do is retrieve the request's `Context` via its `Context` method. Conveniently, this `Context` is canceled when the client's connection closes, when the request is canceled (with HTTP/2), or when the `ServeHTTP` method returns.

From this we create a derived context, applying our own explicit timeout, which will cancel the `Context` after 10 seconds, no matter what.

Because the derived context is passed to the `UserName` function, we are able to draw a direct causative line between closing the HTTP request and closing the database connection: if the request's `Context` closes, all derived `Contexts` close as well, ultimately ensuring that all open resources are released as well in a loosely coupled manner.

Timing out HTTP/REST client calls

Back in "A Possible Pitfall of Convenience Functions" on page 229, we presented one of the pitfalls of the `http` "convenience functions" like `http.Get` and `http.Post`: that they use the default timeout. Unfortunately, the default timeout value is 0, which Go interprets as "no timeout."

The mechanism we presented at the time for setting timeouts for client methods was to create a custom `Client` value with a nonzero `Timeout` value, as follows:

```
var client = &http.Client{
    Timeout: time.Second * 10,
}

response, err := client.Get(url)
```

This works perfectly fine, and in fact, will cancel a request in exactly the same way as if its `Context` is canceled. But what if you want to use an existing or derived `Context` value? For that you'll need access to the underlying `Context`, which you can get by using `http.NewRequestWithContext`, the `Context`-accepting equivalent of `http.New Request`, which allows a programmer to specify a `Context` that controls the entire lifetime of the request and its response.

This isn't as much of a divergence as it might seem. In fact, looking at the source code for the `Get` method on the `http.Client` shows that under the covers, it's just using `NewRequest`:

```
func (c *Client) Get(url string) (resp *Response, err error) {
    req, err := NewRequest("GET", url, nil)
```

```
    if err != nil {
        return nil, err
    }

    return c.Do(req)
}
```

As you can see, the standard Get method calls NewRequest to create a *Request value, passing it the method name and URL (the last parameter accepts an optional io.Reader for the request body, which we don't need here). A call to the Do function executes the request proper.

Not counting an error check and the return, the entire method consists of just one call. It would seem that if we wanted to implement similar functionality that also accepts a Context value, we could do so without much hassle.

One way to do this might be to implement a GetContext function that accepts a Context value:

```
type ClientContext struct {
    http.Client
}

func (c *ClientContext) GetContext(ctx context.Context, url string)
        (resp *http.Response, err error) {

    req, err := http.NewRequestWithContext(ctx, "GET", url, nil)
    if err != nil {
        return nil, err
    }

    return c.Do(req)
}
```

Our new GetContext function is functionally identical to the canonical Get, except that it also accepts a Context value, which it uses to call http.NewRequestWithContext instead of http.NewRequest.

Using our new ClientContext would be very similar to using a standard http.Client value, except instead of calling client.Get we'd call client.GetContext (and pass along a Context value, of course):

```
func main() {
    client := &ClientContext{}
    ctx, cancel := context.WithTimeout(context.Background(), 5*time.Second)
    defer cancel()

    response, err := client.GetContext(ctx, "http://www.example.com")
    if err != nil {
        log.Fatal(err)
    }
```

```
    bytes, _ := ioutil.ReadAll(response.Body)
    fmt.Println(string(bytes))
}
```

But does it work? It's not a *proper* test with a testing library, but we can manually kick the tires by setting the deadline to 0 and running it:

```
$ go run .
2020/08/25 14:03:16 Get "http://www.example.com": context deadline exceeded
exit status 1
```

And it would seem that it does! Excellent.

Timing out gRPC client calls

Just like http.Client, gRPC clients default to "no timeout," but also allow timeouts to be explicitly set.

As we saw in "Implementing the gRPC client" on page 239, gRPC clients typically use the grpc.Dial function to establish a connection to a client, and that a list of grpc.DialOption values—constructed via functions like grpc.WithInsecure and grpc.WithBlock—can be passed to it to configure how that connection is set up.

Among these options is grpc.WithTimeout, which can be used to configure a client dialing timeout:

```
opts := []grpc.DialOption{
    grpc.WithInsecure(),
    grpc.WithBlock(),
    grpc.WithTimeout(5 * time.Second),
}
conn, err := grpc.Dial(serverAddr, opts...)
```

However, while grpc.WithTimeout might seem convenient on the face of it, it's actually been deprecated for some time, largely because its mechanism is inconsistent (and redundant) with the preferred Context timeout method. We show it here for the sake of completion.

> The grpc.WithTimeout option is deprecated and will eventually be removed. Use grpc.DialContext and context.WithTimeout instead.

Instead, the preferred method of setting a gRPC dialing timeout is the very convenient (for us) grpc.DialContext function, which allows us to use (or reuse) a context.Context value. This is actually doubly useful, because gRPC service methods accept a Context value anyway, so there really isn't even any additional work to be done:

```
func TimeoutKeyValueGet() *pb.Response {
    // Use context to set a 5-second timeout.
    ctx, cancel := context.WithTimeout(context.Background(), 5 * time.Second)
    defer cancel()

    // We can still set other options as desired.
    opts := []grpc.DialOption{grpc.WithInsecure(), grpc.WithBlock()}

    conn, err := grpc.DialContext(ctx, serverAddr, opts...)
    if err != nil {
        grpclog.Fatalf(err)
    }
    defer conn.Close()

    client := pb.NewKeyValueClient(conn)

    // We can reuse the same Context in the client calls.
    response, err := client.Get(ctx, &pb.GetRequest{Key: key})
    if err != nil {
        grpclog.Fatalf(err)
    }

    return response
}
```

As advertised, TimeoutKeyValueGet uses grpc.DialContext—to which we pass a con text.Context value with a 5-second timeout—instead of grpc.Dial. The opts list is otherwise identical except, obviously, that it no longer includes grpc.WithTimeout.

Note the client.Get method call. As we mentioned previously, gRPC service methods accept a Context parameter, so we simply reuse the existing one. Importantly, reusing the same Context value will constrain both operations under the same timeout calculation—a Context will time out regardless of how it's used—so be sure to take that into consideration when planning your timeout values.

Idempotence

As we discussed at the top of Chapter 4, cloud native applications by definition exist in and are subject to all of the idiosyncrasies of a networked world. It's a plain fact of life that networks—all networks—are unreliable, and messages sent across them don't always arrive at their destination on time (or at all).

What's more, if you send a message but don't get a response, you have no way to know what happened. Did the message get lost on its way to the recipient? Did the recipient get the message, and the response get lost? Maybe everything is working fine, but the round trip is just taking a little longer than usual?

In such a situation, the only option is to send the message again. But it's not enough to cross your fingers and hope for the best. It's important to plan for this inevitability by making it safe to resend messages by designing the functions for *idempotence*.

You might recall that we briefly introduced the concept of idempotence in "What Is Idempotence and Why Does It Matter?" on page 108, in which we defined an idempotent operation as one that has the same effect after multiple applications as a single application. As the designers of HTTP understood, it also happens to be an important property of any cloud native API that guarantees that any communication can be safely repeated (see "The Origins of Idempotence on the Web" on page 287 for a bit on that history).

The actual means of achieving idempotence will vary from service to service, but there are some consistent patterns that we'll review in the remainder of this section.

The Origins of Idempotence on the Web

The concepts of idempotence and safety, at least in the context of networked services, were first defined way back in 1997 in the HTTP/1.1 standard.[13]

An interesting aside: that ground-breaking proposal, as well as the HTTP/1.0 "informational draft" that preceded it the year before,[14] were authored by two greats.

The primary author of the original HTTP/1.0 draft (and the last author of the proposed HTTP/1.1 standard) was Sir Timothy John Berners-Lee, who is credited for inventing the World Wide Web, the first web browser, and the fundamental protocols and algorithms allowing the Web to scale—for which he was awarded with an ACM Turing Award, a knighthood, and various honorary degrees.

The primary author of the proposed HTTP/1.1 standard (and the second author of the original HTTP/1.0 draft) was Roy Fielding, then a graduate student at the University of California Irvine. Despite being one of the original authors of the World Wide Web, Fielding is perhaps known for his doctoral dissertation, in which he invented REST.[15]

---

13 Fielding, R., et al. "Hypertext Transfer Protocol — HTTP/1.1," Proposed Standard, RFC 2068, June 1997. *https://oreil.ly/28rcs*.

14 Berners-Lee, T., et al. "Hypertext Transfer Protocol — HTTP/1.0," Informational, RFC 1945, May 1996. *https://oreil.ly/zN7uo*.

15 Fielding, Roy Thomas. "Architectural Styles and the Design of Network-Based Software Architectures." *UC Irvine*, 2000, pp. 76–106. *https://oreil.ly/swjbd*.

How do I make my service idempotent?

Idempotence isn't baked into the logic of any particular framework. Even in HTTP—and by extension, REST—idempotence is a matter of convention and isn't explicitly enforced. There's nothing stopping you from—by oversight or on purpose—implementing a nonidempotent GET if you really want to.[16]

One of the reasons that idempotence is sometimes so tricky is because it relies on logic built into the core application, rather than at the REST or gRPC API layer. For example, if back in Chapter 5 we had wanted to make our key-value store consistent with traditional CRUD (create, read, update, and delete) operations (and therefore *not* idempotent) we might have done something like this:

```go
var store = make(map[string]string)

func Create(key, value string) error {
    if _, ok := store[key]; ok {
        return errors.New("duplicate key")
    }

    store[key] = value
    return nil
}

func Update(key, value string) error {
    if _, ok := store[key]; !ok {
        return errors.New("no such key")
    }

    store[key] = value
    return nil
}

func Delete(key string) error {
    if _, ok := store[key]; ok {
        return errors.New("no such key")
    }

    delete(store, key)
    return nil
}
```

This CRUD-like service implementation may be entirely well-meaning, but if any of these methods have to be repeated the result would be an error. What's more, there's also a fair amount of logic involved in checking against the current state which wouldn't be necessary in an equivalent idempotent implementation like the following:

---

16 You monster.

```
var store = make(map[string]string)

func Set(key, value string) {
    store[key] = value
}

func Delete(key string) {
    delete(store, key)
}
```

This version is a *lot* simpler, in more than one way. First, we no longer need separate "create" and "update" operations, so we can combine these into a single Set function. Also, not having to check the current state with each operation reduces the logic in each method, a benefit that continues to pay dividends as the service increases in complexity.

Finally, if an operation has to be repeated, it's no big deal. For both the Set and Delete functions, multiple identical calls will have the same result. They are idempotent.

What about scalar operations?

"So," you might say, "that's all well and good for operations that are either *done* or *not done*, but what about more complex operations? Operations on scalar values, for example?"

That's a fair question. After all, it's one thing to PUT a thing in a place: it's either been PUT, or it hasn't. All you have to do is not return an error for re-PUTs. Fine.

But what about an operation like "add $500 to account 12345"? Such a request might carry a JSON payload that looks something like the following:

```
{
    "credit":{
        "accountID": 12345,
        "amount": 500
    }
}
```

Repeated applications of this operation would lead to an extra $500 going to account 12345, and while the owner of the account might not mind so much, the bank probably would.

But consider what happens when we add a transactionID value to our JSON payload:

```
{
    "credit":{
        "accountID": 12345,
        "amount": 500,
        "transactionID": 789
```

```
        }
    }
```

It may require some more bookkeeping, but this approach provides a workable solution to our dilemma. By tracking `transactionID` values, the recipient can safely identify and reject duplicate transactions. Idempotence achieved!

Service Redundancy

Redundancy—the duplication of critical components or functions of a system with the intention of increasing reliability of the system—is often the first line of defense when it comes to increasing resilience in the face of failure.

We've already discussed one particular kind of redundancy—messaging redundancy, also known as "retries"—in "Play It Again: Retrying Requests" on page 275. In this section, however, we'll consider the value of replicating critical system components so that if any one fails, one or more others are there to pick up the slack.

In a public cloud, this would mean deploying your component to multiple server instances, ideally across multiple zones or even across multiple regions. In a container orchestration platform like Kubernetes, this may even just be a matter of setting your replica count to a value greater than one.

As interesting as this subject is, however, we won't actually spend too much time on it. Service replication is an architectural subject that's been thoroughly covered in many other sources.[17] This is supposed to be a Go book, after all. But still, we'd be remiss to have an entire chapter about resilience and not even mention it.

A Word of Caution: Fault Masking

Fault masking occurs when a system fault is invisibly compensated for without being explicitly detected.

For example, imagine a system with three service nodes, all performing a share of the tasks. If one node goes bad and the other nodes can compensate, you might never notice anything wrong. The fault has been masked.

Fault masking can conceal possibly progressive faults, and may eventually—and quietly—result in a loss of protective redundancy, often with a sudden and catastrophic outcome.

---

17 *Building Secure and Reliable Systems: Best Practices for Designing, Implementing, and Maintaining Systems* (*https://oreil.ly/YPKyr*) by Heather Adkins—and a host of other authors—is one excellent example.

To prevent fault masking, it's important to include service health checks—which we'll discuss in "Healthy Health Checks" on page 294—that accurately report the health of a service instance.

Designing for Redundancy

The effort involved in designing a system so that its functions can be replicated across multiple instances can yield significant dividends. But exactly how much? Well…a lot. You can feel free to take a look at the following box if you're interested in the math, but if you don't, you can just trust me on this one.

Reliability by the Numbers

Imagine, if you will, a service with "two-nines"—or 99%—of availability. Any given request to this system it has a theoretical probability of success of 0.99, which is denoted A_s. This actually isn't very good, but that's the point.

What kind of availability can you get if two of these identical instances are arranged in parallel, so that both have to be down to interrupt service?[18] This kind of arrangement can be diagrammed as shown here:

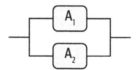

What's the resulting system availability? What we really want to know is: what's the probability that both instances will be *unavailable*? To answer this, we take the product of each component's probability of failure:

$$U_s = (1 - A_1) \times (1 - A_2)$$

This method generalizes to any number of components arranged in parallel, so that the availability of any N components is equal to one minus the product of their unavailabilities:

$$A_s = 1 - \prod_{1}^{N} (1 - A_i)$$

18 Brace yourself. We're going in.

When all A_i are equal, then this can be simplified to:

$$A_s = 1 - (1 - A_i)^N$$

So what about our example? Well, with two components, each with a 99% availability, we get the following:[19]

$$A_s = 1 - (1 - 0.99)^2 = 0.9999$$

99.99%. Four nines. That's an improvement of two orders of magnitude, which isn't half bad. But what if we added a third replica? Extending this out a little, we get some interesting results, summarized in the following table:

Components	Availability	Downtime per year	Downtime per month
One component	99% ("2-nines")	3.65 days	7.31 hours
Two parallel components	99.99% ("4-nines")	52.60 minutes	4.38 minutes
Three parallel components	99.9999% ("6-nines")	31.56 seconds	2.63 seconds

Incredibly, three parallel instances, each of which isn't exactly awesome on its own, can provide a very impressive 6-nines of availability! This is why cloud providers advise customers to deploy their applications with three replicas.

But what if the components are arranged serially, like a load balancer in front of our components? This might look something like the following:

In this kind of arrangement, if either component is unavailable, the entire system is unavailable. Its availability is the product of the availabilities of its components:

$$A_s = \prod_1^N A_i$$

When all A_i are equal, then this can be simplified to:

$$A_s = A^N$$

---

19 This assumes that the failure rates of the components are absolutely independent, which is very unlikely in the real world. Treat as you would spherical cows in a vacuum.

So what if we slapped a dodgy load balancer instance in front of our fancy 99.9999% available set of service replicas? As it turns out, the result isn't so good:

0.99 × 0.999999 = 0.98999901

That's even lower than the load balancer by itself! This is important, because as it turns out:

The total reliability of a sequential system cannot be higher than the reliability of any one of its sequences of subsystems.

Autoscaling

Very often, the amount of load that a service is subjected to varies over time. The textbook example is the user-facing web service where load increases during the day and decreases at night. If such a service is built to handle the peak load, it's wasting time and money at night. If it's built only to handle the nighttime load, it will be overburdened in the daytime.

Autoscaling is a technique that builds on the idea of load balancing by automatically adding or removing resources—be they cloud server instances or Kubernetes pods—to dynamically adjust capacity to meet current demand. This ensures that your service can meet a variety of traffic patterns, anticipated or otherwise.

As an added bonus, applying autoscaling to your cluster can save money by rightsizing resources according to service requirements.

All major cloud providers provide a mechanism for scaling server instances, and most of their managed services implicitly or explicitly support autoscaling. Container orchestration platforms like Kubernetes also include support for autoscaling, both for the number of pods (horizontal autoscaling) and their CPU and memory limits (vertical autoscaling).

Autoscaling mechanics vary considerably between cloud providers and orchestration platforms, so a detailed discussion of how to gather metrics and configure things like predictive autoscaling is beyond the scope of this book. However, some key points to remember:

- Set reasonable maximums, so that unusually large spikes in demand (or, heaven forbid, cascade failures) don't completely blow your budget. The throttling and load shedding techniques that we discussed in "Preventing Overload" on page 270 are also useful here.

- Minimize startup times. If you're using server instances, bake machine images beforehand to minimize configuration time at startup. This is less of an issue on Kubernetes, but container images should still be kept small and startup times reasonably short.

- No matter how fast your startup, scaling takes a nonzero amount of time. Your service should have *some* wiggle room without having to scale.

- As we discussed in "Scaling Postponed: Efficiency" on page 197, the best kind of scaling is the kind that never needs to happen.

Healthy Health Checks

In "Service Redundancy" on page 290, we briefly discussed the value of redundancy—the duplication of critical components or functions of a system with the intention of increasing overall system reliability—and its value for improving the resilience of a system.

Multiple service instances means having a load-balancing mechanism—a service mesh or dedicated load balancer—but what happens when a service instance goes bad? Certainly, we don't want the load balancer to continue sending traffic its way. So what do we do?

Enter the *health check*. In its simplest and most common form, a health check is implemented as an API endpoint that clients—load balancers, as well as monitoring services, service registries, etc.—can use to ask a service instance if it's alive and healthy.

For example, a service might provide an HTTP endpoint (`/health` and `/healthz` are common naming choices) that returns a `200 OK` if the replica is healthy, and a `503 Service Unavailable` when it's not. More sophisticated implementations can even return different status codes for different states: HashiCorp's Consul service registry interprets any 2XX status as a success, a `429 Too Many Requests` as a warning, and anything else as a failure.

Having an endpoint that can tell a client when a service instance is healthy (or not) sounds great and all, but it invites the question of what, exactly, does it mean for an instance to be "healthy"?

Health checks are like bloom filters. A failing health check means a service isn't up, but a health check passing means the service is *probably* "healthy." (Credit: Cindy Sridharan[20])

What Does It Mean for an Instance to Be "Healthy"?

We use the word "healthy" in the context of services and service instances, but what exactly do we mean when we say that? Well, as is so often the case, there's a simple answer and a complex answer. Probably a lot of answers in between, too.

We'll start with the simple answer. Reusing an existing definition, an instance is considered "healthy" when it's "available." That is, when it's able to provide correct service.

Unfortunately, it isn't always so clear cut. What if the instance itself is functioning as intended, but a downstream dependency is malfunctioning? Should a health check even make that distinction? If so, should the load balancer behave differently in each case? Should an instance be reaped and replaced if it's not the one at fault, particularly if all service replicas are affected?

Unfortunately, there aren't any easy answers to these questions, so instead of answers, I'll offer the next best thing: a discussion of the three most common approaches to health checking and their associated advantages and disadvantages. Your own implementations will depend on the needs of your service and your load-balancing behavior.

The Three Types of Health Checks

When a service instance fails, it's usually because of one of the following:

- A local failure like an application error or resource—CPU, memory, database connections, etc.—depletion.
- A remote failure in some dependency—a database or other downstream service —that affects the functioning of the service.

These two broad categories of failures give rise to three (yes, three) health checking strategies, each with its own fun little pros and cons.

Liveness checks do little more than return a "success" signal. They make no additional attempt to determine the status of the service, and say nothing about the service

---

20 Sridharan, Cindy (@copyconstruct). "Health checks are like bloom filters…" 5 Aug 2018, 3:21 AM. Tweet. *https://oreil.ly/Qpw3d.*

except that it's listening and reachable. But, then again, sometimes this is enough. We'll talk more about liveness checks in "Liveness checks" on page 296.

Shallow health checks go further than liveness checks by verifying that the service instance is likely to be able to function. These health checks only test local resources, so they're unlikely to fail on many instances simultaneously, but they can't say for certain whether a particular request service instance will be successful. We'll wade into shallow health checks in "Shallow health checks" on page 297.

Deep health checks provide a much better understanding of instance health, since they actually inspect the ability of a service instance to perform its function, which also exercises downstream resources like databases. While thorough, they can be expensive, and are susceptible to false positives. We'll dig into deep health checks in "Deep health checks" on page 298.

Liveness checks

A liveness endpoint always returns a "success" value, no matter what. While this might seem trivial to the point of uselessness—after all, what is the value of a health check that doesn't say anything about health—liveness probes actually can provide some useful information by confirming:

- That the service instance is listening and accepting new connections on the expected port
- That the instance is reachable over the network
- That any firewall, security group, or other configurations are correctly defined

This simplicity comes with a predictable cost, of course. The absence of any active health checking logic makes liveness checks of limited use when it comes to evaluating whether a service instance can actually perform its function.

Liveness probes are also dead easy to implement. Using the `net/http` package, we can do the following:

```
func healthLivenessHandler(w http.ResponseWriter, r *http.Request) {
    w.WriteHeader(http.StatusOK)
    w.Write([]byte("OK"))
})

func main() {
    r := mux.NewRouter()
    http.HandleFunc("/healthz", healthLivenessHandler)
    log.Fatal(http.ListenAndServe(":8080", r))
}
```

The previous snippet shows how little work can go into a liveness check. In it, we create and register a /healthz endpoint that does nothing but return a 200 OK (and the text OK, just to be thorough).

 If you're using the gorilla/mux package, any registered middleware (like the load shedding function from "Load shedding" on page 274) can affect your health checks!

Shallow health checks

Shallow health checks go further than liveness checks by verifying that the service instance is *likely* to be able to function, but stop short of investigating in any way that might exercise a database or other downstream dependency.

Shallow health checks can evaluate any number of conditions that could adversely affect the service, including (but certainly not limited to):

- The availability of key local resources (memory, CPU, database connections)
- The ability to read or write local data, which checks disk space, permissions, and for hardware malfunctions such as disk failure
- The presence of support processes, like monitoring or updater processes

Shallow health checks are more definitive than liveness checks, and their specificity means that any failures are unlikely to affect the entire fleet at once.[21] However, shallow checks are prone to false positives: if your service is down because of some issue involving an external resource, a shallow check will miss it. What you gain in specificity, you also sacrifice in sensitivity.

A shallow health check might look something like the following example, which tests the service's ability to read and write to and from local disk:

```
func healthShallowHandler(w http.ResponseWriter, r *http.Request) {
    // Create our test file.
    // This will create a filename like /tmp/shallow-123456
    tmpFile, err := ioutil.TempFile(os.TempDir(), "shallow-")
    if err != nil {
        http.Error(w, err.Error(), http.StatusServiceUnavailable)
        return
    }
    defer os.Remove(tmpFile.Name())

    // Make sure that we can write to the file.
```

---

21 Though I've seen it happen.

```
    text := []byte("Check.")
    if _, err = tmpFile.Write(text); err != nil {
        http.Error(w, err.Error(), http.StatusServiceUnavailable)
        return
    }

    // Make sure that we can close the file.
    if err := tmpFile.Close(); err != nil {
        http.Error(w, err.Error(), http.StatusServiceUnavailable)
        return
    }

    w.WriteHeader(http.StatusOK)
}

func main() {
    r := mux.NewRouter()
    http.HandleFunc("/healthz", healthShallowHandler)
    log.Fatal(http.ListenAndServe(":8080", r))
}
```

This simultaneously checks for available disk space, write permissions, and malfunctioning hardware, which can be a very useful thing to test, particularly if the service needs to write to an on-disk cache or other transient files.

An observant reader might notice that it writes to the default directory to use for temporary files. On Linux, this is /tmp, which is actually a RAM drive. This might be a useful thing to test as well, but if you want to test for the ability to write to disk on Linux you'll need to specify a different directory, or this becomes a very different test.

Deep health checks

Deep health checks directly inspect the ability of a service to interact with its adjacent systems. This provides much better understanding of instance health by potentially identifying issues with dependencies, like invalid credentials, the loss of connectivity to data stores, or other unexpected networking issues.

However, while thorough, deep health checks can be quite expensive. They can take a long time and place a burden on dependencies, particularly if you're running too many of them, or running them too often.

 Don't try to test *every* dependency in your health checks: focus on the ones that are required for the service to operate.

When testing multiple downstream dependencies, evaluate them concurrently if possible.

What's more, because the failure of a dependency will be reported as a failure of the instance, deep checks are especially susceptible to false positives. Combined with the lower specificity compared to a shallow check—issues with dependencies will be felt by the entire fleet—and you have the potential for a cascading failure.

If you're using deep health checks, you should take advantage of strategies like circuit breaking (which we covered in "Circuit Breaking" on page 280) where you can, and your load balancer should "fail open" (which we'll discuss in "Failing Open" on page 300) whenever possible.

Here we have a trivial example of a possible deep health check that evaluates a database by calling a hypothetical service's `GetUser` function:

```
func healthDeepHandler(w http.ResponseWriter, r *http.Request) {
    // Retrieve the context from the request and add a 5-second timeout
    ctx, cancel := context.WithTimeout(r.Context(), 5*time.Second)
    defer cancel()

    // service.GetUser is a hypothetical method on a service interface
    // that executes a database query
    if err := service.GetUser(ctx, 0); err != nil {
        http.Error(w, err.Error(), http.StatusServiceUnavailable)
        return
    }

    w.WriteHeader(http.StatusOK)
}

func main() {
    r := mux.NewRouter()
    http.HandleFunc("/healthz", healthDeepHandler)
    log.Fatal(http.ListenAndServe(":8080", r))
}
```

Ideally, a dependency test should execute an actual system function, but also be lightweight to the greatest reasonable degree. In this example, the `GetUser` function triggers a database query that satisfies both of these criteria.[22]

"Real" queries are generally preferable to just pinging the database for two reasons. First, they're a more representative test of what the service is doing. Second, they

---

22 It's an imaginary function, so let's just agree that that's true.

allow the leveraging of end-to-end query time as a measure of database health. The previous example actually does this—albeit in a very binary fashion—by using `Context` to set a hard timeout value, but you could choose to include more sophisticated logic instead.

Failing Open

What if all of your instances simultaneously decide that they're unhealthy? If you're using deep health checks, this can actually happen quite easily (and, perhaps, regularly). Depending on how your load balancer is configured, you might find yourself with zero instances serving traffic, possibly causing failures rippling across your system.

Fortunately, some load balancers handle this quite cleverly by "failing open." If a load balancer that fails open has *no* healthy targets—that is, if *all* of its targets' health checks are failing—it will route traffic to all of its targets.

This is slightly counterintuitive behavior, but it makes deep health checks somewhat safer to use by allowing traffic to continue to flow even when a downstream dependency may be having a bad day.

Summary

This was an interesting chapter to write. There's quite a lot to say about resilience, and so much crucial supporting operational background. I had to make some tough calls about what would make it in and what wouldn't. At about 37 pages, this chapter still turned out a fair bit longer than I intended, but I'm quite satisfied with the outcome. It's a reasonable compromise between too little information and too much, and between operational background and actual Go implementations.

We reviewed what it means for a system to fail, and how complex systems fail (that is, one component at a time). This led naturally to discussing a particularly nefarious, yet common, failure mode: cascading failures. In a cascade failure, a system's own attempts to recover hasten its collapse. We covered common measures of preventing cascading failures on the server side: throttling and load shedding.

Retries in the face of errors can contribute a lot to a service's resilience, but as we saw in the DynamoDB case study, can also contribute to cascade failures when applied naively. We dug deep into measures that can be taken on the client side as well, including circuit breakers, timeouts, and especially exponential backoff algorithms. There were several pretty graphs involved. I spent a lot of time on the graphs.

All of this led to conversations about service redundancy, how it affects reliability (with a little math thrown in, for fun), and when and how to best leverage autoscaling.

Of course, you can't talk about autoscaling without talking about resource "health." We asked (and did our best to answer) what it means for an instance to be "healthy," and how that translated into health checks. We covered the three kinds of health checks and weighed their pros and cons, paying particular attention to their relative sensitivity/specificity tradeoffs.

In Chapter 10 we'll take a break from the operational topics for a bit and wade into the subject of manageability: the art and science of changing the tires on a moving car.

CHAPTER 10
Manageability

> Everyone knows that debugging is twice as hard as writing a program in the first place. So if you're as clever as you can be when you write it, how will you ever debug it?[1]
>
> —Brian Kernighan, *The Elements of Programming Style (1978)*

In a perfect world, you'd never have to deploy a new version of your service or (heaven forbid!) shut down your entire system to fix or modify it to meet new requirements.

Then again, in a perfect world, unicorns would exist and four out of five dentists would recommend we eat pie for breakfast.[2]

Clearly, we don't live in a perfect world. But while unicorns might never exist,[3] you don't have to resign yourself to a world where you have to update your code whenever you need to alter your system's behavior.

While you'll probably always have to make code changes to update core logic, it is possible to build your systems so that you—or, critically, somebody else—can change a surprising variety of behaviors without having to recode and redeploy.

You may recall that we introduced this important attribute of cloud native systems back in "Manageability" on page 10, where we defined it as the ease with which a system's behavior can be modified to keep it secure, running smoothly, and compliant with changing requirements.

---

1 Kernighan, Brian W., and P. J. Plauger. *The Elements of Programming Style.* McGraw-Hill, 1978.

2 Staff, America's Test Kitchen. *Perfect Pie: Your Ultimate Guide to Classic and Modern Pies, Tarts, Galettes, and More.* America's Test Kitchen, 2019. *https://oreil.ly/rl5TP.*

3 They're doing some pretty amazing things with genetic engineering. Don't stop believing.

While this sounds straightforward, there's actually quite a bit more to manageability than you might think. It goes far beyond configuration files (though that's certainly part of it). In this chapter, we'll discuss what it means to have a manageable system, and we'll cover some of the techniques and implementations that can allow you to build a system that can change *almost* as quickly as its requirements.

Manageability Is Not Maintainability

It can be said that manageability and maintainability have some "mission overlap" in that they're both concerned with the ease with which a system can be modified. But where they differ somewhat is exactly *how* the system is modified:

- *Manageability* describes the ease with which changes can be made to the behavior of a system, typically without having to resort to changing its code. In other words, it's how easy it is to change to a system *from the outside*.
- *Maintainability* describes the ease with which a software system or component can be modified to change or add capabilities, correct faults or defects, or improve performance,[4] usually by making changes to the code. In other words, it's how easy it is to change a system *from the inside*.

What Is Manageability and Why Should I Care?

When considering manageability, it's common to think in terms of a single service. Can my service be configured easily? Does it have all the knobs and dials that it might need?

However, this misses the larger point by focusing on the component at the expense of the system. Manageability doesn't end at the service boundary. For a system to be manageable, the entire system has to be considered.

Take a moment to reconsider manageability with a complex system in mind. Can its behavior be easily modified? Can its components be modified independently of one another? Can they be easily replaced, if necessary? How do we know when that is?

Manageability encompasses all possible dimensions of a system's behavior. Its functions can be said to fall into four broad categories:[5]

---

4 "Systems and Software Engineering: Vocabulary." ISO/IEC/IEEE 24765:2010(E), 15 Dec. 2010. *https://oreil.ly/NInvC*.

5 Radle, Byron, et al. "What Is Manageability?" *NI*, National Instruments, 5 Mar. 2019. *https://oreil.ly/U3d7Q*.

Configuration and control

It's important that setting up and configuring a system—and each of its components—should be easily configurable for optimal availability and performance. Some systems need regular or real-time control, so having the right "knobs and levers" is absolutely fundamental. This is where we'll focus most of our attention in this chapter.

Monitoring, logging, and alerting

These functions keep track of the system's ability to do its job, and are critical to effective system management. After all, without them, how would we know when our system requires management? As vital as these features are to manageability, we won't discuss them in this chapter. Instead, they get an entire chapter of their own in Chapter 11, *Observability*.

Deployment and updates

Even in the absence of code changes, the ability to easily deploy, update, roll back, and scale system components is valuable, especially when there are many systems to manage. Obviously, this is useful during the initial deployment, but it comes into effect throughout a system's lifetime any time it has to be updated. Fortunately, its lack of external runtimes and singular executable artifacts make this an area in which Go excels.

Service discovery and inventory

A key feature of cloud native systems is their distributed nature. It's critical that components be able to quickly and accurately detect one another, a function called *service discovery*. Since service discovery is an architectural feature rather than a programmatic one, we won't go too deeply into it in this book.

Because this is more of a Go book than it is an architecture book,[6] it focuses largely on service implementations. For that reason only—*not because it's more important*—most of this chapter will similarly focus on service-level configuration. Unfortunately, an in-depth discussion of these is beyond the scope of this book.[7]

Managing complex computing systems is generally difficult and time-consuming, and the costs of managing them can far exceed the costs of the underlying hardware and software. By definition, a system designed to be manageable can be managed more efficiently, and therefore more cheaply. Even if you don't consider management costs, complexity reduction can have a huge impact on the likelihood of human error, making it easier and faster to undo when it inevitably creeps in. In that way,

---

6 Or so I told my editors. Hi, Amelia! Hi, Zan!

7 This makes me sad. These are important topics, but we have to focus.

manageability directly impacts reliability, availability, and security, making it a key ingredient of system dependability.

Configuring Your Application

The most basic function of manageability is the ability to configure an application. In an ideally configurable application, anything that's likely to vary between environments—staging, production, developer environments, etc.—will be cleanly separated from the code and be externally definable in some way.

You may recall that *The Twelve-Factor App*—a set of twelve rules and guidelines for building web applications that we introduced way back in Chapter 6—had quite a bit to say on this subject. In fact, the third of its twelve rules—"III. Configuration" on page 180—was concerned entirely with application configuration, about which it says:

> Store configuration in the environment.

As written, *The Twelve-Factor App* insists that all configurations should be stored in environment variables. There are a plenty of opinions on this, but in the years since its publication the industry seems to have reached a general consensus that what really matters is:

Configuration should be strictly separated from the code
Configuration—anything that's likely to vary between environments—should always be cleanly separated from the code. While configuration can vary substantially across deploys, code does not. Configuration shouldn't be baked into the code. Ever.

Configurations should be stored in version control
Storing configurations in version control—separately from the code—allows you to quickly roll back a configuration change if necessary, and aids system recreation and restoration. Some deployment frameworks, like Kubernetes, make this distinction naturally and relatively seamless by providing configuration primitives like the ConfigMap.

These days, it's still quite common to see applications configured mainly by environment variables, but it's just as common to see command-line flags and configuration files with various formats. Sometimes an application will even support more than one of these options. In the subsequent sections, we'll review some of these methods, their various pros and cons, and how they can be implemented in Go.

Configuration Good Practice

When you're building an application, you have a lot of options in how you define, implement, and deploy your application configurations. However, in my experience, I've found that certain general practices produce better long- and short-term outcomes:

Version control your configurations
> Yes, I'm repeating myself, but this bears repeating. Configuration files should be stored in version control before being deployed to the system. This makes it possible to review them before deployment, to quickly reference them afterwards, and to quickly roll back a change if necessary. It's also helpful if (and when) you need to re-create and restore your system.

Don't roll your own format
> Write your configuration files using a standard format like JSON, YAML, or TOML. We'll cover some of these later in the chapter. If you *must* roll your own format, be sure that you're comfortable with the idea of maintaining it—and forcing any future maintainers to deal with it—forever.

Make the zero value useful
> Don't use nonzero default values unnecessarily. This is actually a good rule in general; there's even a "Go proverb" about it.[8] Whenever possible, the behavior that results from an undefined configuration should be acceptable, reasonable, and unsurprising. A simple, minimal configuration makes errors less likely.

Configuring with Environment Variables

As we discussed in Chapter 6, and reviewed previously, using environment variables to define configuration values is the method advocated for in *The Twelve-Factor App*. There's some merit to this preference: environment variables are universally supported, they ensure that configurations don't get accidentally checked into the code, and using them generally requires less code than using a configuration file. They're also perfectly adequate for small applications.

On the other hand, the process of setting and passing environment variables can be ugly, tedious, and verbose. While some applications support defining environment variables in a file, this largely defeats the purpose of using environment variables in the first place.

The implicit nature of environment variables can introduce some challenges as well. Since you can't easily learn about the existence and behavior of environment

---

8 Pike, Rob. "Go Proverbs." Gopherfest, 18 Nov. 2015, YouTube. *https://oreil.ly/5bOxW*.

variables by looking at an existing configuration file or checking the help output, applications that reply on them can sometimes be harder to use, and errors in them harder to debug.

As with most high-level languages, Go makes environment variables easily accessible. It does this through the standard os package, which provides the os.Getenv function for this purpose:

```
name := os.Getenv("NAME")
place := os.Getenv("CITY")

fmt.Printf("%s lives in %s.\n", name, place)
```

The os.Getenv function retrieves the value of the environment variable named by the key, but if the variable isn't present, it'll return an empty string. If you need to distinguish between an empty value and an unset value, Go also provides the os.LookEnv function, which returns both the value and a bool that's false if the variable isn't set:

```
if val, ok := os.LookupEnv(key); ok {
    fmt.Printf("%s=%s\n", key, val)
} else {
    fmt.Printf("%s not set\n", key)
}
```

This functionality is pretty minimal, but perfectly adequate for many (if not most) purposes. If you're in need of more sophisticated options, like default values or typed variables, there are several excellent third-party packages that provide this functionality. Viper (spf13/viper) (*https://oreil.ly/bS4RY*)—which we'll discuss in "Viper: The Swiss Army Knife of Configuration Packages" on page 329—is particularly popular.

Configuring with Command-Line Arguments

As configuration methods go, command-line arguments are definitely worth considering, at least for smaller, less-complex applications. After all, they're explicit, and details of their existence and usage are usually available via a --help option.

The standard flag package

Go includes the flag package, which is a basic command-line parsing package, in its standard library. While flag isn't particularly feature-rich, it's fairly straightforward to use, and—unlike os.Getenv—supports typing out-of-the-box.

Take, for example, the following program, which uses flag to implement a basic command that reads and outputs the values of command-line flags:

```
package main

import (
    "flag"
```

```
    "fmt"
)

func main() {
    // Declare a string flag with a default value "foo"
    // and a short description. It returns a string pointer.
    strp := flag.String("string", "foo", "a string")

    // Declare number and Boolean flags, similar to the string flag.
    intp := flag.Int("number", 42, "an integer")
    boolp := flag.Bool("boolean", false, "a boolean")

    // Call flag.Parse() to execute command-line parsing.
    flag.Parse()

    // Print the parsed options and trailing positional arguments.
    fmt.Println("string:", *strp)
    fmt.Println("integer:", *intp)
    fmt.Println("boolean:", *boolp)
    fmt.Println("args:", flag.Args())
}
```

As you can see from the previous code, the flag package allows you to register command-line flags with types, default values, and short descriptions, and to map those flags to variables. We can see a summary of these flags by running the program and passing it the -help flag:

```
$ go run . -help
Usage of /var/folders/go-build618108403/exe/main:
  -boolean
        a boolean
  -number int
        an integer (default 42)
  -string string
        a string (default "foo")
```

The help output presents us with a list of all of the available flags. Exercising all of these flags gives us something like the following:

```
$ go run . -boolean -number 27 -string "A string." Other things.
string: A string.
integer: 27
boolean: true
args: [Other things.]
```

It works! However, the flag package seems to have a couple of issues that limit its usefulness.

First, as you may have noticed, the resulting flag syntax seems a little...nonstandard. Many of us have come to expect command-line interfaces to follow the GNU argument standard, (*https://oreil.ly/evqk4*) with long-named options prefixed by two dashes (--version) and short, single-letter equivalents (-v).

Second, all `flag` does is parse flags (though to be fair, it doesn't claim to do any more than that), and while that's nice, it's not as powerful as it could be. It sure would be nice if we could map commands to functions, wouldn't it?

The Cobra command-line parser

The `flags` package is perfectly fine if all you need to do is parse flags, but if you're in the market for something a little more powerful to build your command-line interfaces, you might want to consider the Cobra package (*https://oreil.ly/4oCyH*). Cobra has a number of features that make it a popular choice for building fully featured command-line interfaces. It's used in a number of high-profile projects, including Kubernetes, CockroachDB, Docker, Istio, and Helm.

In addition to providing fully POSIX-compliant flags (short *and* long versions), Cobra also supports nested subcommands, and automatically generates help (--help) output and autocomplete for various shells. It also integrates with Viper, which we'll cover in "Viper: The Swiss Army Knife of Configuration Packages" on page 329.

Cobra's primary downside, as you might imagine, is that it's quite complex relative to the `flags` package. Using Cobra to implement the program from "The standard flag package" on page 308 looks like the following:

```
package main

import (
    "fmt"
    "os"
    "github.com/spf13/cobra"
)

var strp string
var intp int
var boolp bool

var rootCmd = &cobra.Command{
    Use:  "flags",
    Long: "A simple flags experimentation command, built with Cobra.",
    Run:  flagsFunc,
}

func init() {
    rootCmd.Flags().StringVarP(&strp, "string", "s", "foo", "a string")
    rootCmd.Flags().IntVarP(&intp, "number", "n", 42, "an integer")
    rootCmd.Flags().BoolVarP(&boolp, "boolean", "b", false, "a boolean")
}

func flagsFunc(cmd *cobra.Command, args []string) {
    fmt.Println("string:", strp)
    fmt.Println("integer:", intp)
    fmt.Println("boolean:", boolp)
```

```
        fmt.Println("args:", args)
}

func main() {
    if err := rootCmd.Execute(); err != nil {
        fmt.Println(err)
        os.Exit(1)
    }
}
```

In contrast to the `flags`-package version, which basically just reads some flags and prints the results, the Cobra program has a bit more complexity, with several distinct parts.

First, we declare the target variables with package scope, rather than locally within a function. This is necessary because they have to be accessible to both the `init` function and the function that implements the command logic proper.

Next, we create a `cobra.Command` struct, `rootCmd`, that represents the *root command*. A separate `cobra.Command` instance is used to represent every command and sub-command that the CLI makes available. The `Use` field spells out the command's one-line usage message and `Long` is the long message displayed in the help output. `Run` is a function of type `func(cmd *Command, args []string)` that implements the actual work to be done when the command is executed.

Typically, commands are constructed in an `init` function. In our case, we add three flags—`string`, `number`, and `boolean`—to our root command along with their short flags, default values, and descriptions.

Every command gets an automatically generated help output, which we can retrieve using the `--help` flag:

```
$ go run . --help
A simple flags experimentation command, built with Cobra.

Usage:
  flags [flags]

Flags:
  -b, --boolean         a boolean
  -h, --help            help for flags
  -n, --number int      an integer (default 42)
  -s, --string string   a string (default "foo")
```

This makes sense, and it's also pretty! But does it run as we expect? Executing the command (using the standard flags style), gives us the following output:

```
$ go run . --boolean --number 27 --string "A string." Other things.
string: A string.
integer: 27
```

```
boolean: true
args: [Other things.]
```

The outputs are identical; we have achieved parity. But this is just a single command. One of the benefits of Cobra is that it also allows *subcommands*.

What does this mean? Take, for example, the git command. In this example, git would be the root command. By itself, it doesn't do much, but it has a series of sub-commands—git clone, git init, git blame, etc.—that are related but are each distinct operations of their own.

Cobra provides this capability by treating commands as a tree structure. Each command and subcommand (including the root command) are represented by a distinct cobra.Command value. These are attached to one another using the (c *Command) Add Command(cmds ...*Command) function. We demonstrate this in the following example by turning the flags command into a subcommand of a new root, which we call cng (for *Cloud Native Go*).

To do this, we first have to rename the original rootCmd to flagsCmd. We add a Short attribute to define its short description in help output, but it's otherwise identical. But now we need a new root command, so we create that as well:

```
var flagsCmd = &cobra.Command{
    Use:   "flags",
    Short: "Experiment with flags",
    Long:  "A simple flags experimentation command, built with Cobra.",
    Run:   flagsFunc,
}

var rootCmd = &cobra.Command{
    Use:   "cng",
    Long: "A super simple command.",
}
```

Now we have two commands: the root command, cng, and a single subcommand, flags. The next step is to add the flags subcommand to the root command so that it's immediately beneath the root in the command tree. This is typically done in an init function, which we demonstrate here:

```
func init() {
    flagsCmd.Flags().StringVarP(&strp, "string", "s", "foo", "a string")
    flagsCmd.Flags().IntVarP(&intp, "number", "n", 42, "an integer")
    flagsCmd.Flags().BoolVarP(&boolp, "boolean", "b", false, "a boolean")

    rootCmd.AddCommand(flagsCmd)
}
```

In the preceding init function, we keep the three Flags methods, except we now call them on flagsCmd.

What's new, however, is the AddCommand method, which allows us to add flagsCmd to rootCmd as a subcommand. We can repeat AddCommand as many times as we like with multiple Command values, adding as many subcommands (or sub-subcommands, or sub-sub-subcommands) as we want.

Now that we've told Cobra about the new flags subcommand, its information is reflected in the generated help output:

```
$ go run . --help
A super simple command.

Usage:
  cng [command]

Available Commands:
  flags       Experiment with flags
  help        Help about any command

Flags:
  -h, --help   help for cng

Use "cng [command] --help" for more information about a command.
```

Now, according to this help output, we have a top-level root command named cng that has *two* available subcommands: our flags command, and an automatically-generated help subcommand that lets a user view any subcommand's help. For example, help flags provides us with information and instructions for the flags subcommand:

```
$ go run . help flags
A simple flags experimentation command, built with Cobra.

Usage:
  cng flags [flags]

Flags:
  -b, --boolean          a boolean
  -h, --help             help for flags
  -n, --number int       an integer (default 42)
  -s, --string string    a string (default "foo")
```

Kind of neat, huh?

This is a tiny, tiny sample of what the Cobra library is capable of, but it's more than sufficient to let us to build a robust set of configuration options. If you're interested in learning more about Cobra and how you can use it to build powerful command-line interfaces, take a look at its GitHub repository (*https://oreil.ly/oy7EN*) and its listing on GoDoc (*https://oreil.ly/JOeoJ*).

Configuring with Files

Last but not least, we have what is probably the most commonly used configuration option: the configuration file.

Configuration files have a lot of advantages over environment variables, particularly for more complex applications. They tend to be more explicit and comprehensible by allowing behaviors to be logically grouped and annotated. Often, understanding how to use a configuration file is just a matter of looking at its structure or an example of its use.

Configuration files are particularly useful when managing a large number of options, which is an advantage they have over both environment variables and command-line flags. Command-line flags in particular can sometimes result in some pretty long statements that can be tedious and difficult to construct.

Files aren't the perfect solution though. Depending on your environment, distributing them at scale in a way that maintains parity across a cluster can be a challenge. This situation can be improved by having a single "source of truth," such as a distributed key/value store like etcd or HashiCorp Consul, or a central source code repository from which the deployment automatically draws its configuration, but this adds complexity and a dependency on another resource.

Fortunately, most orchestration platforms provide specialized configuration resources—such as Kubernetes' `ConfigMap` object—that largely alleviate the distribution problem.

There are probably dozens of file formats that have been used for configuration over the years, but in recent years, two in particular have stood out: JSON and YAML. In the next few sections, we'll go into each of these—and how to use them in Go—in a little more detail

Our configuration data structure

Before we proceed with a discussion of file formats and how to decode them, we should discuss the two general ways in which configurations can be unmarshalled:

- Configuration keys and values can be mapped to corresponding fields in a specific struct type. For example, a configuration that contains the attribute `host: localhost`, could be unmarshalled into a struct type that has a `Host string` field.

- Configuration data can be decoded and unmarshalled into one or more, possibly nested, maps of type `map[string]interface{}`. This can be convenient when you're working with arbitrary configurations, but it's awkward to work with.

If you know what your configuration is likely to look like in advance (which you generally do), then the first approach to decoding configurations, mapping them to a data structure created for that purpose, is by far the easiest. Although it's possible to decode and do useful work with arbitrary configuration schemas, doing so can be very tedious and isn't advisable for most configuration purposes.

So, for the remainder of this section, our example configurations will correspond to the following `Config` struct:

```
type Config struct {
    Host string
    Port uint16
    Tags map[string]string
}
```

 For a struct field to be marshallable or unmarshallable by *any* encoding package, it *must* begin with a capital letter to indicate that it's exported by its package.

For each of our examples we'll start with the `Config` struct, occasionally enhancing it with format-specific tags or other decorations.

Working with JSON

JSON (JavaScript Object Notation) was invented in the early 2000s, growing out of the need for a modern data interchange format to replace XML and other formats in use at the time. It's based on a subset of the JavaScript scripting language, making it both relatively human-readable and efficient for machines to generate and parse, while also offering the semantics for lists and mappings that were absent from XML.

As common and successful as JSON is, it does have some drawbacks. It's generally considered less user-friendly than YAML. Its syntax is especially unforgiving and can be easily broken by a misplaced (or missing) comma, and it doesn't even support comments.

However, of the formats presented in this chapter, it's the only one that's supported in Go's standard library.

What follows is a very brief introduction into encoding and decoding data to and from JSON. For a somewhat more thorough review, take a look at Andrew Gerrand's "JSON and Go" on *The Go Blog* (*https://oreil.ly/6Uvl2*).

Encoding JSON. The first step to understanding how to decode JSON (or any configuration format) is understanding how to *encode* it. This may seem strange, particularly in a section about reading configuration files, but encoding is important to the general subject of JSON encoding, and provides a handy means of generating, testing, and debugging your configuration files.[9]

JSON encoding and decoding is supported by Go's standard encoding/json package, which provides a variety of helper functions useful for encoding, decoding, formatting, validating, and otherwise working with JSON.

Among these is the json.Marshal function, which accepts an interface{} value v, and returns a []byte array containing a JSON-encoded representation of v:

```
func Marshal(v interface{}) ([]byte, error)
```

In other words, a value goes in, and JSON comes out.

This function really is as straightforward to use as it looks. For example, if we have an instance of Config, we can pass it to json.Marshal to get its JSON encoding:

```
c := Config{
    Host: "localhost",
    Port: 1313,
    Tags: map[string]string{"env": "dev"},
}

bytes, err := json.Marshal(c)

fmt.Println(string(bytes))
```

If everything works as expected, err will be nil, and bytes will be a []byte value containing the JSON. The fmt.Println output will look something like the following:

```
{"Host":"localhost","Port":1313,"Tags":{"env":"dev"}}
```

 The json.Marshal function traverses the value of v recursively, so any internal structs will be encoded as well as nested JSON.

That was pretty painless, but if we're generating a configuration file it sure would be nice if the text was formatted for human consumption. Fortunately, encoding/json

---

9 Neat trick, huh?

also provides the following `json.MarshalIndent` function, which returns "pretty-printed" JSON:

```
func MarshalIndent(v interface{}, prefix, indent string) ([]byte, error)
```

As you can see, `json.MarshalIndent` works a lot like `json.Marshal`, except that also takes `prefix` and `indent` strings, as demonstrated here:

```
bytes, err := json.MarshalIndent(c, "", "   ")
fmt.Println(string(bytes))
```

The preceding snippet prints exactly what we'd hope to see:

```
{
    "Host": "localhost",
    "Port": 1313,
    "Tags": {
        "env": "dev"
    }
}
```

The result is prettily printed JSON, formatted for humans like you and me[10] to read. This is a very useful method for bootstrapping configuration files!

Decoding JSON.   Now that we know how to encode a data structure into JSON, let's take a look at how to decode JSON as an existing data structure.

To do that, we use the conveniently named `json.Unmarshal` function:

```
func Unmarshal(data []byte, v interface{}) error
```

The `json.Unmarshal` function parses the JSON-encoded text contained in the `data` array and stores the result in the value pointed to by v. Importantly, if v is `nil` or isn't a pointer, `json.Unmarshal` returns an error.

But, what type should v be, exactly? Ideally, it would be a pointer to a data structure whose fields exactly correspond to the JSON structure. While it's possible to unmarshal arbitrary JSON into an unstructured map, as we'll discuss in "Decoding Arbitrary JSON" on page 318, this really should only be done if you really don't have any other choice.

As we'll see, though, if you have a data type that reflects your JSON's structure, then `json.Unmarshal` is able to update it directly. To do this, we first have to create an instance where our decoded data will be stored:

```
c := Config{}
```

---

10 Well, like you.

Now that we have our storage value, we can call `json.Unmarshal`, to which we pass a `[]byte` that contains our JSON data and a pointer to c:

```
bytes := []byte(`{"Host":"127.0.0.1","Port":1234,"Tags":{"foo":"bar"}}`)
err := json.Unmarshal(bytes, &c)
```

If `bytes` contains valid JSON, then `err` will be `nil` and the data from `bytes` will be stored in the struct c. Printing the value of c should now provide output like the following:

```
{127.0.0.1 1234 map[foo:bar]}
```

Neat! But what happens when the structure of the JSON doesn't exactly match the Go type? Let's find out:

```
c := Config{}
bytes := []byte(`{"Host":"127.0.0.1", "Food":"Pizza"}`)
err := json.Unmarshal(bytes, &c)
```

Interestingly, this snippet doesn't produce an error as you might expect. Instead, c now contains the following values:

```
{127.0.0.1 0 map[]}
```

It would seem that the value of `Host` was set, but `Food`, which has no corresponding value in the `Config` struct, was ignored. As it turns out, `json.Unmarshal` will only decode the fields that it can find in the target type. This behavior can actually be quite useful if you want to cherry pick a few specific fields out of a big JSON blob.

Decoding Arbitrary JSON

As we briefly mentioned in "Our configuration data structure" on page 314, it's *possible* to decode and do useful work with arbitrary JSON, but doing so can be pretty tedious and should only be done if you don't know the structure of your JSON beforehand.

Take, for example, this entirely arbitrary JSON data:

```
bytes := []byte(`{"Foo":"Bar", "Number":1313, "Tags":{"A":"B"}}`)
```

Without knowing this data's structure ahead of time, we can actually use `json.Unmarshal` to decode it into an `interface{}` value:

```
var f interface{}
err := json.Unmarshal(bytes, &f)
```

Outputting the new value of f with `fmt.Println` yields an interesting result:

```
map[Number:1313 Foo:Bar Tags:map[A:B]]
```

It would seem that the underlying value of f is now a map whose keys are strings and values are stored as empty interfaces. It's functionally identical to a value defined as:

```
f := map[string]interface{}{
    "Foo":    "Bar",
    "Number":  1313,
    "Tags": map[string]interface{}{"A": "B"},
}
```

But even though its underlying value is a map[string]interface{}, f still has a type of interface{}. We'll need to use a type assertion to access its values:

```
m := f.(map[string]interface{})

fmt.Printf("<%T> %v\n", m, m)
fmt.Printf("<%T> %v\n", m["Foo"], m["Foo"])
fmt.Printf("<%T> %v\n", m["Number"], m["Number"])
fmt.Printf("<%T> %v\n", m["Tags"], m["Tags"])
```

Executing the previous snippet produces the following output:

```
<map[string]interface {}> map[Number:1313 Foo:Bar Tags:map[A:B]]
<string> Bar
<float64> 1313
<map[string]interface {}> map[A:B]
```

Field formatting with struct field tags. Under the covers, marshalling works by using reflection to examine a value and generate appropriate JSON for its type. For structs, the struct's field names are directly used as the default JSON keys, and the struct's field values become the JSON values. Unmarshalling works essentially the same way, except in reverse.

What happens when you marshal a zero-value struct? Well, as it turns out, when you marshal a Config{} value, for example, this is the JSON you get:

```
{"Host":"","Port":0,"Tags":null}
```

This isn't all that pretty. Or efficient. Is it really necessary to even output the empty values at all?

Similarly, struct fields have to be exported—and therefore capitalized—to be written or read. Does that mean that we're stuck with uppercase field names?

Fortunately, the answer to both questions is "no."

Go supports the use of *struct field tags*—short strings that appear in a struct after the type declaration of a field—that allow metadata to be added to specific struct fields. Field tags are most commonly used by encoding packages to modify encoding and decoding behavior at the field level.

Go struct field tags are special strings containing one or more keys/values pairs enclosed in backticks, after a field's type declaration:

```
type User struct {
    Name string `example:"name"`
}
```

In this example, the struct's Name field is tagged with `example:"name"`. These tags can be accessed using run-time reflection via the `reflect` package, but their most common use case is to provide encoding and decoding directives.

The `encoding/json` package supports several such tags. The general format uses the `json` key in the struct field's tag, and a value that specifies the name of the field, possibly followed by a comma-separated list of options. The name may be empty in order to specify options without overriding the default field name.

The available options supported by `encoding/json` are shown here:

Customizing JSON keys
> By default, a struct field will case-sensitively map to a JSON key of the exact same name. A tag overrides this default name by setting the first (or only) value in the tag's options list.
>
> Example: `CustomKey string `json:"custom_key"``

Omitting empty values
> By default, a field will always appear in the JSON, even if it's empty. Using the `omitempty` option will cause fields to be skipped if they contain a zero-value. Note the leading comma in front of `omitempty`!
>
> Example: `OmitEmpty string `json:",omitempty"``

Ignoring a field
> Fields using the - (dash) option always will be completely ignored during encoding and decoding.
>
> Example: `IgnoredName string `json:"-"``

A struct that uses all of the previous tags might look like the following:

```
type Tagged struct {
    // CustomKey will appear in JSON as the key "custom_key".
    CustomKey   string `json:"custom_key"`

    // OmitEmpty will appear in JSON as "OmitEmpty" (the default),
    // but will only be written if it contains a nonzero value.
    OmitEmpty   string `json:",omitempty"`

    // IgnoredName will always be ignored.
    IgnoredName string `json:"-"`

    // TwoThings will appear in JSON as the key "two_things",
    // but only if it isn't empty.
```

```
    TwoThings   string `json:"two_things,omitempty"`
}
```

For more information on how how `json.Marshal` encodes data, take a look at the function's documentation on golang.org (*https://oreil.ly/5QeJ4*).

Working with YAML

YAML (YAML Ain't Markup Language[11]) is an extensible file format that's popular with projects like Kubernetes that depend on complex, hierarchical configurations. It's highly expressive, though its syntax can also be a bit brittle, and configurations that use it can start to suffer from readability issues as they scale up.

Unlike JSON, which was originally created as a data interchange format, YAML is largely a configuration language at heart. Interestingly, however, YAML 1.2 is a superset of JSON, and the two formats are largely inter-convertible. YAML does have some advantages over JSON though: it can self-reference, it allows embedded block literals, and it supports comments and complex data types.

Unlike JSON, YAML isn't supported in Go's core libraries. While there are a few YAML packages to choose from, the standard choice is Go-YAML (*https://oreil.ly/yhERJ*). Version 1 of Go-YAML started in 2014 as an internal project within Canonical to port the well-known `libyaml` C library to Go. As a project, it's exceptionally mature and well maintained. Its syntax is also conveniently very similar to `encoding/json`.

Encoding YAML. Using Go-YAML to encode data is a *lot* like encoding JSON. Exactly like it. In fact, the signatures for both packages' `Marshal` functions are identical. Like its `encoding/json` equivalent, Go-YAML's `yaml.Marshal` function also accepts an `interface{}` value, and returns its YAML encoding as a `[]byte` value:

```
func Marshal(v interface{}) ([]byte, error)
```

Just as we did in "Encoding JSON" on page 316, we demonstrate its use by creating an instance of `Config`, which we pass to `yaml.Marshal` to get its YAML encoding:

```
c := Config{
    Host: "localhost",
    Port: 1313,
    Tags: map[string]string{"env": "dev"},
}

bytes, err := yaml.Marshal(c)
```

---

11 Seriously, that really is what it stands for.

Once again, if everything works as expected, err will be nil and bytes will be a []byte value containing the YAML. Printing the string value of bytes will provide something like the following:

```
host: localhost
port: 1313
tags:
  env: dev
```

Also, just like the version provided by encoding/json, Go-YAML's Marshal function traverses the value v recursively. Any composite types that it finds—arrays, slices, maps, and structs—will be encoded appropriately and will be present in the output as nested YAML elements.

Decoding YAML. In keeping with the theme we've established with the similarity of the Marshal functions from encoding/json and Go-YAML, the same consistency is evident between the two packages' Unmarshal functions:

```
func Unmarshal(data []byte, v interface{}) error
```

Again, the yaml.Unmarshal function parses the YAML-encoded data in the data array and stores the result in the value pointed to by v. If v is nil or not a pointer, yaml.Unmarshal returns an error. As shown here, the similarities are very clear:

```
// Caution: Indent this YAML with spaces, not tabs.
bytes := []byte(`
host: 127.0.0.1
port: 1234
tags:
    foo: bar
`)

c := Config{}
err := yaml.Unmarshal(bytes, &c)
```

Just as we did in "Decoding JSON" on page 317, we pass yaml.Unmarshal a pointer to a Config instance, whose fields correspond to the fields found in the YAML. Printing the value of c should (once again) provide output like the following:

```
{127.0.0.1 1234 map[foo:bar]}
```

There are other behavioral similarities between encoding/json and Go-YAML:

- Both will ignore attributes in a source document that cannot be mapped to the Unmarshal function. Again, this can be useful if you only care about a subset of the document, but it can be a "gotcha," too: if you forget to export the struct field, Unmarshal will always silently ignore it, and it'll never get set.

- Both are capable of unmarshalling arbitrary data by passing an interface{} value to Unmarshal. However, while json.Unmarshal will provide a `map[string]interface{}`, `yaml.Unmarshal` will return a `map[inter face{}]interface{}`. A minor difference, but another potential gotcha!

Struct field tags for YAML. In addition to the "standard" struct field tags—custom keys, `omitempty`, and - (dash)—detailed in "Field formatting with struct field tags" on page 319, Go-YAML supports two additional tags particular to YAML marshal formatting:

Flow style
> Fields using the `flow` option will be marshalled using the flow style (*https:// oreil.ly/zyUpd*), which can be useful for structs, sequences, and maps.
>
> Example: `Flow map[string]string ` + "`" + `yaml:"flow"` + "`"

Inlining structs and maps
> The `inline` option causes all of a struct or map fields or keys to be processed as if they were part of the outer struct. For maps, keys must not conflict with the keys of other struct fields.
>
> Example: `Inline map[string]string ` + "`" + `yaml:",inline"` + "`"

A struct that uses both of these options might look like the following:

```
type TaggedMore struct {
    // Flow will be marshalled using a "flow" style
    // (useful for structs, sequences and maps).
    Flow map[string]string `yaml:"flow"`

    // Inlines a struct or a map, causing all of its fields
    // or keys to be processed as if they were part of the outer
    // struct. For maps, keys must not conflict with the yaml
    // keys of other struct fields.
    Inline map[string]string `yaml:",inline"`
}
```

As you can see, the tagging syntax is also consistent, except that instead of using the `json` prefix, Go-YAML tags use the `yaml` prefix.

Watching for configuration file changes

When working with configuration files, you'll inevitably be confronted with a situation in which changes have to be made to the configuration of a running program. If it doesn't explicitly watch for and reload changes, then it'll generally have to be restarted to reread its configuration, which can be inconvenient at best, and introduce downtime at worst.

At some point, you're going to have to decide how you want your program to respond to such changes.

The first (and least complex) option is to do nothing, and just expect the program to have to restart when its configuration changes. This is actually a fairly common choice, since it ensures that no trace of the former configuration exists. It also allows a program to "fail fast" when an error is introduced into the configuration file: the program just has to spit out an angry error message and refuse to start.

However, you might prefer to add logic to your program that detects changes in your configuration file (or files) and reloads them appropriately.

Making your configuration reloadable. If you'd like your internal configuration representations to reload whenever the underlying file changes, you'll have to plan a little ahead.

First, you'll want to have a single global instance of your configuration struct. For now, we'll use a Config instance of the kind we introduced in "Our configuration data structure" on page 314. In a slightly larger project, you might even put this in a config package:

```
var config Config
```

Very often you'll see code in which an explicit config parameter is passed to just about every method and function. I've seen this quite a lot; often enough to know that this particular antipattern just makes life harder. Also, because the configuration now lives in N places instead of one, it also tends to make configuration reloading more complicated.

Once we have our config value, we'll want to add the logic that reads the configuration file and loads it into the struct. Something like the following loadConfiguration function will do just fine:

```
func loadConfiguration(filepath string) (Config, error) {
    dat, err := ioutil.ReadFile(filepath)   // Ingest file as []byte
    if err != nil {
        return Config{}, err
    }

    config := Config{}

    err = yaml.Unmarshal(dat, &config)      // Do the unmarshal
    if err != nil {
        return Config{}, err
    }

    return config, nil
}
```

Our loadConfiguration function works almost the same way that we discussed in "Working with YAML" on page 321, except that it uses the ioutil.ReadFile function from the io/ioutil standard library to retrieve the bytes that it passes to yaml.Unmarshal. The choice to use YAML here was entirely arbitrary.[12] The syntax for a JSON configuration would be practically identical.

Now that we have logic to load our configuration file into a canonical struct, we need something to call it whenever it gets a notification that the file has changed. For that we have startListening, which monitors an updates channel:

```
func startListening(updates <-chan string, errors <-chan error) {
    for {
        select {
        case filepath := <-updates:
            c, err := loadConfiguration(filepath)
            if err != nil {
                log.Println("error loading config:", err)
                continue
            }
            config = c

        case err := <-errors:
            log.Println("error watching config:", err)
        }
    }
}
```

As you can see, startListening accepts two channels: updates, which emits the name of a file (presumably the configuration file) when that file changes, and an errors channel.

It watches both channels in a select inside of an infinite loop so that if a configuration file changes, the updates channel sends its name, which is then passed to load Configuration. If loadConfiguration doesn't return a non-nil error, then the Config value it returns replaces the current one.

Stepping back another level, we have an init function that retrieves the channels from a watchConfig function and passes them to startListening, which it runs as a goroutine:

```
func init() {
    updates, errors, err := watchConfig("config.yaml")
    if err != nil {
        panic(err)
    }

    go startListening(updates, errors)
}
```

---

12 Also, I just love JSON *so much.*

But what's this `watchConfig` function? Well, we don't quite know the details yet. We'll figure that out in the next couple of sections. We do know that it implements some configuration watching logic, and that it has a function signature that looks like the following:

```
func watchConfig(filepath string) (<-chan string, <-chan error, error)
```

The `watchConfig` function, whatever its implementation, returns two channels—a `string` channel that sends the path of the updated configuration file, and an `error` channel that notifies about invalid configurations—and an `error` value that reports if there's a fatal error on startup.

The exact implementation of `watchConfig` can go a couple of different ways, each with its pros and cons. Now let's take a look at the two most common of those.

Polling for configuration changes.   Polling, where you check for changes in your configuration file on some regular cadence, is a common way of watching a configuration file. A standard implementation uses a `time.Ticker` to recalculate a hash of your configuration file every few seconds and reload if the hash changes.

Go makes a number of common hash algorithms available in its `crypto` package, each of which lives in its own subpackage of `crypto` and satisfies both the `crypto.Hash` and `io.Writer` interfaces.

For example, Go's standard implementation of SHA256 can be found in `crypto/sha256`. To use it, you use its `sha256.New` function to get a new `sha256.Hash` value, into which you then write the data you want to calculate the hash of, just as you would any `io.Writer`. When that's complete, you use its `Sum` method to retrieve the resulting hash sum:

```go
func calculateFileHash(filepath string) (string, error) {
    file, err := os.Open(filepath)  // Open the file for reading
    if err != nil {
        return "", err
    }
    defer file.Close()                 // Be sure to close your file!

    hash := sha256.New()               // Use the Hash in crypto/sha256

    if _, err := io.Copy(hash, file); err != nil {
        return "", err
    }

    sum := fmt.Sprintf("%x", hash.Sum(nil))  // Get encoded hash sum

    return sum, nil
}
```

Generating a hash for a configuration has three distinct parts. First, we get a []byte source in the form of an io.Reader. In this example we use an io.File. Next, we copy those bytes from the io.Reader to our sha256.Hash instance, which we do with a call to io.Copy. Finally, we use the Sum method to retrieve the hash sum from hash.

Now that we have our calculateFileHash function, creating our watchConfig implementation is just a matter of using a time.Ticker to concurrently check it on some cadence, and emit any positive results (or errors) to the appropriate channel:

```
func watchConfig(filepath string) (<-chan string, <-chan error, error) {
    errs := make(chan error)
    changes := make(chan string)
    hash := ""

    go func() {
        ticker := time.NewTicker(time.Second)

        for range ticker.C {
            newhash, err := calculateFileHash(filepath)
            if err != nil {
                errs <- err
                continue
            }

            if hash != newhash {
                hash = newhash
                changes <- filepath
            }
        }
    }()

    return changes, errs, nil
}
```

The polling approach has some benefits. It's not especially complex, which is always a big plus, and it works for any operating system. Perhaps most interestingly, because hashing only cares about the configuration's contents, it even can be generalized to detect changes in places like remote key/value stores that aren't technically files.

Unfortunately, the polling approach can be a little computationally wasteful, especially for very large or many files. By its nature, it also incurs also a brief delay between the time the file is changed and the detection of that change. If you're definitely working with local files, it would probably be more efficient to watch OS-level filesystem notifications, which we discuss in the next section.

Watching OS filesystem notifications. Polling for changes works well enough, but this method has some drawbacks. Depending on your use case, you may find it more efficient to instead monitor OS-level filesystem notifications.

Actually doing so, however, is complicated by the fact that each operating system has a different notification mechanism. Fortunately, the fsnotify (*https://oreil.ly/ziw4J*) package provides a workable abstraction that supports most operating systems.

To use this package to watch one or more files, you use the fsnotify.NewWatcher function to get a new fsnotify.Watcher instance, and use the Add method to register more files to watch. The Watcher provides two channels, Events and Errors, which sends notifications of file events and errors, respectively.

For example, if we wanted to watch our config file, we could do something like the following:

```
func watchConfigNotify(filepath string) (<-chan string, <-chan error, error) {
    changes := make(chan string)

    watcher, err := fsnotify.NewWatcher()        // Get an fsnotify.Watcher
    if err != nil {
        return nil, nil, err
    }

    err = watcher.Add(filepath)                  // Tell watcher to watch
    if err != nil {                              // our config file
        return nil, nil, err
    }

    go func() {
        changes <- filepath                      // First is ALWAYS a change

        for event := range watcher.Events {      // Range over watcher events
            if event.Op&fsnotify.Write == fsnotify.Write {
                changes <- event.Name
            }
        }
    }()

    return changes, watcher.Errors, nil
}
```

Note the statement event.Op & fsnotify.Write == fsnotify.Write, which uses a bitwise AND (&) to filter for "write" events. We do this because the fsnotify.Event can potentially include multiple operations, each of which is represented as one bit in an unsigned integer. For example, a simultaneous fsnotify.Write (2, binary 0b00010) and fsnotify.Chmod (16, binary 0b10000) would result in an event.Op value of 18 (binary 0b10010). Because 0b10010 & 0b00010 = 0b00010, the bitwise AND allows us to guarantee that an operation includes a fsnotify.Write.

Viper: The Swiss Army Knife of Configuration Packages

Viper (spf13/viper) (*https://oreil.ly/pttZM*) bills itself as a complete configuration solution for Go applications, and justifiably so. Among other things, it allows application configuration by a variety of mechanisms and formats, including, in order of precedence:

Explicitly set values

This takes precedence over all other methods, and can be useful during testing.

Command-line flags

Viper is designed to be a companion to Cobra, which we introduced in "The Cobra command-line parser" on page 310.

Environment variables

Viper has full support for environment variables. Importantly, Viper treats environment variables as case-sensitive!

Configuration files, in multiple file formats

Out of the box, Viper supports JSON and YAML with the packages we introduced previously; as well as TOML, HCL, INI, envfile, and Java Properties files. It can also write configuration files to help bootstrap your configurations, and even optionally supports live watching and rereading of configuration files.

Remote key/value stores

Viper can access key/value stores like etcd or Consul, and can watch them for changes.

It also supports features like default values and typed variables, which the standard packages typically don't provide.

Keep in mind though, that while Viper does *a lot*, it's also a pretty big hammer that brings in a lot of dependencies. If you're trying to build a slim, streamlined application, Viper may be more than you need.

Explicitly setting values in Viper

Viper allows you to use the `viper.Set` function to explicitly set values from, for example, command-line flags or the application logic. This can be pretty handy during testing:

```
viper.Set("Verbose", true)
viper.Set("LogFile", LogFile)
```

Explicitly set values have the highest priority, and override values that would be set by other mechanisms.

Working with command-line flags in Viper

Viper was designed to be a companion to the Cobra library (*https://oreil.ly/67LFI*), which we briefly discussed in the context of constructing command-line interfaces in "The Cobra command-line parser" on page 310. This close integration with Cobra makes it straightforward to bind command-line flags to configuration keys.

Viper provides the `viper.BindPFlag` function, which allows individual command-line flags to be bound to a named key, and `viper.BindPFlags`, which binds a full flag set using each flag's long name as the key.

Because the actual value of the configuration value is set when the binding is accessed, rather than when it's called, you can call `viper.BindPFlag` in an `init` function as we do here:

```
var rootCmd = &cobra.Command{ /* omitted for brevity */ }

func init() {
    rootCmd.Flags().IntP("number", "n", 42, "an integer")
    viper.BindPFlag("number", rootCmd.Flags().Lookup("number"))
}
```

In the preceding snippet, we declare a `&cobra.Command` and define an integer flag called "number." Note that we use the `IntP` method instead of `IntVarP`, since there's no need to store the value of the flag in an external value when Cobra is used in this way. Then, using the `viper.BindPFlag` function, we bind the "number" flag to a configuration key of the same name.

After it's been bound (and the command-line flags parsed), the value of the bound key can be retrieved from Viper by using the `viper.GetInt` function:

```
n := viper.GetInt("number")
```

Working with environment variables in Viper

Viper provides several functions for working with environment variables as a configuration source. The first of these is `viper.BindEnv`, which is used to bind a configuration key to an environment variable:

```
viper.BindEnv("id")                      // Bind "id" to var "ID"
viper.BindEnv("port", "SERVICE_PORT")    // Bind "port" to var "SERVICE_PORT"

id := viper.GetInt("id")
id := viper.GetInt("port")
```

If only a key is provided, `viper.BindEnv` will bind to the environment variable matching the key. More arguments can be provided to specify one or more environment variables to bind to. In both cases, Viper automatically assumes that the name of the environment variable is in all caps.

Viper provides several additional helper functions for working with environment variables. See the Viper GoDoc (*https://oreil.ly/CGpPS*) for more details on these.

Working with configuration files in Viper

Out of the box, Viper supports JSON and YAML using the packages we introduced previously; as well as TOML, HCL, INI, envfile, and Java Properties files. It can also write configuration files to help bootstrap your configurations, and even optionally supports live watching and rereading of configuration files.

A discussion of local configuration files may seem unexpected in a book on cloud native, but files are still a commonly used structure in any context. After all, shared filesystems—be they Kubernetes ConfigMaps or NFS mounts—are quite common, and even cloud native services can be deployed by a configuration management system that installs a read-only local copy of a file for all service replicas to read. A configuration file could even be baked or mounted into a container image in a way that looks—as far as a containerized service is concerned—exactly like any other local file.

Reading configuration files. To read configurations from files, Viper just needs to know the names of the files, and where to look for them. Also, it needs to know its type, if that can't be inferred from a file extension. The `viper.ReadInConfig` function instructs Viper to find and read the configuration file, potentially returning an `error` value if something goes wrong. All of those steps are demonstrated here:

```
viper.SetConfigName("config")

// Optional if the config has a file extension
viper.SetConfigType("yaml")

viper.AddConfigPath("/etc/service/")
viper.AddConfigPath("$HOME/.service")
viper.AddConfigPath(".")

if err := viper.ReadInConfig(); err != nil {
    panic(fmt.Errorf("fatal error reading config: %w", err))
}
```

As you can see, Viper can search multiple paths for a configuration file. Unfortunately, at this time, a single Viper instance only supports reading a single configuration file.

Watching and rereading configuration files in Viper. Viper natively allows your application to watch a configuration file for modifications and reload when changes are detected, which means that configurations can change without having to restart the server for them to take effect.

By default, this functionality is turned off. The `viper.WatchConfig` function can be used to enable it. Additionally, the `viper.OnConfigChange` function allows you to specify a function that's called whenever the configuration file is updated:

```
viper.WatchConfig()
viper.OnConfigChange(func(e fsnotify.Event) {
    fmt.Println("Config file changed:", e.Name)
})
```

 Make sure that any calls to `viper.AddConfigPath` are made *before* calling `viper.WatchConfig`.

Interestingly, Viper actually uses the `fsnotify/fsnotify` package behind the scenes, the same mechanism that we detailed in "Watching for configuration file changes" on page 323.

Using remote key/value stores with Viper

Perhaps the most interesting feature of Viper is its ability to read a configuration string written in any supported format from a path in a remote key/value store, like etcd (*https://etcd.io*) or HashiCorp Consul (*https://consul.io*). These values take precedence over default values, but are overridden by configuration values retrieved from disk, command-line flags, or environment variables.

To enable remote support in Viper, you first have to do a blank import of the `viper/remote` package:

```
import _ "github.com/spf13/viper/remote"
```

A remote key/value configuration source can then be registered using the `viper.AddRemoteProvider` method, whose signature is as follows:

```
func AddRemoteProvider(provider, endpoint, path string) error
```

- The `provider` parameter can be one of `etcd`, `consul`, or `firestore`.
- The `endpoint` is the URL of the remote resource. An odd quirk of Viper is that the etcd provider requires the URL to include a scheme (`http://ip:port`), while Consul requires *no scheme* (ip:port).
- The `path` is the path in the key-value store to retrieve the configuration from.

To read a JSON-formatted configuration file from an etcd service, for example, you'll do something like the following:

```
viper.AddRemoteProvider("etcd", "http://127.0.0.1:4001","/config/service.json")
viper.SetConfigType("json")
err := viper.ReadRemoteConfig()
```

Note that even though the configuration path includes a file extension, we also use viper.SetConfigType to explicitly define the configuration type. This is because from Viper's perspective, the resource is just a stream of bytes, so it can't automatically infer the format.[13] As of the time of writing, the supported formats are *json*, *toml*, *yaml*, *yml*, *properties*, *props*, *prop*, *env*, and *dotenv*.

Multiple providers may be added, in which case they're searched in the order in which they were added.

This is just a very basic introduction to what Viper can do with remote key/value stores. For more details about how to use Viper to read from Consul, watch for configuration changes, or read encrypted configurations, take a look at Viper's README (*https://oreil.ly/1iE2y*).

Setting defaults in Viper

Unlike all of the other packages we reviewed in this chapter, Viper optionally allows default values to be defined for a key, by way of the SetDefault function.

Default values can sometimes be useful, but care should be taken with this functionality. As mentioned in "Configuration Good Practice" on page 307, useful zero values are generally preferable to implicit defaults, which can lead to surprising behaviors when thoughtlessly applied.

A snippet of Viper showing default values in action might look like the following:

```
viper.BindEnv("id")           // Will be upper-cased automatically
viper.SetDefault("id", "13")  // Default value is "13"

id1 := viper.GetInt("id")
fmt.Println(id1)              // 13

os.Setenv("ID", "50")         // Explicitly set the envvar

id2 := viper.GetInt("id")
fmt.Println(id2)              // 50
```

Default values have the lowest priority, and will only take effect if a key isn't explicitly set by another mechanism.

---

13 Or that feature just hasn't been implemented. I don't know.

Feature Management with Feature Flags

Feature flagging (or *feature toggling*[14]) is a software development pattern designed to increase the speed and safety with which new features can be developed and delivered by allowing specific functionality to be turned on or off during runtime, without having to deploy new code.

A feature flag is essentially a conditional in your code that enables or disables a feature based on some external criteria, often (but not always) a configuration setting. By setting the configuration to different values, a developer can, for example, choose to enable an incomplete feature for testing and disable it for other users.

Having the ability to release a product with unfinished features provides a number of powerful benefits.

First, feature flags allow many small incremental versions of software to be delivered without the overhead of branching and merging that comes with using feature branches. In other words, feature flags decouple the release of a feature from its deployment. Combined with the fact that feature flags, by their very nature, require code changes to be integrated as early as possible, which both encourages and facilitates continuous deployment and delivery. As a result, developers get more rapid feedback about their code, which in turn allows smaller, faster, and safer iterations.

Second, not only can feature flags allow features to be more easily tested before they're deemed ready for release, but they can also do so dynamically. For example, logic can be used to build feedback loops that can be combined with a circuit breaker–like pattern to enable or disable flags automatically under specific conditions.

Finally, logically executing flags can even be used to target feature rollouts to specific subsets of users. This technique, called *feature gating*, can be used as an alternative to proxy rules for canary deployments and staged or geographically based rollouts. When combined with observability techniques, feature gating can even allow you to more easily execute experiments like A/B testing or targeted tracing that instrument particular slices of user base, or even single customers.

The Evolution of a Feature Flag

In this section, we'll step through the iterative implementation of a feature flag with a function taken directly from the key-value REST service that we built in Chapter 5. Starting with the baseline function, we'll progress through several evolutionary

---

14 I've also seen "feature switch," "feature flipper," "conditional feature," and more. The industry seems to be settling on "flag" and "toggle," probably because the other names are just a little silly.

stages, from flaglessness all the way to a dynamic feature flag that toggles on for a particular subset of users.

In our scenario, we've decided that we want to be able to scale our key-value store, so we want to update the logic so that it's backed by a fancy distributed data structure instead of a local map.

Generation 0: The Initial Implementation

For our first iteration, we'll start with the keyValueGetHandler function from "Implementing the read function" on page 120. You may recall that keyValueGetHandler is an HTTP handler function that satisfies the HandlerFunc interface defined in the net/http package. If you're a little rusty on what that means, you may want to take a look back at "Building an HTTP Server with net/http" on page 112.

The initial handler function, copied almost directly from Chapter 5 (minus some of its error handling, for brevity) is shown here:

```
func keyValueGetHandler(w http.ResponseWriter, r *http.Request) {
    vars := mux.Vars(r)                    // Retrieve "key" from the request
    key := vars["key"]

    value, err := Get(key)                 // Get value for key
    if err != nil {                        // Unexpected error!
        http.Error(w,
            err.Error(),
            http.StatusInternalServerError)
        return
    }

    w.Write([]byte(value))                 // Write the value to the response
}
```

As you can see, this function has no feature toggle logic (or indeed anything to toggle *to*). All it does is retrieve the key from the request variables, use the Get function to retrieve the value associated with that key, and write that value to the response.

In our next implementation, we'll start testing a new feature: a fancy distributed data structure to replace the local map[string]string that'll allow the service to scale beyond a single instance.

Generation 1: The Hard-Coded Feature Flag

In this implementation, we'll imagine that we've built our new and experimental distributed backend, and made it accessible via the NewGet function.

Our first attempt at creating a feature flag introduces a condition that allows us to use a simple Boolean value, useNewStorage, to switch between the two implementations:

```go
// Set to true if you're working on the new storage backend
const useNewStorage bool = false;

func keyValueGetHandler(w http.ResponseWriter, r *http.Request) {
    vars := mux.Vars(r)
    key := vars["key"]

    var value string
    var err error

    if useNewStorage {
        value, err = NewGet(key)
    } else {
        value, err = Get(key)
    }

    if err != nil {
        http.Error(w,
            err.Error(),
            http.StatusInternalServerError)
        return
    }

    w.Write([]byte(value))
}
```

This first iteration shows some progress, but it's far from where we want to be. Having the flag condition fixed in the code as a hard-coded value makes it possible to toggle between implementations well enough for local testing, but it won't be easy to test both together in an automated and continuous manner.

Plus, you'll have to rebuild and redeploy the service whenever you want to change the algorithm you're using in a deployed instance, which largely negates the benefits of having a feature flag in the first place.

Practice good feature flag hygiene! If you haven't updated a feature flag in a while, consider removing it.

Generation 2: The Configurable Flag

A little time has gone by, and the shortcomings of hard-coded feature flags have become evident. For one thing, it would be really nice if we could use an external mechanism to change the value of the flag so we can test *both* algorithms in our tests.

In this example, we use Viper to bind and read an environment variable, which we can now use to enable or disable the feature at runtime. The choice of configuration mechanism isn't really important here. All that matters is that we're able to externally update the flag without having to rebuild the code:

```
func keyValueGetHandler(w http.ResponseWriter, r *http.Request) {
    vars := mux.Vars(r)
    key := vars["key"]

    var value string
    var err error

    if FeatureEnabled("use-new-storage", r) {
        value, err = NewGet(key)
    } else {
        value, err = Get(key)
    }

    if err != nil {
        http.Error(w,
            err.Error(),
            http.StatusInternalServerError)
        return
    }

    w.Write([]byte(value))
}

func FeatureEnabled(flag string, r *http.Request) bool {
    return viper.GetBool(flag)
}
```

In addition to using Viper to read the environment variable that sets the use-new-storage flag, we've also introduced a new function: FeatureEnabled. At the moment all this does is perform viper.GetBool(flag), but more importantly it also concentrates the flag reading logic in a single place. We'll see exactly what the benefit of this is in the next iteration.

You might be wondering why FeatureEnabled accepts an *http.Request. Well, it doesn't use it yet, but it'll make sense in the next iteration.

Generation 3: Dynamic Feature Flags

The feature is now deployed, but turned off behind a feature flag. Now we'd like to be able to test it in production on a specific subset of your user base. It's clear that we're not going to be able to implement this kind of flag with a configuration setting. Instead, we'll have to build dynamic flags that can *figure out for themselves* if they should be set. That means associating flags with functions.

Dynamic flags as functions

The first step in building dynamic flag functions is deciding what the signature of the functions will be. While it's not strictly required, it's helpful to define this explicitly with a function type like the one shown here:

```
type Enabled func(flag string, r *http.Request) (bool, error)
```

The Enabled function type is the prototype for all of our dynamic feature flags functions. Its contract defines a function that accepts the flag name as a string and the *http.Request, and it returns a bool that's true if the requested flag is enabled.

Implementing a dynamic flag function

Using the contract provided by the Enabled type, we can now implement a function that we can use to determine whether a request is coming from a private network by comparing the request's remote address against a standard list of IP ranges allocated for private networks:

```
// The list of CIDR ranges associated with internal networks.
var privateCIDRs []*net.IPNet

// We use an init function to load the privateCIDRs slice.
func init() {
    for _, cidr := range []string{
        "10.0.0.0/8",
        "172.16.0.0/12",
        "192.168.0.0/16",
    } {
        _, block, _ := net.ParseCIDR(cidr)
        privateCIDRs = append(privateCIDRs, block)
    }
}

// fromPrivateIP receives the flag name (which it ignores) and the
// request. If the request's remote IP is in a private range per
// RFC1918, it returns true.
func fromPrivateIP(flag string, r *http.Request) (bool, error) {
    // Grab the host portion of the request's remote address
    remoteIP, _, err := net.SplitHostPort(r.RemoteAddr)
    if err != nil {
        return false, err
    }

    // Turn the remote address string into a *net.IPNet
    ip := net.ParseIP(remoteIP)
    if ip == nil {
        return false, errors.New("couldn't parse ip")
    }

    // Loopbacks are considered "private."
```

```
    if ip.IsLoopback() {
        return true, nil
    }

    // Search the CIDRs list for the IP; return true if found.
    for _, block := range privateCIDRs {
        if block.Contains(ip) {
            return true, nil
        }
    }

    return false, nil
}
```

As you can see, the fromPrivateIP function conforms to Enabled by receiving a string value (the flag name) and an *http.Request (specifically, the instance associated with the initiating request). It returns true if the request originates from a private IP range (as defined by RFC 1918 (*https://oreil.ly/lZ5PQ*)).

To make this determination, the fromPrivateIP function first retrieves the remote address, which contains the network address that sent the request, from the *http.request. After parsing off the host IP with net.SplitHostPort and using net.ParseIP to parse it into a *net.IP value, it compares the originating IP against each of the private CIDR ranges contained in privateCIDRs, returning true if a match is found.

> This function also returns true if the request is traversing a load balancer or reverse proxy. A production-grade implementation will need to be aware of this, and would ideally be proxy protocol-aware (*https://oreil.ly/S3btg*).

Of course, this function is just an example. I used it because it's relatively simple, but a similar technique can be used to enable or disable a flag for a geographic region, a fixed percentage of users, or even for a specific customer.

The flag function lookup

Now that we have a dynamic flag function in the form of fromPrivateIP, we have to implement some mechanism of associating flags with it, by name. Perhaps the most straightforward way of doing this is to use a map of flag name strings to Enabled functions:

```
var enabledFunctions map[string]Enabled

func init() {
    enabledFunctions = map[string]Enabled{}
```

```
    enabledFunctions["use-new-storage"] = fromPrivateIP
}
```

Using a map in this manner to indirectly reference functions provides us with a good deal of flexibility. We can even associate a function with multiple flags, if we like. This could be useful if we want a set of related features to always be active under the same conditions.

You may have noticed that we're using an `init` function to fill the `enabledFunctions` map. But wait, didn't we already have an `init` function?

Yes, we did, and that's okay. The `init` function is special: you're allowed to have multiple `init` functions if you like.

The router function

Finally, we get to tie everything together.

We do this by refactoring the `FeatureEnabled` function to look up the appropriate dynamic flag function, call it if it finds it, and return the result:

```go
func FeatureEnabled(flag string, r *http.Request) bool {
    // Explicit flags take precedence
    if viper.IsSet(flag) {
        return viper.GetBool(flag)
    }

    // Retrieve the flag function, if any. If none exists,
    // return false
    enabledFunc, exists := enabledFunctions[flag]
    if !exists {
        return false
    }

    // We now have the flag function: call it and return
    // the result
    result, err := enabledFunc(flag, r)
    if err != nil {
        log.Println(err)
        return false
    }

    return result
}
```

At this point, `FeatureEnabled` has become a full-fledged router function that can dynamically control which code path is live according to explicit feature-flag settings and the output of flag functions. In this implementation, flags that have been explicitly set take precedence over everything else. This allows automated tests to verify both sides of a flagged feature.

Our implementation uses a simple in-memory lookup to determine the behavior of particular flags, but this could just as easily be implemented with a database or other data source, or even a sophisticated managed service like LaunchDarkly. Keep in mind, though, that these solutions do introduce a new dependency.

> ### Feature Flags as a Service?
>
> If you're interested in implementing some of the more sophisticated dynamic feature flags but (probably wisely) would prefer not to roll your own, LaunchDarkly (*https://oreil.ly/0xKeq*) provides an excellent "feature flags as a service" service.

Summary

Manageability isn't the most glamorous subject in the cloud native world—or any world, really—but I still really enjoyed how much we got our hands dirty with details in this chapter.

We dug into some of the nuts and bolts of various configuration styles, including environment variables, command-line flags, and variously formatted files. We even went over a couple of strategies for detecting configuration changes to trigger a reload. That's not to mention Viper, which pretty much does all of that and more.

I do feel like there may be some potential to go a lot deeper on some things, and I might have had it not been for the constraints of time and space. Feature flags and feature management are a pretty big subject, for example, and I definitely would have liked to have been able to explore them a bit more. Some subjects, like deployments and service discovery, we couldn't even cover at all. I guess we have some things to look forward to in the next edition, right?

As much as I enjoyed this chapter, I'm especially excited about Chapter 11, in which we'll get to dive into observability in general, and OpenTelemetry in particular.

Finally, I'll leave you with some advice: always be yourself, and remember that luck comes from hard work.

Observability

> Data is not information, information is not knowledge, knowledge is not understanding, understanding is not wisdom.[1]
>
> —Clifford Stoll, *High-Tech Heretic: Reflections of a Computer Contrarian*

"Cloud native" is still a pretty new concept, even for computing. As far as I can tell (*https://oreil.ly/sPxg7*), the term "cloud native" only started entering our vocabulary just after the founding of the Cloud Native Computing Foundation in the middle of 2015.[2]

As an industry, we're largely still trying to figure out exactly what "cloud native" means, and with each of the major public cloud providers regularly launching new services—each seeming to offer more abstraction than the last—even what little agreement we have is shifting over time.

One thing is clear, though: the functions (and failures) of the network and hardware layers are being increasingly abstracted and replaced with API calls and events. Every day we move closer to a world of software-defined *everything*. All of our problems are becoming software problems.

While we certainly sacrifice a fair share of control over the platforms our software runs on, we win *big* in overall manageability and reliability,[3] allowing us to focus our limited time and attention on our software. However, this also means that most of our failures now originate from within our own services and the interactions between

---

1 Stoll, Clifford. *High-Tech Heretic: Reflections of a Computer Contrarian.* Random House, September 2000.

2 Interestingly, this was also just after the AWS launched its Lambda functions as a service (FaaS) offering. Coincidence? Maybe.

3 Assuming of course that all of our network and platform configurations are correct!

them. No amount of fancy frameworks or protocols can solve the problem of bad software. As I said way back in Chapter 1, a kludgy application in Kubernetes is still kludgy.

Things are complicated in this brave new software-defined, highly distributed world. The software is complicated, the platforms are complicated, together they're *really* complicated, and more often than not we have no idea what's going on. Gaining visibility into our services has become more important than ever, and about the only thing that we *do* know is that the existing monitoring tools and techniques simply aren't up to the task. Clearly, we need something new. Not just a new technology, or even a new set of techniques, but an entirely new way of thinking about how we understand our systems.

What Is Observability?

Observability is the subject of an awful lot of buzz right now. It's kind of a big deal. But what is observability, actually? How is it different from (and how is it like) traditional monitoring and alerting with logs and metrics and tracing? Most importantly, how do we "do observability"?

Observability isn't just marketing hype, although it's easy to think that based on all the attention it's getting.

It's actually pretty simple. Observability is a system property, no different than resilience or manageability, that reflects how well a system's internal states can be inferred from knowledge of its external outputs. A system can be considered *observable* when it's possible to quickly and consistently ask novel questions about it with minimal prior knowledge and without having to reinstrument or build new code. An observable system lets you ask it questions that you haven't thought of yet.

Ultimately, observability is more than tooling, despite what some vendors may try to tell you (and sell you). You can't "buy observability" any more than you can "buy reliability." No tooling will make your system observable just because you're using it any more than a hammer will by itself make a bridge structurally sound. The tools can get you partway there, but it's up to you to apply them correctly.

This is much easier said than done, of course. Building observability into a complex system demands moving past searching for "known unknowns," and embracing the fact that we often can't even fully understand its state at a given snapshot in time. Understanding *all possible* failure (or non-failure) states in a complex system is pretty much impossible. The first step to achieving observability is to stop looking for specific, expected failure modes—the "known unknowns"—as if this isn't the case.

Why Do We Need Observability?

Observability is the natural evolution of traditional monitoring, driven by the new challenges introduced by cloud native architectures.

The first of these is simply the pure scale of many modern cloud native systems, which increasingly have too much *stuff* for our limited human brains with their limited human attention spans to handle. All of the data generated by multiple concurrently operating interconnected systems provides more things than we can reasonably watch, more data than we can reasonably process, and more correlations than we can reasonably make.

More importantly, however, is that the nature of cloud native systems is fundamentally different from the more traditional architectures of not-so-long-ago. Their environmental and functional requirements are different, the way they function—and the way they fail—is different, and the guarantees they need to provide are different.

How do you monitor distributed systems given the ephemerality of modern applications and the environments in which they reside? How can you pinpoint a defect in a single component within the complex web of a highly distributed system? These are the problems that "observability" seeks to address.

How Is Observability Different from "Traditional" Monitoring?

On its face, the line between monitoring and observability seems fuzzy. After all, both are about being able to ask questions of a system. The difference is in the types of questions that are and can be asked.

Traditionally, monitoring focuses on asking questions in the hope of identifying or predicting some expected or previously observed failure modes. In other words, it centers on "known unknowns." The assumption is that the system is expected to behave—and therefore fail—in a specific, predictable way. When a new failure mode is discovered—usually the hard way—its symptoms are added to the monitoring suite, and the process begins again.

This approach works well enough when a system is fairly simple, but it has some problems. First, asking a new question of a system often means writing and shipping new code. This isn't flexible, it definitely isn't scalable, and it's super annoying.

Second, at a certain level of complexity the number of "unknown unknowns" in a system starts to overwhelm the number of "known unknowns." Failures are more often unpredicted, less often predictable, and are nearly always the outcome of many things going wrong. Monitoring for every possible failure mode becomes effectively impossible.

Monitoring is something you *do to a system* to find out it isn't working. Observability techniques, on the other hand, emphasize understanding a system by allowing you to correlate events and behaviors. Observability is a *property a system has* that lets you ask why it isn't working.

The "Three Pillars of Observability"

The *Three Pillars of Observability* is the collective name by which the three most common (and foundational) tools in the observability kit—logging, metrics, and tracing—are sometimes referred. These three parts are, in the order that we'll be discussing them:

Tracing
> Tracing (or *distributed tracing*) follows a request as it propagates through a (typically distributed) system, allowing the entire end-to-end request flow to be reconstructed as a directed acyclic graph (*https://oreil.ly/exjvV*) (DAG) called a *trace*. Analysis of these traces can provide insight into how a system's components interact, making it possible to pinpoint failures and performance issues.
>
> Tracing will be discussed in more detail in "Tracing" on page 350.

Metrics
> Metrics involves the collection of numerical data points representing the state of various aspects of a system at specific points in time. Collections of data points, representing observations of the same subject at various times, are particularly useful for visualization and mathematical analysis, and can be used to highlight trends, identify anomalies, and predict future behavior.
>
> We'll discuss more about metrics in "Metrics" on page 369.

Logging
> Logging is the process of appending records of noteworthy events to an immutable record—the log—for later review or analysis. A log can take a variety of forms, from a continuously appended file on disk to a full-text search engine like Elasticsearch (*https://oreil.ly/Hf4Pn*). Logs provides valuable, context-rich insight into application-specific events emitted by processes. However, it's important that log entries are properly structured; not doing so can sharply limit their utility.
>
> We'll dive into logging in more detail in "Logging" on page 387.

While each of these methods is useful on its own, a truly observable system will interweave them so that each can reference the others. For example, metrics might be used to track down a subset of misbehaving traces, and those traces might highlight logs that could help to find the underlying cause of the behavior.

If you take nothing else away from this chapter, remember that observability is *just a system property*, like resilience or manageability, and that no tooling, framework, or

---

vendor can "give you" observability. The so-called "Three Pillars" are just techniques that can be used to build in that property.

> ## The (So-Called) "Three Pillars"
>
> This name "Three Pillars of Observability" is often criticized—with good reason, I think—because it's easy to interpret it as suggesting that they're how you can "do observability." But while just having logging, metrics, and tracing won't necessarily make a system more observable, each of the "three pillars" are powerful tools that, if well understood and used well together, can provide deep insight into the internal state of your system.
>
> Another common criticism is that the term implies that observability is the combination of three very different things, when each of the three tools simply provides a different view of the same thing, which ultimately enhances a singular ability to understand the state of your system. It's through the integration of these three approaches that it becomes possible to take the first steps towards observability.

OpenTelemetry

As of the time of writing, OpenTelemetry (or "OTel," as the cool kids are calling it[4]) is one of about four dozen "Sandbox" member projects of the Cloud Native Computing Foundation, and arguably one of the most interesting projects in the entire CNCF project catalog.

Unlike most CNCF projects, OpenTelemetry isn't a service, *per se*. Rather, it's an effort to standardize how telemetry data—traces, metrics, and (eventually) logs—are expressed, collected, and transferred. Its multiple repositories (*https://oreil.ly/GpGD5*) include a collection of specifications, along with APIs and reference implementations in various languages, including Go (*https://oreil.ly/vSO7k*).[5]

The instrumentation space is a crowded one, with perhaps dozens of vendors and tools that have come and gone over the years, each with their own unique implementations. OpenTelemetry seeks to unify this space—and all of the vendors and tools within it—around a single vendor-neutral specification that standardizes how telemetry data is collected and sent to backend platforms. There have been other attempts to standardize before. In fact, OpenTelemetry is the merger of two such

---

4 I'm not one of the cool kids.

5 In addition to Go, implementations exist for Python, Java, JavaScript, .NET, C++, Rust, PHP, Erlang/Elixir, Ruby, and Swift.

earlier projects: OpenTracing and OpenCensus, which it unifies and extends into a single set of vendor-neutral standards.

In this chapter, we'll review each of the "three pillars," their core concepts, and how to use OpenTelemetry to instrument your code and forward the resulting telemetry to a backend of your choice. However, it's important to note that OpenTelemetry is a *big* subject that deserves a book of its own to truly do it justice, but I'll do my best to provide sufficient coverage to at least make it a practical introduction. At the time of this writing, there weren't any comprehensive resources available about OpenTelemetry, but I've gathered what I can from examples and a handful of articles (and a fair amount of digging through the source code).

 As I was writing this chapter, I learned that Charity Majors[6] and Liz Fong-Jones were hard at work on *Observability Engineering* (*https://oreil.ly/FZw86*), planned for release by O'Reilly Media in January 2022.

The OpenTelemetry Components

OpenTelemetry extends and unifies earlier attempts at creating telemetry standards, in part by including abstractions and extension points in the SDK where you can insert your own implementations. This makes it possible to, for example, implement custom exporters that can interface with a vendor of your choice.

To accomplish this level of modularity, OpenTelemetry was designed with the following core components:

Specifications
> The OpenTelemetry specifications describe the requirements and expectations for all OpenTelemetry APIs, SDKs, and data protocols.

API
> Language-specific interfaces and implementations based on the specifications that can be used to add OpenTelemetry to an application.

SDK
> The concrete OpenTelemetry implementations that sit between the APIs and the Exporters, providing functionality like (for example) state tracking and batching data for transmission. An SDK also offers a number of configuration options for behaviors like request filtering and transaction sampling.

---

6 If you've never seen Charity Majors' blog (*https://charity.wtf*), I recommend that you check it out immediately. It's one part genius plus one part experience, tied together with rainbows, cartoon unicorns, and a generous helping of rude language.

Exporters

In-process SDK plug-ins that are capable of sending data to a specific destination, which may be local (such as a log file or `stdout`), or remote (such as Jaeger (*https://oreil.ly/uMAfg*), or a commercial solution like Honeycomb (*https://oreil.ly/cBlnX*) or Lightstep (*https://oreil.ly/KScdI*)). Exporters decouple the instrumentation from the backend, making it possible to change destinations without having to reinstrument your code.

Collector

An optional, but very useful, vendor-agnostic service that can receive and process telemetry data before forwarding it to one or more destinations. It can be run either as a sidecar process alongside your application or as a standalone proxy elsewhere, providing greater flexibility for sending the application telemetry. This can be particularly useful in the kind of tightly controlled environments that are common in the enterprise.

You may have noticed the absence of an OpenTelemetry backend. Well, there isn't one. OpenTelemetry is only concerned with the collection, processing, and sending of telemetry data, and relies on you to provide a telemetry backend to receive and store the data.

There are other components as well, but the above can be considered to be OpenTelemetry's core components. The relationships between them are illustrated in Figure 11-1.

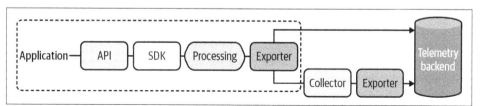

Figure 11-1. A high-level view of OpenTelemetry's core components for data instrumentation (API), processing (SDK), and exporting (exporter and collectors); you have to bring your own backend

Finally, broad language support is a central aim of the project. As of the time of this writing, OpenTelemetry provides APIs and SDKs for Go, Python, Java, Ruby, Erlang, PHP, JavaScript, .NET, Rust, C++, and Swift.

Tracing

Throughout this book, we've spent a lot of time talking about the benefits of microservices architectures and distributed systems. But the unfortunate reality—as I'm sure has already become clear—is that such architectures also introduce a variety of new and "interesting" problems.

It's been said that fixing an outage in a distributed system can feel like solving a murder mystery, which is a glib way of saying that when *something* isn't working, *somewhere* in the system, it's often a challenge just knowing where to start looking for the source of the problem before you can find and fix it.

This is exactly the kind of problem that *tracing* was invented to solve. By tracking requests as they propagate through the system—even across process, network, and security boundaries—tracing can help you to (for example) pinpoint component failures, identify performance bottlenecks, and analyze service dependencies.

 Tracing is usually discussed in the context of distributed systems, but a complex monolithic application can also benefit from tracing, especially if it contends for resources like network, disk, or mutexes.

In this section, we'll go into more depth on tracing, its core concepts, and how to use OpenTelemetry to instrument your code and forward the resulting telemetry to a backend of your choice.

Unfortunately, the constraints of time and space permit us to only dig so far into this topic. But if you'd like to learn more about tracing, you might be interested in *Distributed Tracing in Practice* by Austin Parker, Daniel Spoonhower, Jonathan Mace, Ben Sigelman, and Rebecca Isaacs (O'Reilly).

Tracing Concepts

When discussing tracing, there are two fundamental concepts you need to know about, *spans* and *traces*:

Spans
> A span describes a unit of work performed by a request, such as a fork in the execution flow or hop across the network, as it propagates through a system. Each span has an associated name, a start time, and a duration. They can be (and typically are) nested and ordered to model causal relationships.

Traces
> A trace represents all of the events—individually represented as spans—that make up a request as it flows through a system. A trace may be thought of as a

directed acyclic graph (DAG) of spans, or more concretely as a "stack trace" in which each span represents the work done by one component.

This relationship between a request trace and spans is illustrated in Figure 11-2, in which we see two different representations of the same request as it flows through five different services to generate five spans.

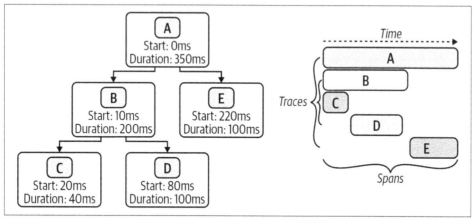

Figure 11-2. Two representations of a trace of a request as it traverses five services, resulting in five spans; the full traces are visualized as a DAG (left), and as a bar diagram (right) with a time axis illustrating start times and durations

When a request begins in the first (edge) service, it creates the first span—the *root span*—which will form the first node in the span trace. The root span is automatically assigned a globally unique trace ID, which is passed along with each subsequent hop in the request lifecycle. The next point of instrumentation creates a new span with the provided trace ID, perhaps choosing to insert or otherwise enrich the metadata associated with the request, before sending the trace ID along again with the next request.

Each hop along the flow is represented as one span. When the execution flow reaches the instrumented point at one of these services, a record is emitted with any metadata. These records are usually asynchronously logged to disk before being submitted out of band to a collector, which can then reconstruct the flow of execution based on different records emitted by different parts of the system.

Figure 11-2 demonstrates the two most common ways of illustrating a trace containing five spans, lettered A through E in the order that they were created. On the left side, the trace is represented in DAG form; the root span A starts at time 0 and lasts for 350ms, until the response is returned for the last service E. On the right, the same data is illustrated as a bar diagram with a time axis, in which the position and length of the bars reflect the start times and durations, respectively.

Tracing with OpenTelemetry

Using OpenTelemetry to instrument your code includes two phases: configuration and instrumentation. This is true whether you're instrumenting for tracing or metrics (or both), although the specifics change slightly between the two. For both tracing and metric instrumentation, the configuration phase is executed exactly once in a program, usually in the `main` function, and includes the following steps:

1. The first step is to retrieve and configure the appropriate exporters for your target backends. Tracing exporters implement the `SpanExporter` interface (which in OpenTelemetry v0.17.0 is located in the `go.opentelemetry.io/otel/sdk/export/trace` package, often aliased to `export`). As we'll discuss in "Creating the tracing exporters" on page 353, several stock exporters are included with OpenTelemetry, but custom implementations exist for many telemetry backends.

2. Before instrumenting your code for tracing, the exporters—and any other appropriate configuration options—are passed to the SDK to create the "tracer provider," which, as we'll show in "Creating a tracer provider" on page 355, will serve as the main entry point for the OpenTelemetry tracing API for the lifetime of your program.

3. Once you've created your tracer provider, it's a good practice to set it as your "global" tracer provider. As we'll see in "Setting the global tracer provider" on page 356, this makes it discoverable via the `otel.GetTracerProvider` function, which allows libraries and other dependencies that also use the OpenTelemetry API to more easily discover the SDK and emit telemetry data.

Once the configuration is complete, instrumenting your code requires only a few small steps:

1. Before you can instrument an operation, you first have to obtain a `Tracer`, which has the central role of keeping track of trace and span information, from the (usually global) tracer provider. We'll discuss this in more detail in "Obtaining a tracer" on page 356.

2. Once you have a handle to your `Tracer` you can use it to create and start the `Span` value that is the actual value that you'll use to instrument your code. We'll cover this in some detail in "Starting and ending spans" on page 357.

3. Finally, you can also choose to add metadata to your spans, including human-readable, timestamped messages called *events*, and key/value pairs called *attributes*. We'll cover span metadata in "Setting span metadata" on page 358.

Creating the tracing exporters

The first thing you have to do when using OpenTelemetry is create and configure your exporters. Tracing exporters implement the SpanExporter interface, which in OpenTelemetry v0.17.0 lives in the go.opentelemetry.io/otel/sdk/export/trace package, which is often aliased to export to reduce package naming collisions.

You may recall from "The OpenTelemetry Components" on page 348 that OpenTelemetry exporters are in-process plug-ins that know how to convert metric or trace data and send it to a particular destination. This destination may be local (stdout or a log file) or remote (such as Jaeger, or a commercial solution like Honeycomb or Lightstep).

If you want to do anything worthwhile with the instrumentation data you collect, you'll need at least one exporter. One is usually enough, but you can define as many as you like, should you have the need. Exporters are instantiated and configured once at program startup, before being passed to the OpenTelemetry SDK. This will be covered in more detail in "Creating a tracer provider" on page 355.

OpenTelemetry comes with a number of included exporters for both tracing and metrics. Two of these are demonstrated in the following.

The Console Exporter. OpenTelemetry's Console Exporter allows you to write telemetry data as JSON to standard output. This is very handy for debugging or writing to log files. The Console Exporter is noteworthy in that it can also be used to export metric telemetry, as we'll see in "Metrics" on page 369.

Creating an instance of the Console Exporter is just a matter of calling `stdout.NewEx porter`, which in OpenTelemetry v0.17.0 lives in the `go.opentelemetry.io/otel/exporters/stdout` package.

Like most exporters' creation functions, `stdout.NewExporter`, is a variadic function that can accept zero or more configuration options. We demonstrate with one of these—the option to "pretty-print" its JSON output—here:

```
stdExporter, err := stdout.NewExporter(
    stdout.WithPrettyPrint(),
)
```

In the preceding snippet, we use the `stdout.NewExporter` function, which returns both our exporter and an `error` value. We'll see what its output looks like when we run our example in "Putting It All Together: Tracing" on page 363.

> For more information about the Console Exporter, please refer to its page in the relevant OpenTelemetry documentation (*https://oreil.ly/PEfAI*).

The Jaeger Exporter. The Console Exporter may be useful for logging and debugging, but OpenTelemetry also includes a number of exporters designed to forward data to specialized backends, such as the Jaeger Exporter.

The Jaeger Exporter (as its name suggests) knows how to encode tracing telemetry data to the Jaeger (*https://oreil.ly/uMAfg*) distributed tracing system. You can retrieve an exporter value using the `jaeger.NewRawExporter` function, as shown here:

```
jaegerEndpoint := "http://localhost:14268/api/traces"
serviceName := "fibonacci"

jaegerExporter, err := jaeger.NewRawExporter(
    jaeger.WithCollectorEndpoint(jaegerEndpoint),
    jaeger.WithProcess(jaeger.Process{
        ServiceName: serviceName,
    }),
)
```

In OpenTelemetry v0.17.0, the Jaeger Exporter can be found in the `go.opentelemetry.io/otel/exporter/trace/jaeger` package.

You may have noticed that `jaeger.NewRawExporter` works a lot like `stdout.NewEx porter` in that it's a variadic function that accepts zero or more configuration options, returning an `export.SpanExporter` (the Jaeger Exporter) and an `error` value.

The options passed to `jaeger.NewRawExporter` are:

- `jaeger.WithCollectorEndpoint`, which is used to define the URL that points to the target Jaeger process's HTTP collector endpoint
- `jaeger.WithProcess`, which allows you to set information about the exporting process, in this case the service's name

There are quite a few other configuration options available, but only two are used for the sake of brevity. If you're interested in more detail, please refer to its page in the relevant OpenTelemetry documentation (*https://oreil.ly/dOpd5*).

What Is Jaeger?

Jaeger (*https://oreil.ly/uMAfg*) is an open source distributed tracing system inspired by Google's seminal 2010 paper[7] describing its Dapper distributed systems tracing infrastructure, and the earlier OpenZipkin (*https://zipkin.io*) project.

Originally developed (in Go) as an internal project by Uber Technologies, it was released as open source under the Apache license in November 2016. In September of 2017, it became the Cloud Native Computing Foundation's 12th hosted project, and advanced to graduated status in October 2019.

Among its features is support for multiple storage backends (including in-memory storage for testing setups) and a modern web UI.

Creating a tracer provider

In order to generate traces, you first have to create and initialize a *tracer provider*, represented in OpenTelemetry by the `TracerProvider` type. In OpenTelemetry v0.17.0, it lives in the `go.opentelemetry.io/otel/sdk/trace` package, which is usually aliased to `sdktrace` to avoid naming collisions.

A `TracerProvider` is a stateful value that serves as the main entry point for the OpenTelemetry tracing API, including, as we'll see in the next section, providing access to the `Tracer` that in turn serves as the provider for new `Span` values.

---

7 Sigelman, Benjamin H., et al. "Dapper, a Large-Scale Distributed Systems Tracing Infrastructure." *Google Technical Report*, Apr. 2010. *https://oreil.ly/Vh7Ig*.

To create a tracer provider, we use the `sdktrace.NewTracerProvider` function:

```
tp := sdktrace.NewTracerProvider(
    sdktrace.WithSyncer(stdExporter),
    sdktrace.WithSyncer(jaegerExporter))
```

In this example, the two exporters that we created in "Creating the tracing exporters" on page 353—`stdExporter` and `jaegerExporter`—are provided to `sdktrace.NewTracerProvider`, instructing the SDK to use them for exporting telemetry data.

There are several other options that can be provided to `sdktrace.NewTracerProvider`, including defining a `Batcher` or a `SpanProcessor`. These are (reluctantly) beyond the scope of this book, but more information on these can be found in the OpenTelemetry SDK Specification (*https://oreil.ly/BaL9M*).

Setting the global tracer provider

Once you've created your tracer provider, it's generally a good practice to set it as your global tracer provider via the `SetTracerProvider` function. In OpenTelemetry v0.17.0, this and all of OpenTelemetry's global options live in the `go.opentelemetry.io/otel` package.

Here we set the global tracer provider to be the value of `tp`, which we created in the previous section:

```
otel.SetTracerProvider(tp)
```

Setting the global tracer provider makes it discoverable via the `otel.GetTracerProvider` function. This allows libraries and other dependencies that use the OpenTelemetry API to more easily discover the SDK and emit telemetry data:

```
gtp := otel.GetTracerProvider(tp)
```

 If you don't explicitly set a global tracer provider, `otel.GetTracer Provider` will return a no-op `TracerProvider` implementation that returns a no-op `Tracer` that provides no-op `Span` values.

Obtaining a tracer

In OpenTelemetry, a `Tracer` is a specialized type that keeps track of trace and span information, including what span is currently active. Before you can instrument an operation you first have to use a (usually global) tracer provider's `Tracer` method to obtain a `trace.Tracer` value:

```
tr := otel.GetTracerProvider().Tracer("fibonacci")
```

TracerProvider's Tracer method accepts a string parameter to set its name. By convention, Tracers are named after the component they are instrumenting, usually a library or a package.

Now that you have your tracer, your next step will be to use it to create and start a new Span instance.

Starting and ending spans

Once you have a handle to a Tracer, you can use it to create and start new Span values representing named and timed operations within a traced workflow. In other words, a Span value represents the equivalent of one step in a stack trace.

In OpenTelemetry v0.17.0, both the Span and Tracer interfaces can be found in the go.opentelemetry.io/otel/trace. Their relationship can be deduced by a quick review of Tracer's definition code:

```
type Tracer interface {
    Start(ctx context.Context, spanName string, opts ...trace.SpanOption)
        (context.Context, trace.Span)
}
```

Yes, that's really all there is. Tracer's only method, Start, accepts three parameters: a context.Context value, which is the mechanism that Tracer uses to keep track of spans; the name of the new span, which by convention is usually the name of the function or component being evaluated; and zero or more span configuration options.

> Unfortunately, a discussion of the available span configurations is beyond the scope of this book, but if you're interested, more detail is available in the relevant Go Documentation (*https://oreil.ly/ksmfV*).

Importantly, Start returns not just the new Span, but also a context.Context. This is a new Context instance derived from the one that was passed in. As we'll see shortly, this is important when we want to create child Span values.

Now that you have all of the pieces in place, you can begin instrumenting our code. To do this, you request a Span value from your Tracer via its Start method, as shown in the following:

```
const serviceName = "foo"

func main() {
    // EXPORTER SETUP OMITTED FOR BREVITY

    // Retrieve the Tracer from the otel TracerProvider.
```

```
tr := otel.GetTracerProvider().Tracer(serviceName)

// Start the root span; receive a child context (which now
// contains the trace ID), and a trace.Span.
ctx, sp := tr.Start(context.Background(), "main")
defer sp.End()      // End completes the span.

SomeFunction(ctx)
}
```

In this snippet we use Tracer's Start method to create and start a new Span, which returns a derived context and our Span value. It's important to note that we ensure that the Span is ended by calling it in a defer, so that SomeFunction is entirely captured in the root Span.

Of course, we'll also want to instrument SomeFunction. Since it receives the derived context we got from the original Start, it can now use that Context to create its own subspan:

```
func SomeFunction(ctx context.Context) {
    tr := otel.GetTracerProvider().Tracer(serviceName)
    _, sp := tr.Start(ctx, "SomeFunction")
    defer sp.End()

    // Do something MAGICAL here!
}
```

The only differences between main and SomeFunction are the names of the spans and the Context values. It's significant that SomeFunction uses the Context value derived from the original Start call in main.

Setting span metadata

Now that you have a Span, what do you do with it?

If you do nothing at all, that's okay. As long as you've remembered to End your Span (preferably in a defer statement) a minimal timeline for your function will be collected.

However, the value of your span can be enhanced with the addition of two types of metadata: *attributes* and *events*.

Attributes. Attributes are key/value pairs that are associated with spans. They can be used later for aggregating, filtering, and grouping traces.

If known ahead of time, attributes can be added when a span is created by passing them as option parameters to the tr.Start method using the WithAttributes function:

```
ctx, sp := tr.Start(ctx, "attributesAtCreation",
    trace.WithAttributes(
        label.String("hello", "world"), label.String("foo", "bar")))
defer sp.End()
```

Here we call `tr.Start` to start a new span, passing it our active `context.Context` value and a name. But `Start` is also a variadic function that can accept zero or more options, so we opt to use the `WithAttributes` function to pass two string attributes: `hello=world` and `foo=far`.

The `WithAttributes` function accepts a `label.KeyValue` type, from OpenTelemetry's `go.opentelemetry.io/otel/label` package. Values of this type can be created using the various type methods, such as `label.String` as above. Methods exist for all Go types (and more). See the label package's documentation (*https://oreil.ly/AVkTG*) for more information.

Attributes don't have to be added at span creation time. They can be added later in a span's lifecycle as well, as long as the span hasn't yet been completed:

```
answer := LifeTheUniverseAndEverything()
span.SetAttributes(label.Int("answer", answer))
```

Events.   An *event* is a timestamped, human-readable message on a span that represents *something* happening during the span's lifetime.

For example, if your function requires exclusive access to a resource that's under a mutex, you might find it useful to add events when you acquire and release the lock:

```
span.AddEvent("Acquiring mutex lock")
mutex.Lock()

// Do something amazing.

span.AddEvent("Releasing mutex lock")
mutex.Unlock()
```

If you like, you can even add attributes to your events:

```
span.AddEvent("Canceled by external signal",
    label.Int("pid", 1234),
    label.String("signal", "SIGHUP"))
```

Autoinstrumentation

Autoinstrumentation, broadly, refers to instrumentation code that you didn't write. This is a useful feature that can spare you from a fair amount of unnecessary bookkeeping.

OpenTelemetry supports autoinstrumentation through various wrappers and helper functions around many popular frameworks and libraries, including ones that we cover in this book, like net/http, gorilla/mux, and grpc.

While using these functionalities doesn't free you from having to configure OpenTelemetry at startup, they do remove some of the effort associated with having to manage your traces.

Autoinstrumenting net/http and gorilla/mux. In OpenTelemetry 0.17.0, autoinstrumentation support for both the standard net/http library and gorilla/mux, both of which we first covered in Chapter 5 in the context of building a RESTful web service, is provided by the go.opentelemetry.io/contrib/instrumentation/net/http/otelhttp package.

Its use is refreshingly minimalist. Take, for example, this standard idiom in net/http for registering a handler function to the default mux[8] and starting the HTTP server:

```go
func main() {
    http.HandleFunc("/", helloGoHandler)
    log.Fatal(http.ListenAndServe(":3000", nil))
}
```

In OpenTelemetry, a handler function can be autoinstrumented by passing it to the otelhttp.NewHandler function, the signature for which is shown here:

```go
func NewHandler(handler http.Handler, operation string, opts ...Option)
    http.Handler
```

The otelhttp.NewHandler function accepts and returns a handler function. It works by wrapping the passed handler function in a second handler function that creates a span with the provided name and options, so that the original handler acts like middleware within the returned span-handling function.

A typical application of the otelhttp.NewHandler function is shown in the following:

```go
func main() {
    http.Handle("/",
        otelhttp.NewHandler(http.HandlerFunc(helloGoHandler), "root"))
    log.Fatal(http.ListenAndServe(":3000", nil))
}
```

You'll notice that we have to cast the handler function to a http.HandlerFunc before passing it to otelhttp.NewHandler. This wasn't necessary before because http.HandleFunc performs this operation automatically before itself calling http.Handle.

---

8 Recall that the name "mux" is short for "HTTP request multiplexer."

If you're using `gorilla/mux`, the change is almost the same, except that you're using the `gorilla` mux instead of the default mux:

```
func main() {
    r := mux.NewRouter()
    r.Handle("/",
        otelhttp.NewHandler(http.HandlerFunc(helloGoHandler), "root"))
    log.Fatal(http.ListenAndServe(":3000", r))
}
```

You'll need to repeat this for each handler function you want to instrument, but either way the total amount of code necessary to instrument your entire service is pretty minimal.

Autoinstrumenting gRPC. In OpenTelemetry 0.17.0, autoinstrumentation support for gRPC, which we introduced in Chapter 8 in the context of loosely coupled data interchange, is provided by the `go.opentelemetry.io/contrib/instrumentation/google.golang.org/grpc/otelgrpc` package.[9]

Just like autoinstrumentation for `net/http`, autoinstrumentation for gRPC is very minimalist, leveraging *gRPC interceptors*. We haven't talked about gRPC interceptors at all yet, and unfortunately a full treatment of gRPC interceptors is beyond the scope of this book. They can be described as the gRPC equivalent to middleware in `gorilla/mux`, which we leveraged in "Load shedding" on page 274 to implement automatic load shedding.

As their name implies, gRPC interceptors can intercept gRPC requests and responses to, for example, inject information into the request, update the response before it's returned to the client, or to implement a cross-cutting functionality like authorization, logging, or caching.

 If you'd like to learn a little more about gRPC interceptors, the article "Interceptors in gRPC-Web" on the gRPC blog (*https://oreil.ly/R0MGm*) offers a good introduction to the subject. For a more in-depth coverage, you might want to invest in a copy of *gRPC: Up and Running* (*https://oreil.ly/N50q7*) by Kasun Indrasiri and Danesh Kuruppu (O'Reilly).

Taking a look at a slice of the original service code from "Implementing the gRPC service" on page 236, you can see two of the operative functions:

```
s := grpc.NewServer()
pb.RegisterKeyValueServer(s, &server{})
```

---

9 That wins the record for longest package name, at least in this book.

In the above snippet, we create a new gRPC server, and pass that along to our auto-generated code package to register it.

Interceptors can be added to a gRPC server using the `grpc.UnaryInterceptor` and/or `grpc.StreamInterceptor`, the former of which is used to intercept unary (standard request–response) service methods, and the latter of which is used for intercepting streaming methods.

To autoinstrument your gRPC server, you use one or both of these functions to add one or more off-the-shelf OpenTelemetry interceptors, depending on the types of requests your service handles:

```
s := grpc.NewServer(
    grpc.UnaryInterceptor(otelgrpc.UnaryServerInterceptor()),
    grpc.StreamInterceptor(otelgrpc.StreamServerInterceptor()),
)

pb.RegisterKeyValueServer(s, &server{})
```

While the service we built in Chapter 8 uses exclusively unary methods, the preceding snippet adds interceptors for both unary and stream methods for the sake of demonstration.

Getting the current span from context. If you're taking advantage of autoinstrumentation, a trace will automatically be created for each request. While convenient, this also means that you don't have your current `Span` immediately on hand for you to enhance with application-specific attribute and event metadata. So, what do you do?

Fear not! Since your application framework has conveniently placed the span data inside the current context, the data is easily retrievable:

```
func printSpanHandler(w http.ResponseWriter, req *http.Request) {
    ctx := req.Context()                         // Get the request Context

    span := trace.SpanFromContext(ctx)      // Get the current span

    fmt.Printf("current span: %v\n", span)  // Why not print the span?
}
```

What About the Clients?

For a complete distributed tracing experience, tracing metadata has to be forwarded across service boundaries. That means you have to instrument on the client side as well.

The good news is that OpenTelemetry supports autoinstrumentation of `http` and gRPC clients.

Unfortunately, there isn't enough space available in this chapter to cover client auto-instrumentation in any detail. Examples of both `http` and `gRPC` client autoinstrumentation are available in the GitHub repository associated with this book (*https://oreil.ly/SznMj*), however.

Putting It All Together: Tracing

Using all the parts that we've discussed in this section, let's now build a small web service. Because we're going to instrument this service with tracing, the ideal service would make a whole lot of function calls, but would still be pretty small.

We're going to build a Fibonacci service. Its requirements are very minimal: it will be able to accept an HTTP GET request, in which the *n*th Fibonacci number can be requested using parameter n on the GET query string. For example, to request the sixth Fibonacci number, you should be able to `curl` the service as: `http://local host:3000?n=6`.

To do this, we'll use a total of three functions. Starting from the inside and working our way out, these are:

The service API
> This will do the Fibonacci computation proper—at the request of the service handler—by recursively calling itself, with each call generating its own span.

The service handler
> This is an HTTP handler function as defined by the `net/http` package, which will be used just like in "Building an HTTP Server with net/http" on page 112 to receive the client request, call the service API, and return the result in the response.

The main function
> In the `main` function, the OpenTelemetry exporters are created and registered, the service handler function is provided to the HTTP framework, and the HTTP server is started.

The Fibonacci service API

The service API at the very core of the service is where the actual computation is performed. In this case, it's a concurrent implementation of the Fibonacci method to calculate the *n*th Fibonacci number.

Just like any good service API, this function doesn't know (or care) how it's being used, so it has no knowledge of HTTP requests or responses:

```
func Fibonacci(ctx context.Context, n int) chan int {
    ch := make(chan int)
```

```
go func() {
    tr := otel.GetTracerProvider().Tracer(serviceName)

    cctx, sp := tr.Start(ctx,
        fmt.Sprintf("Fibonacci(%d)", n),
        trace.WithAttributes(label.Int("n", n)))
    defer sp.End()

    result := 1
    if n > 1 {
        a := Fibonacci(cctx, n-1)
        b := Fibonacci(cctx, n-2)
        result = <-a + <-b
    }

    sp.SetAttributes(label.Int("result", result))

    ch <- result
}()

    return ch
}
```

In this example, the Fibonacci function doesn't know how it's being used, but it *does* know about the OpenTelemetry package. Autoinstrumentation can only trace what it wraps. Anything within the API will need to instrument itself.

This function's use of otel.GetTracerProvider ensures that it'll get the global TracerProvider, assuming that it was configured by the consumer. If no global tracer provider has been set, these calls will be no-ops.

 For extra credit, take a minute to add support for Context cancellation to the Fibonacci function.

The Fibonacci service handler

This is an HTTP handler function as defined by the net/http package.

It'll be used in our service just like in "Building an HTTP Server with net/http" on page 112: to receive the client request, call the service API, and return the result in the response:

```
func fibHandler(w http.ResponseWriter, req *http.Request) {
    var err error
    var n int

    if len(req.URL.Query()["n"]) != 1 {
```

```
        err = fmt.Errorf("wrong number of arguments")
    } else {
        n, err = strconv.Atoi(req.URL.Query()["n"][0])
    }

    if err != nil {
        http.Error(w, "couldn't parse index n", 400)
        return
    }

    // Retrieve the current context from the incoming request
    ctx := req.Context()

    // Call the child function, passing it the request context.
    result := <-Fibonacci(ctx, n)

    // Get the Span associated with the current context and
    // attach the parameter and result as attributes.
    if sp := trace.SpanFromContext(ctx); sp != nil {
        sp.SetAttributes(
            label.Int("parameter", n),
            label.Int("result", result))
    }

    // Finally, send the result back in the response.
    fmt.Fprintln(w, result)
}
```

Note that it doesn't have to create or end a Span; autoinstrumentation will do that for us.

It *does*, however, set some attributes on the current span. To do this, it uses `trace.SpanFromContext` to retrieve the current span from the request context. Once it has the span, it's free to add whatever metadata it likes.

> The `trace.SpanFromContext` function will return `nil` if it can't find a Span associated with the `Context` passed to it.

The service Main function

At this point, all of the hard work has been done. All we have left to do is configure OpenTelemetry, register the handler function with the default HTTP mux, and start the service:

```
const (
    jaegerEndpoint = "http://localhost:14268/api/traces"
    serviceName    = "fibonacci"
)
```

```
func main() {
    // Create and configure the console exporter
    stdExporter, err := stdout.NewExporter(
        stdout.WithPrettyPrint(),
    )
    if err != nil {
        log.Fatal(err)
    }

    // Create and configure the Jaeger exporter
    jaegerExporter, err := jaeger.NewRawExporter(
        jaeger.WithCollectorEndpoint(jaegerEndpoint),
        jaeger.WithProcess(jaeger.Process{
            ServiceName: serviceName,
        }),
    )
    if err != nil {
        log.Fatal(err)
    }

    // Create and configure the TracerProvider exporter using the
    // newly created exporters.
    tp := sdktrace.NewTracerProvider(
        sdktrace.WithSyncer(stdExporter),
        sdktrace.WithSyncer(jaegerExporter))

    // Now we can register tp as the otel trace provider.
    otel.SetTracerProvider(tp)

    // Register the autoinstrumented service handler
    http.Handle("/",
        otelhttp.NewHandler(http.HandlerFunc(fibHandler), "root"))

    // Start the service listening on port 3000
    log.Fatal(http.ListenAndServe(":3000", nil))
}
```

As you can see, the majority of the main method is dedicated to creating our (console and Jaeger) exporters and configuring the tracer provider as we did in "Creating the tracing exporters" on page 353. Note the value of jaegerEndpoint, which assumes that you'll have a local Jaeger service running. We'll do that in the next step.

The last two lines are spent autoinstrumenting and registering the handler function and starting the HTTP service, just as we did in "Autoinstrumentation" on page 359.

Starting your services

Before we continue, we'll want to start a Jaeger service to receive the telemetry data provided by the Jaeger exporter that we included. For a little more background on Jaeger, see "What Is Jaeger?" on page 355.

If you have Docker installed, you can start a Jaeger service with the following command:

```
$ docker run -d --name jaeger   \
  -p 16686:16686                 \
  -p 14268:14268                 \
  jaegertracing/all-in-one:1.21
```

Once the service is up and running, you'll be able to access its web interface by browsing to `http://localhost:16686`. Obviously, there won't be any data there yet, though.

Now for the fun part: start your service by running its main function:

```
$ go run .
```

Your terminal should pause. As usual, you can stop the service with a Ctrl-C.

Finally, in another terminal, you can now send a request to the service:

```
$ curl localhost:3000?n=6
13
```

After a short pause, you should be rewarded with a result. In this case, 13.

Be careful with the value of n. If you make it n too large, it might take the service a long time to respond, or even crash.

Console exporter output

Now that you've issued a request to your service, take a look at the terminal you used to start your service. You should see several JSON blocks that resemble the following:

```
[
    {
        "SpanContext":{
            "TraceID":"4253c86eb68783546b8ae3b5e59b4a0c",
            "SpanID":"817822981fc2fb30",
            "TraceFlags":1
        },
        "ParentSpanID":"0000000000000000",
        "SpanKind":1,
        "Name":"main",
        "StartTime":"2020-11-27T13:50:29.739725-05:00",
        "EndTime":"2020-11-27T13:50:29.74044542-05:00",
        "Attributes":[
            {
                "Key":"n",
                "Value":{
                    "Type":"INT64",
                    "Value":6
                }
            },
```

```
        {
            "Key":"result",
            "Value":{
                "Type":"INT64",
                "Value":13
            }
        }
    ],
    "ChildSpanCount":1,
    "InstrumentationLibrary":{
        "Name":"fibonacci",
        "Version":""
    }
  }
}
]
```

These JSON objects are the output of the Console Exporter (which, remember, we've configured to pretty-print). There should be one per span, which is quite a few.

The preceding example (which has been pruned slightly) is from the root span. As you can see, it includes quite a few interesting bits of data, including its start and end times, and its trace and span IDs. It even includes the two attributes that we explicitly set: the input value n, and the result of our query.

Viewing your results in Jaeger

Now that you've generated your trace and sent it to Jaeger, it's time to visualize it. Jaeger just happens to provide a slick web UI for exactly that purpose!

To check it out, browse to `http://localhost:16686` with your favorite web browser. Select Fibonacci in the Service dropdown, and click the Find traces button. You should be presented with output similar to that shown in Figure 11-3.

Each bar in the visualization represents a single span. You can even view a specific span's data by clicking on it, which reveals the same data that was contained in the (quite verbose) console output that you saw in "Console exporter output" on page 367.

Figure 11-3. Screenshot of the Jaeger interface, displaying the results of a concurrent Fibonacci call

Metrics

Metrics is the collection of numerical data about a component, process, or activity over time. The number of potential metric sources is vast, and includes (but isn't limited to) things like computing resources (CPU, memory used, disk and network I/O), infrastructure (instance replica count, autoscaling events), applications (request count, error count), and business metrics (revenue, customer sign-ups, bounce rate, cart abandonment). Of course, these are just a handful of trivial examples. For a complex system, the *cardinality* can range into the many thousands, or even millions.

A metric data point, representing one observation of a particular aspect of the target (such as the number of hits an endpoint has received), is called a *sample*. Each sample has a name, a value, and a millisecond-precision timestamp. Also—at least in modern systems like Prometheus (*https://prometheus.io*)—a set of key-value pairs called *labels*.

Cardinality

Cardinality is an important concept in observability. It has its origins in set theory, where it's defined as the number of elements in a set. For example, the set $A = \{1, 2, 3, 5, 8\}$ contains five elements, so A therefore has a cardinality of five.

The term was later adopted by database designers to refer to the number of distinct values in a table column.[10] For example, "eye color" would have a low cardinality, while "username" would be quite high.

More recently, however, the term "cardinality" has been adopted for monitoring, where it's come to refer to the number of unique combinations of metric names and dimensions—the number of distinct label values attached to a particular metric—in your monitoring system. High cardinality information is critical for observability because it means that the data has many different ways that it can be queried, making it all the more likely that you'll be able to ask it a question that you'd never thought to ask before.

By itself, a single sample is of limited use, but a sequence of successive samples with the same name and labels—a *time series*—can be incredibly useful. As illustrated in Figure 11-4, collecting samples as a time series allows metrics to be easily visualized by plotting the data points on a graph, in turn making it easier to see trends or to observe anomalies or outliers.

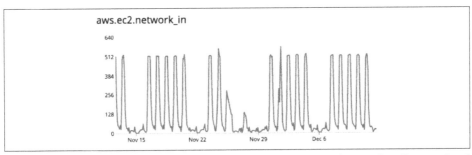

Figure 11-4. Arranging samples as a time series allows them to be graphically visualized

In the above figure, we show a time series of the metric `aws.ec2.network_in` for one AWS EC2 instance. Time is on the x-axis (specifically, one month spanning November–December 2020). The y-axis represents the instantaneous rate at which the instance is receiving network data at that moment. Visualizing the time series this way, it becomes obvious that traffic to the instance spikes each weekday.

---

10 It can *also* refer to the numerical relationship between two database tables (i.e., *one-to-one*, *one-to-many*, or *many-to-many*), but that definition is arguably less relevant here.

Interestingly, November 25–27—the days spanning the day before to the day after Thanksgiving in the United States—are the exceptions.

The true power of metrics, however, isn't its ability to be visually represented for human eyes: it's that its numerical nature makes it particularly amenable to mathematical modeling. For example, you might use trend analysis to detect anomalies or predict future states, which in turn can inform decisions or trigger alerts.

Push Versus Pull Metric Collection

There are two primary architectures in the universe of metrics: push-based and pull-based (so called because of the relationship between the components being monitored and the collector backend).

In push-based metrics, monitored components "push" their data to a central collector backend. In pull-based metrics, the inverse is true: the collector actively retrieves metrics by "pulling" them from HTTP endpoints exposed by the monitored components (or by sidecar services deployed for this purpose, also confusingly called "exporters"; see "Prometheus Exporters" on page 377). Both approaches are illustrated in Figure 11-5.

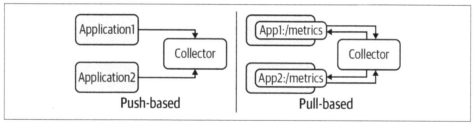

Figure 11-5. Push-based metrics (left) send telemetry directly to a central collector backend; pull-based metrics (right) are actively scraped by the collector from exposed metric endpoints

What follows is a short description of each of these approaches, along with a very limited list of some arguments for and against each approach. Unfortunately, there are bounteous arguments, many quite nuanced—far too nuanced to delve into here—so we'll have to be content with some of the common ones.

Push-based metric collection

In push-based metric collection, an application, either directly or via a parallel agent process, periodically sends data to a central collector backend. Push implementations, like Ganglia, Graphite, and StatsD, tend to be the most common (even default) approach, perhaps in part because the push model tends to be quite a bit easier to reason about.

Push messages are typically unidirectional, being emitted by the monitored components or monitoring agent and sent to a central collector. This places a bit less burden on the network relative to the (bidirectional) pull model, and can reduce the complexity of the network security model, since components don't have to make a metrics endpoint accessible to the collector. It's also easier to use the push model to monitor highly ephemeral components such as short-lived containers or serverless functions.

There are some downsides to the push model, though. First, you need to know where to send your request. While there are lots of ways of doing this, each has its downside, ranging from hardcoded addresses (which are hard to change) to DNS lookups or service discovery (which may add unacceptable latency). Scaling can also sometimes be an issue, in that it's entirely possible for a large number of components to effectively DDoS your collector backend.

Pull-based metric collection

In the pull-based collection model, the collector backend periodically (on some configurable cadence) scrapes a metric endpoint exposed by a component, or by a proxy deployed for this purpose. Perhaps the best-known example of a pull-based system is Prometheus (*https://prometheus.io*).

The pull approach offers some notable advantages. Exposing a metric endpoint decouples the components being observed from the collector itself, which provides all of the benefits of loose coupling. For example, it becomes easier to monitor a service during development, or even manually inspect a component's health with a web browser. It's also much easier for a pull model to tell if a target is down.

However, the pull approach has a discovery issue of its own, in that the collector has to somehow know where to find the services it's supposed to monitor. This can be a bit of a challenge, particularly if your system isn't using dynamic service discovery. Load balancers are of little help here, either, since each request will be forwarded to a random instance, greatly reducing the effective collection rate (since each of N instance receives 1/N of the pulls) and severely muddying what data is collected (since all of the instances tend to look like a single target). Finally, pull-based collection can make it somewhat harder to monitor very short-lived ephemeral things like serverless functions, necessitating a solution like the push gateway.

What Is Prometheus?

Prometheus (*https://prometheus.io*) is an open source monitoring and alerting toolkit. It uses a pull model over HTTP to scrape metric data, storing it as high-dimensionality values in its time series database.

Prometheus consists of a core server, which is responsible for the acquisition and storage of data, as well as a variety of other optional components, including a push gateway for supporting data pushes by short-lived jobs, and an alertmanager for handling alerts. While Prometheus isn't intended as a dashboarding solution, it also provides a basic web UI and query language, PromQL, to make data more easily accessible.

In January of 2015, SoundCloud publicly released Prometheus as an open source project under the Apache license, and in May 2016, Prometheus joined the Cloud Native Computing Foundation as its second hosted project (after Kubernetes). It advanced to graduated status in August 2018.

But which is better?

Since the push and pull approaches are, it would seem, polar opposites of one another, it's common for people to wonder which is better.[11] That's a hard question, and as is often the case when comparing technical methodologies, the answer is a resounding "it depends."

Of course, that's never stopped a sufficiently motivated programmer from stridently arguing one side or another, but at the end of the day, the "better" approach is the one that satisfies the requirements of your system. Of course (and quite unsatisfyingly) that could be both. We technical types abhor ambiguity, yet it stubbornly insists on existing anyway.

So, I will close this section with the words of Brian Brazil, a core developer of Prometheus:

> From an engineering standpoint, in reality, the question of push versus pull largely doesn't matter. In either case, there's advantages and disadvantages, and with engineering effort, you can work around both cases.[12]

---

11 Whatever "better" means.

12 Kiran, Oliver. "Exploring Prometheus Use Cases with Brian Brazil." *The New Stack Makers*, 30 Oct. 2016. *https://oreil.ly/YDlek*.

Metrics with OpenTelemetry

As of the time of writing, the OpenTelemetry metrics API is still in alpha, so it still has a few rough spots to be ironed out and a few inconsistencies with the tracing API that are yet to be resolved.

That being said, the considerable private and community support behind OpenTelemetry, coupled with its quite impressive rate of development, make it appropriate not just for inclusion in this book, but as the most likely candidate to become the gold standard for metric telemetry for the next several years at least.

For the most part, OpenTelemetry metrics work a lot like traces, but are different enough to possibly cause some confusion. For both tracing and metric instrumentation, the configuration phase is executed exactly once in a program, usually in the `main` function, and includes the following steps:

1. The first step is to create and configure the appropriate exporter for the target backend. Metric exporters implement the `metric.Exporter` interface, which in OpenTelemetry v0.17.0 is located in the `go.opentelemetry.io/otel/sdk/export/metric` package. As we'll discuss in "Creating the metric exporters" on page 375, several stock exporters are included with OpenTelemetry, but unlike trace exporters, you can currently only use one metric exporter at a time.

2. Before instrumenting your code for metrics, the exporter is used to define the global "meter provider," which will serve as your program's main entry point into the OpenTelemetry metric API throughout its lifetime. As we'll see in "Setting the global meter provider" on page 376, this makes the meter exporter discoverable via the `otel.GetMeterProvider` function, which allows libraries and other dependencies that use the OpenTelemetry API to more easily access the SDK and emit telemetry data.

3. If your metric backend uses a pull-based design like Prometheus, you'll have to expose a metric endpoint that it can pull from. You'll see how the Prometheus exporter leverages Go's standard `http` package to do this in "Exposing the metrics endpoint" on page 376.

Once the configuration is complete, instrumenting your code requires only a few small steps:

1. Before you can instrument an operation, you first have to obtain a `Meter`, the structure through which all metric collection is configured and reported, from the meter provider. We'll discuss this in more detail in "Obtaining a meter" on page 378.

2. Finally, once you have a `Meter`, you can use it to instrument your code. There are two ways this can be done, either by explicitly recording measurements, or by

creating *observers* that can autonomously and asynchronously collect data. Both of these approaches are covered in "Metric instruments" on page 379.

OpenTelemetry Metrics Imports

There are many, many packages in the OpenTelemetry framework. Fortunately, for the purposes of this section, we'll be able to focus on just a subset of these.

The examples in this section were created using OpenTelemetry v0.17.0, which was the latest release at the time of writing. If you choose to follow along with this section, you'll need to import the following packages from that release:

```
import (
    "go.opentelemetry.io/otel"
    "go.opentelemetry.io/otel/exporters/metric/prometheus"
    "go.opentelemetry.io/otel/label"
    "go.opentelemetry.io/otel/metric"
)
```

As usual, the complete code examples are available in the GitHub repository (*https://oreil.ly/SznMj*) associated with this book.

Creating the metric exporters

Just like with tracing, the first thing you have to do when using OpenTelemetry for metrics is create and configure your exporters. Metric exporters implement the `metric.Exporter` interface, which in OpenTelemetry v0.17.0 lives in the `go.opentelemetry.io/otel/sdk/export/metric` package.

The way that you create metric exporters varies a little between implementations, but it's typical for an exporter to have a `NewExportPipeline` builder function, at least in the standard OpenTelemetry packages.

To get an instance of the Prometheus exporter, for example, you would use the `NewExportPipeline` function from the `go.opentelemetry.io/otel/exporters/metric/prometheus` package:

```
prometheusExporter, err := prometheus.NewExportPipeline(prometheus.Config{})
```

The above snippet creates the exporter and configures it according the directions specified by the passed `prometheus.Config` value. Any behaviors not overridden by the `Config` will use the recommended options.

The `prometheus.Config` parameter also allows you to specify a variety of custom behaviors. Unfortunately, the specifics are beyond the scope of this book, but if you're interested the exporter Config code (*https://oreil.ly/fKIzt*) and the code for the Prometheus Go client (*https://oreil.ly/biCJn*) are fairly straightforward.

Setting the global meter provider

Where OpenTelemetry tracing has the "tracer provider" that provides `Tracer` values, OpenTelemetry metrics has the *meter provider*, which provides the `Meter` values through which all metric collection is configured and reported.

You may recall that when working with tracing exporters, defining the global tracer provider requires two steps: creating and configuring a tracer provider instance, and then setting that instance as the global tracer provider.

The meter provider works a little differently: rather than using one or more exporters to create and define a provider (as is the case with the `TracerProvider`), a meter provider is typically retrieved *from* the metric exporter, and then passed directly to the `otel.SetMeterProvider` function:

```
// Get the meter provider from the exporter.
mp := prometheusExporter.MeterProvider()

// Set it as the global meter provider.
otel.SetMeterProvider(mp)
```

An unfortunate consequence of this design is that you're limited to using only one metric exporter at a time, since the meter provider is provided by the exporter instead of the other way around. Obviously, this is a significant deviation from how the tracing API works, and I expect it to change as the OpenTracing metrics API moves into beta.

 There's also a `prometheus.InstallNewPipeline` convenience function that can be used instead of explicitly calling the `prometheus.NewExportPipeline` and `otel.SetMeterProvider` functions.

Exposing the metrics endpoint

Because Prometheus is pull-based, any telemetry data we want to send it must be exposed through an HTTP endpoint that the collector can scrape.

To do this, we can make use of Go's standard `http` package, which, as we've shown several times in this book, requires minimal configuration, and is rather straightforward to use.

To review what we first introduced in "Building an HTTP Server with net/http" on page 112, starting a minimal HTTP server in Go requires at least two calls:

- `http.Handle` to register a handler function that implements the `http.Handler` interface

- `http.ListenAndServe` to start the server listening

But the OpenTelemetry Prometheus exporter has a pretty nifty trick up its sleeve: it implements the `http.Handler` interface, which allows it to be passed directly to `http.Handle` to act as a handler function for the metric endpoint! See the following:

```
// Register the exporter as the handler for the "/metrics" pattern.
http.Handle("/metrics", prometheusExporter)

// Start the HTTP server listening on port 3000.
log.Fatal(http.ListenAndServe(":3000", nil))
```

In this example, we pass the Prometheus exporter directly into `http.Handle` to register it as the handler for the pattern "/metrics." It's hard to get more convenient than that.

 Ultimately, the name of your metrics endpoint is up to you, but `metrics` is the most common choice. It's also where Prometheus looks by default.

Prometheus Exporters

It's relatively straightforward to expose a metrics endpoint if your application is a standard web service written in Go. But what if you want to collect JMX data from a JVM-based application, query metrics from a PostgreSQL database, or system metrics from a deployed Linux or Windows instance?

Unfortunately, not all of the things you'll want to collect data on are things that you control, and very few of them natively expose their own metrics endpoints.

In this (very common) scenario, the typical pattern is to deploy a *Prometheus exporter*. A Prometheus exporter (not to be confused with an OpenTelemetry exporter) is a specialized adapter that runs as a service to collect the desired metric data and expose it on a metrics endpoint.

As of the time of writing, there are over 200 different Prometheus exporters listed in the Prometheus documentation (*https://oreil.ly/ZppOm*), and many more community-built exporters that aren't. You can check that page for an up-to-date list, but some of the most popular are:

Node Exporter (https://oreil.ly/lq2Rv)
  Exposes hardware and OS metrics exposed by *NIX kernels.

Windows Exporter (https://oreil.ly/2LIFK)
  Exposes hardware and OS metrics exposed by Windows.

JMX Exporter (https://oreil.ly/rY0jg)
  Scrapes and expose MBeans of a JMX (*https://oreil.ly/11HLz*) target.

PostgreSQL Exporter (https://oreil.ly/yhZrn)
  Retrieves and exposes PostgreSQL server metrics.

Redis Exporter (https://oreil.ly/XRkfl)
  Retrieves and exposes Redis server metrics.

Blackbox Exporter (https://oreil.ly/VuM0U)
  Allows blackbox probing of endpoints over HTTP, HTTPS, DNS, TCP, or ICMP.

Push Gateway (https://oreil.ly/JxO3w)
  A metrics cache that lets ephemeral and batch jobs expose their metrics by pushing them to an intermediary. Technically a core component of Prometheus rather than a distinct exporter.

Obtaining a meter

Before you can instrument an operation, you first have to obtain a `Meter` value from a `MeterProvider`.

As you'll see in "Metric instruments" on page 379, the `metric.Meter` type, which lives in the `go.opentelemetry.io/otel/metric` package, is the means by which all metric collection is configured and reported, either as record batches of synchronous measurements or asynchronous observations.

You can retrieve a `Meter` value as follows:

```
meter := otel.GetMeterProvider().Meter("fibonacci")
```

You may have noticed that snippet looks almost exactly like the expression used to get a `Tracer` back in "Obtaining a tracer" on page 356. In fact, `otel.GetMeterProvider` is exactly equivalent to `otel.GetTracerProvider`, and works pretty much the same way.

The `otel.GetMeterProvider` function returns the registered global meter provider. If none is registered then a default meter provider is returned that forwards the `Meter` interface to the first registered `Meter` value.

The provider's `Meter` method returns an instance of the `metric.Meter` type. It accepts a string parameter representing the instrumentation name, which by convention is named after the library or package it's instrumenting.

Metric instruments

Once you have a `Meter`, you can create *instruments*, which you can use to make measurements and to instrument your code. However, just as there are several different types of metrics, there are several types of instruments. The type of instrument you use will depend on the type of measurement you're making.

All told, there are 12 *kinds* of instruments available, each with some combination of *synchronicity*, *accumulation* behavior, and data type.

The first of these properties, *synchronicity*, determines how an instrument collects and transmits data:

- *Synchronous instruments* are explicitly called by the user to record a metric, as we'll see in "Synchronous instruments" on page 381.
- *Asynchronous instruments*, also called *observers*, can monitor a specific property and are asynchronously called by the SDK during collection. We'll demonstrate in "Asynchronous instruments" on page 383.

Second, each instrument has an *accumulation* behavior that describes how it tracks the acquisition of new data:

- *Additive* instruments are used to track a sum that can go arbitrarily up or down, like a gauge. They're typically used for measured values like temperatures or current memory usage, but also "counts" that can go up and down, like the number of concurrent requests.
- *Additive monotonic* instruments track monotonically increasing (*https://oreil.ly/RESQ1*) values that can only increase (or be reset to zero on restart), like a counter. Additive monotonic values are often used for metrics like the number of requests served, tasks completed, or errors.
- *Grouping* instruments are intended for capturing a distribution, like a histogram. A grouping instrument samples observations (usually things like request durations or response sizes) and counts them in configurable buckets. It also provides a sum of all observed values.

Finally, each of the previous six kinds of instruments has types that support either `float64` or `int64` input values, for a total of 12 kinds of instruments. Each has an associated type in the `go.opentelemetry.io/otel/metric` package, summarized in Table 11-1.

Table 11-1. The 12 kinds of OpenTelemetry metric instruments, by synchronicity and accumulation behavior.

	Synchronous	Asynchronous
Additive	Float64UpDownCounter, Int64UpDownCounter	Float64UpDownSumObserver, Int64UpDownSumObserver
Additive, Monotonic	Float64Counter, Int64Counter	Float64SumObserver, Int64SumObserver
Grouping	Float64ValueRecorder, Int64ValueRecorder	Float64ValueObserver, Int64ValueObserver

Each of the 12 types has an associated constructor function on the `metric.Meter` type, all with a similar signature. For example, the `NewInt64Counter` method looks like the following:

```
func (m Meter) NewInt64Counter(name string, options ...InstrumentOption)
    (Int64Counter, error)
```

All 12 constructor methods accept the name of the metric as a `string`, and zero or more `metric.InstrumentOption` values, just like the `NewInt64Counter` method. Similarly, each returns an instrument value of the appropriate type with the given name and options, and can return an error if the name is empty or otherwise invalid, or if the instrument is duplicate registered.

For example, a function that uses the `NewInt64Counter` method to get a new `metric.Int64Counter` from a `metric.Meter` value looks something like the following:

```
// The requests counter instrument. As a synchronous instrument,
// we'll need to keep it so we can use it later to record data.
var requests metric.Int64Counter

func buildRequestsCounter() error {
    var err error

    // Retrieve the meter from the meter provider.
    meter := otel.GetMeterProvider().Meter(serviceName)

    // Get an Int64Counter for a metric called "fibonacci_requests_total".
    requests, err = meter.NewInt64Counter("fibonacci_requests_total",
        metric.WithDescription("Total number of Fibonacci requests."),
    )

    return err
}
```

Note how we retain a reference to the instrument in the form of the `requests` global variable. For reasons I'll discuss shortly, this is generally specific to synchronous instruments.

But while the `metric.Int64Counter` happens to be a synchronous instrument, the takeaway here is that synchronous and asynchronous instruments are both obtained in the same way: via the corresponding `Metric` constructor method. How they're used, however, differs significantly, as we'll see in the subsequent sections.

Synchronous instruments. The initial steps to using a synchronous instrument— retrieving a meter from the meter provider and creating an instrument—are largely the same for both synchronous and asynchronous instruments. We saw these in the previous section.

However, using synchronous instruments differs from using asynchronous instruments in that they're explicitly exercised in your code logic when recording a metric, which means you have to be able to refer to your instrument after it's been created. That's why the above example uses a global `requests` variable.

Perhaps the most common application is to record individual events by incrementing a counter when an event occurs. The additive instruments even have an `Add` method for this. The following example uses the `requests` value that we created in the previous example by adding a call to `requests.Add` to the API's `Fibonacci` function that was originally defined in "The Fibonacci service API" on page 363:

```
// Define our labels here so that we can easily reuse them.
var labels = []label.KeyValue{
    label.Key("application").String(serviceName),
    label.Key("container_id").String(os.Getenv("HOSTNAME")),
}

func Fibonacci(ctx context.Context, n int) chan int {
    // Use the Add method on out metric.Int64Counter instance
    // to increment the counter value.
    requests.Add(ctx, 1, labels...)

    // The rest of the function...
}
```

As you can see, the `requests.Add` method—which is safe for concurrent use— accepts three parameters:

- The first parameter is the current context in the form of a `context.Context` value. This is common for all of the synchronous instrument methods.

- The second parameter is the number to increment by. In this case, each call to `Fibonacci` increases the call counter by one.

- The third parameter is zero or more `label.KeyValue` values that represent the labels to associate with the data points. This increases the cardinality of the metrics, which, as discussed in "Cardinality" on page 370, is incredibly useful.

Data labels are a powerful tool that allow you to describe data beyond which service or instance emitted it. They can allow you to ask questions of your data that you hadn't thought of before.

It's also possible to group multiple metrics and report them as a batch. This works slightly differently than the Add method you saw in the previous example, though. Specifically, for each metric in the batch, you need to:

1. Collect the value or values you want to record.

2. Pass each value to its appropriate instrument's Measurement method, which returns a metric.Measurement value that wraps your metric and provides some supporting metadata.

3. Pass all of the metric.Measurement values to the meter.RecordBatch, which atomically records the entire batch of measurements.

These steps are demonstrated in the following example, in which we use the runtime package to retrieve two values—the amount of memory and the number of goroutines used by the process—and emit them to the metrics collector:

```
func updateMetrics(ctx context.Context) {
    // Retrieve the meter from the meter provider.
    meter := otel.GetMeterProvider().Meter(serviceName)

    // Create the instruments that we'll use to report memory
    // and goroutine values. Error values ignored for brevity.
    mem, _ := meter.NewInt64UpDownCounter("memory_usage_bytes",
        metric.WithDescription("Amount of memory used."),
    )
    goroutines, _ := meter.NewInt64UpDownCounter("num_goroutines",
        metric.WithDescription("Number of running goroutines."),
    )

    var m runtime.MemStats

    for {
        runtime.ReadMemStats(&m)

        // Report the values to the instruments, and receive
        // metric.Measurement values in return.
        mMem := mem.Measurement(int64(m.Sys))
        mGoroutines := goroutines.Measurement(int64(runtime.NumGoroutine()))

        // Provide the measurements (and teh context and
        // labels) to the meter.
        meter.RecordBatch(ctx, labels, mMem, mGoroutines)
```

```
        time.Sleep(5 * time.Second)
    }
}
```

When run as a goroutine, the `updateMetrics` function executes in two parts: an initial setup, and an infinite loop in which it generates and records measurements.

In the set-up phase, it retrieves the `Meter`, defines some metric labels, and creates the instruments. All of these values are created exactly once and are reused in the loop. Note that in addition to types, the instruments are created with names and descriptions indicating the metrics they're instrumenting.

Inside the loop, we first use the `runtime.ReadMemStats` and `runtime.NumGoroutine` functions to retrieve the metrics we want to record (the amount of memory used and the number of running goroutines, respectively). With those values, we use the instruments' `Measurement` methods to generate `metrics.Measurement` values for each metric.

With our `Measurement` values in hand, we pass them into the `meter.RecordBatch` method—which also accepts the current `context.Context` and any labels that we want to attach to the metrics—to officially record them.

Asynchronous instruments. Asynchronous instruments, or *observers*, are created and configured during setup to measure a particular property, and are subsequently called by the SDK during collection. This is especially useful when you have a value you want to monitor without managing your own background recording process.

Just like synchronous instruments, asynchronous instruments are created from a constructor method attached to a `metric.Meter` instance. In total, there are six such functions: a `float64` and `int64` version for each of the three accumulation behaviors. All six have a very similar signature, of which the following is representative:

```
func (m Meter) NewInt64UpDownSumObserver(name string,
    callback Int64ObserverFunc, opts ...InstrumentOption)
    (Int64UpDownSumObserver, error)
```

As you can see, the `NewInt64UpDownSumObserver` accepts the name of the metric as a `string`, something called a `Int64ObserverFunc`, and zero or more instrument options (such as the metric description). Although it returns the observer value, this isn't actually used all that often, though it can return a non-`nil` error if the name is empty, duplicate registered, or otherwise invalid.

The second parameter—the *callback function*—is the heart of any asynchronous instrument. Callback functions are asynchronously called by the SDK upon data collection. There are two kinds, one each for `int64` and `float64`, but they look, feel, and work essentially the same:

```
type Int64ObserverFunc func(context.Context, metric.Int64ObserverResult)
```

When called by the SDK, the callback functions receive the current context.Con text, and either a metric.Float64ObserverResult (for float64 observers) or metric.Int64ObserverResult (for int64 observers). Both result types have an Observe method, which you use to report your results.

This is a lot of little details, but they come together fairly seamlessly. The following function does exactly that, defining two observers:

```
func buildRuntimeObservers() {
    meter := otel.GetMeterProvider().Meter(serviceName)
    m := runtime.MemStats{}

    meter.NewInt64UpDownSumObserver("memory_usage_bytes",
        func(_ context.Context, result metric.Int64ObserverResult) {
            runtime.ReadMemStats(&m)
            result.Observe(int64(m.Sys), labels...)
        },
        metric.WithDescription("Amount of memory used."),
    )

    meter.NewInt64UpDownSumObserver("num_goroutines",
        func(_ context.Context, result metric.Int64ObserverResult) {
            result.Observe(int64(runtime.NumGoroutine()), labels...)
        },
        metric.WithDescription("Number of running goroutines."),
    )
}
```

When called by main, the buildRuntimeObservers function defines two asynchronous instruments—memory_usage_bytes and num_goroutines—each with a callback function that works exactly like the data collection in the updateMetrics function that we defined in "Synchronous instruments" on page 381.

In updateMetrics, however, we used an infinite loop to synchronously report data. As you can see, using an asynchronous approach for non-event data is not only less work to set up and manage, but has fewer moving parts to worry about later, since there isn't anything else to do once the observers (and their callback functions) are defined and the SDK takes over.

Putting It All Together: Metrics

Now that we have an idea what metrics we're going to collect and how, we can use them to extend the Fibonacci web service that we put together in "Putting It All Together: Tracing" on page 363.

The functionality of the service will remain unchanged. As before, it will be able to accept an HTTP GET request, in which the nth Fibonacci number can be requested using parameter n on the GET query string. For example, to request the sixth

Fibonacci number, you should be able to `curl` the service as: `http://localhost:3000?n=6`.

The specific changes we'll be making, and the metrics that we'll be collecting, are as follows:

- Synchronously recording the API request count by adding the `buildRequestsCounter` function to `main` and instrumenting the `Fibonacci` function in the service API as we described in "Synchronous instruments" on page 381

- Asynchronously recording the processes' memory used, and number of active goroutines, by adding the `buildRuntimeObservers` described in "Asynchronous instruments" on page 383 to the `main` function

Starting your services

Once again, start your service by running its main function:

```
$ go run .
```

As before, your terminal should pause. You can stop the service with a Ctrl-C.

Next, you'll start the Prometheus server. But before you do, you'll need to create a minimal configuration file for it. Prometheus has a ton of available configuration options (*https://oreil.ly/h8A7f*), but the following should be perfectly sufficient. Copy and paste it into a file named `prometheus.yml`:

```
scrape_configs:
- job_name: fibonacci
  scrape_interval: 5s
  static_configs:
  - targets: ['host.docker.internal:3000']
```

This configuration defines a single target named `fibonacci` that lives at `host.docker.internal:3000` and will be scraped every five seconds (down from the default of every minute).

What is host.docker.internal?

The name `host.docker.internal` is a special DNS name defined in Docker Desktop for both Mac and Windows that resolves to the internal IP address used by the host, allowing the container to interact with host processes.

Importantly, this address is provided for development convenience and won't work in a production environment outside of Docker Desktop for Mac and Windows (i.e., it's not supported by default in Docker on Linux).

Once you've created the file prometheus.yml, you can start Prometheus. The easiest way to do this is a container using Docker:

```
docker run -d --name prometheus                              \
  -p 9090:9090                                               \
  -v "${PWD}/prometheus.yml:/etc/prometheus/prometheus.yml" \
  prom/prometheus:v2.23.0
```

 If you're using Linux for development, you'll need to add the parameter --add-host=host.docker.internal:host-gateway to the above command. *But do not use this in production.*

Now that your services are both running, you can send a request to the service:

```
$ curl localhost:3000?n=6
13
```

Behind the scenes, OpenTelemetry has just recorded a value for the number of requests (recursive and otherwise) made to its Fibonacci function.

Metric endpoint output

Now that your service is running, you can always examine its exposed metrics directly with a standard curl to its /metrics endpoint:

```
$ curl localhost:3000/metrics
# HELP fibonacci_requests_total Total number of Fibonacci requests.
# TYPE fibonacci_requests_total counter
fibonacci_requests_total{application="fibonacci",container_id="d35f0bef2ca0"} 25
# HELP memory_usage_bytes Amount of memory used.
# TYPE memory_usage_bytes gauge
memory_usage_bytes{application="fibonacci",container_id="d35f0bef2ca0"}
  7.5056128e+07
# HELP num_goroutines Number of running goroutines.
# TYPE num_goroutines gauge
num_goroutines{application="fibonacci",container_id="d35f0bef2ca0"} 6
```

As you can see, all three of the metrics you're recording—as well as their types, descriptions, labels, and values—are listed here. Don't be confused if the value of con tainer_id is empty: that just means you're not running in a container.

Viewing your results in Prometheus

Now that you've started your service, started Prometheus, and run a query or two to the service to seed some data, it's time to visualize your work in Prometheus. Again, Prometheus isn't a full-fledged graphing solution (you'll want to use something like Grafana (*https://grafana.com*) for that), but it does offer a simple interface for executing arbitrary queries.

You can access this interface by browsing to localhost:9090. You should be presented with a minimalist interface with a search field. To see the value of your metric over time, enter its name in the search field, hit enter, and click the "graph" tab. You should be presented with something like the screenshot in Figure 11-6.

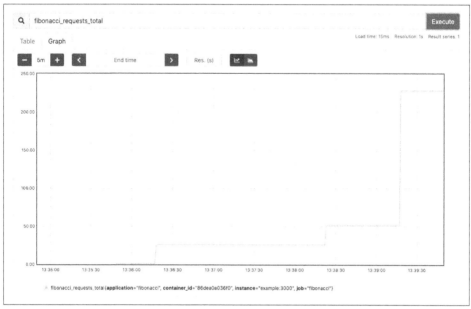

Figure 11-6. Screenshot of the Prometheus interface, displaying the value of the fibonacci_requests_total *metric after three calls to the Fibonacci service*

Now that you're collecting data, take a moment to run a few more queries and see how the graph changes. Maybe even look at some other metrics. Enjoy!

Logging

A *log* is an immutable record of *events*—discrete occurrences that are worth recording—emitted by an application over time. Traditionally, logs were stored as append-only files, but these days, a log is just as likely to take the form of some kind of searchable data store.

So, what's there to say about logging, other than that it's a really good idea that's been around as long as electronic computing has? It's the OG of observability methods.

There's actually quite a bit to say, largely because it's really, really easy to do logging in a way that makes your life harder than it needs to be.

Of the Three Pillars of Observability, logs are by far the easiest to generate. Since there's no initial processing involved in outputting a log event, in its simplest form it's as easy as adding a `print` statement to your code. This makes logs really good at providing lots and lots of context-rich data about what a component is doing or experiencing.

But this free-form aspect to logging cuts both ways. While it's possible (and often tempting) to output whatever you think might be useful, the verbose, unstructured logs are difficult to extract usable information from, especially at scale. To get the most out of logging, events should be structured, and that structure doesn't come for free. It has to be intentionally considered and implemented.

Another, particularly underappreciated, pitfall of logging is that generating lots of events puts significant pressure on disk and/or network I/O. It's not unusual for half or more of available bandwidth to be consumed this way. What's more, this pressure tends to scale linearly with load: `N` users each doing `M` things translates to `N*M` log events being emitted, with potentially disastrous consequences for scalability.

Finally, for logs to be meaningfully useful, they have to be processed and stored in a way that makes them accessible. Anybody who's ever had to manage logs at scale can tell you that it's notoriously operationally burdensome to self-manage and self-host, and absurdly expensive to have somebody else manage and host.

In the remainder of this section, we'll first discuss some high-level practices for logging at scale, followed by how to implement them in Go.

Better Logging Practices

As simple as the act of logging may seem on the face of it, it's also really easy to log in a way that makes life harder for you and anybody who has to use your logs after you. Awkward logging issues, like having to navigate unstructured logs or higher-than-expected resource consumption, which are annoying in small deployments, become major roadblocks at scale.

As you'll see, for this reason and others, the best practices around logging tend to focus on maximizing the quality, and minimizing the quantity, of logging data generated and retained.

 It goes without saying that you shouldn't log sensitive business data or personally identifiable information.

Treat logs as streams of events

How many times have you looked at log output and been confronted with an inscrutable stream of consciousness? How useful was it? Better than nothing, maybe, but probably not by much.

Logs shouldn't be treated as data sinks to be written to and forgotten until something is literally on fire, and they definitely shouldn't be a garbage dump where you send random thoughts and observations.

Instead, as we saw back in Chapter 6, logs should be treated as a *stream of events*, and should be written, unbuffered, directly to `stdout` and `stderr`. Though seemingly simple (and perhaps somewhat counterintuitive), this small change in perspective provides a great deal of freedom.

By moving the responsibility for log management out of the application code, it's freed from concerns about implementation trivialities like routing or storage of its log events, allowing the executor to decide what happens to them.

This approach provides quite a lot of freedom for how you manage and consume your logs. In development, you can keep an eye on your service's behavior by sending them directly to a local terminal. In production, the execution environment can capture and redirect log events to a log indexing system like ELK or Splunk for review and analysis, or perhaps a data warehouse for long-term storage.

Treat logs as streams of events, and write each event, unbuffered, directly to `stdout` and `stderr`.

Structure events for parsing

Logging, in its simplest and most primitive form, is technically possible using nothing more than `fmt.Println` statements. The result, however, would be a set of unformatted strings of questionable utility.

Fortunately, it's more common for programmers to use Go's standard `log` library, which is conveniently located and easy to use, and generates helpful timestamps. But how useful would a terabyte or so of log events formatted like the following be?

```
2020/11/09 02:15:10AM User 12345: GET /help in 23ms
2020/11/09 02:15:11AM Database error: connection reset by peer
```

Certainly, it's better than nothing, but you're still confronted with a mostly unstructured string, albeit an unstructured string with a timestamp. You still have to parse the arbitrary text to extract the meaningful bits.

Compare that to the equivalent messages outputted by a structured logger:[13]

```
{"time":1604888110, "level":"info", "method":"GET", "path":"/help",
       "duration":23, "message":"Access"}
{"time":1604888111, "level":"error", "error":"connection reset by peer",
       "database":"user", "message":"Database error"}
```

The above log structure places all of the key elements into properties of a JavaScript object, each with:

time
: A timestamp, which is a piece of contextual information that's critical for tracking and correlating issues. Note that the JSON example is also in an easily-parsable format that's far less computationally expensive to extract meaning from than the first, barely structured example. When you're processing billions of log events, little things add up.

level
: A log level, which is a label that indicates the level of importance for the log event. Frequently used levels include INFO, WARN, and ERROR. These are also key for filtering out low-priority messages that might not be relevant in production.

One or more contextual elements
: These contain background information that provides insight into the state of the application at the time of the message. The *entire point* of a log event is to express this context information.

In short, the structured log form is easier, faster, and cheaper to extract meaning from, and the results are far easier to search, filter, and aggregate.

Structure your logs for parsing by computers, not for reading by humans.

Less is (way) more

Logging isn't free. In fact, it's very expensive.

Imagine you have a service deployed to a server running in AWS. Nothing fancy, just a standard server with a standard, general-purpose disk capable of a sustained throughput of 16 MiB/second.

Let's say that your service likes to be thorough, so it fastidiously logs events acknowledging each request, response, database call, calculation status, and various other bits of information, totaling sixteen 1024-byte events for each request the service handles. It's a little verbose, but nothing too unusual so far.

---

13 Any wrapping in the example is for the benefit of formatting for presentation only. Don't use line breaks in your log events if you can help it.

But this adds up. In a scenario in which the service handles 512 requests per second—a perfectly reasonable number for a highly concurrent service—your service would produce 8192 events/second. At 16 KiB per event, that's a total of 8 MiB/second of log events, or *half of your disk's I/O capacity*. That's quite a burden.

What if we skip writing to disk and forward events straight to a log-hosting service? Well, the bad news is that we then have to transfer and store our logs, and that gets expensive. If you're sending the data across the internet to a log provider like Splunk or Datadog, you'll have to pay your cloud provider a data transfer fee. For AWS, this amounts to US$0.08/GB, which at an average rate of 8 MiB/s—about 1 TiB every day and a half—comes to almost $250,000/year for a single instance. Fifty such instances would run more than $12 million dollars in data transfer costs alone.

Obviously, this example doesn't take into account fluctuations in load due to hour of day or day of week. But it clearly illustrates that logging can get very expensive very quickly, so log only what's useful, and be sure to limit log generation in production by using severity thresholds. A "warning" threshold is common.

Dynamic sampling

Because the kind of events that are produced by debug events tend to be both high-volume and low-fidelity, it's pretty standard practice to eliminate them from production output by setting the log level to WARNING. But debug logs aren't *worthless*, are they?[14] As it turns out, they become really useful really fast when you're trying to chase down the root cause of an outage, which means you have to waste precious incident time turning debug logs on just long enough for you find the problem. Oh, and don't forget to turn them off afterwards.

However, by *dynamically sampling* your logs—recording some proportion of events and dropping the rest—you can still have your debug logs—but not too many—available in production, which can help drive down the time to recovery during an incident.

Having some debug logs in production can be *really* useful when things are on fire.

Logging with Go's Standard log Package

Go includes a standard logging package, appropriately named log, that provides some basic logging features. While it's very bare bones, it still has just about everything you need to put together a basic logging strategy.

Besides importing the log package, using it doesn't require any kind of setup.

---

14 If they are, why are you producing them at all?

Its most basic functions can be leveraged with a selection of functions very similar to the various `fmt` print functions you may be familiar with:

```
func Print(v ...interface{})
func Printf(format string, v ...interface{})
func Println(v ...interface{})
```

You may have noticed what is perhaps the most glaring omission from the `log` package: that it doesn't support logging levels. However, what it lacks in functionality, it makes up for in simplicity and ease of use.

Here's the most basic logging example:

```
package main

import "log"

func main() {
    log.Print("Hello, World!")
}
```

When run, it provides the following output:

```
$ go run .
2020/11/10 09:15:39 Hello, World!
```

As you can see, the `log.Print` function—like all of the `log` logging functions—adds a timestamp to its messages without any additional configuration.

The special logging functions

Although `log` sadly doesn't support log levels, it does offer some other interesting features. Namely, a class of convenience functions that couple outputting log events with another useful action.

The first of these is the `log.Fatal` functions. There are three of these, each corresponding to a different `log.PrintX` function, and each equivalent to calling its corresponding print function followed by a call to `os.Exit(1)`:

```
func Fatal(v ...interface{})
func Fatalf(format string, v ...interface{})
func Fatalln(v ...interface{})
```

Similarly, `log` offers a series of `log.Panic` functions, which are equivalent to calling its corresponding `log.PrintX` followed by a call to `panic`:

```
func Panic(v ...interface{})
func Panicf(format string, v ...interface{})
func Panicln(v ...interface{})
```

Both of these sets of functions are useful, but they're not used nearly as often as the log.Print functions, typically in error handling where it makes sense to report the error and halt.

Logging to a custom writer

By default, the log package prints to stderr, but what if you want to redirect that output elsewhere? The log.SetOutput function allows you to do exactly that by letting you specify a custom io.Writer to write to.

This allows you to, for example, send your logs to a file if you want to. As we mention in "Less is (way) more" on page 390, writing logs to files generally isn't advisable, but it can be useful under certain circumstances.

This is demonstrated in the following using os.OpenFile to open the target file, and using log.SetOutput to define it as the log writer:

```go
package main

import (
    "log"
    "os"
)

func main() {
    // O_APPEND = Append data to the file when writing
    // O_CREATE = Create a new file if none exists
    // O_WRONLY = Open the file write-only
    flags := os.O_APPEND | os.O_CREATE | os.O_WRONLY

    file, err := os.OpenFile("log.txt", flags, 0666)
    if err != nil {
        log.Fatal(err)
    }

    log.SetOutput(file)

    log.Println("Hello, World!")
}
```

When run, the following is written to the file log.txt:

```
$ go run .; tail log.txt
2020/11/10 09:17:05 Hello, World!
```

The fact that log.SetOutput accepts an interface means that a wide variety of destinations can be supported just by satisfying the io.Writer contract. You could even, if you so desired, create an io.Writer implementation that forwards to a log processor like Logstash or a message broker like Kafka. The possibilities are unlimited.

Log flags

The `log` package also allows you to use constants to enrich log messages with additional context information, such as the filename, line number, date, and time.

For example, adding the following line to our above "Hello, World":

```
log.SetFlags(log.Ldate | log.Ltime | log.Lshortfile)
```

Will result in a log output like the following:

```
2020/11/10 10:14:36 main.go:7: Hello, World!
```

As you can see, it includes the date in the local time zone (`log.Ldate`), the time in the local time zone (`log.Ltime`), and the final file name element and line number of the `log` call (`log.Lshortfile`).

We don't get any say over the order in which the log parts appear or the format in which they are presented, but if you want that kind of flexibility, you probably want to use another logging framework, such as Zap.

The Zap Logging Package

Of the Three Pillars of Observability, logging is the one that's least supported by OpenTelemetry. Which is to say that it isn't supported at all, at least at the time of this writing (though it will be incorporated in time).

So, for now, rather than discuss the OpenTelemetry Logging API, we'll cover another excellent library: Zap (*https://oreil.ly/fjMls*), a JSON-formatted logger designed to allocate memory as infrequently as possible, and to use reflection and string formatting as little as possible.

Zap is currently one of the two most popular Go logging packages, alongside Logrus (*https://oreil.ly/UZt5n*). Logrus is actually a little more popular, but three main factors drove me to choose Zap for this book instead. First, Zap is known for its speed and low memory impact (which is useful at scale). Second, it has a "structured first" philosophy which, as I asserted in "Structure events for parsing" on page 389, is incredibly desirable. Finally, Logrus is now in maintenance mode, and isn't introducing any new features.

How fast is Zap, exactly? It's really fast. For a minimalist example, Table 11-2 shows comparisons of benchmarks between several common structured logging packages, without including any context or `printf`-style templating.

Table 11-2. Relative benchmarks of structured logging packages for a message with no context or `printf`-style templating.

Package	Time	Time % to Zap	Objects Allocated
Zap	118 ns/op	+0%	0 allocs/op
Zap (sugared)	191 ns/op	+62%	2 allocs/op
Zerolog	93 ns/op	-21%	0 allocs/op
Go-kit	280 ns/op	+137%	11 allocs/op
Standard library	499 ns/op	+323%	2 allocs/op
Logrus	3129 ns/op	+2552%	24 allocs/op
Log15	3887 ns/op	+3194%	23 allocs/op

These numbers were developed using Zap's own benchmarking suite (*https://oreil.ly/ uGbA7*), but I did examine, update, and execute the benchmarks myself. Of course, as with any benchmarking, take these numbers with a grain of salt. The two standouts here are Go's own standard `log` library, which had a runtime about triple Zap's standard logger, and Logrus, which took a very significant 25 times Zap's time.

But we're supposed to use context fields, aren't we? What does Zap look like then? Well, those results are even more striking.

Table 11-3. Relative benchmarks of structured logging packages for a message with 10 context fields.

Package	Time	Time % to Zap	Objects Allocated
Zap	862 ns/op	+0%	5 allocs/op
Zap (sugared)	1250 ns/op	+45%	11 allocs/op
Zerolog	4021 ns/op	+366%	76 allocs/op
Go-kit	4542 ns/op	+427%	105 allocs/op
Logrus	29501 ns/op	+3322%	125 allocs/op
Log15	29906 ns/op	+3369%	122 allocs/op

Zap's lead over Logrus has extended to a (very impressive) factor of 33X; the standard `log` library isn't included in this table because it doesn't even support context fields.

Alright then, so how do we use it?

Creating a Zap logger

The first step to logging with Zap is to create a `zap.Logger` value.

Of course, before you do that, you first need to import the Zap package, as follows:

```
import "go.uber.org/zap"
```

Once you've imported Zap, you can build your `zap.Logger` instance. Zap allows you to configure several aspects of your logging behavior, but the most straightforward way to build a `zap.Logger` is to use Zap's opinionated preset constructor functions—`zap.NewExample`, `zap.NewProduction`, and `zap.NewDevelopment`—each of which build a logger via a single function call:

```
logger, err := zap.NewProduction()
if err != nil {
    log.Fatalf("can't initialize zap logger: %v", err)
}
```

Typically, this will be done in an `init` function and the `zap.Logger` value maintained globally. Zap loggers are safe for concurrent use.

The three available presets are usually perfectly fine for small projects, but larger projects and organizations may want a bit more customization. Zap provides the `zap.Config` struct for exactly this purpose, and while the specifics are beyond the scope of this book, the Zap documentation (*https://oreil.ly/q1mHb*) describes its use in some detail.

Writing logs with Zap

One of the more unique aspects of Zap is that every logger actually has two easily interchangeable forms—standard and "sugared"—that vary somewhat in efficiency and usability.

The standard `zap.Logger` implementation emphasizes performance and type safety. It's slightly faster than the `SugaredLogger` and allocates far less, but it only supports structured logging which does make it a little more awkward to use:

```
logger, _ := zap.NewProduction()

// Structured context as strongly typed Field values.
logger.Info("failed to fetch URL",
    zap.String("url", url),
    zap.Int("attempt", 3),
    zap.Duration("backoff", time.Second),
)
```

The output of which will look something like the following:

```
{"level":"info", "msg":"failed to fetch URL",
        "url":"http://example.com", "attempt":3, "backoff":"1s"}
```

In contexts where performance is good but not absolutely critical (which is most of the time, probably) you can use the `SugaredLogger`, which is easily obtainable from a standard logger via its `Sugar` method.

The SugaredLogger still provides structured logging, but its functions for doing so are loosely typed, as opposed to the standard logger's strong context typing. Despite using runtime reflection behind the scenes, its performance is still very good.

The SugaredLogger even includes printf-style logging methods, for convenience. (Remember, though, that when it comes to logging, context is king.)

All of these features are demonstrated in the following:

```
logger, _ := zap.NewProduction()
sugar := logger.Sugar()

// Structured context as loosely typed key-value pairs.
sugar.Infow("failed to fetch URL",
    "url", url,
    "attempt", 3,
    "backoff", time.Second,
)

sugar.Infof("failed to fetch URL: %s", url)
```

The output of which will look something like the following:

```
{"level":"info", "msg":"failed to fetch URL",
        "url":"http://example.com", "attempt":3, "backoff":"1s"}
{"level":"info", "msg":"failed to fetch URL: http://example.com"}
```

 Don't create a new Logger for every function. Instead, create a global instance, or use the zap.L or zap.S functions to get Zap's global standard or sugared loggers, respectively.

Using dynamic sampling in Zap

You may recall from "Dynamic sampling" on page 391 that dynamic sampling is a technique in which incoming log entries are sampled by capping recorded events to some maximum number per unit of time.

If done broadly, this technique can be used to manage the CPU and I/O load of your logging while preserving a representative subset of events. If targeted to a particular class of otherwise high-volume and low-fidelity events, such as debug logs, dynamic sampling can ensure their availability for production troubleshooting without consuming too much storage.

Zap supports dynamic sampling, which is configurable using the zap.SamplingCon fig structure, shown here:

```
type SamplingConfig struct {
    // Initial sets the cap on the number of events logged each second.
    Initial    int
```

```
// Thereafter sets the proportion of events that are logged each second
// after Initial is exceeded. A value of 3 indicates one event in every
// 3 is logged.
Thereafter int

// Hook (if defined) is called after each "log/no log" decision.
Hook        func(zapcore.Entry, zapcore.SamplingDecision)
}
```

Using `zap.SamplingConfig` allows you to define the number of initial events with the same level and message permitted each second (`Initial`), after which only every *n*th message (`Thereafter`) is logged. The rest are dropped.

The following example demonstrates how to build a new `zap.Logger` using a preconfigured `zap.Config` instance:

```go
package main

import (
    "fmt"

    "go.uber.org/zap"
    "go.uber.org/zap/zapcore"
)

func init() {
    cfg := zap.NewDevelopmentConfig()
    cfg.EncoderConfig.TimeKey = ""            // Turn off timestamp output

    cfg.Sampling = &zap.SamplingConfig{
        Initial:    3,                        // Allow first 3 events/second
        Thereafter: 3,                        // Allows 1 per 3 thereafter
        Hook: func(e zapcore.Entry, d zapcore.SamplingDecision) {
            if d == zapcore.LogDropped {
                fmt.Println("event dropped...")
            }
        },
    }

    logger, _ := cfg.Build()                  // Constructs the new logger

    zap.ReplaceGlobals(logger)                // Replace Zap's global logger
}
```

The above example creates a new `zap.Logger` and sets it as Zap's global logger. It does this in several steps.

First, the example creates a new `zap.Config` struct. For convenience, this example uses the predefined `zap.NewDevelopmentConfig` function, which provides a

`zap.Config` value that produces human-readable output and a threshold of `DebugLe`
`vel` and above.

If you like, the `zap.NewProductionConfig` function, which returns a preconfigured
`zap.Config` value with a threshold of `InfoLevel` and encodes events in JSON. If you
really want to, you can even create your own `zap.Config` from scratch.

Next, the example creates a new `zap.SamplingConfig` on the `zap.Config`, which
instructs the Zap sampler to keep the first three of any similar events in a given second, and to drop all but every third message thereafter (each second).

The `Hook` function is invoked after each sampling decision. The
example will write a message if it sees that an event has been dropped.

Finally, the example uses the Config's `Build` method to construct a `zap.Logger` from
the `Config`, and uses `zap.ReplaceGlobals` to replace Zap's global Logger. Zap's
global logger and sugared logger can be accessed by using the `zap.L` and `zap.S` functions, respectively.

But does it work as we expect? Well, let's see:

```
func main() {
    for i := 1; i <= 10; i++ {
        zap.S().Infow(
            "Testing sampling",
            "index", i,
        )
    }
}
```

The above function logs 10 events, but with our sampling configuration we should
see only the first 3 events, and then every third after that (6 and 9). Is that what
we see?

```
$ go run .
INFO    zap/main.go:39    Testing sampling    {"index": 1}
INFO    zap/main.go:39    Testing sampling    {"index": 2}
INFO    zap/main.go:39    Testing sampling    {"index": 3}
event dropped...
event dropped...
INFO    zap/main.go:39    Testing sampling    {"index": 6}
event dropped...
event dropped...
INFO    zap/main.go:39    Testing sampling    {"index": 9}
event dropped...
```

The output is exactly as we expected. Clearly, log sampling is a very powerful technique, and, when used properly, can provide significant value.

Summary

There's a lot of hype around observability, and with its promises to dramatically shorten development feedback loops and generally make complexity manageable again, it's easy to see why.

I wrote a little at the start of this chapter about observability and its promises, and a little more about how observability *isn't* done. Unfortunately, *how to do* observability is a really, really big subject, and the limitations of time and space meant that I wasn't able to say as much about that as I certainly would have liked.[15] Fortunately, with some pretty great books on the horizon (most notably *Observability Engineering* by Charity Majors and Liz Fong-Jones (O'Reilly)), that void won't go unfilled for long.

By far, however, most of this chapter was spent talking about the Three Pillars of Observability in turn, specifically how to implement them using OpenTelemetry (*https://oreil.ly/zEgIp*), where possible.

All told, this was a challenging chapter. Observability is a vast subject about which not that much is written yet, and, as a result of its newness, the same is true of OpenTelemetry. Even its own documentation is limited and spotty in parts. On the plus side, I got to spend a lot of time in the source code.

---

15 This is a Go book, after all. At least that's what I keep telling my incredibly patient editors.

Index

K

key, 125
key pair, 146
key-value store, 108, 256
Kibana (see ELK)
Kubernetes
    applications for, 7, 314
    features of, 24, 151, 162, 293, 306, 310

L

labels, 369
Laprie, Jean-Claude, 169
latency, 205
LaunchDarkly, 341
leaking goroutine, 206-207
Least Recently Used cache (see LRE cache)
len built-in function, 36-41
Lightstep, 349
linguistic stability, 21
Linkerd, 223
Linux binaries, 159
Linux Foundation, 6
ListenAndServe, 113, 148
liveness checks, 295-297
load shedding, 270, 274
lock contention, 101, 205
locks, 102, 122
    (see also read locks, write locks)
log level, 390
logging, 346, 387-400
    (see also Zap logging)
logging packages, 391
    (see also Go log package, Zap logging)
Logrus, 394
logs, 187, 346, 387, 389
    (see also stream of events)
Logstash, 187
looking up plug-ins, 243
loops, 44-46
loose coupling
    definition of, 7-8, 175, 220-221
    hexagonal architecture and, 255-264
    plug-ins, 241-255
LRU cache, 198-201

M

maintainability, 11, 171, 304
make built-in function, 38, 41

make function, 65
manageability
    categories of, 305
        (see also configuration)
    contributions to, 173
    definition of, 10, 303-306
    designs for, 177
    maintainability and, 11, 304
map literals, 42
maps, 36, 41-42, 121-123
matchers, 117
mean time between failures (MTBF), 170
Means of Dependability pyramid, 173
memory, 195
memory leaks, 206-209
Message Transfer System (MTS), 221
messaging redundancy, 290
Meter, 374-379
meter provider, 376
methods, 58-59
metric collection, 371
    pull-based metric collection, 372
    push-based metric collection, 371
metric instruments, 379
    additive instruments, 379, 381
    additive monotonic instruments, 379
    asynchronous instruments, 379, 383-384
    grouping instruments, 379
    synchronous instruments, 379, 381-383
metrics, 346, 369-387
microservice, 209-210
    (see also microservices architecture)
microservices architecture, 8, 209, 211-213
monitoring, 345, 370
monolith, 209, 213
    (see also monolith architecture)
monolith architecture, 210-211, 216
MTBF (mean time between failures), 170
MTS (Message Transfer System), 221
multiple containers, 156
multiple returns, 51
multiplexer (mux), 113
multitiered architecture, 4
mutex, 121, 201, 205
mux (multiplexer), 113

N

network I/O, 195
networked applications, history of, 4-6

About the Author

Matthew A. Titmus is a veteran of the software development industry. Since teaching himself to build virtual worlds in LPC, he's earned a surprisingly relevant degree in molecular biology, written tools to analyze terabyte-sized datasets at a high energy physics laboratory, developed an early web development framework from scratch, wielded distributed computing techniques to analyze cancer genomes, and pioneered machine learning techniques for linked data.

He was an early adopter and advocate of both cloud native technologies in general and the Go language in particular. For the past four years he has specialized in helping companies migrate monolithic applications into a containerized, cloud native world, allowing them to transform the way their services are developed, deployed, and managed. He is passionate about what it takes to make a system production quality, and has spent a lot of time thinking about and implementing strategies for observing and orchestrating distributed systems.

Matthew lives on Long Island with the world's most patient woman, to whom he is lucky to be married, and the world's most adorable boy, by whom he is lucky to be called "Dad."

Colophon

The animal on the cover of *Cloud Native Go* is a member of the tuco-tuco family (*Ctenomyidae*). These neotropical rodents can be found living in excavated burrows across the southern half of South America.

The name "tuco-tuco" refers to a wide range of species. In general, these rodents have heavily built bodies with powerful short legs and well-developed claws. They have large heads but small ears, and though they spend up to 90% of their time underground, their eyes are relatively large compared to other burrowing rodents. The color and texture of the tuco-tucos' fur varies depending on the species, but in general, their fur is fairly thick. Their tails are short and not particularly furry.

Tuco-tucos live in tunnel systems—which are often extensive and complicated—that they dig into sandy and/or loamy soil. These networks often include separate chambers for nesting and food storage. They have undergone a variety of morphological adaptions that help them create and thrive in these underground environments, including an improved sense of smell, which helps them orient themselves in the tunnels. They employ both scratch-digging and skull-tooth excavation when creating their burrows.

The diet of the tuco-tucos consists primarily of roots, stems, and grasses. Today, tuco-tucos are viewed as agricultural pests, but in pre-European South America they were an important foodsource for indigenous peoples, particlarly in Tierra del Fuego. Today, their conservation status is contingent upon species and geographic location. Many species fall into the "Least Concern" category, while others are considered "Endangered." Many of the animals on O'Reilly covers are endangered; all of them are important to the world.

The cover illustration is by Karen Montgomery, based on a black and white engraving from *English Cyclopedia Natural History*. The cover fonts are Gilroy Semibold and Guardian Sans. The text font is Adobe Minion Pro; the heading font is Adobe Myriad Condensed; and the code font is Dalton Maag's Ubuntu Mono.

©2019 O'Reilly Media, Inc. O'Reilly is a registered trademark of O'Reilly Media, Inc. | 175

Milton Keynes UK
Ingram Content Group UK Ltd.
UKHW032207221123
433106UK00002B/6

9 781492 076339